"For more than a hundred years, peo[ple] renewal who are not Hasidic have fou.... ...spir...ion in Hasidism. Now, Arthur Green and Ariel Mayse, both scholars of Hasidism and committed spiritual seekers, have assembled critical texts for the fashioning of neo-Hasidism in the twenty-first century. The result is a landmark contribution to Jewish spirituality."

—DAVID BIALE, Emanuel Ringelblum Distinguished Professor of Jewish History at the University of California, Davis, and editor in chief of *Hasidism: A New History*

"*A New Hasidism* is a treasure for the heart and mind. With this superb two-volume anthology in hand, contemporary seekers and scholars have a broad spectrum of spiritual wisdom with which to contemplate the history and contemporary character of neo-Hasidism. The first volume provides the 'Roots' of the modern reinterpretation of Hasidism in Europe and America; the second displays the 'Branches' spreading over Jewish life in the United States and Israel in our times. Together they mark a major moment of our Jewish religious renaissance."

—MICHAEL FISHBANE, Nathan Cummings Distinguished Service Professor of Jewish Studies at the University of Chicago

"In two sequential volumes, the diamonds of Hasidic spiritual teaching have been skillfully recut and set to offer seekers of all backgrounds entry into a challenging and soul-expanding opportunity. You are invited to enter a multigenerational conversation, deeply engage with the most inspiring teachings of Hasidic and contemporary teachers, build upon these insights, and carry them forward."

—RABBI MARCIA PRAGER, director and dean of the ALEPH Ordination Program and author of *Path of Blessing: Experiencing the Abundance of the Divine*

"The impact of neo-Hasidism on contemporary Jewish life cannot be overstated; its influence has penetrated farther and wider than is usually acknowledged. Yet what is neo-Hasidism really—what are its main teachings, and where do those ideas stem from? Here, brought together for the first time, are the essential texts of neo-Hasidism, from forebears like Hillel Zeitlin and Abraham Joshua Heschel, and from recent and contemporary thinkers like Zalman Schachter-Shalomi and Arthur Green. Whatever their own relationship to neo-Hasidism, students of Jewish thought and contemporary religious life cannot afford to miss these volumes. They are a veritable feast for seeker and scholar alike."

—RABBI SHAI HELD, president and dean of the Hadar Institute and author of *The Heart of Torah: Essays on the Weekly Torah Portion*

"Over the past century, a number of creative spirits have reimagined Hasidism—infusing it with new energy, liberating it from its insularity and dynastic power structure, and translating its radical wisdom into a modern idiom. Now, for the first time, one of those creative spirits, together with his brilliant disciple, have chronicled that transformation and assembled its foundational documents (or 'roots') along with many of its recent literary 'branches.' Dip into these volumes to experience the renewal of Jewish spirituality."

—DANIEL MATT, author of *The Essential Kabbalah* and the annotated translation *The Zohar: Pritzker Edition*

"Just when we are in such dire need of old/new tools for truth telling and loving kindness (*hesed ve'emet*), we receive these wise, passionate, intellectually compelling essays that continue the unfolding of the Neo-Hasidic revolution in our own times. These volumes will open minds, hearts, and even souls."

—RABBI LISA GOLDSTEIN, executive director of the Institute for Jewish Spirituality

"Green and Mayse have masterfully crafted a living tree of neo-Hasidic worldview and practice spanning the sources of neo-Hasidic thought and their manifestations in contemporary neo-Hasidism. These two wonderfully innovative volumes reveal a creatively alive Judaism informed by a deep legacy."

—MELILA HELLNER-ESHED, senior research fellow at the Shalom Hartman Institute and author of *A River Flows from Eden: The Language of Mystical Experience in the Zohar*

"Arthur Green and Ariel Mayse invite us to sit more, read more, think more, and garment more of our blessings. *Roots* and *Branches* are two walking sticks with which we can walk this Creation with wonder and humility. Your mind and heart will coil and uncoil as you enter these crevices of love, faith, devotion, and challenge on a journey to the depths of your being."

—RABBI REB MIMI FEIGELSON, Mashpiah Ruchanit (spiritual mentor) and senior lecturer of Talmud and Chassidic Thought at the Schechter Institute, Jerusalem

A New Hasidism

Roots

University of Nebraska Press
Lincoln

A New Hasidism

Roots

EDITED BY ARTHUR GREEN
AND ARIEL EVAN MAYSE

The Jewish Publication Society
Philadelphia

Library of Congress Cataloging-in-Publication Data
Names: Green, Arthur, 1941–, editor. | Mayse, Ariel
Evan, editor.
Title: A new Hasidism: roots / edited by Arthur Green
and Ariel Evan Mayse.
Description: Philadelphia: Jewish Publication Society;
Lincoln: University of Nebraska Press, [2019] |
Includes bibliographical references.
Identifiers: LCCN 2019005752
ISBN 9780827613065 (pbk.: alk. paper)
ISBN 9780827617841 (epub)
ISBN 9780827617858 (mobi)
ISBN 9780827617865 (pdf)
Subjects: LCSH: Hasidism — Philosophy. |
Hasidism — 21st century.
Classification: LCC BM198.2 .N496
2019 | DDC 296.8/332 — dc23
LC record available at
https://lccn.loc.gov/2019005752

Set in Merope by E. Cuddy.

To a teacher in the Neo-Hasidic life,

Rabbi Zalman Schachter-Shalomi,

הרב משולם זלמן רן שלמה הכהן וגיטל שכטר-שלומי

and to Kathy Green, a partner along the path,

קריינדל בת שמעון ולאה

יהי זכרם ברוך

Contents

Preface

The book before you is a collaboration between two people who began as teacher and student and have become dear friends and literary collaborators. We are grateful to the Master of the Universe for the gift of this friendship, which has taken shape around our shared love for the teachings—and teachers—found here, and for the ability to bring it to completion. We offer this project as a testament to that friendship and to the ideal of spiritual friendship, a value for which our world thirsts so deeply.

This volume and its companion, *A New Hasidism: Branches*, are intended primarily for the personal religious seeker, one who is looking for an old-new approach to the eternal questions of life, presented through a Jewish lens. The editors of this volume are themselves such seekers. Each of us, representing two different generations, would say that our discovery of Hasidism opened the door to Judaism, and to a deeper personal spiritual life. We welcome you to walk through that doorway as well.

Both volumes are also addressed to scholars and students of Judaism and contemporary religious thought. We hope that they, too, may discover different perspectives on a contemporary and future Judaism than those usually presented. We also hope that the publication of these volumes will stir discussion of a Neo-Hasidic approach to Jewish life and inspire a new generation of leaders, thinkers, and teachers to continue to develop such a path.

Acknowledgments

We are grateful to a number of people who have helped bring this project to fruition.

The Martin Buber estate, Professor Susanna Heschel, Neshama Carlebach, Eve Ilsen, and Netanel Miles-Yepez have all generously allowed us to publish material. Sam Berrin Shonkoff wrote the introduction to the chapter on Martin Buber and annotated the accompanying selections, and Nehemia Polen provided a preface to Shlomo Carlebach's "The Torah of the Nine Months."

We are grateful to Ivan Ickovits for the original transcription of the interview with Reb Zalman, and to David Shneer and Stephanie Yuhas of the University of Colorado Archives Project for providing the interview tape. The entire interview text—including many more phrases in Yiddish, Hebrew, and German (with translations)—is available online at artgreen26.com.

From the moment he learned of this project, Rabbi Barry Schwartz of The Jewish Publication Society has offered support and encouragement. Joy Weinberg's editorial hand has been judicious and wise, and her generous attentions have improved the manuscript significantly. The editors are also grateful to the University of Nebraska for publishing the work.

Kevin Wolf helped in the technical matters of retrieving and scanning many of the excerpts reprinted herein. Rabbi David Maayan has worked tirelessly—and insightfully—toward all aspects of preparing the manuscript for publication and has served as a very thoughtful first reader.

Finally, we would like to thank Ruth Feldman (RuthFeldmanArt.com), an artist and an award-winning Jewish educator, for providing the painting *Between the Branches* that appears as the cover art for this book. The image of the forest has played a major role in Hasidic thought ever since the movement's founder, Israel Ba'al Shem Tov, was known to choose it as a place of prayer. *Between the Branches* shows the richness of life within the forest, representing the original Hasidic tradition, out of which this new Hasidism is to spring.

Our thanks to them all.

Introduction

Sometime in the mid-1920s, the Neo-Hasidic writer Hillel Zeitlin (1871–1942) penned the following lines describing Yavneh, a new Jewish movement he was seeking to create:

> Yavneh wants to be for Jewry what Hasidism was a hundred and fifty years ago. This was Hasidism in its origin, that of the BeSHT.[1] This does not mean that Yavneh wants to be that original Hasidism. It rather wants to bring into *contemporary* Jewish life the freshness, vitality, and joyful attachment to God, in accord with the style, concepts, mood, and meaning of the modern Jew, just as the BeSHT did—in his time—according to the style, concepts, mood, and meaning of Jews of that time.[2]

Nearly a century later, and in a world that neither Zeitlin nor the Ba'al Shem Tov could have quite imagined, the editors of the present volume seek to do the same.

Hasidism, the great popular mystical revival of Judaism that began in Eastern Europe 250 years ago, has proven itself a hardy tree in the great orchard or *pardes* of Jewish wisdom that has flourished through the ages. Its original teachers called for a Judaism of inwardness and enthusiasm, a spiritual life marked by the great joy of standing in God's presence and the privilege of serving at the inner altar. They created communities of masters and disciples devoted to the three great loves that the Ba'al Shem Tov, revered as the movement's founder, was said to have proclaimed as the reasons his soul had come into the world: the love of God, the love of Torah, and the love of the People of Israel.[3]

Hasidism as originally taught saw the promulgation of these as its greatest task, and taught them both by word and by the example of the masters' lives. It perceived its greatest enemy in this task to be the life of unthinking and routinized religious behavior. Such a regimen dulled the spirit rather than restoring it to its source in the One that underlies, flows through, and unites all that is.

Born in the semirural Ukraine at the very dawn of the modern era, Hasidism survived the challenges of poverty and oppression, imperial absolutism under the czars and Hapsburgs, and the great transitions wrought by modernity, including industrialization, urbanization, and the emergence of various secular-Jewish identities. After being the dominant force within Jewish life throughout much of Eastern Europe in the nineteenth century, it retreated to minority status in the early twentieth. Identifying with an emerging notion of ultra-Orthodoxy, much of later Hasidism took a hostile and suspicious view of any change or innovation, even any alterations in outward habits of dress and style from those passed down by prior generations.[4]

The Holocaust that destroyed the Jews of Eastern Europe dealt a particularly harsh blow to the Hasidic communities. The vast majority of Hasidim, who had eschewed emigration to the West as a threat to their way of life, fell victim to the slaughter-pits and the gas chambers. After the war, the few remaining survivors gathered first in the displaced persons camps and then chose to leave the bloodied soil of Europe behind, most emigrating either to America or to the new state of Israel.

The greatest miracle of the movement's history, indeed one of the modern world's most important testaments to the renewing power of faith, is the way the Hasidic communities rebuilt themselves on those new shores. No one could have predicted that the small bedraggled groups of survivors, bewildered by their new and alien surroundings, would reconstitute themselves around charismatic leaders and, within a generation, recreate their institutions, produce large new families that mostly remained faithful, and widely extend their influence within world Jewry. Hasidism has again become a major force in contemporary Jewish life.

Understanding Neo-Hasidism

The insights of Hasidism are too important, though, to be left to the Hasidim alone. More than a hundred years ago, as the fierce struggle between Hasidism and Haskalah, or Western "Enlightenment," started to wane, modern Jews began to seek out the inward truths and insights of Hasidic teaching. These Neo-Hasidic Jews then sought to convey their accumulated wisdom to Jews and others whose chosen way of life was far from that of the traditional Hasidic communities. The teachings were presented in universalized fashion and the Hasidic wisdom was shared selectively. Not communicated, for example, was the Hasidic disdain for all things modern, including its rejection of Western education. Traditional Hasidic attitudes toward the gentile world and toward women's roles, in particular, were left aside as relics of an earlier era.

The editors of this volume stand proudly within this Neo-Hasidic tradition. Our intent here is to define that now hundred-year-old tradition called Neo-Hasidism, to trace its history, and to cultivate its further growth. Neo-Hasidism is a wide tent, encompassing Jews who are highly observant and learned within the tradition (some study and teach the Hasidic sources in the original Hebrew and Yiddish) as well as Jews—and others—who know little of such things. Drawing everyone together is a common quest for a Judaism of heart and soul, of *hitlahavut* or fiery spiritual devotion.

As both seekers and editors of this volume, we sense that a new look at Hasidic teachings, updated and expanded for this postmodern era, will provide inspiration and direction for this quest. In an age of great interest in the inner life, spirituality, and meditation, we also believe that an updated, universalized, and accessible version of Hasidic insights might also reach beyond the borders of Judaism and speak to the hearts of non-Jewish seekers. We welcome these readers too.

The Neo-Hasidism that forms the subject of this volume is different from a broader usage of the term that applies it to the influence of Hasidism on modern Jewish culture as a whole, especially as reflected in works of twentieth-century Hebrew and Yiddish literature. Beginning early in that century, various writers used the backdrop of Hasidism to tell their own tales. Well-known authors such as I. L. Peretz, Shmuel Yosef Agnon, and Isaac Bashevis Singer, for example, set many of their fictional creations in the Hasidic world they had known in childhood.[5] Often, though, they combined romantic reconstructions of the Hasidic shtetl (small town) with more and less subtle jibes at the old way of life. Many a modern reader becomes familiar with Hasidism more from their re-creations of it, often filled with ambivalence, than from the Hasidic sources themselves.

The Teachings of Hasidism

What, then, are those essential teachings of original Hasidism, especially as taught in its first few generations, that we cherish, seek to preserve, and believe to be so important for the wider world to know? What, too, are the sources of these key Hasidic teachings, and how were they preserved and transmitted?

Early Hasidism was a semi-spontaneous outburst of popular religious enthusiasm. It crystallized around the image of the Ba'al Shem Tov in the decades following his death in 1760. Most of its leading proponents were at first traveling preachers, wandering from town to town to spread their revivalist message. The more successful among them then established "courts," fixed locations that became places of pilgrimage where disciples would flock to hear their teachings, receive their blessing, and bask in their glory.

The teachings were originally oral, preached in Yiddish. Over the last quarter of the eighteenth century, they began to appear in Hebrew books, some with short aphoristic counsels on how to live the good life in God's sight, others in the form of longer homilies around the cycle of Torah readings.

We offer some of the most important teachings of Hasidism in brief form here:

1. All existence is radiant with divine presence. "The power of the Maker is within the made," a common Hasidic watchword, teaches that all creation reflects the godly hand that in every moment creates it anew. Our ordinary view of existence, one that separates person from God, matter from spirit, subject from object, is essentially superficial. Everything that happens comes from the hand of God; there is no moment, place, or deed in which God is not present. Were our eyes truly open — and the purpose of all religious life is to help in that opening — we would see that there is no reality outside of Y-H-W-H, the God of all being. The indwelling Divine Presence, while hidden from sight, is the ultimate truth of existence.

2. The Divine Presence is to be discovered and joyously celebrated through all of life. The service of God is not limited to the hours of prayer, study, and specific commandments. Even as these precise God-given forms of worship are to be carried out with great devotion, the fulfillment of the specific commandments also serves a broader purpose that touches our every deed: inspiration and example for the sanctification of all the rest of life. God's presence is everywhere, waiting to be revealed. The discovery and uplift-

ing of sparks of divine energy, even in the most unlikely places, is essential to the religious task.

3. Torah, traditional Jewish teaching in both the narrowest and broadest sense, is to guide every aspect of one's life. It is the eternal will and teaching of God, but it is also a mysterious embodiment of God's own self, as is the human soul. Torah is our guide to help us discover the divine message imprinted within our hearts. Constant engagement with Torah, seeking out the light hidden deep within it, inspires an ongoing creative quest for new and deeper meanings that in turn energizes our spiritual lives.

4. Our human task includes uplifting and transforming our emotional selves and our moral way of acting, seeking to become ever more perfect vessels for God's service. This inner process begins with the key devotional pair of love and fear. We need to purify both of these in our lives, coming to understand that all true love derives from and leads back to the love of God and that God alone is the proper subject of our fear or awe. Other loves, desires, needs, and fears are in a "fallen" state and need to be uplifted. All moral growth begins with this insight. Generosity, openheartedness, and compassion, toward ourselves as well as others, are essential religious values. Condescension, judging, and especially anger (even for the sake of righteousness) are to be avoided.

5. A person who fully embodies these teachings and personal qualities (*middot*) is to be considered a *tsaddik* or righteous one. The cultivation of such souls is the great goal of Hasidic teaching. Their presence is a source of blessing to those around them. They are also called upon to serve as models and teachers. The *tsaddik* or spiritual master stands at the center of a circle of *hasidim*, disciples, who are devoted both to their teacher and to the

community they create around him. The relationship between master and disciple is thus complemented by the intense fellowship fostered within the Hasidic community.

These teachings were conveyed by a remarkable array of religious personalities who embodied the role of *tsaddik* across several generations. Many of them were influenced by the BesHT and his principal successor, Dov Baer the *maggid* (preacher) of Mezritch. Other well-known figures of the early movement include Levi Yitzhak of Berdichev, Zusha of Anipolye, Shneur Zalman of Liadi (the founder of Chabad Hasidism), and Nahman of Bratslav.[6] Tales about their lives and those of many other masters were told and later written down. The genre of storytelling became an important vehicle for conveying the Hasidic message, as its truths were inseparable from the lives of those who lived them.[7]

Contemporary Hasidism

The transplanted Eastern European Hasidism that exists today in both Israel and the Diaspora embodies a somewhat pale reflection of these teachings. Contemporary Hasidism largely lives in a very frightened and suspicious relationship with the world around it. Since its alignment with ultra-Orthodoxy early in the nineteenth century, and its fierce battle with emerging secularism as that century proceeded, it has dedicated most of its energies to preserving the old ways of Jewish life in every detail rather than seeking out new realms in which to proclaim God's presence. The creative and spiritually expansive teachings of the first generations came to be replaced by an extreme conservatism. While sparks of the original vision can certainly be found in the surviving and reborn Hasidic communities, the outer shell in which they are housed makes it extremely difficult for outsiders to access the wisdom there.

Small-town Eastern Europe of two hundred years ago, the cradle of Hasidism, was a place and time in which Jews suffered from poverty and oppression. For many, daily sustenance was a constant struggle. Modern medicine was as yet unknown, and the ravages of disease took a terrible toll on both young and old. The surrounding Christian culture was exclusivist in its view of salvation and particularly hostile toward Jews for their ongoing rejection of the Christian message. Ancient magical beliefs and practices were rampant in both Judaism and Christianity.

Hasidism and American Judaism

American Judaism, as it emerged in the nineteenth century, was devoid of almost any awareness of Hasidism and its teachings. Built upon Central rather than Eastern European models, it presented Judaism in rational and liberal categories that had emerged from post-Enlightenment circles, primarily in Germany. The denominational divisions that came to characterize American Jewry had everything to do with degrees of halakhic obligation while having little to say about the inner self, awareness of divine presence, or a life of passionate devotion. These Westernized Jewries tended to look down upon Hasidism, depicting it as rather boorish and superstitious. In such "enlightened" circles the figure of the Hasidic *tsaddik* in particular was an object of derision; he was pictured as a "wonder-rabbi," usually a charlatan preying on the beliefs of unlettered Jews.

This negative image of Hasidism prevailed across the denominational spectrum of American Jewry, from the modern Orthodox to the Reform, well into the latter half of the twentieth century. As a whole, modern Westernized Jews had largely swept the Jewish mystical tradition under the rug. Since it did not belong to what they defined as the "mainstream," they deemed it unworthy of being taught or passed on.

That attitude has changed radically over the course of the past three or four decades. Attempts to reintegrate once-discarded mystical terms, practices, and understandings of the tradition are widespread throughout the Jewish community. Collections of Hasidic teachings are newly available in translation, Hasidic-inspired musical compositions are performed in Reform synagogues, various retreats emphasize personal prayer and meditation, courses in mysticism are offered in rabbinical seminaries and universities, the distinctively mystical practices of all-night study *tikkunim* in Shavuot and Tu b'Shevat seders have become familiar in liberal Jewish circles, and much more.

This growing phenomenon within Judaism must be seen in the broad context of the emergence of postmodern consciousness preceding and following the turn of the twenty-first century. Two elements of this new way of thinking require brief mention here. One is a quest for ancient strands of wisdom, abandoned by Westerners in the move toward a science-based modernity, that might help us recover a lost sense of humanity, perhaps even prevent us from a rush toward nuclear self-annihilation or planetary destruction. Perhaps, it is thought, there is wisdom to be found among the Sufi saints, the Zen Buddhists, the monks of India—or the Hasidic masters—that will offer us some guidance in the very dangerous era we have entered. Second, and no less important, is that the postmodern student of religious traditions no longer requires the sources offering such wisdom to be literally true. Their insights must be translatable into terms and settings that work for the contemporary seeker. Questions of whether they are literally the word of God to Moses or concerning the original meaning of the ancient Scripture become secondary to the depths of wisdom and insight these texts have to offer. This is the moment for a Neo-Hasidic Judaism.

About This Book

The writings of key interpreters of Judaism shaped by intensive contact with the Hasidic tradition are brought together for the first time in this volume, *A New Hasidism: Roots*, as well as in its companion, *A New Hasidism: Branches*. For its part, *Roots* reaches back a hundred years into the Neo-Hasidic past, offering the contemporary seeker a chain of tradition that links back to the first modern readers of the early Hasidic sources. If Hillel Zeitlin, writing in Poland in the 1920s, was already able to broaden and universalize his notions of love of Torah and love of Israel, surely we twenty-first-century Neo-Hasidim may do so as well.

Here we delve into what might be called spiritual or philosophical Neo-Hasidism, an approach to religious questions based on the writings of the early Hasidic masters, but expanded and adjusted to apply to the broader contours of contemporary life. We examine the writings and legacies of key Neo-Hasidic figures, beginning in twentieth-century Europe prior to the First World War and continuing into twenty-first-century North America.

We begin with Neo-Hasidism's two most important European spokesmen, Hillel Zeitlin and Martin Buber, each of whom took a different approach to the Hasidic legacy. Zeitlin, rediscovering and reshaping the Hasidism of his youth after wandering quite far from its moorings, wrote in Hebrew and Yiddish, addressing a knowledgeable and exclusively Jewish readership. While living a life of traditional piety, he was highly critical of the Hasidic community of his own day and strove to create a new Hasidic movement that would revive twentieth-century Judaism with the spirit of Hasidism in its earliest days. Buber, himself an outsider to Hasidism, wrote in German, reaching an audience that included both Westernized Jews and sympathetic Christians. Emphasizing the tales as the most vital record of Hasidism's inner life, he retold them in an attractive and subtly dramatic style. In his essays he offered a distillation of the Hasidic message that largely removed it from its original setting in the context of traditional Jewish lore and observance.

The third visionary in this book, Abraham Joshua Heschel, was himself a scion of several great Hasidic dynasties. After leaving the Hasidism of his Warsaw home to attain a Western higher education and immigrating to America at the outbreak of the Second World War, he began his career as a religious philosopher and a historian of Jewish thought. At that point he did not reference Hasidism specifically. After the Holocaust, however, he increasingly came to see himself as a spokesman for the classic Jewish tradition, especially in its now lost Eastern European form. His presentation of this tradition of faith was largely shaped by his Hasidic roots, and he also became deeply engaged in studying the history of the movement. He became the most influential American Jewish theologian of the postwar era, shaping the ways both Jews and Christians came to see the spiritual legacy of Judaism.

Neo-Hasidism was essentially recreated in North America through the legacy of two remarkable teachers, Shlomo Carlebach and Zalman Schachter-Shalomi, the fourth and fifth thinkers presented in this volume. Both had immigrated from Europe to America as adolescents at the outbreak of World War II and became involved with the Chabad or Lubavitch school within Hasidism. In the late 1940s the sixth Lubavitcher Rebbe, Yosef Yitzchak Schneersohn, called upon them to bring the message of Hasidism to nonobservant Jewish college students. Over the course of the turbulent 1960s, however, both Carlebach and Schachter-Shalomi broke away from Lubavitch and began to teach distinctively new versions of the Hasidic message — retooled visions that would speak to an American-born audience, especially to one shaped by the monumental spiritual and moral revolutions of the era.

The thinking of Arthur Green, a student of both Heschel and Schachter-Shalomi and one of this book's editors, concludes this volume. He wrote the first two of three presented essays at the height of the sixties upheaval. Youthful and self-admittedly unripe expressions, they bear early witness to his quest to appropriate Hasidic language in describing inward journeys that were becoming a familiar part of the American spiritual landscape. These writings also contain his earliest formulations of ideas that were to be developed more fully in his address to a conference on Neo-Hasidism, the third text, delivered some four decades later.

Reinterpreting and expanding upon the values of eighteenth-century Hasidism, we believe the visions of all six thinkers—Zeitlin, Buber, Heschel, Carlebach, Schachter-Shalomi, and Green—still speak to a revival of Judaism, and even to a broader spiritual community, in our own day.

The Companion Volume, *A New Hasidism: Branches*

Carrying the enterprise forward is *A New Hasidism: Branches*. In this companion volume, contemporary Neo-Hasidic teachers treat key issues confronting the spiritual seekers of today and tomorrow: the role of halakhah or normative praxis in contemporary Jewish spirituality, the place for charismatic teachers in an egalitarian religious community, the legitimacy of learning from other traditions in a nontriumphalist interreligious context, the voices of women in contemporary spiritual leadership, and more.

The editors are particularly happy to include, toward the end of this volume, perspectives that emerge from the Israeli encounter with Neo-Hasidism, quite different from the experience in North America.

Using These Books

The selections in this volume, as well as some of the essays to be found in *Branches*, will serve as excellent texts for study and conversation in the synagogue and other adult Jewish educational settings. They will also resonate well with the many seekers among today's university students, and as such could be used well both for university courses and more informal education at Hillels.

Zeitlin's "Rules for Members of Yavneh" and Buber's passionate descriptions in "The Life of the Hasidim" will offer particularly rich fodder for classroom discussion. Schachter-Shalomi's call for his original B'nai Or community would be an especially interesting mirror to hold up to today's "independent minyanim" and *havurot*.

In the companion volume, *Branches*, Green's "Neo-Hasidic Credo" should also provide a rich background for conversation, not only for adult learning groups but also for campus and synagogue leaders who are willing to partake in real self-examination in promulgating their mission. So too Mayse's treatment of halakhah and its place in a contemporary Jewish spirituality. The essays on such specific topics as a Neo-Hasidic approach to ecology or psychotherapy will also evoke interesting conversation, perhaps to be conducted in tandem with experts from those realms who are first being exposed to this Neo-Hasidic Torah.

To guide these conversations, The Jewish Publication Society is offering a Discussion Guide for both volumes, available either at Arthur Green's website, artgreen26.com, or at jps.org/books/a-new-hasidism -roots and jps.org/books/a-new-hasidism-branches.

We invite you to join with us in meeting an array of teachers and fellow-seekers of both past and present. Perhaps you too may choose to follow, build upon, expand, and carry forward their paths into an unknown future.

Editors' Note

All of the introductory material preceding the excerpts in this volume has been written by the editors, with just two exceptions, noted in the acknowledgments. Mostly the authors' original texts have been preserved precisely as they were originally composed. In rare instances we changed the names of places or figures, altered transliterations, or made minor grammatical adjustments within the excerpts, all for purposes of consistency and editorial understanding.

The notes in this book are almost entirely those of the editors, with the following exceptions. In chap. 1, on Hillel Zeitlin, the original text included some notes to "The Fundaments of Hasidism" that the present editors have supplemented. Whenever possible, the editors have updated Zeitlin's references to Hasidic works to more current editions. Added comments are presented in brackets to distinguish them from Zeitlin's. The notes to Zalman Schachter-Shalomi's *Foundations of the Fourth Turning of Hasidism: A Manifesto* are original, as are those of Arthur Green's "Notes from the Jewish Underground: On Psychedelics and Kabbalah" and "After Itzik: Toward a Theology of Jewish Spirituality."

A New Hasidism

Roots

1

Hillel Zeitlin

Introduction

Hillel Zeitlin (1871–1942) was the leading figure of philosophical Neo-Hasidism among Eastern European Jews in the pre-Holocaust era.[1] In many ways his life's work—addressing a Hebrew and Yiddish-reading public that had both a familiar and complicated relationship with its Hasidic past—was parallel to that of the German philosopher and scholar Martin Buber, whose writing on Hasidism and Hasidic tales presented the spiritual legacy of the Ba'al Shem Tov and his disciples to a Western audience (chap. 2). Both men were deeply rooted in the Western philosophical tradition. Both tended toward a certain romanticization of Hasidism, in the spirit of their age. Both had profound insight into the religious heart of Hasidism that has come to be appreciated again in more recent times. The two studied and wrote about Hasidism with a programmatic agenda in mind: the dream of bringing about a new revival of Judaism that would bear within it much of the spiritual energy and enthusiasm that had characterized Hasidism in its early heyday.

Zeitlin, the scion of a Chabad family who had rebelled in his youth, was an autodidact who had read very widely, especially in the thought of his own era. In the first decade of the twentieth century, he saw his task as bringing philosophical enlightenment to the Hebrew reader. His first two significant published works were on Spinoza (*Baruch Spinoza*, 1900) and Nietzsche (a series of articles called "Friedrich

Nietzsche" in *Ha-Zeman*, 1905), both in Hebrew. He was also influenced by Schopenhauer, Tolstoy, Lev Shestov, readings in Buddhism, and various other philosophical-theological currents present in his contemporary culture. All of these studies fed directly into his way of understanding Hasidism and his decision to reappropriate its religious language as his own.

During the decade prior to the First World War, Zeitlin was a member of the circle of Hebrew writers Yosef Chaim Brenner, Uri Gnessin, and others, all of them more-or-less followers of Micha Yosef Berdyczewski, Hebrew literature's Nietzschean rebel against tradition and its authority. In the course of a quest for an authentic Jewish spiritual language, Zeitlin began to reembrace Hasidism. Doing so, he made the very unusual decision for those times to return to a life of traditional religious observance. Until his death on the road to Treblinka in 1942, he lived at the center of Warsaw's teeming intellectual and highly partisan political life, dressed in a Hasidic caftan, a mystical-prophetic figure choosing to operate within an almost entirely secular milieu.[2]

Zeitlin nonetheless disdained the Orthodox of his day almost as fully as he disdained every other party. A tireless author, journalist, and polemicist, he published constantly in both the Yiddish and Hebrew press,[3] taking on enemies from all sides.[4]

In his key 1910 essay on Hasidic thought, "The Fundaments of Hasidism," Zeitlin offers a quasi-systematic presentation of Hasidic mystical theology, woven of quotations from the movement's early sources. He begins with "Being and Nothingness," trying to show that the movement's doctrine grew out of an experiential matrix in which the world of multiplicity gives way to an inner perception of the mysterious underlying oneness of being, the ultimate truth of mystical religion. He continued in this vein in a 1913 essay called "In the Soul's Secret Place," a response to his reading of William James's *Varieties of Religious Experience*, probably in Russian translation.[5] Zeitlin thus shows himself to be both deeply rooted in the Hasidic sources, which he constantly quoted, and a person of modern sophistication who had not relinquished his Western literary tastes when turning back to Hasidism. His volume of personal religious poetry, published in both Hebrew and Yiddish versions, includes adapted translations of several poems from Christian and other non-Jewish sources.

Already in the 1920s, Zeitlin became obsessed by a growing sense of an impending (but undefined) catastrophe about to overwhelm Polish Jewry.[6] This was not difficult to imagine, given the terrible pogroms that had befallen the Polish and Ukrainian Jewish communities between 1918 and 1921. Particularly in the southern and southeastern regions of the newly emergent country (eastern Galicia and Volhynia), the local Jewry was even more badly battered by the bitter Polish-Ukrainian and Polish-Soviet conflicts in the immediate postwar years than it had been during the First World War itself. Both Polish and Ukrainian forces committed significant antisemitic atrocities, including large-scale murder. Vast numbers of Jews fled the region, continuing the ongoing process of urbanization. Warsaw in particular saw a great influx of refugees, including a large youthful population.[7]

Many of these young people were unemployed and footloose. Coming from now-destroyed traditional *shtetlakh*, some were also on the edge of deciding whether to abandon the religious way of life. At the same time, by 1922 it was becoming clear that the loudly touted Minorities Treaty accepted by newly independent Poland would not amount to much, and that Jews both culturally and economically were being left to their own meager resources. Poverty and despair were widespread on the Jewish street.

Yet in these same years of increasingly dire economic and political circumstances, Jewish society was being dramatically transformed by the new intellectual currents rampant in the first half of the twentieth century: nationalist and territorialist movements, linguistic ideologies espousing the rebirth of Yiddish and Hebrew literatures, secular and religious forms of Zionism, and the mass politicization of the ultra-Orthodox bloc. These various movements, and especially their robust and energetic youth cultures, formed a crucial part of the historical backdrop of Zeitlin's project of spiritual renewal.[8]

In the face of both the tragedy and the expansive opportunity, Zeitlin sought to become an activist as well as a literary figure. He was especially concerned with the situation of rootless Jewish youth. Throughout his career as a public figure, beginning shortly after World War I, he issued calls for a new organization of Jewish life under various banners, each addressing different aspects, concerns, and slices of the Jewish community. The conceptions ranged from Ahdut Yisrael, a vision for unifying and recharging the entire Jewish people (perhaps to be seen as an alternative to Zionism), to Beney Heikhala, a group so elite in its religious education that he sought to address it in Zoharic Aramaic! In 1936 he called the group Moshi'im or "saviors" of Israel. Even as the war was about to break out in 1939, he assembled a group of ten *mekhavvenim*, or people of intense prayer, to join him in devotionally withstanding the great destruction he knew was about to come. All of these groups called for transcendence of party loyalties, concern for the entire Jewish people and its fate, and a combination of political and economic reforms coupled with a call for spiritual renewal.

Of special interest is his 1923 call for the formation of an elite Jewish spiritual fraternity to be called *Yavneh*. He first announced this most fully elaborated of his attempts at intentional community[9] in a series of stirring articles entitled "The Call of the Hour" in the Warsaw daily *Der Moment*, where Zeitlin had a weekly column (he had been among the newspaper's founders).[10] These were followed up by two further articles in which he began to suggest more concrete steps for the formation of this would-be movement for the spiritual regeneration of Judaism and Jewry. The fact that this series of articles was published in a widely popular Yiddish daily suggests that Zeitlin was hoping to address the broadest possible readership.

Zeitlin longed for a rarefied and reinvigorated Judaism, one based on his idealized vision of early Hasidism and deeply tied also to the image of the circle around Rabbi Shimon bar Yohai in the Zohar. Zeitlin had a lifelong love affair with the Zohar; in those years he was beginning to translate it from Aramaic into Hebrew.[11] Still, his particular vision of a glorified Neo-Hasidic community very much belonged to Poland of the 1920s. The values of socialism, including supporting oneself by the dignity of one's own labor and disdain for commerce as a form of exploitation, were integral to the rules he composed for the community he sought to create. This idealistic religious community was to serve as a beacon for alienated Jewish youth, presenting Judaism to them at once as both a highly moral and profoundly spiritual way of life. This stood in sharp contrast to the petty and divisive squabbling, as well as to the questionable ethical standards, that he saw in the existing Orthodox and Hasidic communities of his day.[12]

Zeitlin's vision of Yavneh was also the subject of a privately published pamphlet called *Di Teyvah* that appeared in 1924.[13] *Di Teyvah* announced itself as published by the "religious-ethical circle Yavneh of the Ahavat Re'im Society," a group otherwise unidentified. This makes it sound as though Yavneh came into being for some brief amount of time following Zeitlin's call, although it is possible that the title-page pronouncement reflects more wish than reality.

Di Teyvah opens with a small number of evocative Yiddish poems. These reveal Zeitlin's deep longing to draw near to the Divine as well as his increasing frustration with the Jewish people's sufferings and God's seeming indifference to their plight.[14] One such poem, a prayer entitled "Our Wish," is accompanied by a note telling the reader that it "was prayed in a small circle in Warsaw on the new moon of Shevat in 5684 [January 7, 1924]."

In *Di Teyvah* Zeitlin also published the previously mentioned rules: a list of fourteen "commandments for every true follower of Yavneh [a fifteenth was added in a 1928 version found in *Sifran shel Yehidim*]."[15] Preceding these admonitions was an "interview" Zeitlin did with himself, "What Does Yavneh Want . . . ?," which describes the new society as a renewed and more universalized version of the Ba'al Shem Tov's spiritual path.

This was also the subject of a newly discovered manuscript signed by Zeitlin, a single-sheet four-sided text in which he describes more succinctly (brevity was not one of his virtues) and clearly the nature of the group and its intended function.[16] That text is offered in translation here. In it he announces that some tens of Polish Jews have already signed on to the group and are living by its rule. He also refers to a forthcoming prophetic-mystical work of his that is to serve as a guide to the group's members. This is likely *Sifran shel Yehidim*, published in 1928.

The existence of an active Yavneh group in Warsaw is also attested by a letter Zeitlin wrote to Nehemiah Aminoach in Jerusalem in the summer of 1925. Aminoach was one of the founders of the Poel Mizrachi movement, the religious version of Labor Zionism. The two had met during Zeitlin's single visit to the Land of Israel earlier that year, on the occasion of the opening of Hebrew University. Zeitlin writes:

> Now there is something I want to say to you. I think a small Yavneh group should be established in Jerusalem, a society of working people who will live in accord with the fourteen principles that I set forth in my Yiddish composition *Di Teyvah*. Such a group already exists here in Warsaw, but I think that Jerusalem (or the Land of Israel altogether) is its true place. Members of Yavneh may belong to any political party, so long as they recognize the holiness of Israel [i.e., all Jews] and the exaltedness of true Jewish religious life. They should come together to fulfill in life those fourteen principles I set forth in *Di Teyvah*. For people like you, living by the work of your hands and filled with religious feeling and holy fire, it will be easy to live by those rules. [You should] join together for support, to defend these principles, and to distribute them among all the working people of the Holy Land. I am sending you a special package of thirteen copies (since thirteen is

the numerical equivalent of *ehad*) of *Di Teyvah* and ten copies of
the seventh issue of *Mayn Vort* (because it contains a letter to the
members of Yavneh, and there you will see their spiritual side).[17]
Along with these will be a few other booklets that I have published
recently, including *Ha-Hasidut* (in Yiddish), *Hillel Zeitlin's Bletlekh*
(I am missing the first issue), and *Der Sneh*. And what do I want
of you? Please distribute *Di Teyvah* and *Mayn Vort* among your
friends and try to establish a Yavneh society. [Members of] this
group should take upon themselves to strive to live in the spirit
of those ideas and principles outlined in *Di Teyvah*, and to meet
each week (no less) to study together and discuss matters of true
religion (here we study mainly the *Tanya* by the Rav of Liadi, the
Kuzari, the works of the MaHaRaL, and similar things) and life
in the spirit of Yavneh.[18]

Here we learn uniquely of the existence of Yavneh as a group that
met regularly for study in Warsaw. The record of its curriculum is also
most revealing, giving us a glimpse into Zeitlin's own selection of Jewish religious classics.

We do not know how long that group continued to function or what
problems it encountered. Four years later, when Zeitlin published *Sifran
shel Yehidim*, he confessed that his prior efforts had failed and he was
now attempting to revive them:

The Yavneh or Beney Heikhala [Children of the palace] groups that
I suggest founding in this book are not to be confused with the
Ahdut Yisrael [Unity of Israel] of which I have spoken frequently
in the press. Ahdut Yisrael is meant to absorb all within it, since it
is of Jewry as a whole. The Yavneh or Beney Heikhala groups (I call
the elite within the elite Beney Heikhala), if they are founded, will
be societies of unique individuals dedicated to inward elevation
and a quest for solutions to the ills of the nation and the world.

A small attempt was made in this matter in 1923–24, but that attempt did not succeed. A few pure and upright young people responded to my call in the press, but not people of clear consciousness and deep inner awareness.

What did not succeed in the years 1923–24 may succeed now.[19]

There is no indication, however, that the second call for Yavneh was any more successful than the first.[20] In the 1930s Zeitlin became ever more absorbed both in his Hebrew translation of the Zohar and the prophetic call to repentance in the eye of the gathering storm. We no longer hear of Yavneh. One is left with the impression that the lack of response to his call was disappointing to Zeitlin, who struggled throughout his life with periods of depression and disillusionment. The failure of Yavneh likely left him more isolated than ever. It is also probable that aspects of his own personality, including his donning the mantle of prophet of doom, did not encourage others to come to his side.

In his *Demamah ve-Kol*, published in 1936, Zeitlin asks himself:

"Where are the Bonim, Beney Yavneh, Beney Heikhala, Beney ha-Raz, and all the various *yehidim* [special individuals] of yours?

"The wind has blown them away; the stormy times have scattered them . . . but wherever they are, they are better than others.

"And for whom do you wait and hope today?

"For those whom I would like to call 'Ve-'Alu Moshi'im.'

"And who will they be?"[21]

There follows a long paragraph giving yet another description of Zeitlin's imagined vanguard: people freed from all doctrinaire views, dedicating themselves entirely to the Jewish people, having holy fire burning in their hearts, forming a holy society to liberate the people, while "on their lips are whispered prayers that will carry them on the wings of great hope toward the messianic days that are approaching." They are to devote themselves to the ten-point program described earlier in that work, including six suggestions for the physical salvation of Jewry and four devoted to its spiritual restoration.[22] Given the increasing desperation of the times (rabid antisemitism was becoming a dominant political force in Poland as well as across the German border), there is more emphasis on the political program, especially organization toward emigration, than was present in the 1920s documents.

Zeitlin's call for an elite and intimate religious brotherhood places him in a long tradition within the history of Jewish mysticism. His "rules" immediately invoke association with those of the circle around Rabbi Moshe Cordovero and Rabbi Isaac Luria in sixteenth-century Safed,[23] with the Ahavat Shalom circle (the original Bet El) around Rabbi Shalom Shar'abi in eighteenth-century Jerusalem,[24] and with groups that crystallized around such figures as Rabbi Moshe Hayyim Luzzatto in Padua[25] and Rabbi Nahman in Bratslav.[26] All of these, in turn, reflect the fantasy circle of devoted disciples surrounding Rabbi Shimon bar Yohai in the pages of the Zohar, and perhaps, through the mask of that fiction, the real circle of the Zohar writers in late-thirteenth-century Spain.[27] Although rabbinic Judaism defined itself as a religion for married householders, rejecting the monastic option that had existed in Qumran, a thread of quasi-monasticism runs through all of these circles, however diverse in time and place, including also the Hasidey Ashkenaz of the medieval Rhineland, the Mussarniks of nineteenth-century Novarodok in Lithuania, and the Hasidim of Reb Arele Roth in Hungary and Jerusalem.

Zeitlin's quest to establish Yavneh was not the only such effort in Poland during these turbulent years. In the 1920s Rabbi Kalonymous Kalman Shapira of Piasecne, a traditional but highly creative Hasidic leader, wrote a short pamphlet entitled *Beney Mahashavah Tovah*[28] outlining the basic principles and structures of a close-knit mystical fellowship. He called this group the *hevraya*, in obvious reference to the circle of students around Rabbi Shimon bar Yohai in the Zohar. This fellowship was meant to be a part of his larger project of spiritual renewal for Hasidism, which Shapira felt had lost much of its original vitality by the early twentieth century. The text of *Beney Mahashavah Tovah*, not intended for public circulation, was distributed to a select group of Rabbi Shapira's disciples.[29] The fellowship was also meant to be an elite group, though Shapira wrote that entrance must be granted to anyone regardless of his profession, provided that the person was an honest and committed seeker.[30]

Beney Mahashavah Tovah also includes fourteen "points of instruction and rules" (*seder hadrakhah u-khelalim*). This hardly seems coincidental; it is likely that Rabbi Shapira was aware of Zeitlin's writings about Yavneh, especially those then widely available in the Yiddish press. The parallel lists of fourteen points certainly suggest that although Shapira never mentions Zeitlin, Shapira's work, most likely composed just a few years later, was his own response to Zeitlin's call. At the same time, an examination of these specific admonitions makes the difference between his intended fellowship and Zeitlin's project quite clear.[31] Shapira's rule is not "Neo-Hasidic"; instead it addresses individuals who were already living within the Hasidic community and longed to develop a more profound inner life. His more traditional "points" refer to certain books the seeker should study, direct how these works should be approached, describe an impassioned experience of prayer, and promote a type of mindfulness and attentiveness to all of one's actions. Shapira certainly does not promote the virtues of socialism; nor does he warn his readers as explicitly as Zeitlin against political involvement. Elsewhere he does say explicitly that the goal of the group is to rise above ordinary human society; it would not be a place for meting out honors, nor would it have a defined hierarchy.[32]

Zeitlin's Yavneh and its implicit critique of society, on the other hand, were addressed to a broader audience of Warsaw Jews, those alienated from the Hasidic community but still open to tradition. His identification with, even glorification of, the working class is striking. He preached against the spiritual malaise of empty materialism and assimilation, extolling the virtues of a life unencumbered by luxury and unsullied by the exploitation of other workers.

In the highly politicized atmosphere of secular-Jewish Warsaw, Zeitlin felt the need to insist that Yavneh rise above party loyalties.

We cannot be sure if Zeitlin and Rabbi Shapira knew one another, but it is hardly imaginable that they did not meet. Both were very well-known public figures. They did not live far from each other, and both were eventually imprisoned in the Warsaw Ghetto. Zeitlin was certainly aware of Rabbi Shapira's teachings; he published an admiring review of the latter's only published work, *Hovat ha-Talmidim*.[33] We do not know whether Zeitlin might have seen *Beney Mahashavah Tovah*, given its extremely limited distribution, but the possibility cannot be ruled out.

The memory of Zeitlin's dream of a renewed Hasidic community was mostly buried in the ashes of the Warsaw Ghetto, along with his translation of the Zohar and so much else. It would be unfair to say, however, that his efforts bore no later fruit. Zeitlin's *Di Teyvah*, including especially his "monastic" rule, greatly impressed the young Zalman Schachter, then still a Chabad Hasid, when Shmuel Bergman introduced him to Natan Hofshi, its Hebrew translator, during a Jerusalem visit probably in the late 1950s. Schachter's original design for B'nai Or as a Jewish quasi-monastic community, though mostly shaped by his contacts with Christian monastics and named for the newly discovered Qumran document, was also very much influenced by his reading of Zeitlin.[34] That vision in turn influenced the creation of Havurat Shalom in Boston, where Schachter was a visiting member in its crucial founding year (1968-69), and thence the ensuing *havurah* movement. Thus it is fair to say that a spark of Zeitlin's fire is present in both the *havurah* and Jewish Renewal movements,[35] the two most significant attempts at the spiritual regeneration of North American Judaism (other than efforts by Hasidic groups themselves) in the late twentieth and early twenty-first centuries.[36]

Perhaps an apt conclusion to this discussion of Zeitlin's vision for Yavneh is the heartbreaking testimony of a mystical gathering that took place near the end of his life. The explicit goal of this assembly was neither spiritual uplift nor personal transformation. On the eve of the Second World War, Zeitlin called for a group to pray together in an effort to stave off the impending destruction of European Jewry, a disaster he saw approaching with rapid footsteps. Symcha Bunem Urbach, a disciple of Zeitlin's who survived the war, recalled the event:

This happened two months "before the calamity,"[37] two months before the outbreak of the War. As one of his disciples who frequented his house, I was called to Zeitlin's abode for a special gathering. On the invitation slip was inscribed: "This relates to the very existence of the people of Israel. . . ."

Very much surprised by these words, I came to his home. There I beheld a sight that was quite extraordinary, even for me. My surprise was to increase manyfold.

Zeitlin was seated at a table, and there was a group of ten people around him. They included the religious writer and legendary figure Israel Stern, well-known Kabbalists from Warsaw, and a few Bratslaver Hasidim. In a hushed voice both deep and warm, suffused with quiet pathos, in the tone of a seer of visions and looking like a man who is "not present," Zeitlin said to us: "My beloveds, I behold a great catastrophe before me. It is growing nearer and creeping to the gates of the state of Poland. The Nazi enemy is approaching, and it will, heaven forefend, totally destroy the Jewish community on the banks of the Vistula.[38] It will move from city to city, from town to town, from community to community, and it will slaughter us all. It will tear off the heads of elders, smash the skulls of children, and destroy us all, leaving behind no survivors or remnants.

A heavy silence reigned following his words. Suddenly Stern arose, shaken and pierced, and asked with passion, "What must we do to avert this evil?"

"I see no other way," said Zeitlin, "except to pray, to pray, and to pray once more!"

He had assembled us, he added, to establish a fellowship of ten people, *mekhavvenim* [people of intense prayer], who would unite with a single heart and fall before the blessed One in prayer, prayer that would break through the heavens, prayer that would open the closed gates. . . . (He gave me these words in the form of an article entitled *"Mekhavvenim,"* which I published in the journal *Der Nayer Ruf*). . . .

Zeitlin then got up and began to read chapters of Psalms with great passion and trembling, rivers of tears flowing from his eyes: "The prayer of a poor person, when he is faint" (Ps. 102:1), "My God, my God, why have you abandoned me" (Ps. 22:2). . . . We sat together astonished and amazed, for Zeitlin's prayer shook our very heartstrings.

(This whole incident, which I beheld with my own eyes, seemed even to me like an exotic spectacle, and I put it out of my mind. For this I beat my breast and cry out my sin.)

This was our final meeting. (For various reasons I did not see him again. He went off to a summer residence, and I left Warsaw at the very beginning of the war and the German conquest.) But some two months later I was an eyewitness to the catastrophe that Zeitlin had foreseen with his spirit, that came down upon the heads of Polish Jewry. With my own eyes I saw holy communities go up in flames, Jewish towns transformed into graveyards, the heads of sages torn asunder, the skulls of children split open, and Zeitlin's call echoed in my ears. It had been a voice of "desolation in the wilderness. . . ."[39] During my days of wandering through the destroyed villages and forests of Poland, I was reminded of Zeitlin's prayer.

"To pray, and to pray once more"—that was the final testament of Reb Hillel Zeitlin, may the memory of the righteous be a blessing. This was the final chord in the melody of his life.[40]

A testimony published after the war by another survivor, Hillel Seidman, chronicler of the Warsaw Ghetto, related that Zeitlin had called a similar meeting in the Warsaw Ghetto immediately before Rosh Hashanah in the fall of 1941.[41] This gathering, which took place soon after Zeitlin's wife had been deported and his son had died, included many of the same elements. It was preceded by a stirring written invitation, and during the event a group of deeply religious individuals surrounded the wizened Zeitlin, who then delivered a prophetic address that was at once an exhortation to repentance and a prediction of Messiah's imminent arrival. He, too, notes in retrospect the tragedy of the gathering called by Zeitlin, standing as it did on the eve of Jewish Warsaw's destruction. Yet Seidman also recalls the tremendous, even mystical power of Zeitlin's assembly, and speaks with particular reverence of the force and passion of the old man's heartrending prayer.[42]

When Hillel Zeitlin's block was called out to the notorious Umschlagplatz, the gathering point for forced deportations, he appeared, according to Seidman's account, wearing tallit and tefillin and carrying a copy of the Zohar in his hand. He was thus ironically fulfilling the kabbalists' claim, recalled also in the writings of the Bratslav Hasidim, that "with this book Israel will go forth from exile."

Zeitlin died in the course of the forced march to Treblinka on the eve of Rosh Hashanah, 1942.

What Is Yavneh? (Untitled Manuscript, ca. mid-1920s)

This first, short selection from Zeitlin's voluminous writings offers his clearest and most evocative vision for the Yavneh fellowship. The brief text survived as an unknown manuscript written in Zeitlin's own hand until it was purchased at an auction and published in 2016 by the editors of this volume.

Yavneh wants to be for Jewry what Hasidism was a hundred and fifty years ago. This was Hasidism in its origin, that of the BeSHT. This does not mean that Yavneh wants to be that original Hasidism. It rather wants to bring into *contemporary* Jewish life the freshness, vitality, and joyful attachment to God in accord with the style, concepts, mood, and meaning of the modern Jew, just as the BeSHT did—in his time—according to the style, concepts, mood, and meaning of Jews of that time. Yavneh wants especially to revive the *soul* of Jews, not by organizing the masses or agitating among them, but rather by seeking out exceptional individuals in whom Judaism lives not only in their deeds and customs, but in their *hearts*, as the greatest holiness and the purest divine beauty.

Yavneh wants to seek out exceptional individuals who in every aspect of their perceptions, feelings, thoughts, and deeds are willing to serve as a throne for the Infinite. It wants to unify these individuals in a society and to form out of them an example for the entire people.

Yavneh thus wants to devote itself to exceptional individuals, and only to them, recognizing that the Jewish masses today are distant from a higher spirituality, and thus also from deep inner religiosity. In actual fact, the irreligiosity of the Jewish masses is being *especially* strengthened at this moment by the multiple parties on the Jewish street. If leftist, these do battle against religion. Those on the right *marinate* the Jewish religion. That is why Yavneh seeks to find and bring together those Jewish individuals who feel God in their souls, who live in Him. And because of this, because God lives *within* them, the leftist parties will not be able to *rub God off* of them and the right will not be able to *deaden* Him in them.

The ideal of Yavneh is to seek out and unify those individuals who can feel newly born in God each day ("You are my son; this day I give birth to you" [Ps. 2:7]),[43] along with the great joy of that rebirth and the intense holiness that accompanies it.

Furthermore, Yavneh does not intend to remain only a society for inner religious experiences. Yavneh is also a society of Torah. As such, it demands of its members that their inner life in God be expressed in holy and pure actions.

Thus far tens of individuals have been found in Poland who are prepared to live according to the chief ideals of Yavneh, and to form such a society. I have expounded the details of the Yavneh ideal in a series of articles in *Moment* under the title "The Great Call of the Hour."

A prophetic-mystical work of mine is soon to appear. This will be able to serve as a basis for the entire inner and outer life of every single Jew who seeks the spiritual revival of Israel, especially for each member of Yavneh.

—HILLEL ZEITLIN

What Does Yavneh Want? (1924)

Here, in Zeitlin's imagined interview with himself, he describes the new society of Yavneh as a renewed and more universalized version of the Ba'al Shem Tov's spiritual path.

What does Yavneh want?
Yavneh wants to bring the old Hasidism, that of the BeSHT, back to life and establish it on foundations that are more acceptable in the present time of "Messiah's footsteps."

Of what does this old BeSHTian Hasidism consist?
Three loves: the love of God, the love of Israel, and the love of Torah.

How did the BeSHT understand the love of God?
Until the BeSHT, even the purest love of God (and we speak here only of the love of God in its purest form. Those who love God because He gives them health, length of days, glory, and wealth, are not being considered here at all) was conceived only like the love of a glorious king or a great sage. Maybe, in the best case, it was like the way one loves a father. But the BeSHT came and taught that one must love with a terrible thirst, a terrible burning, terrible suffering that fills the entire soul and body in such a way that no room for anything else remains.

Was the BeSHT the first to conceive of the love of God this way?
Long before the BeSHT there were those who saw the love of God as entailing suffering as long as the person remains in the body and does not have an actual "outpouring of the soul."

Who were they?
R. Eleazar Rokeah, R. Yehudah he-Hasid,[44] and in the time of
the BeSHT, R. Hayyim Ibn Attar.[45]

*And how did such enlightened Jews as R. Bahya Ibn Pakuda,[46] Mai-
monides, and many others understand the love of God?*
They understood "love" as an act of the mind, of consciousness, of knowledge.

*And R. Eleazar Rokeah, R. Yehudah he-Hasid, R. Hayyim Ibn Attar,
and the BeSHT think that "love" is not an act of mind, consciousness,
or knowledge?*
They respect these as well. But they demand that the love of
the Most High take in the entire person. It is the highest form
of passion, the desire of all desires. It embraces all particular
wills, all of a person's senses, the totality of passion, all one's
lust for life, all thoughts, all words, all deeds!

*Did they come to this all-consuming love just out of their own souls,
or were they somehow aided by the ancients?*
They saw this love in the words of the poet: "As the hart
pants after streams of water, so does my heart pant for You,
O God." . . . "My soul thirsts for God, for the living God" (Ps.
42:2–3). . . . "Who else do I have in heaven? I want none but
You in the earth. . . . My flesh and heart wear away, O rock of
my heart; God is my portion forever" (Ps. 73:25–26).

*If Rokeah, Yehudah he-Hasid, the BeSHT, and Ibn Attar saw this in
the words of the poet, what did they add to it?*
Everyone knows these words of the poet. But they are taken
as just that: poetry, meaning unique and special moments of
divine inspiration. Along came the Rokeah, R. Yehudah, Ibn

Attar, and the BeSHT, and they made it a requirement for every individual in every hour and moment, like the air we breathe.

And what did the BeSHT in particular add to this?
For the Rokeah, R. Yehudah, and Ibn Attar, this all-consuming love was a positive commandment, alongside all the others. But for the BeSHT it is the foundation of everything. He never stops talking about it in all his teachings, stories, and aphorisms.

And how did the BeSHT understand the love of Israel?
He once said to someone: "Believe me, I love the worst Jew in the world much more than you love your favorite child." This is what love of Israel meant to the BeSHT.

And what did the love of Torah mean to him?
If you understand "Torah" only as sharp-minded, expert, deep learning, you can find love of Torah among other great sages and righteous folk, perhaps even more than in the BeSHT. But the BeSHT's love of Torah touches especially upon the light of Torah, the hidden light, attachment to God through the letters of the Torah, the "worlds, souls, and divinity" that exist within every letter. Those letters combine to form words, and out of the joining of these words are formed awesome unifications, bringing near the coming of messiah.

And why do you call all this a "return to the original Hasidism" of the BeSHT? Why don't you simply say: "to Hasidism"?
Because today's Hasidism is very far from the pure Hasidism of the BeSHT.

In what way has today's official Hasidism turned away from the pure Hasidism of the BeSHT?

Simply in the fact that it no longer possesses that love of God, Israel, and Torah.

What do you mean?
Very simple. Today's Hasidim still *talk* about all these things. But they mix all sorts of incidental things in with them—fanciful interpretations, homilies, intellectual games—until the real point is obscured. Second—and this is really the main thing—for some of today's Hasidim their Hasidism has become a purely external matter. They study without a real taste for it; they pray in the same way. They pursue wealth and glory no less, and sometimes even more, than non-Hasidim. They're always busy praising their own *rebbes* and castigating all the others, along with their disciples. They've set up *rebbes*' courts and dynasties and get all involved in the politics of these. They spend a good part of their lives fighting about rabbis, ritual slaughterers, and other religious officials. They consider only themselves to be proper Jews and everyone else to be nothing at all. They make Hasidism consist entirely of external manners, outer dress, and outward customs. They regularly mix fanaticism with piety. They chase away the young people over petty and foolish matters, sometimes pushing them far from Jewish religious life with their very hands. . . .[47]

Are you claiming that today's Hasidim contain even less true and pure Judaism than the non-Hasidim?
God forbid! First, I'm only speaking here about a portion of today's Hasidim, not about all. Certainly there are other sorts of Hasidim present today as well: those who bear a deep inwardness, a deep attachment, a passionate love of God. They have love for all Jews, a love of truth and a longing for

peace, a strong, clear understanding of all that is happening around them. Second, even the other Hasidim, those of outwardness and dress, still have lots of good qualities, things that belong to all Jews. Whatever failings a contemporary Hasid may have, he still bears a certain sense of shame, a fear of God, a brokenness, something of modesty, humility, a leaning toward lovingkindness, goodness, and love. But all—the inward Hasidim, those who concentrate on the externals, and just ordinary Jews—today need a new light that will shine into their souls, a Hasidism of the future, rays of messiah's light.

Does Yavneh want to be that "Hasidism of the future," that "ray of messiah's light"?
That Hasidism is not yet here. The rays of messiah's light show themselves hardly at all, only to those most pure of sight. But Yavneh wants to prepare for that future. Yavneh seeks, bit by bit, to qualify individuals for it. It wants to create vessels to contain that light, which must come sooner or later.

And in what way will the "Hasidism of the future" be differentiated, not only from today's external Hasidism, but from that which is inward, and even from the Hasidism of the BeSHT?
Differentiated from inward Hasidism and from that of the BeSHT? Not at all! On the contrary, it will be built entirely on the Hasidism of the BeSHT. But what then? It will go farther, broader, and deeper, appropriate to these messianic times.

What will that "going farther," both in breadth and depth, consist of?
In the time of the BeSHT it was enough for Israel to shine a light for itself. In these times, in a time when a world has been destroyed and a new one is being built, Israel has to be

a light for itself and for all peoples, as in the verse: "I the Lord call you in righteousness and hold fast to your hand, making you as a covenantal people, a light to the nations" (Isa. 42:6). And scripture also says: "Is it easy for you to be My servant, to raise up the tribes of Jacob and restore the guarded ones of Israel? I have made you a light unto the nations, so that My salvation reach the ends of the earth" (Isa. 49:6). And it also says: "Then I will turn all the nations toward a clear tongue so that they all might call upon the name of the Lord, to serve Him together" (Zeph. 3:9).

And in what else?

In the time of the BeSHT Jews sought the light of Torah only in the Torah itself. Sometimes they also sought it out in ordinary folk-tales, in which they discovered a hidden light. ("Declare His glory among the nations," Ps. 96:3, according to a profound remark of Rabbi Nahman,[48] means that "the glory of God cries forth from all things, even from tales told by the non-Jews.")[49] But in the times of this final great purification we need to seek out the Torah-light in all the finest works of art, in all forms of worldly knowledge. We need to approach these with a certain light in our hands, with a particular kind of foresight. "A candle of the Lord is the human soul, searching out all the belly's chambers" (Prov. 20:27). It will have to separate, seek out and nullify, casting aside heaps of lies in order to get at the kernel of truth. . . .

And in what else?

In the time of the BeSHT the class conflicts among people were not yet so sharply defined. The demand for social justice had not yet been articulated with full seriousness and honesty. Today we are undergoing horrible evils that are taking place in the world. But these are leading us to a more just and honorable relationship with those who work with sweat on their brows. The "Hasidism of the future" will incorporate all that is healthy, pure, and honorable in Socialism. But it will with great bitterness cast aside all in Socialism that is petty, egotistical, merchant-like in its materialism, unjust, jealous, or vengeful. It will reject the dark and wild tyranny of the masses and of those adventurers who climb up on the backs of the masses.[50]

In the Hasidism of the future the love of God will shine forth and burn even more brightly than it did in the days of the BeSHT. The "Love of Israel" will be transformed into a great worldwide "Love of Humanity." Nevertheless, Israel will always be recognized as the firstborn child of God, the one who has borne, continues to bear, and will continue to bear the godly light. "Love of Torah" will spread forth over all that breathes with sublime wisdom, after the inner light teaches the Jews to distinguish between that within the worldly sciences which is of the divine mind and that which is just self-proclaimed human conviction, error, and lies. "Justice, justice shall you pursue" (Deut. 16:20) will be spread through all social relationships. Justice will be demanded not only of the opposing class (as both the capitalists and the proletariat do today), but people will demand justice of *themselves*. Pursuit of justice will be not only a public matter (as it is today), but rather one of individual concern. Each person will think not about how to avoid being exploited, but rather about how to avoid exploiting the other.

Perhaps you could outline for me, just briefly, how you see the Hasid of the future, that for which the Yavneh member is preparing.

I'll try to do so. The Hasid of the future will live only from his own physical labor. He will exploit no one in the world, doing not even the slightest harm to anyone. He will partake of God's own holiness, living in uninterrupted communion with the Endless. He will walk through divine fire while praying, will study Torah with an inner godly light, will seek and find everywhere the light of Torah and messianic light. In all his thoughts and deeds he will strive only for true peace and unity. He will be filled with love and compassion for every Jew and non-Jew, for every creature. He will long to raise up the form of the *shekhinah* [i.e., the immanent, often feminine, divine Presence] in the holy land and to spread her light through all the world. He will be a great seer and a great knower. In his own eyes he will be as nothing at all, having not just an external veneer of modesty but a deep inner recognition, a full consciousness that he is "just a small creature, lowly, dark, standing with but a weak mind before the One who knows perfectly." In that moment he will be a true "chariot" for the divine, a true servant of God, a faithful messenger.

Admonitions for Every True
Member of Yavneh (1924)

The following list of fourteen admonitions for the members of Yavneh (a fifteenth was added in a 1928 version found in *Sifran shel Yehidim*) was printed together with the previous text in the pamphlet *Di Teyva*.

1. Support yourself only from your own work! Try as hard as you can to support yourself from simple physical labor and not from trade. Trade is based primarily on deception, and deception means lies. And lies completely oppose what the Holy One, who is Absolute Truth, demands of us ("God, our Sovereign, is truth" (Jer. 10:10). And, "the signet of God is truth").[51]

If you are, brother, a worker, try to improve in your craft. Don't look forward, as so many do today, to leaving this work so that you can support yourself through easier professions. If you are not yet a worker, make the effort to become one. If it is difficult for you to join a labor union for religious or ethical reasons, try to establish, together with a few of the members of Yavneh, cooperative workshops, and the like.

If you cannot work as a physical laborer because of old age or infirmity, try at least to choose for yourself a type of livelihood that succeeds with a minimum of commerce in it, and help your friends who *are* laborers in every way you can.

2. Keep away from luxuries! Luxuries consume the mind and the strength of a person. Luxuries drive one to acts of constant deceit, leading easily from there to thievery and robbery. Striving for the true Jewish life, and at the same time for a life of luxuries, is like dipping in a purifying pool while holding a defiling abomination in your hand.[52]

Therefore, choose a life of modesty, simplicity, keeping yourself far away from all external pleasures. Refrain as much as you can from all habits that eat up your money, that do not benefit your body, and only harm your soul. My brother, turn your steps away from the theater and from parties. Guard yourself from smoking, from liquor, from expensive clothes, from adorning yourself with rings, and the like. Seek not to adorn your dwelling with costly decorations. It would be better if you would purify and adorn your soul, my dear brother!

3. Do not exploit anyone! If you support yourself solely by the work of your hands, and in so doing live a life of modesty, tranquility, and humility, abstaining from indulgence, luxury, and pleasure seeking, then it will be easy for you to fulfill the great and holy commandment of every pure ethical system: do not exploit anyone! Do not use people, seeking your own benefit without their agreement, or even with their agreement, if full compensation is not received. Every person has their own purpose. Every person is a complete world. From the standpoint of morality and also in a purely religious sense, all exploitation, in any form whatsoever, is robbery and murder.

A factory boss or artisan who takes advantage of workers by paying them the lowest wage acceptable on the market, and not the **true, full and proper** sum for their work, is exploiting those workers. The merchant who takes unfair advantage in buying or selling exploits the people that merchant is dealing with.

Abuses are sometimes to be found today also among politicians, journalists, doctors, and the rest of the people involved in the free professions. Every pressing of advantage that is not the result of the complete, considered, free, and serious agreement of the person involved is criminal. Protect yourself from all this as you would protect yourself from fire, my dear brother!

4. Purify your family life. The family has always been a strong-hold for the Jew. In the face of work, persecution, and daily troubles, the Jew found rest and comfort in quiet, pleasant, and pure family life. The family has always been the Jew's sanctuary. Even Balaam saw this, and against his will declared: "How good are your dwelling places, O Jacob" (Num. 24:5). Balaam saw this and he became blind from envy ("on account of this the eye of that wicked one was blinded").

Today, sadly, the anarchy of the street has broken into the Jewish family. This bulwark, the pure and pleasant Jewish family of Poland, has started to disintegrate, especially since the time of the German conquest [World War I]. Now, this fall is deepening more and more. Further, this decline is abetted by the general moral ruin of the street, the theater, the movies, the pulp journals, and obscene literature. And a good bit of the so-called better and more serious literature abets this. Knowingly and unknowingly, many of those who declare themselves artists contribute to this decline.

Protect your soul from this danger, my dear brother! Strive to protect the quiet, the peace, and the love in your family!

5. Sanctify your sex life altogether! The preservation and sanctification of the covenant are the exalted bases of both interior and exterior holiness. Concerning this, we are charged: "Be holy" and "One who sanctifies oneself a little here below, will be greatly sanctified from above." "The sexual organ is the fundament of the body, sign of the holy covenant." One who is pure in this matter is holy; one who is impure in this area is defiled. In this one must be guarded not only from actual sin but also from sinful thoughts. And the proven ways to this are always to be occupied with work (at best, physical work), and also with the learning of Torah, with concentration and depth. "There is no room for sin except in a heart that is void of wisdom," says Maimonides.[53] "Torah is good when joined to work; the exertion of both cause sin to be forgotten."[54] Actual work—on no account idleness. Idleness brings on all misfortune.

6. Guard yourself from forbidden foods! "You will be defiled by them" (Lev. 11:43). Read this as, "You will be blocked by them."[55] Forbidden foods defile the body and soul; forbidden foods create vile and impure blood in the human body. If some of today's Jewish youth have more of a tendency now than in the past to go toward evil, this is mainly an outcome of not protecting themselves against forbidden foods. Be careful, my brother, of forbidden foods, and thus you will save yourself from impurity, evil, and harmfulness.

7. Sanctify your Shabbat! The Sabbath is not just an ordinary commandment, but the basic foundation. One who weakens the Sabbath, Heaven forbid, desecrates the God of Israel. A person who doesn't sanctify the Sabbath is like one who worships idols. "Keep" and "remember," the single utterance the one God spoke.[56] Unite with the holiness of the Sabbath, and in this way, commune with the blessed Holy One. The Sabbath, however, must be kept not only on the outside, but also within: pray, learn, truly evaluate your soul, concentrate on holy and pure matters. Shabbat upholds the entire Jewish nation. The Community of Israel and Shabbat are truly a pair, and in them resides the Holy Ancient of Days.

8. Keep your home holy! Not only the synagogue, the house of learning, the prayer room, but also an ordinary Jewish house is a small-scale sanctuary. When can this be said? When the house abounds with words of Torah, prayers, blessings, Kiddush, and Havdalah, and when these are expressed seriously, truthfully, with profound and intent sincerity! When a mother and a father, a brother and a sister, live in calm and true peace (for in a peaceful place, there is the blessing of the Father of Peace); when the children are educated in the spirit of the serious and pure Torah; when all the children of the house speak the Jewish tongue and are full of love, honor, and recognition for every Jewish thing.

But what is today the structure of a house of an average Jewish merchant? Mostly, it is a place of selling and buying, sometimes a feverish stock market, sometimes a club for a game of cards, and sometimes a hall for parties. The father goes out in search of "pleasures," and the mother seeks her own. In the house—a constant ill will, continual arguments behind the backs of others, or to their face. The daughters no longer speak Yiddish; the sons are being prepared for empty careers. Although Shabbat and the holidays are observed in an exterior way, it is without joyous celebration, without soul, without life. They pray, and when they have the opportunity, they fulfill commandments and customs, but everything is mechanical. In a place where there is no light and no fire, no love or devotion—there is no resting place for the almighty God.

Yavnehite! Don't allow your house to become secular and commercial. Let your house look as a Jewish house should—a small sanctuary of the Lord! See that the Jewish language is heard in your house, the voice of Torah, words of peace, heartfelt prayers, suffering on account of the great pain of Israel, and silent hopes for redemption.

9. Live always amid the whole Jewish people and for the whole Jewish people. Don't be concerned about yourself, but about all of Israel. The pain of all should be *your* pain; Israel's joy, your joy. Every single Jewish soul is a part of the *shekhinah*, called *kenesset yisra'el* because She is the totality of Jewish souls.[57] The Community of Israel is the lower *shekhinah*, the kingdom of heaven on earth. The suffering of a Jewish soul is distress to the *shekhinah*, as it were. So how can you, Yavnehite, cause pain to any Jew? Whoever works honestly and wholeheartedly for the redemption of Israel—as he understands it—is working to redeem *shekhinah*. Blessings to anyone who does something good for the Jewish people—even if his views are far from our own! Blessings to any hand that is stretched out to bring help to Israel!

Yavnehite! In all your thoughts, all your longings, all your words and deeds, do not have yourself and only those close to you in mind, but rather the entire great holy Jewish people. Bring yourself and your loved ones into that whole. The salvation of the whole will be yours as well.

10. Remove yourself from party politics. Though you are bound to live as a part of the general society, and work especially for the community, do not join any particular party, even if it is close to your heart. Because as long as the party is occupied with politics, it is bound for the furtherance of those politics to transgress the limits of justice and communion of all of Israel. If you are a member of a party, and you find it difficult to leave it, especially if the main purpose of the party is the building up of the nation—set your heart to scrutinize every act and deed of the party. Your humanity, your Judaism, your pure conscience, is a thousandfold more important than even the best and loftiest party.

Whether you are a member of a party or not, you can and ought to participate in the work of any party, to the extent that it directs deeds to the building of the whole nation, and to the unification of the nation, and you are bound to remove yourself from it when it divides Jews, or when, to achieve its purpose, it uses means that are contrary to the Jewish spirit, which is that of love, justice, and holiness.

11. Remember and never forget the three loves! The Yavnehite is bound to seek perfection in the religious sense: the avoidance of sin and the fulfillment of commandments in actual deeds. Above all, one should be especially imbued with an awareness of the three loves—the love of God, the love of Israel, and the love of Torah.

12. Subdue pride! Pride is the most profound and strongest idol. Pride is the "strange god" within one's own body. Pride has deeply rooted itself in us, and in order to uproot it, concerted effort over decades is necessary. Even more: we must combat it all the days of our lives. As long as it rests in us, it hides God, it hides others, and it hides the world outside ourselves. We cannot reach the light of truth as long as pride rests in us. "Pay attention to this cursed one—and bury it!"

13. Sanctify speech! Speech is the expression of the soul. Guard the covenant of the tongue; the holiness of the tongue. Not one word of evil speech! Not one round of gossip! No idle words at all; and it goes without saying, not to defile your tongue with vulgarities. Do not think that there is no damage from speech. What difference does it make? A vulgar joke? Whom does it hurt? No, dear brother! A word has the power to build and destroy worlds. It is your duty, Yavnehite, to be a builder, a creator, repairing lives that have been destroyed. Therefore, let your words be holy.

14. Sanctify your inner life! Let not a day in life pass without taking stock of your soul. Learn or hear *mussar* [moral teachings] every day. Books like *The Duties of the Hearts*,[58] *The Path of the Upright*,[59] *The Way of the Righteous*,[60] *Tanya*,[61] *Select Counsels*,[62] should always be your companions.

Even if you are busy, steal yourself away for five to ten minutes every day, in your chosen corner, for a short and precise tally of your soul. And at this same time, let there be a short silent prayer in your heart: "Sovereign of the world, set me on the right path, on the path of light."

NOTE: Any reader who has firmly decided to start living in accord with the fourteen principles outlined above, even if not all at once but gradually, may turn in this regard either orally or in writing to Hillel Zeitlin, Szliska 60, Warsaw.

15. Broaden and deepen the activity of "Beney Yavneh." Wherever you encounter a person who is prepared to accept the views offered in this book and to seek to live by them, hold fast to him. Teach him, enlighten him, guide him. When you find a few people in your city ready to live in accord with everything said in this book, cleave to them. Enlighten and guide them; proceed together up the pathway that leads toward God. If the way is too far for you and you find it hard to fulfill everything said here, do not turn back. Fulfill first what is *possible* for you. Afterwards try to go farther. The God of heaven and earth will be there to help you.[63]

Let one small gathering extend its hand to a second, the second to a third, until there is firmly established a whole assemblage of Jews returning to God in truth and wholeness, "doing His word in order to hear the voice of His word (Ps. 103:20)."

The Fundaments of Hasidism (1910)[64]

Next come several chapters from Zeitlin's 1910 essay "The Fundaments of Hasidism." Here he offers a quasi-systematic presentation of Hasidic mystical theology, woven of quotations from the movement's early sources.

Being and Nothingness

"The blessed Creator's life-energy is everywhere. Each thing that exists surely has some taste, smell, appearance, attractiveness, or some other qualities. But when we strip away the physical aspect of that thing and consider it only spiritually—considering, for example, the taste or smell without the physical object itself—we will understand that we are dealing with something that cannot be held in our hands or seen with the eyes of flesh. It is in fact grasped only by our life-force, our human soul. It therefore must indeed be something spiritual, the life-force of our blessed Creator, dwelling within that corporeal thing like the soul within the body."[65]

The meaning: Consider a fruit. Take delight and rejoice in it. What you have before you is a real physical object. But when you think about that fruit, raising it up in your memory, imagining it–that is a spiritual process. Concrete reality has been set aside; only the image remains. Of course that image too can be seen as a product of the senses. But now you analyze that image, keeping in mind its physical form, its species, appearance, size, quality, smell, and taste. When you consider any one of these specifics and go deeply into it, grasping at its very essence, there will be nothing concrete left before you, but only abstraction itself. This is something felt and fully grasped only by the soul, for this is the Nothing within each thing, the divine spark within it.

The Nothing is the spiritual essence of that which is conceived and the spiritual essence of the soul that conceives it.

"There are several rungs within Mind, namely consciousness, intellect, and speech, all of which receive from one another. Speech exists within time. So too does thought, for today you may have one thought and tomorrow another. But there is a quality that connects consciousness to mind, and that quality cannot be grasped.[66] It is the Nothing, the *hyle*, like the way an egg becomes a chicken. There is a moment when it is neither egg nor chick. No one can grab hold of that moment, for it is Nothing. So too when consciousness becomes intellect or when thought is formed into word, you can't grasp that which joins them."[67]

The Nothing is present in each person at that point where the rational intellect, that which is linked to the senses, ends, and higher mind, the divine within, begins. Thus it varies from person to person and from thought to thought.

"*Hokhmah* [wisdom] is called Being, but the life-force within *hokhmah*, that which illumines it, is called Nothing (as Scripture teaches 'Wisdom derives from Nothing'; Job 28:12).[68] 'Nothing' is that which remains beyond the intellect and is not grasped. It sustains and enlightens the soul. All this is in accord with the person's intellect, whether greater or lesser. That which you grasp is considered 'being' to you, while that which remains beyond your intellect is called Infinity, that which gives life to the mind."[69]

Such is the measure of the Nothing in the soul of the one who grasps it and such is its measure within every thing that is grasped. The Nothing is the innermost aspect of creation, the flowing Spring, that which exists beyond the border of what can be grasped by the senses or by ordinary mind. Intellect has a limit. The inward glance — or, more properly, the brilliant flash, the innermost exultation of the spirit, mysterious and hidden—is infinite.

The Nothing is the moment of wonder in creation, a moment that you cannot call by any name. Hence you call it "Nothing." This wondrous moment, precisely because it is so wondrous, cannot be defined, regulated, or placed within bounds of space or time. Thus it constantly unifies opposites. Separations and oppositions have their place within Being, while the Nothing is always the One of equanimity.

"*Hokhmah* links things, making peace even between opposites like the elements. Were *hokhmah* not between them, fire and water could not dwell together. Yet we know that they exist in composite form. That is only because *hokhmah* links them, each of them perceiving the Nothing within it. . . ."[70]

"Each thing in the world, when you take it to its root, can be transformed from what it previously was. Take, for example, the kernel of wheat. When you want to change it, bringing forth from it many more kernels, you need to take it to its root, which lies in the generative power in the soil. Therefore it can grow in the ground, but nowhere else. But there too it will not grow unless rain falls and causes its original form to be disfigured [rotted] and lost. It is reduced to Nothing, to the *hyle*, which is the category of *hokhmah*. Thus Scripture says: 'You made them all in wisdom' [Ps. 104:24]."[71]

"Every thing that exists passes from one nature into another. The linking of these natures is called Wonder. In the language of the Kabbalists it was known as *keter*, the power that links opposites and joins them in a wondrous unity."[72]

"Hylic matter is neither potential nor actual, but lies between the two. It is the starting point of all existent beings. Everything, from *keter 'elyon* downward, exists only because of it.

Hyle does not pass away or go in and out of existence, since it is the beginning of existence itself."[73]

Because the Nothing is the essence of Creation and its innermost soul, it—the Nothing—is in fact the real Being, true existence, essential reality. That which we call "Being" —revealed existence, the sensory, visible to the eyes of flesh and grasped by the rational mind—is in fact naught but the blindness of the senses, illusory existence. It is a cosmic error that we must recognize and negate in order to be free of it.

All that we call existence, with all its charming and entrapping attractions: the blue heavens over our heads, the earth beneath our feet, endless stars, light and radiance, joy and pleasure, beautiful textures, plays of color, sorrow and tears, the roar of the sea and the whisper of springs, all that we pursue and seek out until flesh and spirit are wearied, all that we delight in attaining and all that we moan for when we lack— all of it is naught but illusion.

The more you reach the Nothing that lies within all being, the divine inwardness, the closer you are to truth, to the Godly, to the essence of creation. You reveal the mask and see before you the King in His glory, the endless light.

"There was a certain king who created an optical illusion consisting of walls, towers, and gates. He commanded that those who came in to him would have to pass through these gates and towers. Then he had the royal treasures scattered about at each gate. Some only came up to the first gate, gathered up some coins, and went back. Others—etc. Along came the king's only son; he struggled hard to get to his father the king. Then he saw that there was no real separation between him and his father, that it was all illusion. The blessed Holy One hides behind various garments and partitions. Yet it is known that God fills all the world, that every movement and thought comes from His blessed self. So all the angels and all the palaces are formed of God's own self, like the locust who spins his cocoon out of himself. In fact there is no partition that separates man from God."[74]

"God emanated the worlds and created Being out of Nothingness. The main purpose was so that the *tsaddik* could make Nothingness out of Being."[75]

"If you want to prepare to have God dwell upon you, the main thing is to understand deeply that you contain nothing but life-giving divinity. Without this you are truly nothing. That is the proper preparation for the indwelling of divinity. This 'dwelling' is as in 'Like an eagle rouses his nest, hovering over his chicks' [Deut. 32:11] — touching and not touching. If you grasp this (constantly and with all its power) you will be negated from 'reality.'"[76]

"Everything you see with your eyes, heaven and earth and all within them, are the outer garments of the King, the blessed Holy One. Through them you will come to take constant note of their inner selves, the life-force within them."[77]

Tsimtsum

The world was created *ex nihilo*, being out of nothingness. But just how did the Nothing become being? There is no place for this question when we understand the "Nothing" as the essence of being, when we see it as *keter 'eylon* [supreme crown, the highest of the divine emanations], the force of "Wonder" within all of Creation.

But there is still room for *this* question: Since all that exists is only illusion, being at its core the divine Nothing, how does Being come to be a separate entity? Why do we see the world as we ordinarily do, rather than always perceiving the divine power that courses through it?

In other words, the world is nothing but an optical illusion. But how did that illusion come about? The king's son breaks down all the partitions and comes to the king. But how did the partitions get there in the first place?

The Kabbalists' answer to this is *tsimtsum*. What do they mean by it?

In the school of Rabbi Isaac Luria we learned: "When it arose in the Emanator's will to create the worlds, there was no empty place in which they might stand. The Emanator's light flowed without limit. So He withdrew His own light, like that insect who spins his cocoon out of his own self.[78] He lifts the lights out of that space at the center and removes them to the sides. In this way a void is created in which the worlds can stand."

But this is still not enough. God is — all; "there is no place devoid of Him." Then it is still hard to understand how the lights were removed to the sides. How did that place become empty?

Furthermore, even if we accept that there came to be an "empty space," by what power did it exist? In the end it too relied on the power of God (since "there is no place devoid of Him!"). But in that case, everything is back where we started, and the question still stands: How did existence come to be imagined? How is it that we can think the world to be separate from God? How did that cosmic error come to be?

Hasidism thus explains *tsimtsum* in a different way. *Tsimtsum* is only from our point of view, that of the receivers, the created. *Tsimtsum* exists only in thought. The supreme Emanator sought to bring about diverse and separate entities, displaying His light before all creatures. Everything was thus created in a limited way, in accord with each recipient's power. Just like a father, when explaining some deep concept to his young child, reduces his own profound mind to the limits of that of the child, so does Mind—which is One[79]—descend from its high rung to a lower one.

Another explanation, by way of "king and servants":

"The Zohar says that when the King is in His castle, He is called the great King. But when He goes down among his servants, he is the little King. This was what they meant: The letters of Thought [the unspoken language of the mind] are large, since they transcend the letters of Speech. The King on His own has no need to speak. But for the sake of those who receive from Him, He has to reduce Himself from Thought to Sound and from Sound to Speech. Even though all is a simple unity and all is the King Himself, the vessels [i.e., the recipients of His light] are divided. 'When He is in His castle'—in Thought—[He is the great King.] 'But when He goes down'—into speech, so that His servants can grasp Him—He is called the little King."[80]

The act of cosmic illusion takes place in this way: the young child, as the great thought of the father flows into him, grasps the thought in his own small-minded way. When creatures see the world and its fullness, they grasp only its external nature, the outer garb of things, imagining that is all there is.

But all of these are only examples to offer the ear what it is capable of hearing, making analogy between the spiritual quality of humans and that of the cosmos. Thus we try to understand divine *tsimtsum* based on the reduction of the mind and its going down from expanded to ordinary consciousness, from thought to verbalization to speech. But we still do not know how the One became many. How did such varied and differentiated things come to be, each having its own existence and unique nature?

Tsimtsum is nothing other than the imaging forth of being, the act by which it became possible for being itself to appear as a distinct entity, separate from God. But that still does not give us the key to understand multiplicity, distinction, and the unique "personality" of each thing. We see not only a world, but also endless particular entities, each one (from the archangel Michael down to the smallest urchin in the sea) appearing as its very own world, a living reality all enclosed in its own microcosm. The question remains: How did the "All" split apart into all these tiny pieces?

The Hasidic answer to this is "the breaking of the vessels." This doctrine, taken from Kabbalah, has a distinct meaning in Hasidism. The best of the Kabbalists explained the breaking this way: the vessels were not able to withstand the intensity of the light that flowed ceaselessly into them, and they were broken. This is like a person unable to withstand a sudden burst of joy that overwhelms him. But the Hasidim explain the breaking of the vessels in a more inward and deeper way. The essence of their idea will best be understood by comparison with more recent modes of thought.

What is the innermost, most natural and instinctive desire of each thing that is? The desire to exist. But what is the nature of that desire for existence? "Each thing tries as much as it can to continue forever in its own existence . . . since by that force of being it will continue to exist, so long as it is not destroyed by some external force,"[81] says Spinoza. The desire for existence is thus an inherent power, the force of eternity. Because the thing exists, because it is filled with the feeling of its own reality, it fears being lost.

Schopenhauer added that the desire to live is the absolute inner essence of all existence, realized in each in an individualized way. This cosmic desire, which creates the illusion of being as a whole, also creates the illusion of particular existence. The one who exists also thinks he can attain some understanding—

and comes up with crumbs. The desire for life is no longer an inherent force, one that makes for eternity, but rather an active force, a power that spreads forth, flows, bears fruit and fructifies.

Nietzsche came along and taught that the innermost nature of each thing is not the desire to live, but to rule. What is this "will to power?" It should not be understood in a popular and vulgar sense. Nietzsche's will to power is really the desire to reveal the "I," to manifest one's full inner powers, to have them rule and master the powers of others.

"The tree by my window—and this is its very nature—reveals its 'I,'" says Oscar Wilde.[82]

The desire to rule, that is, the desire for self-manifestation, the feeling of being, is the heritage of everything that exists. This is the secret of personhood, of individuality.

Here we come to the true meaning of *malkhut* ["kingship" of God; the tenth *sefirah*] according to the Hasidim. *Malkhut* is the manifestation of that which is, the spreading forth [of the self], the feeling of power, utterance, imperative, spiritual rule.

Now we come to the Hasidic understanding of the "breaking of the vessels." These vessels are what the modern philosophers and poets see as the beauty of creation, the individual identity of each creature. To the Hasidim this is cosmic sin, the fall, the descent, the brokenness. *Malkhut* belongs only to the One who truly exists, the Creator. But since the creatures also rose up to seek rule, it was smashed into the tiniest fragments, each of them saying "I will rule!"

"The brokenness comes about because each one says: 'I will rule.' The term *malkhut* [kingship] applies to each thing insofar as it is a thing in itself, with no need for anyone or anything else. But in truth this term properly applies only to God, because all others are needy, requiring nourishment from their divine Source. Each quality [or "being"] has within it, from the moment it flows forth from that source, the inherent claim of 'I will rule,' which it had as part of its original Source. There in the Root the claim was appropriate; all of them were raised up there within that Root. In this way they came to have that natural sense about themselves even when it was no longer accurate, after they had been cut off from the Root and had their own force of life."[83]

The Power of the Maker Within the Made

The Hasidim do not understand *tsimtsum* in the ordinary way. Divinity did not really remove itself; it fills being with its light in accord with the abilities and mental capacity of each creature. Rather than a limiting of Divinity, what takes place is a special revelation of the Divine.

But while the Hasidim take *tsimtsum* out of its original sense, they do interpret "the whole earth is filled with His glory" (Isa. 6:3) quite literally. The Gaon of Vilna[84] followed others before him in understanding "His glory" as referring to providence. The Hasidim said no, it is His glory *itself* that is truly present. Divinity is everywhere; it fills everything. Everything you see and hear, touch and feel, think and contemplate—all of it is God.

One of these depends upon the other. Because they do not take *tsimtsum* literally, they become literalists when it comes to "He fills all the worlds." Since the removal of divine light takes place only insofar as our eyes can see, but is not the absolute truth, divinity continues to dwell even in the very lowest of rungs, just as it does in the highest. From its point of view all is equal: heaven and earth, creation of the world, the time before and after creation, "I Y-H-W-H have not changed." "You are He before the world was created; You are He since the world was created...."

"The blessed Creator's glory fills all the worlds. No place is devoid of Him. When you look at the world, you are looking at the Creator, bless His name. When you are talking to a person, you are addressing the soul within him."[85]

"This is a high rung: When a person considers himself to be near to God, God is surrounding him from all sides. He (the person) is at the center of the heavens and God is 'the place of the world.' God was there before the world was created and the world stands in the midst of God."[86]

"Whatever a person sees, he sees it only by power of the life-energy flowing forth from the blessed Creator. If you see people, for example, you notice their form, hear their voices and speech, learn from their wisdom—all this is the life-force flowing through them. This is true of everything you see or hear, for each thing has the structure and purpose befitting it, a particular appearance or smell. All of this is the life-energy of the Creator within each thing, since all is from Him, just dressed up in diverse garments."[87]

"The *shekhinah* is called 'the total picture,' since all depictions appear within the *shekhinah* like a polished mirror, as it were, reflecting back the form of that person who stands before it."[88]

God is called *El 'Olam*, "God of world," to teach you that "God" is world and world is "God."[89]

"'Forever, O Lord, Your word stands in the heavens' (Ps. 119:89) —Your word that You spoke in saying 'Let there be a firmament' (Gen. 1:7)—those very words and letters stand firmly within the skies forever. The words are 'garbed' within all the worlds, giving them life. Were those words to disappear even for an instant, returning to their Source, all of the heavens would be naught, as though they had never come to be. The same is true of all that is created in all worlds above and below, including inanimate objects in this very physical world. If the letters of the ten utterances through which the world was created in those six days were to disappear, they would return to absolute non-existence."[90]

"Every creature and existing thing is considered truly non-existent with regard to the power of the Maker and the spirit of His mouth within the made. It is this that constantly brings it into being and leads it forth from non-existence. The fact that each creature and object appears to us as extant and real is because we, looking with eyes of flesh, cannot see the power of God and the spirit of His mouth within the creature. Were the eye permitted to see and grasp the life-energy and spirituality flowing through each creature, proceeding from God's mouth and its spirit, the physical, corporeal dimension of things would not appear before our eyes at all."[91]

The angels ask: "Where is the place of His glory?"[92] All the worlds are called "place," since each receives its revelation from the one above it and is nullified before it. All are called "place" [because each serves as a container or embodiment of that which comes from above]. But when the angels attain that rung where they realize that all is One and there is no category of "place" at all (for "I Y-H-W-H have not changed" [Mal. 3:6], and before Him, blessed be He, all is equal, as He equalizes great and small), they *then* ask "Where is the 'place' of His glory?" for they understand that there is no category of "place" at all.[93]

Mystery of Thought (1928)

Our selections conclude with "Mystery of Thought," a stirring account of the contemplative life addressed to the readers of Yavneh and beyond.

Thought is a person's inward palace (Temple); the innermost point of his thoughts is that person's holy of holies. That innermost point cleaves to the Endless with a love that never ceases. This is a "strap that ties one to the blessed Holy One."[94] But even if the person does not have the strength and the power to rise to such a rung, but has shame, longings, and pains, and afflictions and they break his spirit at the level of "Their heart cried out to God (Lam. 2:18)" — God dwells here, and this person's soul too dwells within God. They are "One within one"[95] — the Endless within the person; the person within the Endless.

If you, O child of the palace, do not yet have the power and strength to stand firmly on the rung of the "link that joins one" to God, be then on the rung of "his heart is troubled within him."[96] Let your eyes fill with tears — like the "lower waters" that cried out "We too want to be before the King!"[97]

At this time of messiah's approaching footsteps, especially in these final years when those steps' imprint is revealed in the sands of "nations' desert (Ez. 20:35)," overwhelming darkness surrounds us. Darkness perceives that its final hour has arrived; it rushes to send forth all its hosts and forces, both above and below. Seeing the kingdom of light drawing nearer, darkness trembles and stirs and sets out to do battle with the light. It sends forth its shadow to swallow up all of light's forces, to consume all the world's goodness, to wreck, ruin, and demolish all that the "light sown for the righteous" (Ps. 97:11) has planted.

When the darkness sees that it cannot defeat a person, since such a one stands up like a firm pillar and does not allow evil desires or passions of the flesh to rule, then the darkness appears in the form of a good angel, stealing its way into your heart and distancing you from God by way of sadness, a state of melancholy or small-mindedness that derives from the evil side.

Child of the palace, do not let that thief enter your heart! Keep your heart always both "broken" and "joyous." It was taught in Rabbi Shimon bar Yoḥai's name: "Have weeping firmly rooted in one side of your heart, while joy is in the other." Sadness and brokenheartedness are not the same. The holy lion Rabbi Shneur Zalman taught that "sadness is having a heart as dull as stone with no life-energy within it, while a certain acidity and a broken heart, on the contrary, show there is enough life in that heart to turn it sour!"

When your heart is broken so that it has the energy to weep and plead before God, "the palace that it is not possible to open except by tears" immediately will open before you. Once the wellsprings of your heart are opened, a melody of attachment to God will burst forth on its own. Then a "palace opened only by melody" will become accessible to you. And then a holy melody will be heard throughout the upper worlds, causing a "palace attained only by joy" to open before you. As that palace opens, all forces of judgment and negativity will pass away, all accusing [or "guilt-producing"] forces will be hidden in the rocks, and the "shells" will be hidden in the cavity of the great deep. Then holy angels will come down among humans to hear words of Torah spoken by the faithful shepherd and all the other sages of that generation. They will rejoice and exult, dancing as at a festival of bride and groom. Forces of love will be revealed throughout the world, great blessings from above. Abundant love, desire, and grace will pour forth from before our Father in Heaven upon the holy people and upon all who live.

Remember, O child of the palace, what the pious of old have

taught: "All the gates are sealed except those of tears." "Tears *open* the gates—but joy *smashes* all gates. . . ." You, child of the palace, must not forget even for a moment that "God is your shadow" (Ps. 121:5)[98]—the blessed Holy One is your shadow, being and acting toward you as you are toward Him. If you desire God, God will desire you. Everyone knows this, but they do not grasp it in an *inner* way. Even if they know it deeply, they do not *live* in accord with that knowing. Their knowledge and their life remain separate. Even when there is light in them, this light is only surface light and not inner light. For you, child of the palace, your awareness that "God is your shadow" must be your life, both within and without. It must be your inner light, the desire of your desires, your soul and the soul within your soul.

When this simple awareness becomes your inner light, one light from above will descend and surround you. Your life of holiness and good deeds will allow you to absorb that light until it shines from within you. Then another light will descend, surrounding you again, and it too will be absorbed and united with the soul of man and it will be the inner light. And so onward, to the highest of rungs![99]

The most important rule: Let the blessed Holy One in every single moment be your *life*, the very *air* that gives you life. Let every breath you take be in God. There is no quick way to achieve this, but only that of lengthy service and ceaseless prayer, an inward prayer of the very simplest words, yet penetrating and descending into the very depths.

Pray like this:

My beloved Father, desire of my soul! You sent me to this world. For what purpose have You sent me? Surely to bear Your message! Teach me, beloved Father, what I am supposed to do this day and every day to fulfill Your will. What should I be saying to people–all of them my brothers [and sisters] and Your children? What should I be doing—right now and at all times—to make my life pure and holy, as You desire?

My Father, my Heart! Give me all those heavenly lights and all that contains them. May I have the brilliance of soul, bodily health, clarity of mind, and clear awareness—all the abilities and powers needed to do that with which You command me.

And you, holy souls of each generation! You who have fulfilled God's will throughout your lives, in holiness and purity, accompany me on my path! Help me in my actions! Pray with me and be with me in all the good I seek to do.

Light of lights! Soul of all souls! Send me all those holy souls who are close to my own soul-root! Let them hold fast to me, and I to them. Raise us all up and carry us on the wings of endless love.

This is the sort of inward prayer that a child of the palace should offer every day. It may be prayed with these words and phrases or others; the main thing is that it be *constant*.

It is the prayer of the poor and brokenhearted, yet at the same time the burning desire of a child to see his Father's smiling face.

Suggestions for Further Reading

Green, Arthur. "Hillel Zeitlin and Neo-Hasidic Readings of the Zohar." *Kabbalah* 22 (2010): 59–78.

———. "Three Warsaw Mystics." In *Kolot Rabbim: Essays in Memory of Rivka Schatz-Uffenheimer*, edited by Rachel Elior, 1–58. Jerusalem: Magnes, 1997.

Green, Arthur, and Ariel Evan Mayse. "'The Great Call of the Hour': Hillel Zeitlin's Yiddish Writings on *Yavneh*." *In geveb: A Journal of Yiddish Studies,* Spring 2016, online (https://ingeveb.org/articles/the-great-call-of -the-hour-hillel-zeitlins-yiddish-writings-on-yavneh).

Zeitlin, Hillel. *Hasidic Spirituality for a New Era: The Religious Writings of Hillel Zeitlin.* Edited and translated by Arthur Green. New York: Paulist, 2012.

2

Martin Buber

Introduction

Martin Buber (1878–1965) was born in Vienna, but his parents' separation three years later sent the little boy eastward to live with his paternal grandparents in Lemberg, Galicia (present-day Lviv, Ukraine). Buber recalled later that his grandparents were "disinclined to talk over the affairs of their own existence"—they never spoke about what happened between his parents, they never mentioned that his mother would not return. Buber learned only a year later from a neighborhood girl that his mother "will never come back." That moment of utter rupture, according to Buber, set in motion his lifelong yearning to know the meaning of genuine "meeting"—spiritual, interpersonal, and eventually the inseparability of the two.[1]

Buber continued to live with his grandparents throughout his youth, spending only summers on his father's estate starting at age nine. His grandfather Salomon Buber was a prodigious and prolific scholar of Midrash. And despite the fact that he was a "Westernized" intellectual of the Haskalah (Jewish Enlightenment), Buber recalls, "he used to take me with him into his *klaus* [Hasidic prayer room], where he, the *maskil* [enlightened one], prayed exclusively among Hasidim—from a prayerbook full of *kavvanot* [mystical intentions]."[2]

Salomon's erudition, studiousness, and religiosity had a profound impact on Buber, yet it seems that the grandson was somewhat skeptical about his grandfather's solitary bookishness. He preferred the intellect of his grandmother, Adele, who taught him "what it means really to express something." Although Salomon was the renowned scholar, Buber appreciated Adele's more relational mode of thinking: "My grandfather was a true philologist, a 'lover of the word,' but my grandmother's love for the genuine word affected me even more strongly than his: because this love was so direct and so devoted."[3] Raised in Sasov, a small Galician town only a few miles from the city of Zolochev, both of which housed significant Hasidic communities where girls were prohibited from reading anything but "edifying popular books," Adele devoured philosophical and literary works in secrecy, and she later instilled in her sons and grandson a "respect for the authentic word that cannot be paraphrased."[4]

It is evident from his scattered autobiographical reflections and anecdotes that Buber's life transformed quite radically when he was fourteen years old. The most concrete change was his leaving his grandparents' home to live full-time with his father Carl, now remarried and a very successful agriculturalist. Buber ceased his traditional Jewish observance that very same year,[5] and it is hard to imagine that this timing was merely coincidental. Given the adolescent's traumatic memories of abandonment in his first home, perhaps he was especially quick to abandon his Hasidic-inflected practices for fear of disappointing his father. Indeed, Carl himself had diverged sharply from Salomon's ways, and Buber still recounted nearly thirty years later how he had caused "offense" at his father's bourgeois liberal "temple" when he embodied the pietistic postures he had picked up in his grandfather's *klaus*.[6]

However, Buber's detachment from Jewish observance was also bound up with a precocious philosophical crisis and awakening. When he was "about fourteen years of age," Buber recalls that he was maddeningly overwhelmed—nearly to the point of suicide—by his inability to visualize the infinities of space and time.[7] Following this wunderkind's anxiety-ridden efforts to wrap his mind around these supposedly foundational dimensions of existence, he found "salvation" the following year in Kant's declaration that space and time are not properties inherent to nature but rather categories inherent to human perception that facilitate cognition of nature.

Buber himself supposed that this philosophical revelation eroded the earnestness that had animated his youthful religiosity. After describing to his friend Franz Rosenzweig an intensely powerful Yom Kippur from when he was thirteen, Buber reflected, "And do you think I was a 'child' then? Less so than now, perhaps, in a crucial sense; in those days I took space and time seriously, and did not just dismiss them from my mind, as I do now."[8] Moreover, Buber suggested specifically that his early intellectualism desensitized him to the spiritual vitality of Hasidism. Although he had previously glimpsed true community and leadership in the movement — "as a child realizes such things, not as thought, but as image and feeling"[9] — he later lost touch, as it were, with such primordial intuitions. "I looked down on [Hasidism] from the heights of a rational man. I now saw nothing more of its life, even when I passed quite close to it — because I did not want to see anything."[10]

In any case, when fourteen-year-old Buber left his grandfather Salomon's house, his reality transformed: "So long as I lived with him, my roots were firm, although many questions and doubts also jogged about in me. Soon after I left his house, the whirl of the age took me in."[11]

Another profound year of change for Buber took place when he was twenty-one, as the nineteenth century turned into the twentieth. After semesters of studying philosophy, literature, and art history at the Universities of Vienna and Leipzig, Buber spent the summer of 1899 at the University of Zurich. He met a woman there named Paula Winkler. She had come to Zurich after living in an Alpine "colony" revolving around Omar al-Raschid Bey (née Friedrich Arndt-Kürnberg), a long-bearded and colorfully cloaked mystic who expounded an orientalist blend of Muslim, Buddhist, and Hindu wisdoms after converting from Judaism to Islam years earlier in Constantinople. Paula had been one of al-Raschid's most gifted disciples, and apparently the guru himself brought her to Zurich to study Eastern languages before she struck off on her own.[12] A Bavarian Catholic by birth and a year older than Buber, Paula matched him intellectually yet humbled him at that time spiritually and interpersonally. They fell in love that summer—Buber's first love, it seems—and they interlaced their lives almost immediately. Within the next two years they had two children, and seven years later they were legally married following Paula's conversion to Judaism (Buber was a citizen of Austria, where Catholics and Jews were not permitted to marry).[13]

In the fall of 1899, the very first semester after meeting Paula, Buber immersed himself in the study of mysticism, and the chronology suggests that this new phase of his spiritual development was a direct result of their relationship.[14] Moreover, while Buber's mind had been intellectually and philosophically aflame for years, Paula inspired him to see the world of ideas as being only truly alive if it is embedded and embodied in personal relations. He would write to her three years later from the "prison cell" of his grandparents' estate in Lemberg:

> In general, one must tie the whole riddle of the universe to a single person, otherwise one is in a bad way. In the Talmud it says: "He who meditates upon four things, for him it would have been better had he not come into the world; these four are what is above, what is below, what was before, and what will be after."[15] I would prefer to say: Meditate upon all mysteries, but in one person who is yours, and you lie upon the heart of the universe. For everything is in everyone and only love can extract it.[16]

With all these elements and more in motion, Buber confessed to Paula in 1902, "Not until you came to me did I find my soul."[17]

Also within months of meeting Paula, Buber started to participate in the Neue Gemeinschaft (New community), a group of young bohemians in Berlin who celebrated mystical experience as a way to resist and transcend what they deemed the alienation, hyper-rationalism, and spiritual barrenness of modernity.[18] There Buber connected with the captivating revolutionary, philosopher, and "prophet" Gustav Landauer (1870–1919), who became one of the most important and influential friends of his life.[19] It was surely this effervescent confluence of the Neue Gemeinschaft, Landauer, and Paula that inspired Buber to write his doctoral thesis on the Christian mystics Nicholas of Cusa and Jacob Böhme.

Remarkably, it was also in 1899 that Buber first emerged as a prominent Zionist activist. He had become enamored with the movement only a year earlier—through reading, of course—but already delivered an address in August 1899 at the Third Zionist Congress in Basel. Buber's words and visions resonated powerfully for many in the room. Paula, already an impassioned supporter of the cultural movement, was present for the speech and described how it touched her personally: "This was no longer an individual human being; with primordial violence the tremendous longing, wishes, and will of a whole people poured over me like a raging torrent."[20] A less biased audience member, Theodor Herzl, invited Buber just two years later to be editor of *Die Welt*, the official newspaper of Zionism.

If Buber's closeness with Paula nourished for him a new nexus of spirit and relation, his involvement with Zionism solidified that bond at the level of community. Like so many others of his generation, Buber's personal (re)turn to Judaism was coterminous with his turn to Zionism, and the significance of the movement was for him never so much about the establishment of a Jewish nation-state in Palestine as it was a revolution of Jewish spiritual-cultural renewal.[21] Before then, Buber says, his head swarmed with thoughts and his "spirit was in steady and multiple movement," but all this hovered aimlessly, "carried off into the upper atmosphere by the intellect." Zionism was the beginning of his "liberation," fostering for him "the restoration of the connection, the renewed taking root in the community."[22]

Yet Buber realized quickly that even this communal connection remained ungrounded. "I professed Judaism before I really knew it," he confesses years later.[23] Never satisfied with petty chauvinism or knee-jerk nationalism, Buber turned to texts. He relearned the Hebrew that his grandfather had taught him in his youth, but meditated anew on the roots, sounds, and significance of that sacred tongue. Hebrew language proved to be his gateway.

Until one day I opened a little book entitled the *Tsava'at ha-RIVaSH*—that is the testament of Rabbi Israel Baal-Shem—and the words flashed toward me, "He takes unto himself the quality of fervor. He arises from sleep with fervor, for he is hallowed and become another man and is worthy to create and is become like the Holy One, blessed be He, when He created His world." It was then that, overpowered in an instant, I experienced the Hasidic soul. The primally Jewish opened to me, flowering to newly conscious expression in the darkness of exile: man's being created in the image of God I grasped as deed, as becoming, as task. And this primally Jewish reality was a primal human reality, the content of human religiosity. Judaism as religiosity, as "piety," as *hasidut* opened to me there.[24]

This encounter with Hasidic sources changed Buber's life forever. Significantly, the line from *Tsava'at ha-RIVaSH* that astonished him is all about renewal—renewal of self, renewal of community, renewal of world.[25] Buber conceives of renewal here as readiness to "create" new modes of being out of the very primal depths of what it means to be human and, in his case, Jewish. And the "primally Jewish" (*Urjüdisches*) here is most certainly not, for Buber, the institutional and systematic structures of Jewish "religion," but the spontaneous and dynamic impulses of Jewish "religiosity." Whereas, according to Buber, religion seeks power and preservation, religiosity seeks truth and holiness, and it is therefore the latter that fuels real renewal.[26]

For Buber the whole history of Judaism is a dialectic of prophets and priests, religiosity and religion. Although the latter appear to dominate consistently, the former always rumble beneath the surface and erupt at times in explosions of mythic imagination and daring reinterpretation. Buber suggests that traces of primal, "underground" Judaism are perceptible in the Hebrew Bible, Midrash, and Kabbalah— and Hasidism is the most recent and one of the most stirring eruptions of all.[27]

This is not to say that Buber wanted to become a Hasid. As far as he was concerned, the movement was already in steep decline, smothered by the dead weight of religion that always follows great religious awakenings. But he wanted to fan the still glowing coals and kindle a new blaze. "The Hasidic teaching is the proclamation of rebirth," Buber declares. "No renewal of Judaism is possible that does not bear in itself the elements of Hasidism."[28]

With such intention and direction, Buber retreated from all other work at the age of twenty-six to immerse himself in Hasidic sources for the next five years. He was drawn primarily to the legendary literature (*ma'asiyot*) as opposed to the theoretical sermons (*derashot*), and during these early years of study he published his first two books, *The Tales of Rabbi Nachman* (1906) and *The Legend of the Baal-Shem* (1908). Buber's discovery of Hasidism ignited a fire in him that never died. To be sure, he had encountered the movement in his youth, but now it was his own. The textual traces of Hasidism's original stirrings seduced him, and he romanticized them in turn.

It is difficult to exaggerate the extent to which Buber's early honeymoon with Hasidism was a shared experience with Paula. She was always a careful editor of his writings (indeed, German was not the

mother tongue of that great "German Jewish" philosopher, and Paula
herself became an accomplished author under the pseudonym Georg
Munk), but more importantly, she even wrote drafts of some of the tales
for Buber's early Hasidic anthologies.[29] The fact of her involvement in
the work sheds light on a nostalgic poem that Buber penned decades
later in her copy of his *Tales of the Hasidim* (1946)[30]:

> Remember how in youth we set our sails
> Together on the ocean of these tales?
> We saw fantastic sights, grand and awry,
> And we beheld each other, you and I.
> How image fitted image in our hearts!
> Each kindling each, with each one adding parts
> To new descriptions, a new entity
> Came into being between you and me.[31]

Paula, with her own background in mystical exploration, her own
passion for the written word, and her own interests in Jewish culture,
seems to have welcomed this opportunity to "discover" Hasidic literature with Buber, although her utter invisibility in the published books
ought to disturb us today.[32] For her husband, in any case, the experience
was clearly one of profound personal integration.

Buber's embrace of Hasidism was radical in the full sense of the
word, bearing both roots and revolution. In some ways his plunge into
Hasidic sources linked him back to his upbringing. Not only did he pray
beside his grandfather in the Lemberg *klaus*; Salomon's own life work
was steeped in Jewish legendary literature. When Buber describes in
his essay "My Way to Hasidism" how Salomon "edited text after text of
Midrash, those books of Bible interpretation, comparable to no other
literature, abounding in legends, sayings, and noble parables," he fore-
shadows his own work with Hasidic tales.[33]

Moreover, Salomon was quite encouraging of his grandson's project on Hasidism. He (along with Carl) supported Buber financially during those years of textual immersion and sent him books from Lemberg, then the publishing epicenter of Hasidic tales during the so-called "Lemberg period" of 1864–1912.[34]

However, even before Buber's work on Hasidism, the grandson detected dissonance between his Zionist activism and his grandfather's historical-philological labor. "You have mined and refined treasures from the culture of the Jewish past," Buber wrote to Salomon in 1900, but "I, who am young and still long more for action than for knowledge, want to help forge the Jewish future."[35] This dynamic of warm admiration and determined differentiation is manifest on the dedication page of Buber's first Hasidic book: "To my grandfather, Salomon Buber, the last of the great scholars in the old-style Haskalah, I offer this work of *Hasidut* with reverence and love."[36]

There were much deeper complexities surrounding Buber's turn to Hasidism in relation to his father. True, he seems to have recognized in Carl's down-to-earth, unpretentious simplicity some of the sensibilities and values he loved so much in Hasidic tales.[37] However, while Carl took Buber as a child to behold the Hasidic community in the "dirty village of Sadagora,"[38] Buber's active celebration of Hasidic spirituality clashed strongly with Carl's own liberal Judaism and bourgeois sensibilities. "I would be happy if you would free yourself from these Hasidic and Zohar [Kabbalah] matters," Carl implored Buber on his thirtieth birthday, just before the release of his first Hasidic book, "since they can only have a mind-destroying and evil influence, and it is a pity to waste your abilities on such a sterile subject and consume so much labor and time, useless to yourself and the world."[39]

For generations of Europeans, the opposition between Western "progressive" and Eastern "traditional" Jews was a matter of grave sociopolitical significance. The European Jewish struggle for emancipation in their home countries continued well into Carl's adulthood and, in some cases, even into Buber's. For many Jews and non-Jews alike, those disheveled mystics back east looked like the very antithesis of "Enlightenment," undermining all claims that Jews were worthy of integration into the modern world. The Hasidim embodied everything that Western, assimilated Jews had sought to jettison for generations.

Such conformist aspirations and apologetic postures were, however, repulsive to Buber and many others of his generation. In contrast to their parents, who had placed great faith in nineteenth-century visions of "progress" through the promises of universal reason, assimilation, and material comfort, a new generation sensed that modern industrialization, urbanization, and rationalist abandonment of "superstitious" folk traditions brought little more than spiritual impoverishment, alienation from the natural world, and the withering of inner vitality. Seekers of all stripes—philosophers, poets, musicians, and activists—looked longingly to epochs and regions they saw as untouched by the modern malaise. They regarded those cultures as "primitive" in the sense of primal and pristine. Whereas previous generations may have looked down on the "East" as unenlightened and uncivilized, many young Europeans at the turn of the century now glorified "oriental" wisdom and folklore as primordial expressions of premodern authenticity.[40]

The Neue Gemeinschaft in Berlin was a classic incarnation of such "Neo-Romantic" fervor, and it was also in this zeitgeist that Zionists imagined a Jewish renaissance in Palestine. To the discomfort of his father and the titillation of his contemporaries, Buber scribed his enchanting tales of the Hasidim, and he became thereafter a sort of spiritual representative of Judaism in Germany, complete with the growing, graying beard.[41] To be sure, Buber himself remained personally distant from the singing, dancing, and ecstatic expression, let alone the ritual observance, that were so definitive of Hasidic spirituality, yet his literary representations of the movement energized countless readers. Even decades later, English translations of his Hasidic books were taken up by American Protestant theologians and Jewish hippies of the 1960s,[42] and one contemporary scholar demonstrates that Hebrew translations of Buber's tales have even commanded a "covert reception" among Orthodox Jews.[43] There is literally no one in history who has done more than Martin Buber did to introduce non-Hasidim to Hasidism.

In order to attract such broad and diverse readerships, however, he did not simply translate Hasidic tales word for word or portray the movement in purely historical terms. According to his own outlooks and spiritual sensibilities over the course of more than four decades, Buber presented Hasidism anew.

In the introduction to his first anthology, *The Tales of Rabbi Nachman*, Buber declared that "Hasidism is the Kabbalah become ethos," and he stood by this statement over the rest of his life.[44] His point was that Hasidism transformed mystical gnosis—or "knowledge" of divine mysteries—into an "agnostic" ethical-cum-spiritual *way of life*.[45] The essence of religiosity was no longer in esoteric knowledge or abstract concepts, but in immanent presence and concrete community. Buber acknowledged, of course, that Hasidic sages incorporated various terms and images from earlier Jewish mysticism, but he insisted that they revolutionized the meaning of that material. If medieval kabbalists fashioned imaginative maps of the spiritual universe and developed elaborate practices to influence the "upper worlds," Hasidism employed those very elements to illuminate deep dynamics of psychological life and to enrich one's existence here and now in corporeal reality. The gnostic-kabbalistic lexicon that Hasidism absorbed was transmuted from "spiritualities enthroned in the unbinding" to the "core of authentications [*Bewährungen*]."[46] *Bewährung*, a barely translatable term throughout Buber's writings whose meaning is approximately "putting to proof in action," denotes the embodied enactment of spiritual truth.[47] In short, defining Hasidism as "Kabbalah become ethos" affirms that there is nothing more religiously potent or theologically expressive than the very concrete moments of everyday existence.

Buber emphasized this foundation of Hasidic spirituality with increasing depth and boldness over time. In the wake of World War I, he underwent a profound shift "from mysticism to dialogue."[48] While the details of this transformation are beyond the scope of this introduction, we can detect the changes by comparing his essays "The Life of the Hasidim" (1908) and "Spirit and Body of the Hasidic Movement" (1922), included in this volume. The first appeared originally as the introduction to his book *The Legend of the Baal-Shem*, published in the heart of his mystical years. Buber suggests therein that the "basic principle of Hasidic life" is "ecstasy" (*hitlahavut*), a deeply personal, inward, and even antisocial mystical state in which one is lifted "above everything earthly." In contrast, Buber's 1922 essay affirms that the mystic who remains satisfied with such solitary spirituality "is not a true *tsaddik*," and Buber suggests now that the essence of Hasidic life is no more and no less than "the hallowing of the everyday." Thus, for Buber in his later years, the "agnostic" quality of Hasidism is not only a resistance to dogmatic "knowledge" of divine mysteries but also an unshakeable drive to anchor all holiness to the wholeness of earthly life.

From this perspective we can appreciate more fully why Buber preferred the legendary literature over the theoretical literature of Hasidism. To some extent one can attribute this to the historical context of his project amid cultural Zionism and the Neo-Romantic reevaluation of folktales.[49] No less significant, however, are the theological reasons for Buber's embrace of the tales. If the essence of Hasidism was a shift from static schemas and systems to the ever-changing moments of (inter)personal existence, then one is hard pressed to think of a more appropriate genre of theological discourse than narrative.

Indeed, for Buber, it is no coincidence that Hasidism celebrated the act and art of storytelling more than any other movement in Jewish history, at least since biblical times.[50] Hasidic legends—those terse, rarely reflective descriptions of moments in the lives of *tsaddikim*—articulate Hasidic religious sensibilities without stepping back to say so. The Hasidic tale functions for Buber as a sort of *narrative theology*, rendering the embodied wisdom of the Hasidic ethos into transmissible language. Indeed, Buber translates the Hebrew term *tsaddikim* into German as "die Bewährten," the ones in whom truth is put to proof in action,[51] and he celebrates Hasidic narrative as "at once reality and teaching," capturing "events in which . . . even the dumb happening spoke."[52]

These issues lie at the core of a famous debate about the nature of Hasidism between Buber and Gershom Scholem (1897–1982), the founder of the academic study of Jewish mysticism. Buber, drawing mostly from the legendary literature, claimed that Hasidism hallowed bodily life in the everyday, but Scholem pointed exasperatedly to the theoretical literature that celebrated the "annihilation of being" and contemplation of divine nothingness beyond materiality.[53] In this regard it is helpful to note that Scholem, in his case against Buber, differentiates sharply between genuine Hasidic "theology" and "theory," on the one hand, and "popular and vulgar mood" and "praxis," on the other.[54] Scholem suggests that a religious movement's "legends should by no means seduce us into thinking that they represent the real doctrines," nor can a selection of such legends facilitate a "real and scholarly understanding" of a movement.[55] In direct contrast to Scholem's methodology, Buber warns, "it is not always good to begin with a central religious content; it may be more fruitful to proceed from life itself, from the relation to concrete reality, and only finally to ask concerning the central content."[56] Thus, in his rebuttal to Scholem (included later in this chapter), Buber emphasizes his efforts to present the personal relations and communities of Hasidim, to "convey the reality of the way of life that was once informed by [Hasidic] teachings."[57] For Buber the boundaries between theory and practice, spiritual thought and relational life, are blurred in genuine religiosity.

In the wake of Scholem's forceful campaign against him, many have debated if and to what extent Buber distorted Hasidism. The fact is, both the historical phenomenon and the religious phenomenology of Hasidism were and are far more complex than either Buber or Scholem allowed.[58] Moreover, the inclusion of Buber in a volume on "Neo-Hasidism" beckons us beyond such interrogations and invites us to shift from a stance of criticism to one of curiosity. Now, more than half a century after Buber's death, it may be more fruitful to take for granted that this mere mortal looked upon Hasidic sources through the prism of his own personal-spiritual sensibilities, and to take interest in *how* he did so and *what* emerged from that encounter. While his textual-philological familiarity with the movement was stronger than some of his critics wished to admit, it remains true that Buber was first and foremost not a historian but a visionary. What makes Buber such a profound progenitor of Neo-Hasidism is that he engaged intimately with the sources and yet renewed them with his own breath of life. And we are still listening.

The Life of the Hasidim (1908)

The essays here exhibit three distinct domains of Buber's Neo-Hasidic thought. First, "The Life of the Hasidim" showcases his early mystical portrayal of Hasidism. Illuminating four distinct dimensions of Hasidic spirituality, it is filled with references to the tales and teachings in which Buber was so immersed at that time.

Hitlahavut: Ecstasy

Hitlahavut is "the inflaming," the ardor of ecstasy. It is the goblet of grace and the eternal key.

A fiery sword guards the way to the tree of life. It scatters into sparks before the touch of *hitlahavut,* whose light finger is more powerful than it. To *hitlahavut* the path is open, and all bounds sink before its boundless step. The world is no longer its place: it is the place of the world.

Hitlahavut unlocks the meaning of life. Without it even heaven has no meaning and no being. "If a man has fulfilled the whole of the teaching and all the commandments but has not had the rapture and the inflaming, when he dies and passes beyond, paradise is opened to him but, because he has not felt rapture in the world, he also does not feel it in paradise."

Hitlahavut can appear at all places and at all times. Each hour is its footstool and each deed its throne. Nothing can stand against it, nothing hold it down; nothing can defend itself against its might, which raises everything corporeal to spirit. He who is in it is in holiness. "He can speak idle words with his mouth, yet the teaching of the Lord is in his heart at this hour; he can pray in a whisper, yet his heart cries out in his breast; he can sit in a community of men, yet he walks with God: mixing with the creatures yet secluded from the world." Each thing and each deed is thus sanctified. "When a man attaches himself to God, he can allow his mouth to speak what it may speak and his ear to hear what it may hear, and he will bind the things to their higher root."

Repetition, the power which weakens and decolors so much in human life, is powerless before ecstasy, which catches fire again and again from precisely the most regular, most uniform events. Ecstasy overcame one *tsaddik* in reciting the Scriptures, each time that he reached the words, "And God spoke." A Hasidic wise man who told this to his disciples added to it, "But I think also: if one speaks in truth and one receives in truth, then one word is enough to uplift the whole world and to purge the whole world from sin." To the man in ecstasy the habitual is eternally new. A *tsaddik* stood at the window in the early morning light and trembling cried, "A few hours ago it was night and now it is day—God brings up the day!" And he was full of fear and trembling. He also said, "Every creature should be ashamed before the Creator: were he perfect, as he was destined to be, then he would be astonished and awakened and inflamed because of the renewal of the creature at each time and in each moment."

But *hitlahavut* is not a sudden sinking into eternity: it is an ascent to the infinite from rung to rung. To find God means to find the way without end. The Hasidim saw the "world to come" in the image of this way, and they never called that world a Beyond.

One of the pious saw a dead master in a dream. The latter told him that from the hour of his death he went each day from world to world. And the world which yesterday was stretched out above his gaze as heaven is today the earth under his foot; and the heaven of today is the earth of tomorrow. And each world is purer and more beautiful and more profound than the one before.

The angel rests in God, but the holy spirits go forward in God. "The angel is one who stands, and the holy man is one who travels on. Therefore the holy man is higher than the angel."

Such is the way of ecstasy. If it appears to offer an end, an arriving, an attaining, an acquiring, it is only a final no, not a final yes: it is the end of constraint, the shaking off of the last chains, the detachment which is lifted above everything earthly. "When man moves from strength to strength and ever upward and upward until he comes to the root of all teaching and all command, to the I of God, the simple unity and boundlessness—when he stands there, then all the wings of command and law sink down and are as if destroyed. For the evil impulse is destroyed since he stands above it."

"Above nature and above time and above thought"—thus is he called who is in ecstasy. He has cast off all sorrow and all that is oppressive. "Sweet suffering, I receive you in love," said a dying *tsaddik*, and Rabbi Susya cried out amazed when his hand slipped out of the fire in which he had placed it, "How coarse Susya's body has become that it is afraid of fire." The man of ecstasy rules life, and no external happening that penetrates into his realm can disturb his inspiration. It is told of a *tsaddik* that when the holy meal of the teaching prolonged itself till morning, he said to his disciples, "We have not stepped into the limits of the day, rather the day has stepped into our limits, and we need not give way before it."

In ecstasy all that is past and that is future draws near to the present. Time shrinks, the line between the eternities disappears, only the moment lives, and the moment is eternity. In its undivided light appears all that was and all that will be, simple and composed. It is there as a heartbeat is there and becomes manifest like it.

The Hasidic legend has much to tell of those wonderful ones who remembered their earlier forms of existence, who were aware of the future as of their own breath, who saw from one end of the earth to the other and felt all the changes that took place in the world as something that happened to their own bodies. All this is not yet that state in which *hitlahavut* has overcome the world of space and time. We can perhaps learn something of this latter state from two simple anecdotes which supplement each other. It is told of one master that he had to look at a clock during the hour of withdrawal in order to keep himself in this world; and of another that when he wished to observe individual things he had to put on spectacles in order to restrain his spiritual vision; "for otherwise he saw all the individual things of the world as one."

But the highest rung which is reported is that in which the withdrawn one transcends his own ecstasy. When a disciple once remarked that a *tsaddik* had "grown cold" and censured him for it, he was instructed by another, "There is a very high holiness; if one enters it, one becomes detached from all being and can no longer become inflamed." Thus ecstasy completes itself in its own suspension.

At times it expresses itself in an action that it consecrates and fills with holy meaning. The purest form—that in which the whole body serves the aroused soul and in which each of the soul's risings and bendings creates a visible symbol corresponding to it, allowing one image of enraptured meaning to emerge out of a thousand waves of movement—is the dance. It is told of the dancing of one *tsaddik*, "His foot was as light as that of a four-year-old child. And among all who saw his holy dancing, there was not one in whom the holy turning was not accomplished, for in the hearts of all who saw he worked both weeping and rapture in one." Or the soul lays hold of the voice of a man and makes it sing what the soul has experienced in the heights, and the voice does not know what it does. Thus one *tsaddik* stood in prayer in the "days of awe" (New Year and the Day of Atonement) and sang new melodies, "wonder of wonder, that he had never heard and that no human ear had ever heard, and he did not know at all what he sang and in what way he sang, for he was bound to the upper world."

But the truest life of the man of ecstasy is not among men. It is said of one master that he behaved like a stranger, according to the words of David the King: A sojourner am I in the land. "Like a man who comes from afar, from the city of his birth. He does not think of honors nor of anything for his own welfare; he only thinks about returning home to the city of his birth. He can possess nothing, for he knows: That is alien, and I must go home." Many walk in solitude, in "the wandering." Rabbi Susya used to stride about in the woods and sing songs of praise with such great ardor "that one would almost say that he was out of his mind." Another was only to be found in the streets and gardens and groves. When his father-in-law reproved him for this, he answered with the parable of the hen who hatched out goose eggs, "And when she saw her children swimming about on the surface of the water, she ran up and down in consternation seeking help for the unfortunate ones; and did not understand that this was their whole life to them: to roam there on the surface of the water."

There are still more profoundly solitary ones whose *hitlahavut*, for all that, is not yet fulfilled. They become "unsettled and fugitive." They go into exile in order "to suffer exile with the *shekhinah*." It is one of the basic conceptions of the Kabbalah that the *shekhinah*, the exiled glory of God, wanders endlessly, separated from her "lord," and that she will be reunited with him only in the hour of redemption. So these men of ecstasy wander over the earth, dwelling in the silent distances of God's exile, companions of the universal and holy happening of existence. The man who is detached in this way is the friend of God, "as a stranger is the friend of another stranger on account of their strangeness on earth." There are moments in which he sees the *shekhinah* face to face in human form, as that *tsaddik* saw it in the holy land "in the shape of a woman who weeps and laments over the husband of her youth."

But not only in faces out of the dark and in the silence of wandering does God give Himself to the soul afire with Him. Rather out of all the things of the earth His eye looks into the eye of him who seeks, and every being is the fruit in which He offers Himself to the yearning soul. Being is unveiled in the hand of the holy man. "The soul of him who longs very much for a woman and regards her many-colored garment is not turned to its gorgeous material and its colors but to the splendor of the longed-for woman who is clothed in it. But the others see only the garment and no more. So he who in truth longs for and embraces God sees in all the things of the world only the strength and the pride of the Creator who lives in the things. But he who is not on this rung sees the things as separate from God."

This is the earthly life of *hitlahavut* which soars beyond all limits. It enlarges the soul to the all. It narrows the all down to nothing. A Hasidic master speaks of it in words of mystery: "The creation of heaven and of earth is the unfolding of something out of nothing, the descent of the higher into the lower. But the holy men who detach themselves from being and ever cleave to God see and comprehend Him in truth, as if in the nothing before creation. They turn the something back into nothing. And this is the more wonderful: to raise up what is beneath. As it is written in the Gemara: "The last wonder is greater than the first."

'Avodah: Service

Hitlahavut is envelopment in God beyond time and space. *'Avodah* is the service of God in time and space.

Hitlahavut is the mystic meal. *'Avodah* is the mystic offering.

These are the poles between which the life of the holy man swings.

Hitlahavut is silent since it lies on the heart of God. *'Avodah* speaks, "What am I and what is my life that I wish to offer you my blood and my fire?"

Hitlahavut is as far from *'avodah* as fulfillment is from longing. And yet *hitlahavut* streams out of *'avodah* as the finding of God from the seeking of God.

The Baal-Shem told, "A king once built a great and glorious palace with numberless chambers, but only one door was opened. When the building was finished, it was announced that all princes should appear before the king who sat enthroned in the last of the chambers. But when they entered, they saw that there were doors open on all sides which led to winding passages in the distance, and there were again doors and again passages, and no end arose before the bewildered eyes. Then came the king's son and saw that all the labyrinth was a mirrored illusion, and he saw his father sitting in the hall before him."

The mystery of grace cannot be interpreted. Between seeking and finding lies the tension of a human life, indeed the thousandfold return of the anxious, wandering soul. And yet the flight of a moment is slower than the fulfillment. For God wishes to be sought, and how could he not wish to be found?

When the holy man brings ever new fire that the glowing embers on the altar of his soul may not be extinguished, God Himself says the sacrificial speech.

God governs men as He governed chaos at the time of the infancy of the world. "And as when the world began to unfold and He saw that if it flowed further asunder it would no longer be able to return home to its roots, then he spoke, 'Enough!'—so it is that when the soul of man in its suffering rushes headlong, without direction, and evil becomes so mighty in it that it soon could no longer return home, then His compassion awakens, and he says, 'Enough!'"

But man too can say "Enough!" to the multiplicity within him. When he collects himself and becomes one, he draws near to the oneness of God—he serves his Lord. This is 'avodah.

It was said of one *tsaddik*, "With him, teaching and prayer and eating and sleeping are all one, and he can raise the soul to its root."

All action bound in one and the infinite life carried into every action: this is 'avodah. "In all the deeds of man—speaking and looking and listening and going and remaining standing and lying down—the boundless is clothed."

From every deed an angel is born, a good angel or a bad one. But from half-hearted and confused deeds which are without meaning or without power angels are born with twisted limbs or without a head or hands or feet.

When through all action the rays of the universal sun radiate and the light concentrates in every deed, this is service. But no special act is elected for this service. God wills that one serve Him in all ways.

"There are two kinds of love: the love of a man for his wife, which ought properly to express itself in secret and not where spectators are, for this love can only fulfill itself in a place secluded from the creatures; and the love for brothers and sisters and for children, which needs no concealment. Similarly, the are two kinds of love for God: the love through the teaching and prayer and the fulfillment of the commandments—this love ought properly to be consummated in silence and not in public, in order that it may not tempt one to glory and pride—and the love in the time when one mixes with the creatures, when one speaks and hears, gives and takes with them, and yet in the secret of one's heart one cleaves to God and does not cease to think of Him. And this is a higher rung than that, and of it, it is said, 'Oh, that thou wert as my brother that sucked on the breasts of my mother! When I should find thee without I would kiss thee; yea, and none would despise me.'"

This is not to be understood, however, as if there were in this kind of service a cleavage between the earthly and the heavenly deed. Rather each motion of the surrendered soul is a vessel of holiness and of power. It is told of one *tsaddik* that he had so sanctified all his limbs that each step of his feet wed worlds to one another. "Man is a ladder, placed on earth and touching heaven with its head. And all his gestures and affairs and sneaking leave traces in the higher world."

Here the inner meaning of *'avodah* is intimated, coming from the depths of the old Jewish secret teaching and illuminating the mystery of that duality of ecstasy and service, of having and seeking.

God has fallen into duality through the created world and its deed: into the essence of God, Elohim, which is withdrawn from the creatures, and the presence of God, the *shekhinah*, which dwells in things, wandering, straying, scattered. Only redemption will reunite the two in eternity. But it is given to the human spirit, through its service, to be able to bring the *shekinah* near to its source, to help it to enter it. And in this moment of homecoming, before it must again descend into the being of things, the whirlpool which rushes through the life of the stars becomes silent, the torches of the great devastation are extinguished, the whip in the head of fate drops down, the world-pain pauses and listens: the grace of graces has appeared, blessing pours down out of infinity. Until the power of entanglement begins to drag down the *shekhinah* and all becomes as before.

This is the meaning of service. Only the prayer that takes place for the sake of the *shekhinah* truly lives. "Through his need and his want he knows the want of the *shekhinah*, and he prays that the want of the *shekhinah* will be satisfied and that through him, the praying man, the unification of God with His presence will take place." Man should know that his suffering comes from the suffering of the *shekhinah*. He is "one of her limbs," and the stilling of her need is the only true stilling of his. "He does not think about the satisfaction of his needs, neither the lower nor the higher ones, that he might not be like him who cuts off the eternal plants and causes separation. Rather he does all for the sake of the want of the *shekhinah*, and all will be resolved of itself, and his own suffering too will be stilled out of the stilling of the higher roots. For all, above and below, is one unity." "I am prayer," speaks the *shekhinah*. A *tsaddik* said, "Men think they pray before God, but it is not so, for prayer itself is divinity."

In the narrow room of self no prayer can thrive. "He who prays in suffering because of the melancholy which governs him and thinks that he prays in fear of God, or he who prays in joy because of the brightness of his mood and thinks he prays in love of God—his prayer is nothing at all. For this fear is only melancholy and this love is only empty joy."

74

It is told that the Baal-Shem once remained standing on the threshold of a house of prayer and did not want to enter. He spoke in aversion: "I cannot enter there. The house is full to the brim of teaching and prayer." And when his companions were astonished, because it appeared to them that there could be no greater praise than this, he explained to them, "During the day the people speak here words without true devotion, without love and compassion, words that have no wings. They remain between the walls, they squat on the floor, they grow layer by layer like decaying leaves until the decay has packed the house to overflowing and there is no longer room for me in there."

Prayer may be held down in two different ways: if it is spoken without inner intention and if the earlier deeds of the praying man spread themselves like a thick cloud between him and heaven. The obstacle can only be overcome if the man grows upward into the sphere of ecstasy and purifies himself in its grace, or if another soul who is in ecstasy sets the fettered prayers free and carries them upward along with his own. Thus it is told of one *tsaddik* that he stood for a long time silent and without movement during communal prayer and only then began himself to pray, "just as the tribe of Dan lay at the end of the camp and gathered all that was lost." His word became a garment to whose folds the prayers that were held below would cling and be borne upward. This *tsaddik* used to say of prayer, "I bind myself with the whole of Israel, with those who are greater than I that through them my thoughts may ascend, and with those who are lesser than I that they may be uplifted through me."

But this is the mystery of community: not only do the lower need the higher, but the higher also need the lower. Here lies another distinction between the state of ecstasy and the state of service. *Hitlahavut* is the individual way and goal; a rope is stretched over the abyss, tied to two slender trees shaken by the storm: it is trod in solitude and dread by the foot of the venturer. Here there is no human community, neither in doubt nor in attainment. Service, however, is open to many souls in union. The souls bind themselves to one another for greater unity and might. There is a service that only the community can fulfill.

The Baal-Shem told a parable: "Some men stood under a very high tree. And one of the men had eyes to see. He saw that in the top of the tree stood a bird, glorious with genuine beauty. But the others did not see it. And a great longing came over the man to reach the bird and take it; and he could not go from there without the bird. But because of the height of the tree this was not in his power, and a ladder was not to be found. Still out of his great and powerful longing he found a way. He took the men who stood around him and placed them on top of one another, each on the shoulder of a comrade. He, however, climbed to the top so that he reached the bird and took it. And although the men had helped him, they knew nothing of the bird and did not see it. But he, who knew it and saw it, would not have been able to reach it without them. If, moreover, the lowest of them had left his place, then those above would have fallen to the earth. 'And the Temple of the Messiah is called the bird's nest in the book Zohar.'"

But it is not as if only the *tsaddik*'s prayer is received by God or as if only this prayer is lovely in His eyes. No prayer is stronger in grace and penetrates in more direct flight through all the worlds of heaven than that of the simple man who does not know anything to say and only knows to offer God the unbroken promptings of his heart. God receives them as a king receives the singing of a nightingale in his gardens at night, a singing that sounds sweeter to him than the homage of the princes in his throne room. The Hasidic legend cannot give enough examples of the favor that shines on the undivided person and of the power of his service. One of these we shall set down here.

A villager who year after year attended the prayer house of the Baal-Shem in the "days of awe" had a boy who was dull in understanding and could not even learn the shape of the letters, let alone understand the holy words. The father did not take him to the city on the "days of awe," for he knew nothing. Still when he was thirteen years old and of age to receive God's law, the father took him with him on the Day of Atonement that he might not eat something on the day of penance through lack of knowledge and understanding. Now the boy had a little whistle on which he always whistled during the time when he sat in the field and pastured the sheep and calves. He had brought it with him in his pocket without his father's knowing it. The boy sat in the prayer house during the holy hours and did not know anything to say. But when the *Mussaf* prayer was begun, he spoke to his father, "Father, I have my whistle with me, and I wish to play on it."

Then the father was very disturbed and commanded him, "Take care that you do not do so."

And he had to hold himself in. But when the *Minhah* prayer came, he spoke again: "Father, allow me now to take my whistle."

When the father saw that his soul desired to whistle, he became angry and asked him, "Where do you keep it?" and when the boy showed him the place, he laid his hand on the pocket and held it over it from then on to guard the whistle. But the *Ne'ilah* prayer began, and the lights burned trembling in the evening, and the hearts burned like the lights, unexhausted by the long waiting. And through the house the eighteen benedictions strode once again, weary but erect. And the great confession returned for the last time and, before the evening descended and God judged, lay yet once more before the ark of the Lord, its forehead on the floor and its hands extended. Then the boy could no longer suppress his ecstasy, he tore the whistle from his pocket and let its voice powerfully resound. All stood startled and bewildered. But the Baal-Shem raised himself above them and spoke, "The judgment is suspended, and wrath is dispelled from the face of the earth."

Thus every service which proceeds from a simple or a unified soul is sufficient and complete. But there is a still higher one. For he who has ascended from 'avodah to hitlahavut has submerged his will in it and receives his deed from it alone, having risen above every separate service. "Each tsaddik has his special way of serving. But when the tsaddik contemplates his root and attains to the Nothing, then he can serve God on all rungs." Thus one of them said, "I stand before God as a messenger boy." For he had attained to completion and to the Nothing so that he no longer possessed any special way. "Rather he stood ready for all ways which God might show him, as a messenger boy stands ready for all that his master will command him." He who thus serves in perfection has conquered the primeval duality and has brought hitlahavut into the heart of 'avodah. He dwells in the kingdom of life, and yet all walls have fallen, all boundary-stones are uprooted, all separation is destroyed. He is the brother of the creatures and feels their glance as if it were his own, their step as if his own feet walked, their blood as if it flowed through his own body. He is the son of God and lays his soul anxiously and securely in the great hand beside all the heavens and earths and unknown worlds, and stands on the flood of the sea into which all his thoughts and the wanderings of all beings flow. "He makes his body the throne of life and life the throne of the spirit and the spirit the throne of the soul and the soul the throne of the light of God's glory, and the light streams round about him, and he sits in the midst of the light and trembles and rejoices."

Kavvanah: Intention

Kavvanah is the mystery of a soul directed to a goal.

Kavvanah is not will. It does not think of transplanting an image into the world of actual things, of making fast a dream as an object so that it may be at hand, to be experienced at one's convenience in satiating recurrence. Nor does it desire to throw the stone of action into the well of happening that its waters may for a while become troubled and astonished, only to return then to the deep command of their existence, nor to lay a spark on the fuse that runs through the succession of the generations, that a flame may jump from age to age until it is extinguished in one of them without sign or leave-taking. Not this is *kavvanah's* meaning, that the horses pulling the great wagon should feel one impulse more or that one building more should be erected beneath the overfull gaze of the stars. *Kavvanah* does not mean purpose but goal.

But there are no *goals*, only *the goal*. There is only one goal that does not lie, that becomes entangled in no new way, only one into which all ways flow, before which no byway can forever flee: redemption.

Kavvanah is a ray of God's glory that dwells in each man and means redemption.

This is redemption, that the *shekhinah* shall return home from its exile. "That all shells may withdraw from God's glory and that it may purify itself and unite itself with its owner in perfect unity." As a sign of this the Messiah will appear and make all beings free.

To many a Hasid it is, for the whole of his life, as if this must happen here and now. For he hears the voice of becoming roaring in the gorges and feels the seed of eternity in the ground of time as if it were in his blood. And so he can never think otherwise than that *this* moment and now *this* one will be the chosen moment. And his imagination compels him ever more fervently, for ever more commanding speaks the voice and ever more demandingly swells the seed.

It is told of one *tsaddik* that he awaited redemption with such eagerness that when he heard a tumult in the street, he was at once moved to ask what it was and whether the messenger had not come; and each time that he went to sleep he commanded his servant to awaken him at the very moment when the messenger came. "For the coming of the redeemer was so deeply implanted in his heart that it was as when a father awaits his only son from a distant land and stands on the watchtower with longing in his eyes and peers through all the windows and, when one opens the door, hurries out to see whether his son has not come." Others, however, are aware of the progress of the stride, see the place and hour of the path and know the distance of the Coming One. Each thing shows them the uncompleted state of the world, the need of existence speaks to them, and the breath of the winds bears bitterness to them. The world in their eyes is like an unripe fruit. Inwardly they partake in the glory—then they look outward: all lies in battle.

When the great *tsaddik* Rabbi Menahem was in Jerusalem, it happened that a foolish man climbed the Mount of Olives and blew the shofar trumpet. No one had seen him. A rumor spread among the people that this was the shofar blast which announced the redemption. When this came to the ears of the rabbi, he opened a window and looked out into the air of the world. And he said at once, "Here is no renewal."

This is the way of redemption: that all souls and all sparks of souls which have sprung from the primeval soul and have sunk and become scattered in all creatures at the time of the original darkening of the world or through the guilt of the ages should conclude their wandering and return home purified. The Hasidim speak of this in the parable of the prince who allows the meal to begin only when the last of the guests has entered.

All men are the abode of wandering souls. These dwell in many creatures and strive from form to form toward perfection. But those which are not able to purify themselves are caught in the "world of confusion" and make their homes in lakes of water, in stones, in plants, in animals, awaiting the redeeming hour.

It is not only souls that are everywhere imprisoned but also sparks of souls. Nothing is without them. They live in all that is. Each form is their prison.

And this is the meaning and mission of *kavvanah*: that it is given to men to lift up the fallen and to free the imprisoned. Not only to wait, not only to watch for the Coming One: man can work toward the redemption of the world.

Just that is *kavvanah*: the mystery of the soul that is directed to redeem the world.

It is told of some holy men that they imagined that they might bring about redemption by storm and force—in this world, when they were so afire with the grace of ecstasy that to them, who had even embraced God, nothing appeared unattainable any longer, or in the coming world. A dying *tsaddik* said, "My friends have gone hence, intending to bring the Messiah, and have forgotten to do so in their rapture. But I shall not forget."

In reality, however, each can only be effective in his domain. Each man has a sphere of being, far extended in space and time, which is allotted to him to be redeemed through him. Places which are heavy with unraised sparks and in which souls are fettered wait for the man who will come to them with the word of freedom. When a Hasid cannot pray in one place and goes to another, then the first place demands of him, "Why would you not speak the holy words over me? And if there is evil in me, then it is for you to redeem me." But also all journeys have secret destinations of which the traveler is unaware.

It was said of some *tsaddikim* that they had a helping power over the wandering souls. At all times, but especially when they stood in prayer, the wanderers of eternity appeared imploring before them, wishing to receive salvation from their hands. But they also knew how to find the voiceless among the banished in the exile of a tired body or in the darkness of the elements and to upraise them.

This help is an awesome venture, set down in the midst of threatening dangers, which only the holy man can enter upon without going under. "He who has a soul may let himself down into the abyss, bound fast to the rim above through his thoughts, as through a strong rope, and will return. But he who only has life or only life and spirit, he who has not yet attained the rung of thought, for him the bond will not hold and he will fall into the depths."

But, though it is only those blessed ones who can plunge tranquilly into the darkness in order to aid a soul which is abandoned to the whirlpool of wandering, it is not denied to even the least of persons to raise the lost sparks from their imprisonment and send them home.

The sparks are to be found everywhere. They are suspended in things as in sealed-off springs; they stoop in the creatures as in walled-up caves, they inhale darkness and they exhale dread; they wait. And those that dwell in space flit hither and thither around the movements of the world, like light-mad butterflies, looking to see which of them they might enter in order to be redeemed through them. They all wait expectantly for freedom.

"The spark in a stone or a plant or another creature is like a complete figure which sits in the middle of the thing as in a block, so that its hands and feet cannot stretch themselves and the head lies on the knees. He who is able to lift the holy spark leads this figure into freedom, and no setting free of captives is greater than this. It is as when a king's son is rescued from captivity and brought to his father."

But the liberation does not take place through formulae of exorcism or through any kind of prescribed and special action. All this grows out of the ground of otherness, which is not the ground of *kavvanah*. No leap from the everyday into the miraculous is required. "With his every act man can work on the figure of the glory of God that it may step forth out of its concealment." It is not the matter of the action, but only its dedication that is decisive. Just that which you do in the uniformity of recurrence or in the disposition of events, just this answer of the acting person to the manifold demands of the hour—an answer acquired through practice or won through inspiration—just this continuity of the living stream, when accomplished in dedication, leads to redemption. He who prays and sings in holiness, eats and speaks in holiness, in holiness takes the prescribed ritual bath and in holiness is mindful of his business, through him the fallen sparks are raised and the fallen worlds redeemed and renewed.

Around each man—enclosed within the wide sphere of his activity—is laid a natural circle of things which, before all, he is called to set free. These are the creatures and objects that are spoken of as the possessions of this individual: his animals and his walls, his garden and his meadow, his tools and his food. In so far as he cultivates and enjoys them in holiness, he frees their souls. "For this reason a man should always have mercy on his tools and all his possessions."

But also in the soul itself there appear those that need liberation. Most of these are sparks which have fallen through the guilt of this soul in one of its earlier lives. They are the alien, disturbing thoughts that often come to man in prayer. "When man stands in prayer and desires to join himself to the Eternal, and the alien thoughts come and descend on him, these are holy sparks that have sunken and that wish to be raised and redeemed by him; and the sparks belong to him, they are kindred to the roots of his soul: it is his power that will redeem them." He redeems them when he restores each troubled thought to its pure source, allows each impulse intent on a particular thing to flow into the divine creative impulse, allows everything alien to be submerged in the divine self-identity.

This is the *kavvanah* of receiving: that one redeem the sparks in the surrounding things and the sparks that draw near out of the invisible. But there is yet another *kavvanah*, the *kavvanah* of giving. It bears no stray soul-rays in helpful hands; it binds worlds to one another and rules over the mysteries, it pours itself into the thirsty distance, it gives itself to infinity. But it too has no need of miraculous deeds. Its path is creation, and the word before all other forms of creation.

From time immemorial speech was for the Jewish mystic a rare and awe-inspiring thing. A characteristic theory of letters existed which dealt with them as with the elements of the world and with their intermixture as with the inwardness of reality. The word is an abyss through which the speaker strides. "One should speak words as if the heavens were opened in them.

And as if it were not so that you take the word in your mouth, but rather as if you entered into the word." He who knows the secret melody that bears the inner into the outer, who knows the holy song that merges the lonely, shy letters into the singing of the spheres, he is full of the power of God, "and it is as if he created heaven and earth and all worlds anew." He does not find his sphere before him as does the freer of souls, he extends it from the firmament to the silent depths. But he also works toward redemption. "For in each letter are the three: world, soul, and divinity. They rise and join and unite themselves, and they become the word, and the words unite themselves in God in genuine unity, since a man has set his soul in them, and worlds unite themselves and ascend, and the great rapture is born." Thus the acting person prepares the final oneness of all things.

And as 'avodah flowed into hitlahavut, the basic principle of Hasidic life, so here too kavvanah flows into hitlahavut. For creating means to be created: the divine moves and overcomes us. And to be created is ecstasy: only he who sinks into the Nothing of the Absolute receives the forming hand of the spirit. This is portrayed in parable. It is not given to anything in the world to be reborn and to attain to a new form unless it comes first to the Nothing, that is, to the "form of the in between." No creature can exist in it, it is the power before creation and is called chaos. Thus the perishing of the egg into the chick and thus the seed, which does not sprout before it has gone down into the earth and decayed. "And this is called wisdom, that is, a thought without revelation. And so it is: if man desires that a new creation come out of him, then he must come with all his potentiality to the state of nothing, and then God brings forth in him a new creation, and he is like a fountain that does not run dry and a stream that does not cease to flow."

Thus the will of the Hasidic teaching of *kavvanah* is twofold: that enjoyment, the internalizing of that which is without, should take place in holiness and that creation, the externalizing of that which is within, should take place in holiness. Through holy creation and through holy enjoyment the redemption of the world is accomplished.

Shiflut: Humility

God never does the same thing twice, said Rabbi Nachman of Bratzlav.

That which exists is unique, and it happens but once. New and without a past, it emerges from the flood of returnings, takes place, and plunges back into it, unrepeatable. Each thing reappears at another time, but each transformed. And the throws and falls that rule over the great world-creations, and the water and fire which shape the form of the earth, and the mixings and unmixings which brew the life of the living, and the spirit of man with all its trial-and-error relation to the yielding abundance of the possible — none of these can create an identical thing nor bring back one of the things that have been sealed as belonging to the past. It is because things happen but once that the individual partakes in eternity. For the individual with his inextinguishable uniqueness is engraved in the heart of the all and lies forever in the lap of the timeless as he who has been created thus and not otherwise.

Uniqueness is thus the essential good of man that is given to him to unfold. And just this is the meaning of the return, that his uniqueness may become ever purer and more complete; and that in each new life the one who has returned may stand in ever more untroubled and undisturbed incomparability. For pure uniqueness and pure perfection are one, and he who has become so entirely individual that no otherness any longer has power over him or place in him has completed the journey and is redeemed and rests in God.

"Every man shall know and consider that in his qualities he is unique in the world and that none like him ever lived, for had there ever before been someone like him, then he would not have needed to exist. But each is in truth a new thing in the world, and he shall make perfect his special characteristics, for it is because they are not perfect that the coming of the Messiah tarries."

Only in his own way and not in any other can the one who strives perfect himself. "He who lays hold of the rung of his companion and lets go of his own rung, through him neither the one nor the other will be realized. Many acted like Rabbi Simeon ben Yochai and in their hands it did not turn out well, for they were not of the same nature as he but only acted as they saw him act out of his nature."

But as man seeks God in lonely fervor and yet there is a high service that only the community can fulfill, and as man accomplishes enormous things with his everyday actions, yet does not do so alone but needs for such action the world and the things in it, so the uniqueness of man proves itself in his life with others. For the more unique a man really is, so much the more can he give to the other and so much the more will he give him. And this is his one sorrow, that his giving is limited by the one who takes. For "the bestower is on the side of mercy and the receiver is on the side of rigor. And so it is with each thing. As when one pours out of a large vessel into a goblet: the vessel pours from out of its fullness, but the goblet limits the gift."

The individual sees God and embraces Him. The individual redeems the fallen worlds. And yet the individual is not a whole, but a part. And the purer and more perfect he is, so much the more intimately does he know that he is a part and so much the more actively there stirs in him the community of existence. That is the mystery of humility.

"Every man has a light over him, and when the souls of two men meet, the two lights join each other and from them there goes forth one light. And this is called generation." To feel the universal generation as a sea and oneself as a wave, that is the mystery of humility.

But it is not humility when one "lowers himself too much and forgets that man can bring down an overflowing blessing on all the world through his words and his actions." This is called impure humility. "The greatest evil is when you forget that you are the son of a king." He is truly humble who feels the other as himself and himself in the other.

Haughtiness means to contrast oneself with others. The haughty man is not he who knows himself, but he who compares himself with others. No man can presume too much if he stands on his own ground since all the heavens are open to him and all worlds devoted to him. The man who presumes too much is the man who contrasts himself with others, who sees himself as higher than the humblest of things, who rules with measure and weights and pronounces judgment.

"If Messiah should come today," a *tsaddik* said, "and say, 'You are better than the others,' then I would say to him, 'You are not Messiah.'"

The soul of the haughty lives without product and essence; it flutters and toils and is not blessed. The thoughts whose real intent is not what is thought but themselves and their brilliance are shadows. The deed which has in mind not the goal but the profit has no body, only surface, no existence, only appearance. He who measures and weighs becomes empty and unreal like measure and weight. "In him who is full of himself there is no room for God."

It is told of one disciple that he went into seclusion and cut himself off from the things of the world in order to cling solely to the teaching and the service, and he sat alone fasting from Sabbath to Sabbath and learning and praying. But his mind, beyond all conscious purpose, was filled with pride in his action; it shone before his eyes and his fingers burned to lay it on his forehead like the diadem of the anointed. And so all his work fell to the lot of the "other side," and the divine had no share in it. But his heart drove him ever more strongly so that he remained unaware of his fallen state in which the demons played with his acts, and he imagined himself wholly possessed by God. Then it happened once that he leaned outside of himself and became aware of the mute and alienated things around him: Then understanding possessed him and he beheld his deeds piled up at the feet of a gigantic idol, and he beheld himself in the reeling emptiness, abandoned to the nameless. This much is told and no more.

But the humble man has the "drawing power." As long as a man sees himself above and before others, he has a limit, "and God cannot pour His holiness into him, for God is without limit." But when a man rests in himself as in nothing, he is not limited by any other thing, he is limitless and God pours His glory into him.

The humility which is meant here is no willed and practiced virtue. It is nothing but an inner being, feeling, and expressing. Nowhere in it is there a compulsion, nowhere a self-humbling, a self-restraining, a self-resolve. It is indivisible as the glance of a child and simple as a child's speech.

The humble man lives in each being and knows each being's manner and virtue. Since no one is to him "the other," he knows from within that none lacks some hidden value; knows that there "is no man who does not have his hour." For him, the colors of the world do not blend with one another, rather each soul stands before him in the majesty of its particular existence. "In each man there is a priceless treasure that is in no other. Therefore, one shall honor each man for the hidden value that only he and none of his comrades has."

"God does not look on the evil side," said one *tsaddik*; "how should I dare to do so?"

He who lives in others according to the mystery of humility can condemn no one. "He who passes sentence on a man has passed it on himself."

He who separates himself from the sinner departs in guilt. But the saint can suffer for the sins of a man as for his own. Only living with the other is justice.

Living with the other as a form of knowing is justice. Living with the other as a form of being is love. For that feeling that is called love among men, the feeling of being near and of wishing to be near a few, is nothing other than a recollection from a heavenly life: "Those who sat next to one another in Paradise and were neighbors and relatives, they are also near to one another in this world." But in truth love is all-comprehensive and sustaining and is extended to all the living without selection and distinction. "How can you say of me that I am a leader of the generation," said a *tsaddik*, "when I still feel in myself a stronger love for those near me and for my seed than for all men?" That this attitude also extends to animals is shown by the accounts of Rabbi Wolf who could never shout at a horse, of Rabbi Moshe Leib, who gave drink to the neglected calves at the market, of Rabbi Susya who could not see a cage, "and the wretchedness of the bird and its anxiety to fly in the air of the world and to be a free wanderer in accordance with its nature," without opening it. But it is not only the beings to whom the shortsighted gaze of the crowd accords the name of "living" who are embraced by the love of the loving man: "There is no thing in the world in which there is not life, and each has the form of life in which it stands before your eyes. And lo, this life is the life of God."

Thus it is held that the love of the living is love of God, and it is higher than any other service. A master asked one of his disciples, "You know that two forces cannot occupy the human mind at the same time. If then you rise from your couch tomorrow and two ways are before you: the love of God and the love of man, which should come first?" "I do not know," the latter answered. Then spoke the master, "It is written in the prayer book that is in the hands of the people, 'Before you pray, say the words, Love thy companion as one like thyself.' Do you think that the venerable ones commanded that without purpose? If someone says to you that he has love for God but has no love for the living, he speaks falsely and pretends that which is impossible."

Therefore, when one has departed from God, the love of a man is his only salvation. When a father complained to the Baal-Shem, "My son is estranged from God—what shall I do?" he replied, "Love him more."

This is one of the primary Hasidic words: to love more. Its roots sink deep and stretch out far. He who has understood this can learn to understand Judaism anew. There is a great moving force therein.

A great moving force and yet again only a lost sound. It is a lost sound, when somewhere—in that dark windowless room—and at some time—in those days without the power of message—the lips of a nameless, soon-to-be-forgotten man, of the *tsaddik* Rabbi Rafael, formed these words, "If a man sees that his companion hates him, he shall love him the more. For the community of the living is the carriage of God's majesty, and where there is a rent in the carriage, one must fill it, and where there is so little love that the joining comes apart, one must love more on one's own side to overcome the lack."

Once before a journey this Rabbi Rafael called to a disciple that he should sit beside him in the carriage. "I fear I shall make it too crowded for you," the latter responded. But the rabbi now spoke in a stronger voice, "So we shall love each other more: then there will be room enough for us."

They may stand here as a witness, the symbol and the reality, separate and yet one and inseparable, the carriage of the *shekhinah* and the carriage of the friends.

It is the love of a being who lives in a kingdom greater than the kingdom of the individual and speaks out of a knowing deeper than the knowing of the individual. It exists in reality *between* the creatures, that is, it exists in God. Life covered and guaranteed by life, life pouring itself into life, thus first do you behold the soul of the world. What the one is wanting, the other makes up for. If one loves too little, the other will love more.

Things help one another. But helping means to do what one does for its own sake and with a collected will. As he who loves more does not preach love to the other, but himself loves and, in a certain sense, does not concern himself about the other, so the helping man, in a certain sense, does not concern himself about the other, but does what he does out of himself with the thought of helping. That means that the essential thing that takes place between beings does not take place through their intercourse, but through each seemingly isolated, seemingly unconcerned, seemingly unconnected action performed out of himself. This is said in parable: "If a man sings and cannot lift his voice and another comes to help him and begins to sing, then this one too can now lift his voice. And that is the secret of co-operation."

To help one another is no task, but a matter of course, the reality on which the life-together of the Hasidim is founded. Help is no virtue, but an artery of existence. That is the new meaning of the old Jewish saying that good deeds save one from death. It is commanded that the helping person not think about the others who could assist him, about God and man. He must not think of himself as a partial power that needs only to contribute; rather each must answer and be responsible for the whole. And one thing more, and this is again nothing other than an expression of the mystery of *shiflut*: not to help out of pity, that is, out of a sharp, quick pain which one wishes to expel, but out of love, that is, out of living with the other. He who pities does not live with the suffering of the sufferer, he does not bear it in his heart as one bears the life of a tree with all its drinking in and shooting forth and with the dream of its roots and the craving of its trunk and the thousand journeys of its branches, or as one bears the life of an animal with all its gliding, stretching, and grasping and all the joy of its sinews and its joints and the dull tension of its brain. He does not bear in his heart this special essence, the suffering of the other; rather he receives from the most external features of this suffering a sharp, quick pain, unbridgeably dissimilar to the original pain of the sufferer. And it is thus that he is moved. But the helper must live with the other, and only help that arises out of living with the other can stand before the eyes of God. Thus it is told of one *tsaddik* that when a poor person had excited his pity, he provided first for all his pressing need, but then, when he looked inward and perceived that the wound of pity was healed, he plunged with great, restful, and devoted love into the life and needs of the other, took hold of them as if they were his own life and needs and began in reality to help.

He who lives with others in this way realizes with his deed the truth that all souls are one; for each is a spark from the original soul, and the whole of the original soul is in each.

Thus lives the humble man, who is the loving man and the helper: mixing with all and untouched by all, devoted to the multitude and collected in his uniqueness, fulfilling on the rocky summits of solitude the bond with the infinite and in the valley of life the bond with the earthly, flowering out of deep devotion and withdrawn from all desire of the desiring. He knows that all is in God and greets His messengers as trusted friends. He has no fear of the before and the after, of the above and the below, of this world and the world to come. He is at home and never can be cast out. The earth cannot help but be his cradle, and heaven cannot help but be his mirror and his echo.

Spirit and Body of the Hasidic Movement (1922)

This second selection derives from the introduction to Buber's anthology *The Great Maggid and His Succession*. It stands on its own as a powerful portrait of Hasidic spirituality, and also reflects how Buber's portrayal of Hasidism changed in the wake of his shift from mysticism to dialogue. The following constitutes an unprecedented annotated version of the essay, equipping curious readers to compare Buber's numerous textual references with the original Hasidic sources.[59]

I. Spirit

Movements that strive for a renewal of society mean by that for the most part that the axe should be laid to the root of the existing order; they set in contrast to what has come into being a fundamentally different product of willed thought. Not so the religious movements that proceed from a renewal of the soul. However much the principle that is advocated by a genuine religious movement may be diametrically opposed to the prevailing religious status of the environment, the movement experiences and expresses this opposition not as an opposition to the essential original content of the tradition; it feels and explains itself rather as summoned to purify this original content of its present distortions, to restore it, to "bring it back." But from this same starting-point the religious movements can progress very differently in their relation to the prevailing faith. On the one hand, the old-new principle may set its own message in bodily opposition to and as the original state of the late stage of the tradition. It presents its message, therefore, as the obscured original truth, now rescued and brought to light, represented by the central man "come" to restore it, and actually identical with him. Then the complete transformation and separation soon takes place. Such movements may be designated as founding ones. On the other hand, the principle may simply return to an older stage of the tradition, to the "pure word" that it has to liberate and whose distortion it combats. Then a partial separation takes place so that the mythical-dogmatic and magical-cultic fundamentals remain for the most part untouched, and, despite the organizational separation, the spiritual unity essentially continues. These movements are called reforming ones.

There is, however, a third possibility. The principle may accept the tradition in its present state with undiminished value; its teachings and precepts may be recognized in their full present extension without examining their historical credentials and without comparing them with an original form; but the principle creates a new illumination of the teachings and precepts, it makes it possible for it to win in this light a new soul, a new meaning, it renews their vitality without changing them in their substance. Here no separation takes place although here too the battle between the old and the new must break out and can take on the most violent forms: the new community remains within the hereditary one and seeks to penetrate it from within—a measuring of two forces against each other, the moving force and the conserving force, a measuring that is soon carried over to the ground of the new community itself and continues among its members, indeed within the heart of each individual. The conditions of the battle naturally become ever more favorable for the force of inertia. Among the movements of this type is the Hasidic which, beginning in Podolia and Wolhynia around the middle of the eighteenth century, by the turn of the century had taken possession of the Jewry of the whole Polish kingdom as well as important parts of North East Hungary and the Moldau and by the middle of the nineteenth century had developed into a structure benumbed in spirit but mighty in numbers that continues in existence to this day.

Genuine religious movements do not want to offer man the solution of the world mystery, but to equip him to live from the strength of the mystery; they do not wish to instruct him about the nature of God, but to show him the path on which he can meet God. But among them is the third type of which I spoke that is most especially concerned not with a universally valid knowledge of what is and what ought to be, but only about the here and now of the human person, the eternally new shoot of the eternal truth. Just for this reason, this movement can take over unchanged a system of general dogmas and precepts from the contemporary stage of the tradition; its own contribution cannot be codified, it is not the material of a lasting knowledge or obligation, only light for the seeing eye, strength for the working hand, appearing ever anew. This announces itself especially clearly in Hasidism. Of highest importance to it is not what has been from of old but what again and again happens; and, again, not what befalls a man but what he does; and not the extraordinary that he does but the ordinary; and more still than what he does, how he does it. Among all the movements of this type probably none has proclaimed as clearly as Hasidism the infinite ethos of the moment.

Hasidism took over and united two traditions without adding anything essentially different to them other than a new light and a new strength: a tradition of religious law — next to the Vedic sacrificial teaching the most gigantic structure of spiritual commands — the ritual formation of Judaism; and a tradition of religious knowledge — inferior to gnosis in the power of its images, superior to it in systematization — the Kabbalah.

These two streams of tradition were, of course, individually united in each Kabbalist, but their real fusion into one reality of life and community first took place in Hasidism.

The fusion took place through the old-new principle that it represented: the principle of the responsibility of man for God's fate in the world. Responsibility, not in a conditioned, moral, but in an unconditioned, transcendent sense, the mysterious, inscrutable value of human action, the influence of the acting man on the destiny of the universe, even on its guiding forces—that is an ancient idea in Judaism. "The righteous increase the might of the upper dominion."[60] There is a causality of the deed that is withdrawn from our experience and only accessible to our intuitive gleanings.

This idea was elaborated in the development of the Kabbalah to the central and sustaining role in which it came forward in Hasidism: through the Kabbalistic concept of God's fate in the world. . . .

How is the world possible? That is the basic question of the Kabbalah, as it was the basic question of all gnosis. How can the world be since God still is? Since God is infinite, how can anything exist outside Him? Since He is eternal, how can time endure? Since He is perfect, how can imperfection come into being? Since He is unconditioned, why the conditioned?

The Kabbalah[61] answers: God contracted Himself to world because He, nondual and relationless unity, wanted to allow relation to emerge; because He wanted to be known, loved, wanted; because He wanted to allow to arise from His primally one Being, in which thinking and thought are one, the otherness that strives to unity.[62] So there radiated from Him the spheres: separation, creation, formation, making, the world of ideas, the forces, the forms, the material, the kingdom of genius, of spirit, of soul, of life; so there was established in them the All, whose "place" God is and whose center He is.[63] The meaning of emanation, according to a Hasidic saying, is "not as the creatures suppose that the upper worlds should be above the lower ones, but the world of making is this one that appears to our material eye; however, if you fathom it deeper and disclose its materiality, then just this is the world of formation, and if you disclose it further, then it is the world of creation, and if you fathom its being still deeper, so it is the world of separation, and so until the Unlimited, blessed be He."[64]

The space-time world of the senses is only the outermost cover of God. There is no evil in itself; the imperfect is only cover and clasp of a more perfect.

By this is not meant that all world being is, in fact, mere appearance, but that it is a system of ever thicker coverings. And yet it is just this system in which God's fate fulfills itself. God has not, Himself fateless, made a world that experiences a fate: He Himself, as far as He has sent it forth out of Himself, has clad Himself in it, dwells in it, He Himself in His *shekhinah* has His fate in the world.

But why was the primal will not satisfied by the pure spheres of separation, the world of ideas, where He who willed to be known could be known face to face? Why must the act bring forth beyond itself ever "lower," more distant, shell-enclosed spheres, down to this obdurate, troubled, burdened world in which we creatures, we things live? Why could we not have remained ethereal genius, why had we one after the other to be rolled and permeated with fiery spirit, watery soul, earthly corporeal life?

To all such questions the Kabbalah answers only: God contracted Himself to world. And it is answered. God wanted to be known, loved, wanted, that is: God willed a freely existing, in freedom knowing, in freedom loving, in freedom willing otherness; *he set it free.* This means the concept of *tsimtsum,* contraction.[65] But while this power, taken away from eternal being, was accorded its freedom, the limitation of its freedom was set by nothing other than its own consequences; it flooded forth beyond its God-near purity. Becoming broke forth out of being, what the Kabbalah calls "the mystery of the Breaking of the Vessels" took place. Sphere extended itself out of sphere, world climbed away over world, shell joined itself to shell, unto the limit of the transformations. Here, in the realm of matter that is extended in space, that endures in time, on the rim of what has become, in the uttermost border-land of sense things, God's wave breaks. The wave that breaks here is God's. As the light from the highest plunged into the lower spheres and shattered them, light-sparks from the primordial being in the immediate presence of God—the genius-natured Adam Kadmon—have fallen into the imprisonment of the things. God's *shekhinah* descends from sphere to sphere, wanders from world to world, banishes itself in shell after shell until it reaches its furthest exile: us. In our world God's fate is fulfilled.

But our world is in truth the world of man . . .

In other teachings the God-soul, sent or released by heaven to earth, could be called home or freed to return home by heaven; creation and redemption take place in the same direction, from "above" to "below." But this is not so in a teaching which, like the Jewish, is so wholly based upon the double-directional relation of the human I and the divine Thou, on the reality of reciprocity, on the meeting. Here man, this miserable man is, by the very meaning of his creation, the helper of God. For his sake, for the sake of the "chooser," for the sake of him who can choose God, the world was created. Its shells are there in order that he may penetrate through them into the kernel. The spheres have withdrawn from one another in order that he may bring them nearer to one another. The creature waits for him. God waits for him. From him, from "below" the impulse toward redemption must proceed. Grace is God's answer.

None of the upper, inner worlds, only this lowest and most external world is capable of providing the thrust to transformation in the 'Olam Ha-Tikkun, the world of completion, in which "the figure of the shekhinah steps out of the hiddenness." For God has contracted Himself to world, He has set it free; now fate rests on its freedom. That is the mystery of man.

In the history of man the history of the world repeats itself. That which has become free overreaches itself. The "Fall into Sin" corresponds to the "Breaking of the Vessels." Both are signs of the necessary way. Within the cosmic exile of the shekhinah stands the earthly exile, into which it is driven through the denial of man, going with him out of Paradise into wandering. And once again the history of the world repeats itself in that of Israel: its falling away is followed time after time—not as punishment but as consequence—by the exile in which the shekhinah accompanies it, until the ultimate exile, where from now on, in the deepest abasement, "all depends on the turning." This joining of a cosmic conception with a historical one, accomplished by the Kabbalah on the basis of ancient Jewish traditions, certainly contributed to making the concept of the system of emanations more direct and emotional; but at the same time the meaning and task of man was narrowed.[66] All eschatology, indeed, is forever in danger, through the confusion of absolute with historical categories, of sacrificing what is above time to the temporal, above all in an epoch where the eschatological vision is replaced by abstract construction. The finitizing of the end means the finitizing of the means: if the inwardness of Messianism, of the turning and transformation of the world, is forgotten, then there easily arises a theurgical praxis which wants to bring about redemption through formal procedures. This praxis exceeds itself in those powerful exaggerations of asceticism, an asceticism that strains after the void, which characterized the pre-Hasidic phase of the Kabbalah and whose aftereffects entered into Hasidism, but mastered by its anti-ascetic tendency. But for the most part the great cosmogonic vision of the primordial man who embraced the spheres stands in contrast to a small scheme of redemption. . . .

Hasidism wants to "reveal God in this low, undermost world, in all things and at the same time in man that in him there be no limb and no movement in which God's strength might not be hidden, and none with which he could not accomplish unification."[67] To the question of what service should come first, the Baal-Shem answered: "For the spiritual man this is the first: love without mortification; for the others this is the first: to learn to see that in all corporality is a holy life and that man can lead everything back to this its root and can hallow it."[68]

One does not need to fast since whoever eats in dedication liberates the fallen sparks that are held captive in the food and that lend it fragrance and taste;[69] even Haman was affected by the holiness of the meal when he was Esther's guest,[70] and it is said of Abraham that he stood "above" the angels to whom he provided hospitality: because he knew the dedication of eating that was unknown to them.[71] One does not need to forego marital love since—as the Talmud already teaches—where a man and a woman are together in holy unity, the *shekhinah* rests over them.[72] After the death of his wife the Baal-Shem would not let himself be comforted and said: "I had hoped to journey to heaven in a thunderstorm like Elijah, but now it has been taken from me, for I am now only half of a body."[73] One shall not mortify himself; "he who does harm to his body, does harm to his soul."[74] The ascetic ecstasy is "from the other side," not of a divine, but of a demonic nature. One shall not murder the "evil urge," the passion in oneself, but serve God with it; it is the force that shall receive direction from man ("You have made the urge evil," God already says to man in the Midrash).[75] The "alien thoughts," the lusts that come to man are pure ideas that are corrupted in the "Breaking of the Vessels" and now desire to be raised again by man. "Even the noblest bitterness touches on melancholy, but even the most common joy grows out of holiness."[76] One cannot reach the kernel of the fruit except through the shell. A *tsaddik* cited the word of a Talmudic sage: "The roads to the firmament are as illumined for me as the roads of the city of Nehardea" and turned it around: The streets of the city should be as light to one as the paths of heaven; for "one cannot come to God except through nature."[77]

"Enoch was a cobbler. With every stitch of his awl that sewed the upper leather and the sole together, he joined God and His *shekhinah*."[78]

This wonderful contribution to the legend of the patriarch who enjoyed companionship with God, was taken away from earth and underwent transformation into the demiurgic powerful Metatron, the fire-bodied "Prince of the Countenance," was readily varied in the Hasidic teaching. For in his earthly image he expresses what was essential to it: that man influences eternity, and he does this not through special works, but through the intention behind all of his work. It is the teaching of the hallowing of the everyday. It is of no value to attain to a new type of action that is sacral or mystical according to its material; what matters is that one does the allotted tasks, the ordinary and obvious ones, in their truth and in their meaning, and that means in the truth and the meaning of all action.

Even one's works are shells; he who performs them with the right dedication, embraces in kernel the boundless.

On the basis of this view it is understandable why Hasidism had no incentive to break loose any stick from the structure of the traditional Law, for according to the Hasidic teaching there could not exist anything that was not to be fulfilled with intention or whose intention could not be discovered. But it is also understandable how just thereby the conserving force secretly remained superior to the moving and renewing one and finally conquered it within Hasidism itself.[79]

Apart from this, no teaching finds it so difficult to preserve its strength as one which places the meaning of life in the working reality of the here and now and does not tolerate man's fleeing before the taxing infinity of the moment into a uniform system of Is and Ought; the inertia soon proves itself the stronger and coerces the teaching. But in the short time of its purity the Hasidic teaching produced an immortal fullness of genuine life that did not withhold itself.

II. Body

A teaching that places the unspecifiable "How" of an act high above the codifiable "What" is not able to hand down what is peculiar to it through writing; it is communicated ever again through life, by the leader to the community, but preferably from teacher to disciple. Not as though the teaching were divided into a part accessible to all and an esoteric realm; it would contradict its meaning, the work for man, if it concealed a secret drawer with hieratic inscription. Rather the mystery that is handed down is just that which is also proclaimed by the enduring word, only, true to its nature as a "How" it is only pointed to by the word, but in its substantial truth it can only be presented through authentication.[80]

Hence a "hidden *tsaddik*" said of the rabbis who "say Torah," that is, interpret the word of the Scriptures, "What is it that the Torah says? Man shall heed that all his conduct should be a Torah and himself a Torah."[81] And another time it says: "The wise man shall aspire that he himself be a perfected teaching and all his deeds bodies of instruction; or, where this is not granted him, that he be a transmission and exposition of the teaching and that the teaching should spread through each of his movements." A sacramental expression of this basic insight appears when the *tsaddik* of Apt lifts up the girdle, fallen to the ground, of the seventeen-year-old Rabbi Israel, later the Rizhiner, girds it round him and says that in so doing he performs the holy action of Gelilah: the unfolding[82] of the Torah-scroll.[83]

The men in whom "being a Torah" fulfills itself are called *tsaddikim*, "the righteous," the legitimate ones. They hear the Hasidic teaching, not only as its apostles, but its working reality. They are the teaching. . . .

The *tsaddik* is not a priest or a man who renews in himself an already-accomplished work of salvation or transmits it to his generation, but the man who is more concentratedly devoted than other men to the task of salvation that is for all men and all ages, the man whose forces, purified and united, are directed toward the one duty. He is, according to the conception of him, the man in whom transcendental responsibility has grown from an event of consciousness into organic existence. He is the true human being, the rightful subject of the act in which God wants to be known, loved, wanted. In him the "lower," earthly man realizes his archetype, the cosmic primordial man who embraces the spheres. He is the turning of the great flood, in him the world returns to its origin. He is "no slave of time, but above it." He hears the lower blessing upward and the upward below; he draws down the Holy Spirit over men. The being of the *tsaddik* works in the higher realms. He must "boil the great pots" with his fire — so one *tsaddik* once spoke of another in a hearty and perceptive jesting word. In him the world renews itself, he is its "foundation" (so the word concerning the "righteous" in Proverbs 10:25 is interpreted).[84] "The *tsaddik* is the foundation because with his works he incessantly awakens the outpouring of the fullness over the world. And if it is perfected in him that all his action takes place only for the sake of uniting the *shekhinah* with God, then there comes over his soul a stream of grace from the holy fullness that pours forth from out of the light of God's unity, and he is become like a new creature and like a little child that was just born. This is that which is written: 'And unto Shem was also born he ...'[85] For whoever values God alone in all his work, he begets himself in the renewal of the light of his soul."[86]

A true man is more important than an angel because the latter is "one who stands," but he is "one who walks"; he advances, penetrates, ascends.[87] Constant renewal is the characteristic life principle of the *tsaddik*. In him creation's event of becoming concentrates itself into creative meaning, the genuine meaning, wholly free from arbitrariness and self-seeking, which is nothing other than just the turning of the creation to the Creator. The *tsaddik* incessantly beholds directly the bodily renewal of all and "is moved at each moment by the renewal of the creature"; his being answers with the renewal of the spirit. And as the bodily renewal in nature is always accompanied by a submersion, a dissolution, a sleep of the elements, so there is no true spiritual becoming without a ceasing to become. "For the *tsaddikim*," says Rabbi Sussya, "who in their service go ever again from holiness to holiness and from world to world, must, to begin with, cast their life from them in order to receive a new spirit, that a new illumination may sweep over them ever again; and this is the mystery of sleep."[88] The symbolic act that corresponds to this event of deep inwardness is the immersion bath. Primeval symbol of rebirth (which is only genuine when it includes death and resurrection), taken up into Kabbalistic praxis out of old traditions, especially those of the Essenes and the "morning-baptists," it is practiced by the *tsaddikim* with a high and joyous passion that has nothing of the ascetic in it. It is told of many how during the severest frost of winter they broke the ice of the stream in order to immerse themselves in flowing water; and the meaning of this fervor is revealed in the statement of a Hasid that one could replace the immersion bath by a spiritual act, that of the "stripping away of bodiliness."[89] What is here expressed in the action is preparation and readiness to enter into the "condition of the nothing," in which alone the divine renewal can take place.

In this ever-new exercise of the "receiving power" of the *tsaddik*, the ever-new dedication of his acting power takes place. Armed with rejuvenated strength, he goes ever again to his work—to his daily work: to the thousandfold work of "unification," the *yihud*.

Yihud means, first of all, both the unity of God and the confession of it that is to the Jew not only the central sun of his religion, but of his life system in general. Even so, however, this confession already represents, not a passive acknowledgment, but an act. It is in no way the statement of a subject about an object; it is not "subjective" at all, but a subjective-objective event, an event of meeting, it is the dynamic form of the divine unity itself. This active character of *yihud* grows in the Kabbalah, matures in Hasidism.[90] Man works on the unity of God, that is: through him takes place the unity of becoming, the divine unity of creation. By its nature, to be sure, *yihud* can always mean only unification of what has been separated. It is a unification, however, which overarches the enduring differences and finds its cosmic counterpart: the unity without multiplicity which dwells in the unification of multiplicity.

It is of fundamental importance to contrast the characteristic conception of *yihud* with *magic* action. The magic act means the influence of a subject on an object, of a man versed in magic on a "power"—a divine or demonic, personal or impersonal power, appearing in the world of things or concealed behind it. Thus it is a constitutive duality of elements of which the one, the human, is, by its fundamental nature, the weaker. But by virtue of this man's magic ability, it becomes the stronger, the compelling. It compels the other, the divine or the demonic, into human service, into human intention, into human work. The man from whom the act proceeds is also its goal and end; the magic act is an isolated, circular causal process which turns back in on itself. *Yihud* signifies not the influence of a subject upon an object, but the working out of the objective in a subjectivity and through it, of existing being in and through what is becoming; a true, serious, and complete working out, indeed, so that what is becoming is not a tool that is moved but a self-mover that is freed, free, acting out of freedom; world history is not God's game, but God's fate. *Yihud* means the ever-new joining of the spheres striving to be apart, the ever-new marriage of the "majesty" with the "Kingdom"[91]— through man; the divine element living in man moves from him to God's service, to God's intention, to God's work; God, in whose name and by whose command of creation the free *yihud* takes place, is his goal and end, he himself turning not in himself but to God, not isolated, but swallowed in the world process, no circle but the swinging back of the divine strength that was sent forth.

This distinction explains why magic must include a qualitative special action that is supposed to produce the special effect: gestures and speeches of a particular nature alien to other men and other moments. *Yihud*, in contrast, means no formula or procedure but nothing other than the ordinary life of man, only concentrated and directed to the goal of unification. Many Kabbalistic traditions of the secret of the letters (of the alphabet), the turning round and joining of the names of God, were taken up and practiced by Hasidism, it is true, in its system of *kavvanot*, or intentions; but this magic ingredient never touched the center of Hasidic teaching. In this center stand no secret formulae but the dedication of everything: no deed is condemned by its nature to remain "profane," each becomes service and influence on the divine if it is directed toward the unification, that means revealed in its inner dedication. The life of the *tsaddik* is borne by this all-pervading might of *yihud*.

It is told of the *tsaddik* of Berditshev how in his youth, while a guest of his friend the Nikolsburger Rabbi, he aroused general indignation because, wrapped in the prayer shawl and with the double phylacteries on his forehead, he went into the kitchen and inquired about the preparation of the food, and because later in the prayer house he entered into a conversation with the most worldly man about all kinds of apparently frivolous things. Desecration of the holy garments, desecration of the holy place and the holy hour were laid to his charge; but the Master spoke: "What I can only do three hours in the day, he can do the whole day: to preserve his spirit collected so that even with talk that passes as idle he can bring about exalted unifications."[92] Hallowing of the worldly is the central motive of the *tsaddik*. His meal is a sacrifice, his table an altar. All his movements lead to salvation. It is told of one that in his youth he went day after day into the villages and transacted business with the peasants; and always, when he had returned home and said the afternoon prayer he felt all his limbs permeated by a blessed fire. He asked his older brother, who was also his teacher, what this was, for he feared that it might come to him from evil and that his service was false. The brother answered: "When you go over the field in a holy state of mind, all the sparks of souls that are in stones, plants and animals cling to you and purify themselves in you to a holy fire."[93]

This consecration of the everyday is above all magic. When in the days of Rabbi Pinhas of Koretz the whole prayer book of Rabbi Isaac Luria, the master of the theurgic Kabbalah, the prayer book composed of letter *kavvanot*, was published, the disciples of the *tsaddik* requested his permission to pray out of it; but after some time they came to him again and complained that since they had prayed out of the book, they had suffered a great loss of the feeling of vital life in their prayers. Rabbi Pinhas answered them: "You have put all your strength and all your striving for the goal of your thoughts into the *kavvanot* of the holy names and the intertwined letters and have fallen away from what is essential: to make the heart whole and to unite it to God—therefore you have lost the life and feeling of holiness."[94] All formulas and arts are patchwork; the true unification rises beyond them. "He who in his prayer," says the Baal-Shem, "employs all the *kavvanot* that he knows, effects only just what he knows. But he who speaks the word with great binding to God, for him all *kavvanah* enters of itself into each word."[95] What matters is not what can be learned, what matters is giving oneself to the unknown.

A *tsaddik* said: "Note well, that the word Kabbalah stems from *kabbel*, to receive, and the word *kavvanah* from *kaven*, to direct outward. For the ultimate meaning of all the wisdom of the Kabbalah is to take upon oneself the yoke of God's kingdom, and the ultimate meaning of all the art of *kavvanah* is to direct one's heart to God. When one says: 'God is mine, and I am His'—how is it that his soul does not leave his body?" As soon as he had said this, he fell into a deep swoon from which he was awakened only with great difficulty.[96]

It becomes clear here that *yihud* means a risk, *the* risk. The unification of God shall take place in the world, man shall work on God's unification out of his own unification—the human, earthly salvation, earthly understanding, earthly life must be risked for the divine. This is manifested most powerfully in prayer. It is told of one *tsaddik* that every day before he went to pray, he ordered his household as if he were going to die. Another taught his disciples how they should pray: "He who speaks the word 'Lord' and at the same time has in mind speaking the word, 'of the world,' this is no speaking. Rather during the time when he says 'Lord,' he should in his mind offer himself wholly to the Lord so that his soul might perish in the Lord and he no longer be able to utter the word 'world' and it would be enough for him that he could say 'Lord.' This is the essence of prayer."[97] The Baal-Shem-tov compared the ecstatic movements of the Hasid, who prayed with his whole body, to the movements of a drowning man.[98]

It was also told of some *tsaddikim,* as before of certain Talmudic masters, how the ecstasy of prayer powerfully governed their bodies and carried them away to movements far beyond those of the ordinary human world. About many in such moments there was a remoteness as about a holy madman. But all this is only an event of the threshold and not the entrance, it is the struggling risk and not the fulfillment. Rabbi Yehuda Loeb tells how once during the Feast of Booths he witnessed in the tabernacle before the benediction the movements of the great *tsaddik* of Lublin who seemed driven as if by a secret dread.[99] All the people stared fixedly at him and themselves fell into a trembling fear, but Rabbi Yehuda Loeb remained seated and waited until the benediction; then he stood up, looked at the now motionless, exalted master and heard the divine blessing. Thus Moses had once paid no attention to the thunder claps and the smoking mountain that the trembling people surrounded and had drawn near the motionless cloud.[100]

The less premeditated the prayer is, the more immediately it breaks forth out of the natural depths of man, out of the cosmic spontaneity of him who bears the image of the sphere-embracing primordial man, so much the more real it is. It is told of a disciple of a disciple of the Lubliner *tsaddik*, Rabbi Mendel of Kotzk, probably the last great figure of Hasidism, that he prayed without effort and strain, as one converses with a comrade, and yet after the prayer was transformed as though he came from another world, and scarcely recognized his own family; "for the nature of his talk proceeds from the root of the soul unintentionally; as one whose soul is occupied with a very important subject at times unintentionally allows words to issue from his mouth between him and himself, and he himself does not notice his talk, and all this because it proceeds from the root of his soul, and the whole soul is wrapped in the speech which ascends in perfect unity." Here, in genuine prayer, there appears most clearly the essential meaning of *yihud*, that it is no "subjective" happening, but the dynamic form of the divine unity itself. "The people imagine," says Rabbi Pinhas of Koretz, "that they pray before God. But this is not so. For prayer itself is the essence of divinity."[101]

Of such kind is the lonely service of the *tsaddik*. But he is not a true *tsaddik* who remains satisfied with this. Man's bond with God authenticates and fulfills itself in the human world.

Rabbi Hayim of Zans was once bothered after the *minhah* prayer by an importunate man with a request. As the man would not desist, the *tsaddik* addressed him angrily. Questioned by a friend who was present as to the cause of his wrath, he answered, that he who prays the *minhah* stands over against the world of primordial separation;[102] how should he not become angry when he comes from it and now is fallen upon by the petty cares of petty people? To this the other said: "After the Bible has told of the first proclamation of God to Moses on Mount Sinai, it says, 'Moses descended from the mountain to the people.'[103] Rashi comments on this as follows: 'This teaches us that Moses turned from the mountain not toward his own affairs but to the people.' How is that to be understood? What sort of business did Moses have in the wilderness that he renounced in order to go to the people? But it is to be understood thus: When Moses descended from the mountain, he still cleaved to the upper worlds and accomplished in it his high work of penetrating the sphere of justice with the element of mercy. That was Moses's business. And still, when he descended to the people, he desisted from his high work, disengaged himself from the upper worlds and turned himself to the people; he listened to all its small cares, stored up all the heaviness of heart of all Israel and then bore them upward in prayer." When Rabbi Hayim heard this, his spirit became serious and profound, he called back the man whom he had addressed angrily, in order to receive his request and almost the whole night through he received the complaints and requests of the assembled Hasidim. . . .[104]

The love of man is not the fulfillment of an other-worldly commandment; it is the work on the completion, it helps the shape of the *shekhinah* to step forth out of the hiddenness, it works on the "wagon":[105] on the cosmic bearer of liberated glory. Therefore it is written: "Love your fellow as one like yourself: *I am the Lord.*"[106] The kingdom is founded on love.

Therefore Rabbi Raphael of Bershad, Rabbi Pinhas' favorite disciple, always used to warn against being "moderate" in one's dealings with one's fellowmen: Excess in love is necessary in order to make up for the lack in the world.[107]

There are three circles in which the love of the *tsaddik* is authenticated.

The first and broadest encompasses the many who come to the *tsaddik* from a distance, partly—especially on the high holidays—to spend a few days near him, "in the shadow of his holiness," partly to ask help from him for their bodily and spiritual needs. In this pilgrimage there is something of that faithful and trusting spirit with which the Palestinians[108] once went to the Temple in Jerusalem three times a year in order through sacrifice to free themselves from evil and join themselves with the divine: "the *tsaddik* takes the place of the altar."[109] To be sure, on the slips of paper they hand in, mostly quite external lacks and wants are set down.[110] But the healing of these lacks at the same time touches the inmost depths and stirs them to transforming reflection. For the understanding of the general phenomenon that underlies this particular working of the *tsaddik*, a working whose factual nature cannot be contested, the concepts "wonder" and "suggestion" con-tribute very little. The first dissipates the irrationality of the phenomenon, the second makes shallow its ability to be rationalized. To try to explain it as the working of the divine on the human offers a much too vague perspective, as the influence of the "stronger" will on the "weaker" a much too narrow one. One can best do justice to its deeper dimension when one bears in mind that the relation of a soul to its organic life depends on the degree of its wholeness and unity. The more dissociated the soul, the more it is at the mercy of its sicknesses and attacks, the more concentrated it is, the more it is able to master them. It is not as if it conquered the body; rather through its unity it ever again saves and protects the unity of the body. . . .

The second, middle circle includes those who live in the neighborhood of the *tsaddik*. This represents, in general, only a part of the Jewish community of that place, the rest consisting of the "opponents" (*mitnaggedim*) and the indifferent, whose official spiritual leader is the "rav." Inside the Jewish community, which is a "compulsory community,"[111] stands the Hasidic, a free, a "chosen community," with the *tsaddik*, the "rebbe" at its head (yet several *tsaddikim* have also exercised the functions of the rav in the Hasidic-dominated communities and have borne his title). This difference corresponds to that between the legitimation of the rav and that of the rebbe. The qualification of the rav is the demonstrated knowledge of the law in its Talmudic roots and in the whole fullness of its rabbinical ramifications. The qualifications of the rebbe are the spontaneously acknowledged leadership of souls, the depth of his "fear of God," that is, the dominant feeling of the *presence* of God, and the fervor of his "heart service," that is, the shaping of his whole life to active prayer. . . .

The third, narrowest circle is that of the disciples, of whom several are usually taken into the household community of the *tsaddik*. This is the proper sphere of the transmission, the communication of the teaching from generation to generation.

Each of the three circles has its unity in the strength of the *reciprocal action*. Of the "journeying ones" Rabbi Pinhas said, "Often when one comes to me to ask advice, I hear how he himself speaks the answer."[112] Of the community, especially those who pray, the Baal-Shem told the parable of the bird's nest that many people set themselves to fetch from the top of a very high tree, each standing on the shoulder of the other and he himself standing at the top; what if the time had been too long for only one of them?[113] But the might of reciprocity is represented at its greatest in the third circle.

Some disciples of Rabbi Nahum of Chernobyl sat once in a distant city at "the farewell meal for the Queen" that unites the pious once again at the departure of the Sabbath, and they talked among themselves of the reckoning that the soul has to render in the innermost self-recollection of the self. Then they were overcome in their fear and humility so that it seemed to them as if their whole life were thrown away and wasted, and they said to one another that there would be no more hope for them if there were not this one consolation and assurance that they might join themselves to the great *tsaddik* Rabbi Nahum. Then they arose with a common impulse and set out on the way to Chernobyl. At the same time Rabbi Nahum sat in his house and rendered the account of his soul. Then it also seemed to him in his fear and humility that his life was thrown away and wasted and all his assurance lay only in this one thing, that these God-impassioned men had joined themselves to him. He went to the door and looked across toward the dwelling-place of the disciples; and when he had stood there awhile, he saw them coming. "In that moment," added the grandson of the *tsaddik* when he related the happening, "the circle was closed."[114]

As the reciprocal value finds expression here, so in another story the reciprocal influence. Rabbi Susya once sat on his chair on one of the days of heart-searching between New Year's and the Day of Atonement, and the Hasidim stood around him from morning till evening. He had raised his eyes and heart to heaven and freed himself from all corporal bonds. Looking at him awakened in one of the disciples the impulse to the turning, and the tears rushed down his face; and as from a burning ember the neighboring coals begin to glow, so the flame of the turning came over one man after another. Then the *tsaddik* looked around him and regarded them all. He raised his eyes again and spoke to God: "Truly, Lord of the world, it is the right time to turn back to you; but you know, indeed, that I have not the strength for atonement—so accept my love and my shame as atonement!"[115] It is this kind of influence that I have pointed to as that hanging on of the mystery that is above words.

Ever again it says in the Hasidic writings that one should "learn from every limb of the *tsaddik*."[116] It is the spontaneity of his existence above all that exercises the purifying and renewing influence; the conscious expression, and above all, that of words, only accompanies it. Even in the word the essence of the unintentional is what is decisive.

"Make me an altar from the earth of the field," it says in the Scripture; "but if you make me an altar of stone, do not build it of hewn stone, for if you have swung your iron over it, then you have profaned it."[117] The altar made out of earth, so the Rishiner expounded, that is what pleases God above all else, it is the altar made out of silence; but if you make an altar out of words, then do not shape them.[118]

The *tsaddik* shunned the "beautiful," the premeditated. A learned man who was a Sabbath guest at Rabbi Baruch's table said to him: "Let us now hear words of teaching; you speak so beautifully!" "Before I speak beautifully," answered the grandson of the Baal-Shem, "may I become dumb!" and spoke no further.[119]

At the holiest of the Sabbath meals, the "third meal," the *tsaddik* usually speaks the teaching only sparingly and disconnectedly, ever again interrupted by silent meditation; a soft song, vibrating with mystery, sounds forth, an enraptured anthem follows. As often as the silence enters the darkening room, it brings a rustling of eternity with it. . . .

Interpreting Hasidism (1963)

Our final selection appeared as an article in *Commentary* magazine in 1963, just two years before Buber died. It represents his response to Scholem's accusations that he misrepresented the nature of Hasidism. The Buber-Scholem debate is one of the most interesting controversies in twentieth-century Jewish thought, and this particular article reveals much about the methods and motivations behind Buber's project.

I.

There are two different ways in which a great tradition of religious faith can be rescued from the rubble of time and brought back into the light. The first is by means of historical scholarship that seeks to be as comprehensive and exact as possible. The scholar takes this former tradition as an object of knowledge; he edits and interprets the texts of its teachings, investigates its origins and background, its phases of development, and the ramifications of its schools. The primary and controlling purpose of this type of investigation is to advance the state of historical knowledge about the body of religious faith in question—though it may also contribute to the instruction of future generations in the faith. Such a task of historical reconstruction and clarification requires the objectivity and detachment that make the scholar what he is. He must, to be sure, decide which materials are important and need to be treated directly and fully, and which are secondary and can be left in the background. In arriving at these decisions, however, he must follow strictly the principles of historical research and present the primary data as comprehensively and exactly as possible.

The other, and essentially different, way of restoring a great buried heritage of faith to the light is to recapture a sense of the power that once gave it the capacity to take hold of and vitalize the life of diverse classes of people. Such an approach derives from the desire to convey to our own time the force of a former life of faith and to help our age renew its ruptured bond with the Absolute. The scholar bent upon unearthing a forgotten or misunderstood body of teaching cannot accomplish this renewal, even if he succeeds in establishing a new interpretation. To effect such a renewal one must convey the reality of the way of life that was once informed by these teachings, the life of faith that was lived by exemplary individuals and by the communities they founded and led.

An adequate knowledge of the tradition in all its spiritual and historical connections is necessary to insure that a genuine renewal may take place. However, the work of transmitting the old faith to one's contemporaries does not require a complete presentation of all these connections, but rather a selection of those manifestations in which its vital and vitalizing element was embodied. And this, in turn, requires an act of judgment which rests not upon the customary objectivity of the scholar, but upon the reliability of the man in the face of his special task. As long as he performs it with fidelity, he should not be judged by external criteria; for what may appear to be mere "subjectivity" to the detached scholar can sooner or later prove to be necessary to the process of renewal.

Secondly, the man who faithfully and adequately tries to communicate the vitality and power of this faith should not be expected to turn away from the traditional reports concerning its former life in order to give primary emphasis to the doctrine to which the founder and his disciples appealed for their authority. Even in the founding of the great world religions (which are not in question here), the essential is not a doctrine comprehensible in itself but an event which is at once life and word. But it is also right to refuse the demand to give primacy to doctrines even where religious life reaches back to a much earlier doctrine in order to establish its legitimacy. An old teaching as such never engenders a new life of faith in a later age. Rather this new way comes into being within the context of personal and community existence and signifies a far-reaching transformation despite the persistence of traditional forms. At the time of its birth, as well as in the stages of development that follow, the new faith assimilates itself to an old doctrine, appeals to it, indeed finds in the doctrine its own origin. Certainly, in the life of the founder, elements of this doctrine already appear to have fused with his own experience of faith, but with modifications characteristic of the way of life that his own mode of existence has initiated. In the following generations of disciples and disciples of disciples, such modifications may be discarded to the point where the original doctrine rigidly prevails, but in the next generation vital experiences of faith may again renew its power.

Such is the case, as the evidence shows, with Hasidism and its relation to the Kabbalah (especially to the later, "Lurianic" Kabbalah). The man who remains true to the special task of renewing the vitality of that Hasidism is obliged to proceed selectively: he must know precisely what he is to include in his work and what he must hand over uncontested to the scholar who follows the principles of historical completeness. . . .

IV.

My presentation of Hasidism is not a historical one, for I do not discuss the Hasidic teaching in its entirety and do not take into account the differences that have prevailed among the various trends within the Hasidic movement.

Since about 1910—the point in my study of Hasidism when I began to deal with basic sources (my earlier work had not been sufficiently grounded in them)—I became conscious that my task would necessarily be a selective one. Though I did not aim to be comprehensive, either historically or hermeneutically, I was ever more firmly convinced that my principle of selection was not derived from a subjective preference, but rather from the same assumptions that informed my work on Judaism in general. In treating the life and teaching of Judaism, I have attempted to keep to what I believe to be its own proper truth and its decisive contribution in the past and future history of the human spirit. It goes without saying that my attitude includes an evaluation of what is the central truth of Judaism and Hasidism. But such evaluation—on this point, no doubt has touched me during the whole time—has its origin in the immovable central existence of values that in the history of the human spirit and in the uniqueness of every great religion has again and again given rise to those basic attitudes concerning the authentic way of man. Since having reached the maturity of this insight, I have not made use of a filter; I *became* a filter.

Still, it must be possible to characterize this filtering activity objectively, i.e., to explain why that which was admitted was rightly admitted, and why that which was left to one side was rightly left to one side.

Gershom Scholem correctly says that Hasidism produced no mystical doctrine that went essentially beyond the Kabbalistic tradition in which "personality takes the place of doctrine."[120] Looked at in terms of its theories, Hasidism is, in fact, purely derivative. But looked at in terms of the personal lives of its leaders—which we are able to reconstruct through the unexampled fullness of the notes of their disciples, once having separated out the purely legendary—Hasidism shows itself to be the bursting forth of a powerful originality of the life of faith, to which very few episodes in the history of religion can be compared. Scholem has described Hasidism as a "revival movement," but where in the world has there ever been a "revival" with such power to inspire individual conduct and communal enthusiasm for seven generations?

As we have seen, the Hasidic literature that relates the lives of the masters can be compared typologically to that of Zen Buddhism, the Sufis, and at fewer points, the Franciscans; but none of these movements was empowered by so enduring, vital, and intimate a connection to everyday human life. One must immediately add that—in contrast to these other movements—the spiritual leaders of Hasidism were not monks: they were the leaders of communities composed of families. In Zen, Sufism, and Hasidism alike, we find a prevailing devotion to the divine that seeks to hallow each day of life; however, in Zen and Sufism the consecration of one's life is borne by an ascetic limitation of conduct, even when it involves going among the people to bring assistance and instruction. Hasidism firmly extends this hallowing to the natural and the social life. Here alone does the whole man, as God has created him, enter into the hallowing of the everyday.

Scholem is right in saying that *devekut*, the "cleaving" of the soul to God, became the central tendency of the Hasidic teaching. But it must be added that this traditional doctrine of Judaism took two different forms in Hasidism. The *tsaddikim* who sought—if, as has been said, unsuccessfully—to elaborate the Kabbalistic teaching, held to the view, already familiar to us from Gnosis, that one must lift oneself out of the "corporeal" reality of human life into the "nothingness" of pure spirit in order to achieve contact with God, whom the Bible had already named "the Lord of spirit in all flesh." In contrast to this form of *devekut*—though there was no explicit contest between them—one also finds in Hasidism the belief that the "constant being with God," as Scholem calls it in connection with Psalm 73, is to be reached by dedicating to God the totality of the life that a man lives. In the Talmud (b. Ket. III) the question of how one could serve God with the evil urge as well as the good had been answered: by doing what one does with the right *kavvanah*, with dedication to God, and thus hallowing it.

The way of spiritualization comes into Hasidism with its great thinker, the Maggid of Mezritch; the second way, the hallowing of all life, was introduced by his teacher, the Baal-Shem-tov. The Baal-Shem often based this teaching on two Biblical sayings: "In all thy ways know Him" (Proverbs 3:6), and "Do all that your hand finds to do with all your strength" (Ecclesiastes 9:10). He interprets the first saying: "It is necessary that even every bodily thing that you do be in the service of a higher need . . . all for the sake of heaven." And the second: "That he acts with all his limbs according to the knowledge, and thereby the knowledge is spread to all his limbs." Of course, only "the completed man," says the Baal-Shem, can wholly fulfill this command. "The completed man may accomplish high unifications [i.e., unite God with His *Shekhinah*, dwelling in the exile of the world] even with his bodily actions, such as eating, drinking, sexual intercourse, and transactions with his fellows over bodily things . . . as it is written: And Adam knew his wife Eve."

Among the *tsaddikim* closely associated with the Baal-Shem, it was above all Rabbi Yehiel Mikhal of Zlotchov who developed this teaching, even though after the Master's death he attached himself to the great Maggid. The word of the Bible, "Be fruitful and multiply," he expounded thus: "Be fruitful, but not like the animals, be more than they, grow upright *and cleave to God as the spring clings to the root,* and dedicate your copulation to him."

From what I have cited, it is evident that the inner dialectic between transcending earthly life and hallowing it does not belong to a later development of Hasidism, but is already apparent in its earliest stages. It is clear, furthermore, that the teaching of hallowing the everyday provides the original thesis, and that the doctrine of spiritualization comes later with the increasing influence of the Kabbalistic tradition. To be sure, the doctrine of spiritualization already accorded to the *tsaddik* a direct influence through the hallowed human life on the divine sphere. But again and again, in sayings, parables, and tales, the Baal-Shem and many of his disciples praise the simple, ignorant man whose life-forces are combined in an original unity and who serves God with this unity. Even in this lower unspiritual form, the undivided existence of man affects the higher spheres.

A real criticism of the Kabbalistic doctrine of spiritualization was made only later, however, and, as it were, incidentally. It did not take the form of a new systematic doctrine that directly challenged the doctrine of spiritualization, but rather was embodied in a new mode of life that had to come to terms over and over again with the received mode of life. This criticism is found in the teachings of a *tsaddik* of the fifth generation, who was concerned with restoring the original meaning of prayer: as man speaking directly to God.

To understand this development, it is necessary to go back a bit. In place of the immediacy found in Biblical prayer between the personal being of the praying man and the being of God, which is not purely personal but which stands in a personal relation, to the praying man, the Kabbalah substituted forms of meditation whose subject is the inner structure of the divinity, the configurations of the *"Sefirot,"* and the dynamic prevailing among them. According to the text of the prayer, God is still the partner in a dialogue between heaven and earth. But the theosophy which has been added to the prayer alters God's role to that of the object of an ecstatic contemplation and action. In line with this change, the text of the traditional liturgy comes to be covered by a net of *kavvanot,* or "intentions," that lead the praying man into an absorption with the words and letters and with the practice of prescribed mutations, especially approximate vocalizations of the Tetragrammaton.

The Hasidic movement took over uncritically the Kabbalistic prayer book that was formed in this manner; the Baal-Shem himself sanctioned it. This state of affairs inevitably divided the community into the simple folk, who used their prayers to still the need of their hearts, and the "higher men," who took upon themselves the meditational or theurgical task of prayer. This division soon threatened the fundamental community between the *tsaddik* and his Hasidim.

Among the great men of prayer in the third generation was R. Shmelke of Nikolsburg, who sought to bridge this gap by raising the level of the community's prayers, on the one hand, to a concern with the *Shekhinah's* return and to other more intense forms of devotion; on the other hand, in the hour of common prayer he himself prayed with the community, or rather came forth from it to lead the prayers. Another *tsaddik,* R. Levi Yitzhak of Berdichev, entered wholly into the free dialogue practiced by the common people. However, R. Shlomo of Karlin regarded his own praying—manifestly no different from the conventional praying of the *tsaddik*—as a theurgical venture which only he could undertake ("perhaps this time too I shall still not die").

It is perhaps not surprising that a disciple of a disciple of R. Shlomo, R. Moshe of Kobryn, should have become the one to warn against this split. Asked about the secret *kavvanot* of prayer by an author of Kabbalistic writings, R. Moshe answered: "You must keep in mind that the word *Kabbalah* is derived from *kabbel*: to accept; and the word *kavvanah* from *kavven*: to direct. For the final meaning of all the wisdom of the *Kabbalah* is to take on oneself the yoke of God's will, and the final meaning of all the art of *kavvanot* is to direct one's heart to God." The life indicated by the primal faith of Israel, the life of devotional cleaving to the Lord of life—to accept whatever happens to me from the hands of God and to do whatever I do as directed to God—is thus opposed to the hypertrophy of faith produced by mystical-magical doctrine. The original insight of the Baal-Shem into the fundamental need for an immediate and reciprocal relation to God that is attainable by man and that is able to encompass his whole life finds its expression in the words of a disciple of the fifth generation who had grasped the simple basic meaning of prayer that had been obscured by later Kabbalistic doctrine.

What is at issue here is not a spiritual matter that affects life to some extent but remains mostly above it: R. Shlomo's teaching is directed to the question of living itself. When one of his disciples was asked what had been most important to his teacher, he replied: "Whatever he happened to be doing at the moment." By accepting and dedicating whatever is happening here and now, intercourse with God is achieved in the experiences of daily life. Of the two modes of behavior—passively accepting and actively dedicating—the active is the more important. "You shall," it is said, '"become an altar for God." On this altar *everything* shall be offered, according to the elaboration made by the Baal-Shem of the

Kabbalistic teaching of the holy sparks present in all things and awaiting redemption.

The rift between God and the world is not closed but bridged over, though with the paradoxical instruction that man constantly set foot on the invisible bridge and thus make it real. It is for this purpose that man is created and so, too, the things of this world that belong to each individual, which, as the Baal-Shem says, "with all their might entreat him to draw near in order that the sparks of holiness that are in them may be raised": in other words, that they may be brought to God through him. Therefore man, according to other sayings of the Baal-Shem, shall "have mercy on his tools and all his possessions," and each action shall be directed "to heaven." We know from the first-person sayings of the Baal-Shem that he excluded nothing corporeal from this intention. Thus in the Polonoyer tradition, which is undoubtedly true to the teaching of the Master, the relation between body and soul is compared to the relation of a husband to a wife: each is only half a being and needs the other half to attain the fulfillment of life.

Is this not "realism" enough? Nor, to use Scholem's term, can one find any "nullification" of the concrete whatsoever in *this* line of Hasidism—which begins with the beginning of Hasidism itself. The beings and things that we hallow continue to exist undiminished; the "holy sparks" that are "raised" are not thereby withdrawn from the forms of man's earthly life. According to the teaching of the Baal-Shem, there is, to be sure, an art of "liberating" the "holy sparks" which otherwise wander "from stone to plant, from plant to animal, from animal to speaking being." But when he says, "All that man has, his servant, his animals, his tools, all conceal sparks that belong to the roots of his soul and wish to be raised by him," and therefore "entreat him with all their might to draw near them," it is certainly clear that no form of annihilation is involved but rather a dedication, a hallowing that transforms without loss of concreteness. Consequently, the Baal-Shem can also include sin in this teaching—although with a different meaning from the one that Sabbatian theology gives to the inclusion of sin in the holy. "And what sort of sparks," he asks, "are those that dwell in sin?" To which he answers: "It is the turning. In the hour when on account of sin you carry out the turning, you raise the sparks that were in it into the upper world." Again, this is not a nullification of the corporeal but a bridging of the two realms.

The essential point has been expressed even more clearly perhaps by a great *tsaddik*, R. Pinchas of Koretz, who is properly regarded as a comrade rather than a disciple of the Baal-Shem. There are no words or actions, he teaches, that are idle in themselves; one only makes them into idle words and actions when one talks and acts idly.

The critical problem of Hasidism, according to Rivka Schatz-Uffenheimer, a disciple of Gershom Scholem, is "that life split apart for it into external action on the one side and inner intention on the other." But this is not true. Hasidism itself was not faced with this problem, only its spiritualistic tendency, which, to be sure, won the upper hand in the school of the Maggid of Mezritch. It is only here, in the doctrine of the Mezritch tradition, that one finds such terms as "sensory appearance." But wherever the new mode of life became stronger than the doctrine that grew out of the Kabbalistic tradition, the world of concrete daily experience was again emphasized for the sake of a hallowing that became a matter of "decision" rather than a "problem." In sum, the inner dialectic of the Hasidic movement is that between an unoriginal Kabbalism that remained the property of "spiritual" men and a religious life with the world which was unprecedented in its capacity to seize hold of one generation after another.

That is the basis of my selection. I have chosen what I have chosen; rather, I have let Hasidism go through my heart as through a filter because here is a way, one only to be sensed, but a way. I have stated this principle time after time with what appeared to be sufficient clarity.[121] It seemed clear enough to me that I was concerned from first to last with restoring immediacy to the relation between man and God, with helping to end "the eclipse of God."

Given this objective, my selection has necessarily emphasized the unjustly despised "anecdotes"—stories of lived experience—and "aphorisms"—sayings in which lived experience documents itself. The "anecdotes" tell of the life of the *tsaddikim*; the "aphorisms," which originally were spoken by the *tsaddikim*, express this life in particularly pregnant ways.

The central significance of the *tsaddikim* is that they constitute the common and sustaining center of the movement from the beginning—provided, of course, one regards Hasidism not only as theory but as practice that is interpreted by the teaching. Among the great *tsaddikim*, two kinds can be clearly distinguished: the *tsaddik* who is essentially a teacher and whose decisive effect is on his disciples, and the *tsaddik* who is essentially a helper and whose decisive effect is on the people. This is no minor distinction, for it expresses, among other things, precisely the inner dialectic we have been bringing to light. The first kind of *tsaddik* is to be identified mainly with the spiritualizing elements; the second kind with *realizing*. In the person of the Baal-Shem both roles are still united; after him they diverge. In the intellectual history of the movement the decisive figures are the great teachers and heads of schools, like the Maggid of Mezritch, R. Elimelekh of Lizhensk, and the "Seer" of Lublin.

The popular life of the movement, however, is concentrated in such figures as the Berdichever, R. Zusya, and R. Moshe Leib of Sasov. The latter are purely unique products of Hasidism.

The *tsaddikim* of the second kind, along with Baal-Shem, seem to me unique in their feeling of the essential relatedness of the elevated man, who has found the unity of the material and spiritual, to the simple man who, from his much lower spiritual position, can still truly devote himself to God. What the Baal-Shem said to his Hasidim about the faithful stocking-weaver—"Today I have seen the foundation stone that bears the holiness until the Redeemer comes"—is preserved, not in the teaching but in the legends, as a statement of primary importance. And a whole garland of similar tales of the Baal-Shem have been handed down, with the legendary ones supplementing the authentic.

V.

The great hasidic contribution to the belief in the redemption of the world is its assertion that each man can work for this redemption but none can effect it. This is an insight common to all the tendencies within Hasidism. Because of the inner dialectic of the movement, however, two different teachings are again evident. The one asserts that man can work for the redemption of the world by exerting a magical influence on the divine configurations; the other asserts that man can do so only by "turning" with his whole being to God and doing everything that he does henceforth for God. He thereby enhances, in a measure corresponding to the strength of his "turning," the capacity of the world to be redeemed: he "brings it nearer" to the heavenly influence.

That is the basic theme of my book *For the Sake of Heaven*, the one full-scale narrative that I have written. I wrote it because I wanted to make the inner dialectic that was visible and coherent to me visible and coherent to the man of today. Let me try here to clarify it once again.

According to the "metaphysics" of the Seer of Lublin, the demonic force already active in the Napoleonic wars could be intensified to the point where it would shake the gate of heaven and God would come forth to redeem the world. In opposition, not to this Kabbalistic doctrine itself, but rather to its magical undertakings, the "holy Yehudi" taught a simple human "existence." He would have nothing to do with the world-historical Gog—whose wars bring the human world to the chaos from which redemption shall proceed—but confronted instead the dark Gog in our own breast. He called for the transformation of this latter Gog through the "turning"—that is, through giving direction to the indispensable passion so that it might become a force of light working directly for redemption. One should not depreciate this message by identifying it with this or that modern train of thought. To call it "anthropocentric" does not make sense to me; it is rather bipolar. The "holy Yehudi" reaches back both to the prophets of Israel—who exhort us to "turn" before God "turns" from the "naming of his wrath"—and to the idea expounded in the Talmudic age that all eschatological combinations having taken place, redemption now depends upon the human "turning" alone. In the teaching of the Baal-Shem this traditional concept finds its mystical expression in the saying: "The beginning is up to you. For if the power of procreation first stirs in the woman, a male child is born."

That the "holy Yehudi" was deeply committed to this way to God is clearly shown by his saying, reliably transmitted by R. Shlomo of Radomsk: "Turn, turn, turn quickly in the turning, for the time is short and there is no longer any leisure for further wanderings of the soul, for redemption is near." According to the tales I heard in my youth, this was in fact the kernel of the sermon that he repeatedly gave in varying contexts on his "great journey" through the Galician villages. The meaning of the call is clearly this: that man must accomplish the decisive movement *now*, without depending on the idea that his soul still has time to ascend to higher forms; for now the sphere of redemption has drawn close to our world and henceforth the important thing is to draw it at once to us.

The interpreter of Hasidism who in deep and dispassionate seriousness attempts to relate this controversy between "metaphysics" and "existence" to the problematic nature of our own world hour will recognize that all forms of magical gnosis in the end only mean an attempt to flee before the command of our human reality into the darkness above the abyss.

Suggestions for Further Reading

Buber, Martin. Hasidism. New York: Philosophical Library, 1948.

———. *Hasidism and Modern Man*. Translated by Maurice Friedman. Princeton: Princeton University Press, 2015.

———. *The Legend of the Baal-Shem*. Translated by Maurice Friedman. Princeton: Princeton University Press, 1995.

———. *The Origin and Meaning of Hasidism*. New York: Horizon, 1960.

———. *Tales of the Hasidim*. 2 vols. New York: Schocken, 1991.

Horwitz, Rivka. *Buber's Way to I and Thou: An Historical Analysis and the First Publication of Martin Buber's Lectures "Religion als Gegenwart."* Heidelberg: Schneider, 1978.

Mendes-Flohr, Paul. *From Mysticism to Dialogue: Martin Buber's Transformation of German Social Thought*. Detroit: Wayne State University Press, 1989.

Urban, Martina. *Aesthetics of Renewal: Martin Buber's Early Representation of Hasidism as Kulturkritik*. Chicago: University of Chicago Press, 2008.

3

Abraham Joshua Heschel

Introduction

Abraham Joshua Heschel is generally seen as an American Jewish religious thinker.[1] When he is taught, it is primarily in the context of American Judaism. His mature works were published in the United States, and his greatest impact was on Americans, Christians as well as Jews.[2]

But Heschel, both the man and the thinker, was formed in Europe. When he arrived in America in 1940 at age thirty-three, the three major influences on his life were already in place: the Hasidic world of his childhood, the (mostly Jewish) intellectual community of Berlin along with the disciplines studied at its university, and the experience of living for five years in, and finally being booted out of, Nazi Germany.

Hasidic Warsaw was the first part of that European experience. Heschel was the scion of several great Hasidic families of Eastern Europe. For at least five or six generations, virtually all his male ancestors had been Hasidic *rebbes*.[3] He was raised to continue in the family tradition, and it was at first assumed that young Heschel, who was a Talmudic as well as a spiritual prodigy, would be a great figure within the Hasidic would. On his mother's side, his uncle was the Novominsker Rebbe, whose court had moved to Warsaw where Heschel was raised. On his father's side were the Kopitshinitser Hasidim who were centered in Vienna, as well as Chortkev and Husiatyn, branches of the Ruzhin family, descendants of the Maggid of Mezritch.

As an adolescent, however, Heschel left this world behind. Something of a rebel, he sought the kind of broader education, including secular subjects, that his extended family would have preferred he do without. The Hasidic world of early-twentieth-century Poland was just too narrow for him; he saw the small-mindedness that necessarily resulted from the tremendous effort expended to shut out the modern world. He also experienced the competition and frequent bickering that went on among the various dynasties, all of them led by men so stationed because of their lineage; only a rare few had retained the charismatic qualities that had turned the progenitors of their lines into *rebbes*.

Hasidism thus existed for Heschel as something of his past, a world to which he no longer fully belonged. Yet it seems he still felt that Hasidism *belonged to him*. In this regard Heschel should be seen as part of a rather remarkable group of *rebbeshe eyneklekh*, descendants of Hasidic *rebbes* who, though no longer part of the community, took pride in their Hasidic legacy and continued to view Judaism through Hasidic eyes.[4]

Certainly Heschel retained much affection for, and a certain loyalty to, Hasidism. At the same time as he was writing his widely read theological classics (*Man Is Not Alone*, 1951; *Man's Quest for God*, 1954; *God in Search of Man*, 1956), he was also publishing, in Hebrew, meticulously researched historical articles on the early generations of Hasidism. Some of this renewed interest in his own closest roots was sharpened, of course, by the terrible sense of loss Heschel felt after the Holocaust.[5]

In 1944, when the dimensions of European Jewry's loss had become clear, leaders of YIVO, the Yiddish Scientific Institute of New York (itself a recent transplant from Vilna), invited Heschel to deliver a memorial lecture. His stirring eulogy for Eastern European Jewry and what he called the "golden period . . . in the history of the Jewish soul" is both a heartbroken lament and a call to action:

A world has vanished. All that remains is a sanctuary hidden in the realm of spirit. We of this generation are still holding the key. Unless we remember, unless we unlock it, the holiness of ages will remain a secret of God. We of this generation are still holding the key—the key to the sanctuary which is also the shelter of our own deserted souls. If we mislay the key, we shall elude ourselves. . . .

We carry the gold of God in our souls to forge the gate of the kingdom. The time for the kingdom may be far off, but the task is plain: to retain our share in God in spite of peril and contempt. There is a war to wage against the vulgar, against the glorification of the absurd, a war that is incessant, universal. Loyal to the presence of the ultimate in the common, we may be able to make it clear that man is more than man, that in doing the finite he may perceive the infinite.[6]

The precious world of Eastern European Jewry was a realm of inwardness and devotion in which words and time were suffused with God's presence. The Nazi death machine turned it all into ashes and cast the future of such Judaism to the wind. Heschel's response to this devastation, however, was neither a pious retreat from all things modern nor a bitter flight from religion altogether. He called his listeners—and readers—to seek moral uplift and healing through the life of the spirit. This magnificent piece of oratory was printed in Yiddish in 1946 as *Der Mizrakh—Eyropeisher Yid (The East European Jew)*, then expanded, translated, and published as *The Earth Is the Lord's* in 1949.

Along with Roman Vishniac's evocative photographs of European Jewish life taken in the years following Hitler's rise to power and published in *Polish Jews: A Historical Record* (1947), Heschel's work served as the most significant *Kaddish* for the Holocaust available to most American Jews for nearly twenty years.[7] In it Heschel overcame any distance, geographical or critical, that the Berlin years had placed between him and the world of his childhood. During these early postwar years Heschel had come to see himself as one of the last who really understood that lost universe; he was the lone survivor in the tale of Job, the one who says, "I alone have escaped to tell thee."

Moreover, during or immediately after the war, Heschel also readopted the middle name Joshua. He had been named for his illustrious forebear Avraham Yehoshua Heschel of Apt (ca. 1748–1825), but the young Abraham Heschel had rarely used this second name during his time in Berlin. Now his name was instantly recognizable to Polish Jews as that of a Hasidic *rebbe*. Heschel's choice to reclaim the entirety of his name revealed a partial willingness to reassume the mantle of family heritage after the terrible loss of so many Jews, including most of his relatives, and the wholesale destruction of the spiritual riches of the Hasidic world.

In the postwar years Heschel had a mixed attitude toward reemergent Hasidism as it existed in New York. He remained personally close to his surviving relatives (some of whom had preceded him to America), leaders in that community, but maintained a silent truce with them on questions of religious values and priorities.

Looking in retrospect at Heschel's mature thought, we may say that the key themes of his complex writings are the loftiest mysteries of existence as perceived, celebrated, and challenged by the questioning religious mind. He sought to create an inspired phenomenology of religious living around such themes as the mutual relationship of God and person, our human need for God, and the question of God's need for humanity.[8]

Possessed of a poetic spirit, in the 1920s and 1930s the young Heschel published a series of Yiddish poems in Eastern European periodicals. In these early works, eventually collected and printed together as *Der Shem ha-Meforash: Mentsh* (The Ineffable Name of God),[9] the themes of sacred and human love and longings are deeply intertwined.

Propounding a subtle vision of inward-looking religious universalism, he was ever fascinated by the claim that each person is God's image: "Bless me, my spirit / With tenderness instead of might!" he wrote. "Tenderness, you ineffable name of God / Be my image of God."[10] This discovery of the interior spirit shared by all humanity, rooted in Hasidic sources but expanded beyond the Jewish people, brought Heschel to reflect profoundly on the nature of humanity and the roles of community and leadership.

What in particular did Heschel cull from the Hasidic traditions he knew so well into these central themes of his future thought?[11] What does it mean to claim Heschel as a Neo-Hasidic figure—a term he never applied to himself?[12] After all, although he wrote scholarly articles on the early history of Hasidism, Heschel did not assume the role of the movement's defender. Neither was he called upon—nor would he have wanted to—champion Hasidism at the expense of any other Jewish movement. Yet still there is a distinctly Hasidic cast to Heschel's Judaism. How is it present in his thought, and in what ways, if any, was he at pains to transform or universalize it?

Heschel's Hasidic roots may be seen as manifesting in his thought in five significant areas. First, his work is Hasidic in that it maintains a sense of wonder about God who fills the universe. The biblical exclamation "The whole earth is filled with His glory!" and the Zohar's "There is no place devoid of Him!" became twin watchwords of Hasidic consciousness. This is the core religious experience of the Ba'al Shem Tov, around which all of Hasidism crystallized: there exists neither time nor place where God cannot be found by one who has the inner training and courage to open the eyes to see. From the *Upright Practices* of Rabbi Menahem Nahum of Chernobyl:

> Believe with a whole and strong faith that "the whole earth is filled with His glory!" and that "there is no place devoid of Him." His blessed glory inhabits all that is. This glory serves as a garment, as the sages taught: "Rabbi Yohanan called his garment 'glory.'" His divine self wears all things as one wears a cloak, as Scripture says: "You give life to them all."[13]

To see this, and to show it to others, is the task of the *tsaddik*. Listen to young Heschel's bold self-description in the poem "Intimate Hymn":

> I have come to sow the seed of sight in the world,
> To unmask the God who disguises Himself as world.

Like many of the lines in Heschel's poems, these have to be read quite carefully. The "I have come" formula is attributed to the Ba'al Shem Tov, although the formulation appears in the speeches of other great religious teachers as well. It is a line of great power and daring, and young Heschel does not appropriate it lightly. As the line reveals, he thinks of himself as having a mission: to bring religious awareness to others. The notion of "unmasking" the God "who disguises Himself as world" is a precisely Hasidic way of seeing the God-world relationship, expressed much more boldly here than in Heschel's later writings.

Simultaneously, the statement of young Heschel's mission is also connected to Psalm 97:11, "Light is sown for the righteous," one of the biblical verses most often quoted and interpreted in Hasidic writings. The divine light (*or ha-ganuz*) is hidden, sown into the ground, buried behind the mask of nature, waiting for the *tsaddik* to reveal it. I am here, Heschel says, "to sow sight,"[14] to help others discover that hidden light. A true *rebbe* is one who can discover that light and make it visible to others. The Ba'al Shem Tov could well have spoken this line about himself. All the world is a cloak or mask, which hides behind it the great light of God.

The sense of wonder, which Heschel well understands to be basic to all religious consciousness, is a key Hasidic response to the sense of divine presence everywhere and in each moment. Here is Rabbi Mordecai Joseph of Izbica (d. 1853–54), originally a disciple of the Kotsker Rebbe:

> [The prayerbook] says: "He does wonders . . . renewing each day the work of Creation." But what renewal is there if Creation is

renewed each day? Doesn't the renewal itself become habitual? What then is left of it? The fact is, however, that God makes the habitual into something new, bringing wonder into the hearts of those who hope in Him, so that of each thing they say: "Who created these?"

Thus it was with Abraham our Father, of blessed memory. The world had gone on for some time before he came along, with no one asking or wondering about its conduct. *In Abraham's heart there was very great wonder.* "Might you say the palace has no owner?" Who is the palace's owner? When God saw that his questions were not those of the natural scientist, but that he *truly* wanted to know "Who created these?" *in order to serve Him*, and had rejected all worldly pleasures for this sake, the blessed Lord had to reveal Himself and show him that He was indeed Master of the palace.[15]

Heschel the mature thinker, viewing the American cultural land-scape, was profoundly disturbed by the secularization of consciousness among modern Jews (and moderns in general). He wanted to recreate for moderns a Jewish life centered on God. For him the only religious question that mattered was the ultimate one: How do we become aware of God's presence in our lives, of God's passionate and compassionate concern for us, and how do we respond and serve?

The cultivation of *da'at*—a true religious mindfulness that goes deeper than intellectual understanding, and the central subject of many early Hasidic works—appears to be the goal of Heschel's writings as well. He wanted Jews to experience God more fully and to be less reticent in talking both *to* God and *about* God. To lead them to this, he had to write about theology in evocative and passionate ways, demonstrating his faith as he expounded upon it. For all of this, one may say at least metaphorically that Heschel had the writings of the Hasidic masters open before him. The "God intoxication" that makes Heschel so distinctive among twentieth-century religious thinkers came directly from Hasidism, from Heschel's lived memory and his ongoing immersion in its literature.

A second aspect of Heschel's Hasidism was his understanding that God's existence and providence are not to be proven. Although he viewed himself as a philosopher (a point long debated among his students and critics), logical argumentation was hardly his forte.[16] The person of faith does not argue but *witnesses*. The God of Hasidism, despite all the quasi-pantheistic formulations, is also the God of Abraham, not that of Aristotle. For this God, postulates mean nothing. The God of Abraham is the God of living faith, not a Deity whose existence is proven through philosophical reason. Again, young Heschel the poet:

> How miniscule my offering,
> My gift, my way of honoring
> Your presence. What can I do
> But go about the world and swear
> Not just believe—but testify and swear.

The Jew as witness who testifies to God's greatness is key to the Hasidic legacy of Ger. The festivals are frequently described by the *Sefat Emet*, the key writing of that tradition, as times of special witnessing, connecting the term *mo'ed* (festival) with *'ed*, meaning "witness."[17] Its author's son, Rabbi Abraham Mordecai of Ger (who was *rebbe* while Heschel studied in the movement's schools), noted that the concluding two paragraphs of the daily liturgy, the *'aleinu*, each of which begins with the letter *'ayin* and ends with the letter *dalet*, form the word *'ed*, serving as the two required witnesses testifying to the sincerity of our prayers.[18] Both Sinai itself and the daily recitation of the *shema'* are taken in the Ger tradition as moments of universal witness.

Third, as his writing makes manifest, Heschel knew the world was in need of great charismatic religious figures. Such people can have tremendous power and effect upon those around them. Heschel himself grew up nourished by tales of such people, "with my mother's milk" as he used to say. In the classic Hasidic tradition, of course, the transformative power of the holy man's words affected not only people but God.

It seems clear that Heschel was not one to take this belief too literally. Without some rebellion, at least on this level, he never could have left Warsaw. Well-trained to the Kotsker's critical view of Hasidism — Rabbi Menahem Mendel of Kotsk decried sham piety, populism, and all expressions of religious insincerity — Heschel regarded such claims as possessing very varied merit. Nonetheless, however, he did not abandon the Hasidic faith in charismatic leadership and its role in human religious community. Much of his intellectual life remained devoted to the prophets, their experience of God, and their message of charismatic leadership deeply intertwined with the human religious community. It is hard to imagine, moreover, that images of the Hasidic masters, especially of the fiery Kotsker, who castigated his students for any moral inadequacy and brooked no compromise in matters of truth or integrity, did not cross his mind as Heschel read and considered the prophets.

Possibly the prophets served a similar role for Heschel to that served by the Hasidic masters for Martin Buber. Each of these men had to look elsewhere — Buber to Hasidic Eastern Europe, Heschel to the distant past of ancient Israel-for examples of the holy and charismatic figures that both men strove to become, knowing they were so much needed in their day. For Heschel, though, the Hasidic masters were too close to be used as his primary example; he knew too much of their failings to put them on the sort of pedestal that the more distant Buber could. Heschel, after all, could have been a Hasidic *rebbe* had he not chosen a different life for himself.

Still, the figure of the prophet, the topic of Heschel's 1936 doctoral dissertation in Berlin and his major book *The Prophets* in 1962 — in particular the prophets' emphasis on divine pathos and identification with God as the core of the prophetic experience — surely bears echoes of

Hasidic religious figures. Heschel's prophets were overwhelmed with God's suffering at human iniquity, and, called to the highest order of moral responsibility, they refused to countenance wrongdoing or transgression—especially when committed by one person against another. The Hasidic yearning for *true* charisma remained deep within Heschel, who sought to rearticulate a spiritual and ethical vision of Torah in a new language for a new generation.

Such a project may well be compared to Zeitlin's statement about the intent of Yavneh explored in chap. 1. Like Zeitlin's dream of spiritual rebirth in Poland, Heschel's American writings reveal him inhabiting a Neo-Hasidic rebbe's—or prophet's—role. Even if Heschel did not claim that mantle openly, he did not flee when it was cast upon him.

A fourth area of evident Hasidic influence is Heschel's great belief in the Hasidic virtues of *hesed* and *simhah* as key to the spiritual life. In the spirit of Levi Yitzhak of Berdichev (also an ancestor) and others, he saw his own role as bringing Jews back to Judaism by means of kind, patient, and openhearted teaching. He never berated Jews for not being observant, but tried to show them the light and beauty he himself found in the religious life. He exemplified a Judaism of joy in God's service. He sought to help people open their eyes in a deeper way, and recognized that this could only be accomplished by positive, nonjudgmental example. In this sense, too, he took on the role of *rebbe*, however reluctantly, for liberal Jews.

There is something very Hasidic, in the original sense of Hasidism, in this approach. Hasidism understands anger, even righteous anger, as a negative characteristic, emerging from too strong a pull to the left side or the presence of too much black bile in the system. It has to be countered by the activation of *hesed*, divine love or compassion, for which Hasidism is named, after all. To be a Hasid is to be an *ish hesed*, a person of love and compassion—what Heschel tried to exemplify all his life.

The fifth and final confluence is encapsulated by the phrase (and book title) *God in Search of Man*. Heschel knew a God who is concerned with and affected by human actions. This God, he believed, creates each human in the divine image so we may fulfill the role of partnership with God, so we may discover God's presence both within the world and our own souls and respond to it, with heart but primarily by deed. God awaits this response.

God in Search of Man may well be Heschel's contemporary rendition of the classic kabbalistic formula *ha-'avodah tsorekh gavoha*, "worship fulfills a divine need." It had been first expressed in this form by Nahmanides, the great thirteenth-century rabbi who lent credibility to Kabbalah by including its secrets within his widely read Torah commentary.[19]

Whence did Heschel derive this notion of God's need for the *mitzvot*, but from within the Hasidic world? In his childhood he had learned about the secret and mysterious power of the *mitzvot*. Hasidic *rebbes* would lavish their special love and devotion upon these *mitzvot*. Although Hasidism by its second generation had abandoned the complex infrastructure of Lurianic *kavvanot* (mystical intentions for prayer and most of daily life), certain *mitzvot* were still treated as mysterious sacraments. Only partially understood *kavvanot* were retained for them, but they came with the promise that the *tsaddik's* performance of them could take the heavens by storm and affect the divine will—even to the point of changing ill decrees in heaven, a very central concern and original intent of the Ba'al Shem Tov.

Of course, Heschel was not a naive or literal believer in the power of the *tsaddik* to repeal the decree of heaven. But he was also unwilling to abandon this dramatic sense of the cosmic importance of human deeds, which added much to the value of humanity and the sense of divine-human partnership. He thus undertook a very interesting shift in the way he read this part of the Hasidic-Kabbalistic legacy. When Hasidic *rebbes* spoke of the commandments as sublime secrets, *razin 'ila'in*, they usually were referring to such mystery-laden religious acts as *teki'at shofar*, the blowing of the ram's horn on the New Year; *na'anu'ey lulav*, the waving of the palm and other branches on Sukkot; or *tevilah be-mikveh*, immersion in the ritual bath. Preparing intensely for these sacred moments, *rebbes* often turned back to the old *kavvanot.* Surely all these needed to be done *le-shem shamayim,* "for the sake of heaven." On the simplest level, this was defined in classical kabbalistic language as *le-shem yihud qudsha brikh hu u-shekhinteyh,* "in order to unify the blessed Holy One and His *Shekhinah.*" Now, Heschel made a brilliant and transformative move: while agreeing with his Hasidic tradition that God longs for us to do the *mitzvot,* that heaven itself is moved by our deeds, he applied this first and foremost to the *mitzvot beyn adam le-havero,* to the commandments that regard the way we treat our fellow humans. Yes, Heschel said, God *needs* you to do the *mitzvot* — to feed the hungry, care for the poor, sustain widows and orphans, and, in our age, oppose unjust war and march with Martin Luther King. These are the essence of *mitzvot;* it is primarily through these that you become God's partner in the world.

As a traditionalist, Heschel never denied the importance of ritual observance. In fact, his works were often used as a buttress to defend it. But the key thrust of the latter part of *God in Search of Man,* combined with *The Prophets* and several of his essays, is what God seeks of us in the first place: those *mitzvot* that demonstrate human decency, compassion for the oppressed and needy, and a response to the prophetic call for justice restored to God's world.

Heschel sought to rescue the notion of *mitzvot tsorekh gavoha* from the obscurantism of the mystics and bring it back to what he believed was its first source — the teachings of the prophets of Israel. Thus Heschel's version of prophetic Judaism, including the pathos with which the prophet identifies with the will of God, is an expression of his Neo-Hasidism. He comes from that place in the Hasidic tradition that loves the commandments. He sees them as God's great gift to us as a means to be close to God, even as a meeting place between the divine and human spirit. Not mere requirements of the law-code or ways to fence about our evil urge, the *mitzvot* are the means by which we reach toward transcendence.[20]

Ever the man of expansive vision, Heschel understands this to mean that God in divine love for all of us humans calls upon us to do transforming deeds, to act in ways that will at once make our lives holy and the world more whole. The hope of humanity is that we can, and will, still respond to that voice, one that has never ceased calling out to us.

Pikuah Neshamah: To Save a Soul (1949)

The three selections that follow are testament to the Hasidic inflection in Heschel's readings of Judaism at various points in his life.

The first of these is Pikuah Neshamah (To Save a Soul), long a favorite within the circle of Heschel's closest disciples, which was published in his almost untranslatably elegant rabbinic Hebrew in 1949, when the pain of Holocaust memory was still fresh and searing. Here Heschel describes the Jew's task as a quest for inwardness, for a refined sense of spiritual beauty that will call upon us to elevate human life and restore humanity's lost sense of moral decency.

The human being is uniquely graced with the ability to search the soul and reflect, For what purpose am I alive? Does my life have a meaning, a reason? Is there a need for my existence? Will anything on earth be impaired by my disappearance? Would my absence create a vacuum in the world? And if we say that there would be a void and an impairment in the world, and that this means that my life has value beyond its simple existence, is it incumbent upon me to fulfill a purpose in this life? Do I exist that I might build or restore?

Every person moves in two domains: in the domain of nature and in the domain of the spirit. Half slave, half king, we are bound by the laws of nature, but at the same time able to subdue and dominate them. As creatures of nature, we are born perforce and have no need for the same legitimacy or self-justification. As the Talmud remarks, "One does not examine applicants for food."[21] As creatures of spirit, however, we take stock of ourselves and of our world. We yearn to find a reward from all our toils, and search for that which is special in our lives. Does existence simply mean to seize and eat, to seize and drink, or does it have a double meaning: to exist and to serve a purpose?[22]

The purpose of human existence is an age-old problem. Kohelet [Ecclesiastes] was not the only one to agonize over it. The debate over this problem is an ancient one and many have debated it at great length. We are not free to ignore it today. One may not appoint a proxy to engage in spiritual struggles. And just as the generations are not equal, so, too, the efforts extended in finding a solution are not equal. The question of the purpose of our lives as Jews is doubly serious and constitutes a double-edged sword over the Jewish scholar. Our continued existence highlights the question to which we cannot close our eyes: Is it worthwhile to live as a Jew? It is a question that stirs in the heart of each one of us.

Our historical experience has taught us that our existence as Jews is not in the category of things which neither help nor hurt. The opposite is true: to be a Jew is either superfluous or essential. Anyone who adds Judaism to humanity is either diminishing or improving it. Being a Jew is either tyranny or holiness. Moreover, the life of a Jew requires focus and direction, and cannot be carried out offhandedly. One who thinks that one can live as a Jew in a lackadaisical manner has never tasted Judaism.

The very existence of a Jew is a spiritual act. The fact that we have survived, despite the suffering and persecution, is itself a sanctification of God's name. We continue to exist, in spite of the scorn of the complacent, the torrents of hatred, and the dangers that constantly lie in wait for us. We always have had the option to solve the "Jewish Question" through conversion, and had we stopped being Jews, we would not have continued as thorns in everyone's flesh, and we would not have remained an object of scorn. As individuals we would have tasted a life of serenity and security. After all, the Jew is an expert at adaptation and assimilation, and it would not be too much for him to mix with the nations, without their taking note of his joining them. Nevertheless, generation upon generation have withstood the test of their faith. Many blows could not douse the flame. With dedication we guard the fire, the truth, and the wonder.

It is out of neither laziness nor habit that we cleave to the root of our soul. We know that even in normal times we have been required to pay a high price for our existence. We know that we are obliged to bear a double burden of responsibility. Yes, Jewish existence comes at a high price; yet Jewish life is dear to us. It is spiced with a unique charm, radiating a light that delights the soul, a light that graces all our actions. Even simple things, like eating and drinking, rise through it toward the Supreme and acquire a spiritual aspect.

To live as a Jew means to feel the soul in everything, in others and in our own existence. And this soul requires spiritual elevation. Everything that has within it the spirit of life longs for repair. Like candlewicks waiting to be lit, so we wait for the action that has a slight bit of pure intention, a grain of refinement. The soul in us will not find satisfaction merely in physical fulfillment. In each of us flickers the longing for Shabbatness, for beauty, for serenity. Anyone who chains and represses these longings and allows the powers of the soul to disperse to no end not only contaminates his self, but also con-

tributes to the world's destruction. For the soul which degenerates is the mother of all sins and the source of all evil. And
all the evil afflictions such as hate, haughtiness, and jealousy
stem from the spirit of human beings.

And people, what do they do? The major part of our energy
we invest in "fixing [*tikkun*] our clothing," i.e., improving the
outer skin while ignoring the inner essence. The soul goes
mad and degenerates while the world continues with business as usual, as if waiting for the Destroyer to arrive and
return it to a formless void (*tohu va-vohu*). The purpose of
Judaism is to destroy the instinct toward madness which
lurks at the gate of the human soul, to cause something of
the world of divine nobility to dwell in this world, and to
prepare the soul to delight in some of the radiance of Eden
while in this world.

What is the meaning of nobility? A person possessing nobility is one whose hidden wealth surpasses his outward wealth,
whose hidden treasures exceed his obvious treasures, whose
inner depth surpasses by far that which he reveals. Refinement is found only where inwardness is greater than outward
appearance. The hidden is greater than the obvious, depth
greater than breadth. Nobility is the redeemed quality which
rises within the soul when it exchanges the transient for the
permanent, the useful for the valuable.

The Satan of publicity dances at the crossroads, moving with
full strength. Who is the wise man who has not gone out after
him, following his drums and dances? We tend to lick the dust
of his feet in order to gain fame. In truth, the soul has only
that which is hidden in its world, that which is sealed in its
treasure houses. The quality of a person is internal. He does
not live by what his mouth says but by the secret. The honor
of a person is a secret.

The whole honor of Judaism is internal, in the depths, in the small containers that are hidden from sight. Even the stone tablets that were given with loud voices were broken. Blessing is not in noise; beauty is not in the top of trees but rather in the roots which are open to the Ancient Fountain.

A person cannot see the beauty of life unless he remembers that the Finite (*Sof*) and the Infinite (*Ein Sof*) kiss each other; that the One who is enthroned on high is concerned with all below. We live always at one with eternity. Eternal life has been planted in our midst. A family table is an altar in our house. Each and every one of us can determine for ourselves and for the whole world whether we become innocent or guilty. And the most common acts that a person does are compared in their importance to things which are eternal. Judaism teaches us to view any injustice — robbery, violence, or human oppression — as a major tragedy, and to feel divine joy at bringing happiness to a mortal. One who curses a human is insulting his Maker and one who loves others gives pleasure to God.

Every human being is a kind of reminder of God (*shiviti*), and all things are like traces of God's footprints in a barren desert. Through all the things in the world it is possible to come close to the Source. It is incumbent upon us, as Jews, to imitate the footprints, and remove the veil from God, who is masked in the costume of the world.[23]

Many eras have passed since our visionaries and prophets began shaking the human conscience with the anguished cry that all flesh had corrupted its ways on earth, that the earth was filled with violence, in religion as in politics, with individuals as with communal affairs. However, along with this, the prophets sparked in us the vision and the desire to repair and improve the world. We clearly are heretics if we believe that human affairs are predetermined in an inviolable manner.

Each day and each era have the potential to be Friday, and it is incumbent upon us to learn how to prepare on a weekday for the Sabbath. We lack the power to prematurely force the advent of the end of days, but we are able to add to the sacred from the profane.[24] And it is possible to accomplish such additions every hour. Preparation is necessary even in commonplace matters, for you cannot reach the significant without beginning with the insignificant. The same heavens that are stretched out over the ocean also cover the dust on an abandoned path. And though the destruction of evil and the eradication of malice are not easy tasks, laving one's hands before eating bread and reciting the blessing over the bread are not to be trampled upon and made light of.

We are faithful to the purpose of the world, not by paying it lip service or by philosophical inquiry. We cling to the secret of life with a cleaving born of fate, whether we are aware of it or not, and therefore we do not stumble in the dark, nor are we frightened by spirits and phantoms. Judaism is as a candle to the soul. It teaches us to hold on to the melody in the cacophony of life, how to burn off the thorns of the fleeting and the vulgar from the midst of the vineyard of our existence. It teaches us to listen for the miraculous pulse of life, which beats demonstratively through the veins of the universe. For the believing Jew, the dreadful feeling that one's life is empty, that one's efforts have been in vain, is foreign. A Jew knows the secret of a blessing—a blessing over all things which benefit us; the joy of a Jew is not in vain.

The life of a Jew is comparable to one who walks through fire: either he will be burned and the flame will immolate him or he will emerge purified and the light will shine above him. Objectively, one could say to every person: If you want to live a spiritual life which is complete and righteous, then live as a Jew.

Our fate is a sign and a mission. That which happened to Israel will happen to the whole world. Mt. Sinai is now suspended above all the nations. If they accept the Torah, good; if not, they will be buried amid the finest elements of their culture.

These days even an infant can see that humanity stands at the edge of an abyss. We have learned that one can be a villain even though very cultured and expert in science. The possibility of saving the world from destruction depends on the recognition that there is a supreme criterion by which we must evaluate all human values and that there is something that rises above all the achievements of the arts and sciences, above all the accomplishments of an individual or a people.

What is this criterion? How does one measure dominion, beauty, wealth, power? The soul of every human being possesses within it the tendency to value those things that it likes, and to bow down to that which appears to be valuable. This is a test that everyone passes. How easy it is to be attracted by outward beauty, and how hard it is to remove the mask and penetrate to that which is inside. If a Greek poet, for example, had arrived at Samaria, the capital of the Kingdom of Israel, he would have been surprised and overcome with emotion; he would have praised and lauded in verse the idols, the beautiful temples and palaces which the kings of Israel and their ministers had built. But the prophet Amos, after visiting Samaria, did not sing, nor did he bow to the glory of the ivory buildings. When he looked at the buildings of carved stone, at the ivory temples and the beautiful orchards, he saw in them the oppression of the poor, robbery and plunder. External magnificence neither entranced him nor led him astray. His whole being cried out in the name of the Lord: "I loathe the pride of Jacob, and I detest his palaces." Could it be that the prophet Amos's heart—the purest of that generation—was not captivated and did not tremble before beauty? Was the prophet Amos lacking all feeling and appreciation for beauty?

When the annual congress of the Nazi Party convened in Nuremberg in 1937, journalists from all over the world, such as *The Times of London*, described with enthusiasm the demonstrations of the various Nazi organizations. They could not find enough adjectives to praise the physical beauty, the order, the discipline, and the athletic perfection of the tens of thousands of young Nazis who marched ceremoniously and festively before the leader of the "movement." These writers who were so excited by the exterior splendor lacked the ability to see the snakes in the form of humans — the poison that coursed through their veins, which not long after would bring death to millions of people.

Judaism teaches us that beauty which is acquired at the cost of justice is an abomination and should be rejected for its loathsomeness.

All values are esteemed only to the extent that they are worthy in the sight of God, for only through the Divine Light is their light seen. Treasures of the world, though they be marked by beauty and charm, when they diminish the image of the divine will not endure. Fortunate is the person who sees with eyes and heart together. Fortunate is the person who is not entranced by the grand façade or repulsed by the appearance of misery. This is the mark of the spiritual personality; chic clothes, smiling faces, and artistic wonders which are filled with evil and injustice do not entrance him. Architectural wonders and monumental temples, which seem to testify to glory and honor, power and strength, are loathsome to him if they were built with the sweat of slaves and the tears of the oppressed, if they were raised with wrongdoing and deceit. Hypocrisy which parades under the veil of righteousness is worse to him than obvious wrongdoing. In his heart any religious rite for which the truth must be sacrificed is revolting. Deeds which Jews are commanded to perform are for the purpose of coupling the beautiful and the good, for the sake of the unification of grace and splendor. The criterion by which we judge beauty is integrity, the criterion by which we judge integrity is truth, and truth is the correspondence of the finite to the infinite, the specific to the general, the cosmos to God.

It is possible that the future of civilization is dependent on this spiritual power, on the ability to achieve this correspondence. It is of the essence of spirituality to perceive the hidden transcendence which is in the habitual, to hear the afflicted voice even in the heralding of victory, to hear the sound of the stone which cries out from the wall.

Those who think that Judaism stands only on the internal virtues, on psychological attributes alone, are mistaken. To be a Jew means to have both a Jewish soul and a Jewish spirit. The soul is created together with the body, but it is incumbent upon the person to acquire the spirit upon which the soul is dependent, and the Jewish soul is dependent upon the Jewish spirit.

What are the roots from which we draw the ability to cleave to the spirit of Judaism? What is the well from which we draw the unique ability to taste its essence and the strength to stay in contact with the endless reality? There are many among us from whom this essence has been taken, but even they tremble with reverence when the storms of suffering pass over them. At that time their confidence in their spirit and power melts away. It is the aim of the Torah of Israel to breathe into us the trembling of holiness and reverence, so that it fills our hearts at all times.

The historical experience of our day teaches us that the person who is only a human being is actually less than human. Judaism teaches us that to remain a people we must be more than a people. Israel is destined to be a holy people. This is the essence of our mission, the essence of our yearnings. From this essence emerges the divine seriousness which hovers above our being, as well as our reverence for our own existence.

What is this reverence? What is the characteristic which determines the honor of a person? This is not an obvious characteristic. We do not honor a person for his countenance, his physical stature, or his natural talents. Our honor as human beings is of an importance that does not stem from within ourselves. A person's honor represents an importance which is greater than his own importance. The glory of a nation rests upon its king, the glory of knowledge rests upon the scholar, and the glory of the Creator rests upon the created.

This sort of importance hovers above every Jew. A Jew represents a value greater than his own value as an individual. A Jew who forgets his nobility—there is no greater transgression than that.[25]

We are partners with God, partners in everyday actions. We do not walk alone. We are not solitary in our toils or forsaken in our efforts. The smallest one is a microcosm of the Greatest One. A reciprocal relationship binds each lowly one with the One on High.

The fate of our people is not fully in our control. From ancient times the children of Israel made a covenant with God. All subsequent generations preserved this relationship, in which they invested the best of energies, thereby transforming Israel's destiny into a holy entity. Holiness is that aspect of something that does not belong to us but, rather, belongs to God. Holiness lies in the apparent trivialities that God receives from us while we are on this earth. The Torah has repeated to us often: Human beings are the source of holiness, and human will—not dreams and visions—is the anvil upon which holiness is formed. A person enters his silo and, referring to a section of the grain, declares: "This portion is *terumah* [the priestly offer-ing]." Immediately his *terumah* is sanctified and may be eaten only by priests. A Jew writes a verse containing the name of God on a piece of parchment, and the parchment becomes holy. The head of the High Court in Jerusalem, when determining the day upon which the new month should begin, declares: "It is holy," and behold, that day is holy.[26] And when Israel declared at Sinai, "We will act and we will understand," it became a holy nation.[27]

For generation after generation, the children of Israel have repeated: "We will act and we will understand." In the acad-emies and in the synagogues, in the flames of the Inquisition and in the concentration camps, in the marketplaces of the far-flung reaches of the Exile, and in the kibbutzim of the land of Israel. And this people became a holy nation.

Many of us detest the idea of holiness and consider it to be a waste of time, a meaningless concept, the invention of primitive man, notwithstanding the fact that this concept is rooted in the heart of every cultured person. Everyone knows the power of the spoken word. What really happens when a person opens his mouth and promises something? Superficially, only sounds emanate from vocal cords, and the lips are merely moving. So what of it? Why do we assume that loyalty to one's word is the basis of all human relationships? The promise that was given, the contract that is made—is sacred, and one who desecrates it destroys the foundation upon which all of communal life is established. Until the moment I speak, the choice is mine, but once the words have left my mouth, I may not rescind or des-ecrate them. Willingly or unwillingly, the word spoken by me controls me. It becomes a sacred power which has dominion over me, lurking at my door and compelling my compliance.

We Jews fully recognize that we are in the grip of a history which cannot be forced into the boundaries of a single civilization. Even at a time when we are imprisoned in a Tower of Babel, in the midst of a cacophony of self-aggrandizers for whom "nothing they may propose to do will be out of their reach," we discern echoes from another world. How is it possible for a mere mortal to perceive an echo emanating from a world which is beyond history and civilization?

The nations of the world have produced many thinkers who have striven to reach God by intellectual inquiry alone. They have, in fact, dived deep into the stormy waters, but have come up with naught. God cannot be grasped by the intellect. The Jews have a different way: "We will act and we shall understand." Reaching God—the understanding—arrives together with the act, emanates from within the act (the Kotsker Rebbe). When we fulfill a *mitzvah* and perform a desirable action, we achieve the cleaving of humanity with God. It is as if in our actions, in the depths of our existence, "we see the thunder."

The life of Israel teaches us of the correspondence between the spiritual power within us and God, who is above all the worlds. He "who chose to dwell in a thick cloud abides with them in the midst of their uncleanness."[28] There exists a harmony between the good deeds of a human and the Infinite Holiness, between the compassion of a human being and the mercy of the Eternal. The spirituality that flows from our actions is not fleeting, transient, or solitary in a silent cosmos. The music of refined actions, the melody of a noble soul, is woven into the tapestry of eternal music which God Himself composed.

We believe in the possibility of unifying the divine within us with the Infinite Divine, which exists outside of us; we believe that a small bit of lovingkindness in a mortal's heart joins with Eternity; and that ordinary actions are no less significant than the most exalted of projects.

In our vocabulary, whether in Hebrew or in Yiddish, one of the most common words is the word *mitzvah*. This word cannot be translated into any other language. The Christians did not accept the idea of the *mitzvah*, only the idea of "sin," and they even transformed the meaning of this term. For them, sin possesses a positive force, an essence. For us, the word "sin" has mainly a negative connotation. To sin means to fail, to take an inappropriate step ("He who moves hurriedly blunders," Prov. 19:2); or it connotes the failure to find a thing in its appropriate place ("You will know that all is well in your tent; when you visit your home you will not fail," Job 5:24); or in *hiph'il*, it means to miss the target ("Every one of them could sling a stone at a hairbreadth and not miss," Judg. 20:25).

The primary connotation of the word *'aveyrah* (transgression) is also negative. *'Aveyrah* means: not to do, to disregard, or to cross the fixed boundary. ("Then the king's courtiers who were in the palace gate said to Mordecai, Why do you disobey [*'over*] the king's order?" (Esther 3:3) "One might think that if one's father or mother orders him to transgress [*la-'avor*] any one of the commandments written in the Torah . . ." (Sifra, Kedoshim, 1). The same word also means forgiveness ("Who is a God like you, forgiving iniquity and remitting [*'over*] transgression," Mic. 7:18).

In Yiddish — from whose expressions one can gain great insight into the soul of the Jewish people — *'aveyrah* means to spoil something, or to do something for naught. For example, a Yiddish adage states: "If you speak to a deaf person, such speech is a sin, an *'aveyrah*" (i.e., for naught). *Mitzvah* in Yiddish means to do what is good, in a positive, concrete sense. "Do me a *mitzvah*, give me a glass of water." In Hebrew we say: "The wise in heart takes *mitzvot*" (Prov. 10:8). "Beautify yourself in His presence through the performance of *mitzvot*"

(b. Shabbat 133). Consider also the expressions: "To perform a *mitzvah*"; "To involve oneself in *mitzvot*"; "To seize a *mitzvah*"; "To acquire a *mitzvah* (in the synagogue)." The real import of this term is revealed through many such expressions. Is it at all possible to do justice in any other language to Resh Lakish's dictum: "Even the empty ones among your people are as filled with *mitzvot* as a pomegranate (is filled with fruit seeds)"?!²⁹

Indeed, internal radiance is not quantifiable and routinized actions do not illuminate. We are even taught that the sins of the pure at heart are more desirable than the good deeds of the arrogant. However, what will become of the artist who lacks tools, or the craftsman who is bereft of materials? Likewise the musician, whose inner world is permeated with overwhelming and inspired musical images: What is such a person able to accomplish or contribute if he or she lacks instruments with which to articulate these images?

Every morning, when Jews recites the prayer "Fortunate are we, how good is our lot!," our mouths and hearts are in sync. What is the nature of this joy? I believe it emanates from the fact that we do not subsist in a hollow, vacuous universe. We do not feel that we are wandering through chaos, that we are building on nothingness, that our lives are just an accidental shrub, and that our culture is the aftergrowth of much ado about nothing. The feeling—which exists among the other nations—that time is a great abyss—does not oppress us. The life of Israel is stretched between two historical poles: the Exodus from Egypt and the messianic kingdom.

There is no forgetting among the community of Israel. We have not abandoned our past nor have we denigrated our heritage. We know where we stand in time and we number our days in accordance with the calendar of eternity. One of the important characteristics of the spirit of Israel is its phenomenal capacity for remembering. Throughout the generations we have remained loyal to our past. A candle, once lit in the temple of our history, is never extinguished. This historical memory was not sustained through Jews filling themselves with knowledge about antiquity. The preservation of the past to which we refer is not a gathering of facts in the mind but, rather, rises out of love; it is the remembering which occurs in the heart.

In this manner our past is preserved in our souls and in our way of life. This preservation takes the form of an inner service, the renewal or remnant of first things, the grasping of the temporary and transient by the eternal. The present is sanctified by the memory of the past.

Belief likewise depends on memory. "I believe" means: "I remember." For what is belief? Every one of us, at least once in our lifetime, has been able to perceive the existence of the Creator. Every one of us, at least once, has merited a glimpse of the beauty, the serenity, and the strength which flow from the souls of those who have walked with God. However, such feelings and inspirations are not common occurrences. In the lives of most people they are as meteors which flare up for a moment and then disappear from sight. There are, however, people for whom these flashes ignite with them a light which will never be extinguished. Faith means: If you ever once merit that the Hidden One appears to you, be faithful to Him all the days of your life. Faith means: To guard forever the echo which once burst upon the deep recesses of our soul.

Just as an individual's memory determines the nature of his personality, so the collective memory determines the destiny of nations. How bitter are the lives of those who do not know who their ancestors were, who their childhood friends were, or who their sisters and brothers were? We see whole nations that have lost the power of memory and therefore who do not know their origins and their destinies. At times they are gripped by horror, feeling as if they were blinded, and they wander aimlessly in deep darkness upon a volcano. Their inner sight is dimmed, and the volcano is within them.

The power of collective memory is one of the characteristics of Israel. Even in the rush of time, we sat on the sturdy rock of memory, and our past has been preserved in our souls and our way of life. It is incumbent upon us to remember those events that occurred to our ancestors, events through which the spirit of God established residence in the history of our people. This ancient echo still rings in our ears, and even if we ignore it or attempt to silence it, our visions never cease to give it voice.

The days of the past and the present are inextricably tied together. The love of the people Israel is inconceivable if we don't walk with the generations that produced us, and vice versa: without love for the Jews of our time — including even the frivolous and vacuous among them — we will not succeed in connecting with the Israel of the past. The unity of all generations and the unity of all those in our generation are dependent on each other. We must walk with the prophet Isaiah, Rabbi Yohanan ben Zakkai, Maimonides, and the Ba'al Shem Tov, just as we must interact with those who live among us today.

We are not of the opinion that everything that has the stamp of antiquity on it is of the finest. Many garments have been worn out, and many areas have been destroyed. Most people, moreover, tend to look upon everything in the past as useless, and they are willing to exchange the glory of ancient days for the shiny newness of today. They forget that it is not within the power of one individual or within the power of a single generation to construct the bridge which leads to Truth. Let us not discriminate against the structure which many generations have nourished and built up. "The sacred entities of the children of Israel — do not profane them!" (Num. 18:32).

Not only the children of Israel in a single generation but all the children of Israel in all generations comprise the nation. We share a single status and destiny. Even a Jew who stands at a distance wraps himself within his soul and prays: "May it be your will that my portion be bound up with the congregation of Israel."

The Jewish National Fund collection box is on a table in many Jewish houses today. Years ago young men, yeshiva students, would go around to houses and exchange empty boxes for the full ones. Once, a young boy went to empty the boxes in the town of Sanuk in Galicia, and as he entered the doorway of a shoemaker he said, "I've come to empty the Jewish National Fund box." At first the shoemaker was silent, then he asked the visitor to sit down. He removed his shoes and began to put new soles on them. The young man was dumbfounded. "What are you doing?" he asked. The shoemaker replied, "I am a poor person and I cannot afford to make contributions to the Jewish National Fund, so I want to put new soles on your shoes. You go around from house to house and your shoes get torn. I also wish to have a portion in this *mitzvah*."

Like this shoemaker, we all must strive to have a portion in the Temple on high and in the glory of the world. This is what our ancestors struggled for in all times and all lands.

Judaism exists only in community. The primary concern of the Jew is not to merit an honorable seat in the Garden of Eden but, rather, that he assure the continued existence of the people Israel. "One who causes a deed to be performed is greater than one who performs it."[30] The teacher is greater than the student. What is the one who looks out only for himself and his own perfection compared to? "To a *tsaddik* in a fur coat" (*tsaddik in pelts*). What is a "*tsaddik* in a fur coat"? If there is a chill in the house and we wish to warm our bodies, we have two choices: to light a fire in the stove or to put on a fur coat. What is the difference between lighting a fire and putting on the fur? When the fire is lit, I am warm and others are warm as well; when I wrap myself in fur, it is only I who am warm (the Kotsker Rebbe).[31]

After the flood of evil swept over the world, that which remained of refinement wandered about as a forlorn dove between heaven and earth, searching for a resting place in the human conscience. This refinement is the Divine Presence (*Shekhinah*). Who will take pity upon this bereft dove if not we, the children of Israel?

The echoes of the terrible cries that came from the gas chambers, screams the like of which had never been heard in the course of human history, are too horrible to bear. Woe unto the generation in whose days human beings have become a dreadful disgrace. And yet never before has the superhuman power of our existence been as clearly manifest as it is in our time.

The millions of Jews who were destroyed bear witness to the fact that as long as people do not accept the commandment "Remember the Sabbath to keep it holy," the commandment "Thou shalt not kill" will likewise fail to be operative in life.[32] Today we, few in number, are the generation upon whom devolves the obligation to preserve, to purify, and to transmit. We are a generation burdened with a weighty responsibility and with a mighty destiny. The future of Judaism is in the hands of the few. Will we be the last Jews?

From the day on which humans have been on this earth no temple has been so pure and sanctified with so much blood as has the existence of the Jewish nation. Every Jew who survived constitutes a remnant of a candle kindled by divine light, an ember snatched from the fire of evil. Unknowingly, every Jew is crowned with a crown of holiness. Every Jew must feel the glory hovering above the face of our existence. Great is our tragedy and great is our mission. And our major task is to save the heart of humanity, the heart that extends "to the heart of heaven" (Deut. 4:11).

Just as it is incumbent upon us to be human beings, so is it our obligation to be Jews. Anyone who separates himself from Judaism commits spiritual suicide. Just as it is impossible to exchange one's body, so is it impossible to divest oneself of the divine image. Every people has a religion which it received from others; but we are the only people which are unified with our Torah. All parts of the nation, not only an elite few, have come to symbolize this unity. By persisting in our Judaism—by continuing as Jews—we contribute more toward the general welfare than we do through all our significant scientific contributions to the general culture.

When we attempt to explain the exalted status of Israel's destiny, we realize the inadequacy of our words. Even what our own eyes have seen is beyond our power of expression. Our life is like a play with many acts, which God, as it were, watches and hears. Who dares evaluate and judge our role in this drama?

It is said in the Talmud: "A person must ask, When will my deeds approach the deeds of the patriarchs?"[33] The "patriarchs" are Abraham, Isaac, and Jacob. In the Torah, nothing is said about books they wrote or ideas they innovated. Instead, we are told tales of their adventures, their deeds, how they wandered from place to place to find food for their households, how they searched for brides, and so on and their actions became Torah. Hence we learn the purpose of Jewish existence: we are obligated to live lives that will become Torah, lives that are Torah.

Perhaps human beings have never been as much in need of Judaism as they are in our generation. The human species is on its deathbed. In order to seek a cure, we should not desecrate the Sabbath; rather, it is incumbent upon us to sanctify the weekdays. Like our ancestors three thousand years ago, we are called upon to be pioneers for the Torah of Israel and for the land of Israel, and bring their power to all the regions of the Diaspora.[34] We must not forget that the hidden secret of our existence is to be found in the admonition: "Be ye holy." Only in holiness will we be. In keeping faith with our Judaism, we guard the hidden divine light and the noblest of visions, which have been saved for humanity's future.

Hasidism as a New Approach to Torah (1972)

This essay reflects on the legacy of Hasidism as a revitalization movement within Judaism through the image of the Ba'al Shem Tov (the BeSHT). Here Heschel treats Torah interpretation as carrying forth this task of spiritual renewal. Hasidism rereads the tradition of *Torah lishmah*, "study for its own sake," as *Torah le-shem heh*, "study for the sake of the letter *he*," which represents the divine name or God's presence in the world.[35] Intellectual endeavor needs to be redeemed from mere display of personal brilliance and reattached to the divine Source from which all human insight is derived.

Hasidism represents a great enigma. It is first of all the enigma of the impact of one great man, the Besht. Of course many attempts have been made to explain this enigma. Here is one man who in a very short time, within twenty years, was able to capture the majority of the Jewish people and to keep them under his spell for generations. What was there about him that was not to be found in other great Jewish personalities like Maimonides or even Reb Isaac Luria or Rebbe Akiva? This one man in a little town brought into the world a new spirit, and that spirit captured, without the use of modern media, a major part of the Jewish people within twenty years. How do you explain that?[36]

The answers given are partly sociological, partly historical; I believe there is also a Hasidic answer to this Hasidic riddle. That answer was given by Rebbe Hirsh of Zhidachov, a very great personality in his own right, who told the following story: In Poland in those days, namely in the eighteenth century, a king was nominated, as a matter not of heritage but of election. Noblemen would get together from all over the country and they would elect a king. The king could also be a citizen of a foreign country, so naturally whenever a king died and there was a possibility of election, many princes and aristocrats from all over Europe would vie for that honor. And this is what happened. The king passed away and immediately various princes eager to become King of Poland would send their representatives to Poland, their public-relations men, if I may say so, each one trying to sing the praises of his candidate. He is the wisest of all men, one representative said. He's the wealthiest, said another; the kindest, said a third. This went on for days, and no decision was reached. Finally, one representative decided he would take his candidate, the prince himself, bring him to the people, and say, Here he is, look at him, see how grand he is. And that man was elected.

Many Jews talked about God, but it was the Besht who brought God to the people. This in a way is an answer, perhaps the best answer to the question of how to explain the unbelievable impact in such a short time of this great man. What was his contribution?

This contribution was that he brought about renewal of man in Judaism. The Jewish people is not the same since the days of the Besht. It is a new people. Other personalities contributed great works, they left behind impressive achievements; the Besht left behind a new people. Other people produced new ideas, new doctrines; the Besht opened sources of creativity, which fortunately to some degree are still open today. He brought a new light into Jewish life.

Many aspects of Jewish existence which seemed petrified he suddenly made almost ethereal, or at least liquid; he liquefied them. To many Jews the mere fulfillment of regulations was as the essence of Jewish living. Along came the Besht and taught that Jewish life is an occasion for exaltation. Observance of the Law is the basis, but exaltation through observance is the goal.

In other words, the greatness of the Besht was that he was the beginning of a long series of events, a long series of moments of inspiration. And he holds us in his spell to this very day. He who really wants to be uplifted by communing with a great person whom he can love without reservation, who can enrich his thought and imagination without end, that person can meditate about the life and being of the Besht. There has been no one like him during the last thousand years.

But I must also say that it is a tragedy that this great movement is essentially an oral movement, one that cannot be preserved in written form. It is ultimately a living movement. It is not contained fully in any of its books. It is more than can enter books. There are shades of meaning in uttering a Hasidic idea, a certain accent, a spirit, even a manner of speaking which is vital to the substance of speaking in Hasidic law.

Hasidism is not given to be an object of lecturing. One can be a witness to it but one cannot lecture about it. In other words, Hasidism has a very personal dimension, it is a very personal experience, it cannot be made the theme of a report. What does it mean to be a Hasid? To be a Hasid is to be in love, to be in love with God and with what God has created. Once you are in love you are a different human being. Do you criticize a person you are in love with? The Hasidim are in love with God. Even, strangely enough, in love with the world. The history of Hasidism is a history of being in love with God's story. That is the history of Hasidism. Indeed, he who has never been in love will not understand and may consider it a madness. That is why there is so much opposition to Hasidism, more than we are willing to admit.

In the eyes of those who are Hasidim, those who oppose it deserve pity more than anything else. Let me give an example. Someone came to a rabbi to complain that certain people tell Hasidic tales, Hasidic stories, and in this way they take time away from the study of Torah, which is a *mitzvah*. "Is it not so that he who interrupts his study of Torah eventually goes to hell, according to the Talmud? How can you tolerate Hasidim, who do not study all the time?" So the rabbi answered this man. "You know, the Hasidim are not afraid of going to hell, because they are building a new *gan eden*, a new heaven." "What is wrong with the old *gan eden?*" "The old *gan eden* isn't enough for Hasidim. The Talmud asks, What is *gan eden? Gan eden* is the place where Jews sit in the halls of the glory and luster of the divine. But to the Hasidim the luster of the divine is not enough. They would like to be attached to God Himself, not just to His luster, so that all paradise and all *gan eden* are not enough." And that *gan eden* experience is very essential.

Most things that have been said about Hasidism, Hasidism is not. To an average superficial writer, Hasidism means to be gay, to drink a little vodka. Hasidism is not that. It is true that it is important to understand that the Hasidim would drink a *le-hayyim* from time to time. But how did they understand it? He who has never been present at the scene, at the moment that Hasidim drink vodka, cannot know what it means to be holding the essence of his world. Vodka in Hebrew is called *yayin saraf; brandt* wine in German. And there are two ways of purification, said a great *rebbe*. One is with water, the ancient Jewish act of purification, submerging in the water. But there is a finer way of purification, because the immersion in water does not last forever. There is a kind of purification that is more lasting—to be on fire. We can clean metal in fire. To Hasidim, to drink *yayin saraf* is to be on fire, to remember that God is a consuming fire. It is not just gaiety, it is great discipline living in a number of extraordinary relations, commitments, entertaining a number of basic convictions. It is above all the cultivation of the inner life, a complex of sensibilities.

Hasidism must be understood in terms of great insights and teachings. It is equally important to remember that Hasidism is preserved not only in the form of teachings but also in the language of stories, tales. Third, Hasidism can be properly understood only if one realizes its leaning upon classics, on interpretations of biblical or rabbinic texts. The most important aspect of Hasidism is that it lives in personalities; without the charismatic person there is no teaching of Hasidism.

In addition, there are many phases of Hasidism. It was first an intellectual revolution. To understand the context of its origin we have to study the documents preserved at the beginning of the eighteenth century. There was a tremendous fascination in those days for what we call *pilpul*, with what may be called sharpness, intellectual wit in the study of the

Torah and Talmud. It represented a desire to sublimate feelings into thoughts, to transpose dreams into syllogisms. The sages expressed their grief in formulating keen theoretical difficulties and their joy in finding solutions to a contradiction of a disagreement between Maimonides, who lived in the twelfth century, and Rabbi Shlomo Aderet, who lived in the thirteenth century. They had to speak to one another, there was no division in time, they were all together. And there were sharp challenges all the time. That was how they sublimated their entire existence. It was sharp but dry as dust, with all other aspects of existence ignored. For example, there were many books published. I myself know of thirty or forty anthologies. What was their favorite topic in those days? *Pshetlakh. Pshetl* is the opposite of *peshat*, although the word *pshetl* is derived from *peshat*. *Peshat* means the literal simple meaning. *Pshetl* says the opposite: there is no literal meaning, there is always something behind it. In other words, when I say, "Give me a piece of bread," I don't really mean a piece of bread. I mean to answer a difficult passage in a commentary written in the twelfth century, which is noted by an authority of the fifteenth century. *Pshetl* is always an attempt to find the dialectics in the most simple things, and this is what the Talmudic scholars used to love.

And when a preacher came to deliver a sermon, would he speak about daily human problems? No, he spoke of the terrible excitement about the fact that Laban, Jacob's father-in-law, did not treat Jacob well. Why didn't he treat Jacob well? Because he had a serious disagreement with him about an obscure subtle issue in Jewish criminal law. Since Jewish criminal law is very complicated, there are fifty-five possibilities of explaining it, and this is what caused the disagreement. Actually, Laban and Jacob disagreed the same way as did Abbaye and Rava in the third century. But it was dry like dust. Anybody who has gone through such an education would know what it means. What is left is astuteness, acumen. It is always syllogisms on top of syllogisms, a pyramid on top of three other pyramids. You're always walking from one roof to another. You don't just walk straight, you're always jumping, leaping; there's no straight thinking. The Jews loved this Talmudic study, but the soul was not rested. There was very little for the heart. It was always so dry, so remote from existence, without the slightest awareness that there was also an inner life in human problems. There were no human problems, only legal problems.

Came the Ba'al Shem and changed the whole thing. He introduced a kind of thinking that is concerned with personal, intimate problems of religion and life. Some of these problems had smaller problems. Hasidism's major revolution was the opposition to what was generally accepted in Judaism—namely, that study is an answer to all problems. Study was considered more important than any other observance, certainly more important than prayer. Prayer was on the decline. It lost its vitality, it was deprived of spontaneity. One of the first tasks the Ba'al Shem faced was to bring about the resurrection of prayer. When he and his disciples went to a town, they would not just deliver a sermon about observance: they would stand and pray, thus setting an example of how to pray. To this day the Ba'al Shem remains one of the greatest masters of prayer in Jewish history.

Why was the study of Torah considered more important than prayer? Because, as mentioned in a beautiful book written in the Middle Ages, what is the difference between Torah and prayer? When you study Torah God speaks to you; when you pray you speak to God. Naturally, the study of Torah must be regarded as more important than prayer. Came the Ba'al Shem and exalted the role of prayer. The marvel of man's uttering words in the presence of God is tremendously important and vital. By stressing the mystery of uttering words, he projected new insights into the importance of speech, of words. The doctrine of prayer and the doctrine of study as developed by the Ba'al Shem are based upon the discovery of the meaning and the reality of a spoken word. Suddenly a word became greater than the person. And he who does not know that a word is greater than a person does not even know how to pray or how to read the Torah.

What is the meaning of studying Torah? the Ba'al Shem asks. You have to study it in a new way. Learning is a means to an end. To study Torah, he says, means to sense that which transcends Torah. When God created heaven and earth He created also a light, the infinite light, the marvelous light that is absolute, ever warming, penetrating, eternal. But because of the failure of creation and the decline of goodness in the world, God hid that eternal light. Where did He hide it? He hid it in the words of the Torah. When the Besht read the words of the Torah, he was able to sense that light. He was able through that light to see everything that goes on in the world and beyond this world.[37] Study, he also insisted, is a means to an end, not an end itself.

What is the means, what is the end? The end is a person himself. There is a famous story of how a man came to a *rebbe* for the first time in his life. He was already advanced in years, he was almost thirty years old. "It's the first time I come to a *rebbe*," the man said. The *rebbe* asked him, "What did you do all your life?" He answered, "I have gone through the Talmud four times." "How much of the Talmud has gone through you?" asked the *rebbe*.

The Ba'al Shem made men very great, he saw men in a new light. He took men seriously, very seriously. And therefore he had an extraordinary appreciation of the nature of the Jew. He maintained that every Jew could be a sanctuary. The ancient Temple in Jerusalem could be rebuilt by every Jew within his own soul. And out of this inner sanctuary would grow the incense, the smoke of the incense, in the rich heaven. Every Jew could rebuild the Temple and establish its altars.

This is why so much is at stake in human existence. The Ba'al Shem took the tradition of Jewish learning, the Talmud and Kabbalah, mysticism, and gave it a new luster and a new meaning. He was very much influenced by and adopted quite a number of ideas from Jewish mysticism, kabbalah, but he gave them a new slant, a new accent. To use a Hasidic term, he tried to consolidate the abstractions and philosophic reflections of Jewish mysticism into what he called a way of worship, an existential way, an application to human terms rather than letting them stay in their naked abstraction.

What is exciting about Hasidism is that it faces existence as it is without camouflage. It is open to tragedy and suffering, it opens up sources of compassion and insight. My father used to tell me a story about our grandfather, the lover of Israel.[38] He was asked by many other *rebbes*, "How come that your prayers are always accepted and our prayers are not?" He gave the following answer: "You see, whenever some Jew comes to me and pours out his heart and tells me of his misery and suffering, I have such compassion that a little hole is created in my heart. Since I have heard and listened to a great many Jews with their problems and anguish, there are a great many holes in my heart. I'm an old Jew, and when I start to pray I take my heart and place it before God. He sees this broken heart, so many holes, so many splits, so He has compassion for my heart and that's why He listens to me. He listens to my prayers."

Compassion, the love of life and the love of people—these are difficult things to comprehend and to attain. It takes a great deal of inner cultivation to attain real love and real compassion. It takes also a new conception about the relevance of beauty and the marvel and mystery of everything that exists. And this is given in Hasidism.

A relatively unknown statement of the Ba'al Shem Tov which I cherish is a comment on the famous verse in the Book of Ecclesiastes: "Vanity, oh vanity, everything is vanity." Said the Ba'al Shem: "This is the true meaning of the verse in the light of the last verse of the whole book. A man who says what God has created is vanity, vanity of vanities, anything he does, his studies, his goodness, his worship are vanity, what chutzpah, what blasphemy! How dare men say that life is vanity?" Life is a great experience and a great opportunity for exaltation for the greatest. In a period of such depression, such cynicism, to rediscover that what God has created has a meaning and to rediscover that God Himself is a meaning without all the mysteries is really something that speaks to modern men. Therefore, ultimately the great message that Hasidism can give to us is hope and exaltation.

Dissent (Date Unknown)

Our final brief essay, "Dissent," found in Heschel's unpublished literary remains, shows the daring and oppositional spirit of Hasidism in its early days. In particular Heschel found this prophetic, courageously contrary voice embodied in the fiery, rebellious teachings of the Kotsker Rebbe, an iconoclastic Hasidic master who refused to countenance sham piety and fought against external and ignorant conformity.

This piece, a more universal recasting of the Kotsker's ethos, contains an implied cry that contemporary society and religion are sorely in need of such a strong dissenting message — one that will carry within it something of the courage that allowed Abraham and his followers to be called by the name 'ivri (Hebrew), which the ancient rabbis insisted on defining as "contrarian": "All the world stood on one side, and Abraham on the other."[39]

Inherent to all traditional religion is the peril of stagnation. What becomes settled and established may easily turn foul. Insight is replaced by clichés, elasticity by obstinacy, spontaneity by habit. Acts of dissent prove to be acts of renewal.

It is therefore of vital importance for religious people to voice and to appreciate dissent. And dissent implies self-examination, critique, discontent.

Dissent is indigenous to Judaism. The prophets of ancient Israel who rebelled against a religion that would merely serve the self-interest or survival of the people continue to stand out as inspiration and example of dissent to this very day.

An outstanding feature dominating all Jewish books composed during the first five hundred years of our era is the fact that together with the normative view a dissenting view is nearly always offered, whether in theology or in law. Dissent continued during the finest periods of Jewish history: great scholars sharply disagreed with Maimonides; Hasidism, which brought so much illumination and inspiration into Jewish life, was a movement of dissent.

In the past centuries, even under conditions of repression and of danger to their very existence, Jews continued to persist in their dissent from both Judaism and Christianity, thus retaining a spiritual loyalty unmatched in the history of humanity.

Judaism in its very essence came into being as an act of dissent, of dissent from paganism, as an act of nonconformity with the surrounding culture.[40] And unless we continue to dissent, unless we continue to say NO to idol worship in the name of a higher YES, we will revert to paganism.

The greatness of the prophets was in their ability to voice dissent and disagreements not only with the beliefs of their pagan neighbors, but also with the cherished values and habits of their own people.

Is there dissent in Judaism today? Creative dissent comes out of love and faith, offering positive alternatives, a vision. The scarcity of creative dissent today may be explained by the absence of assets that make creative dissent possible: deep caring, concern, untrammeled radical thinking informed by rich learning, a degree of audacity and courage, and the power of the word. The dearth of people who are both rooted in Jewish learning and who think clearly and care deeply, who are endowed with both courage and power of the word, may account for the spiritual vacuum, for the state of religious existence today.

Judaism whose stance is audacity is presented as a religion of complacency; Judaism is a call to grandeur, but what we hear is a system of trivialities, commonplaces, clichés.

So much of what is given out as Jewish thinking is obsolete liberalism or narrow parochialism. The education offered in most Jewish schools in insipid, flat, and trivial.

There are dissenters in Judaism today. Yet those who attract the most attention are frivolous, while those who are authentic speak in a small still voice which the Establishment is unable to hear.

Suggestions for Further Reading

Green, Arthur. "Abraham Joshua Heschel: Re-Casting Hasidism for Moderns." *Modern Judaism* 29, no. 1 (2009): 62–79.

———. "God's Need for Man: A Unitive Approach to the Writings of Abraham Joshua Heschel." *Modern Judaism* 35, no. 3 (2015): 247–61.

Held, Shai. *Abraham Joshua Heschel: The Call of Transcendence.* Bloomington: Indiana University Press, 2013.

Heschel, Abraham Joshua. *The Earth Is the Lord's: The Inner World of the Jew in Eastern Europe.* New York: Farrar, Straus & Giroux, 1949.

———. *Moral Grandeur and Spiritual Audacity: Essays.* Edited by Susannah Heschel. New York: Farrar, Straus & Giroux, 1996.

———. *The Sabbath: Its Meaning for Modern Man.* New York: Farrar, Straus & Young, 1951.

Kaplan, Edward K. *Spiritual Radical: Abraham Joshua Heschel in America, 1940–1972.* New Haven: Yale University Press, 2007.

Kaplan, Edward K., and Samuel H. Dresner. *Abraham Joshua Heschel: Prophetic Witness.* New Haven: Yale University Press, 1998.

Marmur, Michael. *Abraham Joshua Heschel and the Sources of Wonder.* Toronto: University of Toronto Press, 2016.

4

Shlomo Carlebach

Introduction

Rabbi Shlomo Carlebach (1925–94) was a gifted musician, teacher, and storyteller.[1] The scion of a great rabbinic family, he was raised in a traditional German Orthodox community but met the spiritually infused religious world of Hasidism in his youth.[2] In the 1960s he came to imagine a renewal of contemporary Jewish life grounded in Hasidic teachings. He spoke frequently of the need to mobilize Hasidism's spiritual legacy to lift the hearts and minds of Israel out of the Holocaust's incomparable damage. Described variously as the Singing Rabbi, the Dancing *Rebbe*, and the Hasidic Troubadour, Reb Shlomo, as he was popularly known, became a worldwide Jewish sensation. His influence spilled across both geographic and denominational boundaries.[3]

Shlomo and his twin brother Eli Chaim were born in Berlin but raised in Baden bei Wien, a town frequented by members and leaders of several Hasidic communities. On the eve of the Second World War, the Carlebach family escaped to Brooklyn, where Shlomo continued his studies, in the academies of Torah Vodaas and Lakewood, under the aegis of the great Rabbi Aharon Kotler.

In the late 1940s, however, he left the insular *yeshivah* world, following his brother to the Chabad court. The Chabad community, while strictly Orthodox, was already beginning to show signs of interest in reaching beyond its own borders to assimilated and secular American Jews. Reb Shlomo later described this move from Lakewood, New Jersey, to Brooklyn's Crown Heights, then a secular enclave with a small Hasidic community, as having been motivated by the desire to help the Jewish people after the Holocaust.[4] Chabad had a message of spiritual uplift and engagement to share with a people shattered by the Nazi death machine.

Before long the young Shlomo was tasked with gaining recruits for Chabad. In this sense he (along with Reb Zalman, the subject of the next chapter) differs from the figures previously discussed. Earlier Neo-Hasidic figures, such as Buber and Zeitlin, had inveighed in writing against the apathetic and spiritually vapid lives of secularized European Jews, but neither had suggested that their readers should actually become *Hasidim*. Heschel and Carlebach, by contrast, sought to bring the values of Hasidic inwardness to Jews who lived outside the Hasidic world.

Shlomo began as a member of, and a recruiter for, an actual Hasidic community. Chabad in America started a novel program of outreach, specifically aimed at turning assimilated, non-Orthodox Jews toward a traditional life of commitment and observance. Created by Rabbi Yosef Yitzchak Schneersohn and blossoming under the leadership of his son-in-law Rabbi Menachem Mendel Schneerson, the initiative had little precedent in the Hasidic world. The Hasidic community of Eastern Europe in the early twentieth century was operating mostly in a defensive posture, struggling hard to maintain the loyalty of its own youth, lacking the strength or the foresight to reach out to others.

Lubavitch, growing in strength in interwar Poland, did attract young people from outside its own orbit, but these were drawn from the traditionally observant community. It was the shock and terrible sense of loss in the Holocaust (perhaps combined with an already incipient messianism) that moved the *rebbes* toward a broader commitment to outreach, first among American Jews and then worldwide. Those who conceived this program came to believe that the Jewish people needed more than great Talmudic or Hasidic scholars: they needed sensitive, dynamic rabbis who could "talk to people about Judaism."[5] Shlomo, especially with guitar in hand, was an ideal model for this approach.

Together with a brilliant and outgoing young colleague named Zalman Schachter (see chap. 5), Reb Shlomo visited college campuses and gave impromptu performances that included Hasidic stories and music. Both originally hoped that Jews inspired by their teachings, melodies, and stories would journey to Crown Heights and devote themselves to traditional lives of observance in the Chabad mold.

However, even in these early years, Reb Shlomo shaped his presentation of the Hasidic tradition so that it would speak to the postwar seekers. He understood that key elements of Hasidism and Hasidic spirituality could address the existential and social questions of his day, but uncovering these messages and translating them into a contemporary key was a creative enterprise. He also understood that certain elements within the Hasidic legacy (especially religious exclusivism and disdain for other traditions) should be played down.

Throughout the 1950s Reb Shlomo continued traveling widely, and his reputation as a talented Jewish performer grew. His impressive musical talent drew him into the orbit of the growing folk-music culture of the 1960s. He received invitations to play (and he always combined some teaching and storytelling with his musical performances) at venues outside the Jewish community and together with well-known personalities.

As his fame and acceptance grew, he began drifting away from Chabad. The first key issue was the Orthodox insistence on strict gender separations and the prohibition against men's listening to the voices of women singing. Shlomo understood that he could not insist on these at his public appearances, and that even attempting to do so would drive a wedge between himself and those he was trying to reach.[6] In the course of his spiritual journey to share the riches of Hasidism with modern seekers, Reb Shlomo was being dramatically reshaped by the new generation of Jewish youth.[7]

In 1966 Reb Shlomo was invited to participate in the Berkeley Folk Festival. There in the Bay Area he saw the counterculture world in all its beauty and complexity: youthful energy, rebellion, drug addiction, sexual liberation, spirituality, the quest to recover one's roots, a longing for peace and universalism, a deep distrust of authority, and the fundamental belief that the world is broken and in need of repair. Deeply attracted to the soulfulness of many young people he met in that world, Reb Shlomo discovered that many were more open to his own sort of spirituality than many Jews in the yeshiva world of his upbringing. At the same time, he was critical of the hippie culture of the 1960s, which he quickly interpreted as a displaced yearning for the sacred among a generation dissatisfied with the empty, closed-minded bourgeois life of their parents.

Throughout the 1960s and 1970s Reb Shlomo attended hippie gatherings and cultural or religious ceremonies of all kinds, performing together with swamis, gurus, and other spiritual sages. He became a unique phenomenon on the American countercultural scene, a rabbi who was viewed not as a representative of the conventional Judaism that so many of his hearers had rejected, but as a profound and loving spiritual figure who could join the ranks of the various Eastern teachers who flocked to North America during those decades. In 1967 he founded the House of Love and Prayer,[8] a synagogue for spiritual seekers in San Francisco, as well as an experiment in communal living and a loving home for lost souls.[9] Although women did not lead its services, the House (which would exist in various forms for nearly ten years) created a far more embracing and welcoming space for them, without the traditional separation of sexes found in Orthodox houses of worship.

Continuing the Hasidic emphasis on the power of prayer, the House of Love and Prayer also allowed Reb Shlomo to emphasize the Shabbat atmosphere as a means of inspiring ecstatic experiences rivaling those induced by psychoactive drugs in the hippie counterculture. One of his popular songs from these years, "Lord, Get Me High," was also sung to the opening words of "A Psalm for the Sabbath Day." Shabbat eve with Shlomo, whether at the House in San Francisco, at the shul in New York, or on the road, was a grand event, featuring singing, teaching, and storytelling, a spiritual love-feast that would go on into all hours of the night.

When the House of Love and Prayer closed its doors in 1977, many of its former members joined other disciples of Reb Shlomo in founding a community in Israel called Moshav Me'or Modi'in. This settlement, located between Jerusalem and Tel Aviv, might be described as part *yeshiva*, part pioneer kibbutz, and part Jewish ashram. It was, at least in part, Reb Shlomo's vision of a Neo-Hasidic community. Life in common involved agricultural labor as well as devoted and joyful worship and study. The rhythms of life—and communal standards—were largely traditional, even though the community was somewhat diverse in its approaches to Jewish practice and life. Reb Shlomo never made Me'or Modi'in his permanent home, but he spent a great deal of time there over the next two decades.

Although he became increasingly interested in Israel after the 1967 Six-Day War, Reb Shlomo had begun to make an impact in the Holy Land considerably earlier.[10] Concerts he gave throughout Israel during a series of visits between 1959 and 1961 attracted both religious and secular young followers. He was especially welcoming of young people from the Middle Eastern Jewish communities and from lower socio-economic strata, who felt like outsiders to an Israel created by the Ashkenazic elite. He was also fiercely active in promoting morale among soldiers in the aftermath of the many wars. Here he drew upon Rav Kook (perhaps more the "spirit" of Rav Kook) in claiming that the work of "secular" people involved in sacred pursuits has a spiritual kernel. Just as this was true for American hippies seeking to live lives of peace and justice, it was equally true of Israeli soldiers who put their lives as risk—and often made the ultimate sacrifice for the Jewish people.[11]

Reb Shlomo saw himself as carrying forward the spiritual legacy of Hasidism. Like the other Neo-Hasidic figures in this book, he understood that Hasidism was primarily grounded in the inward approach to religion.[12] But in addition to this focus on interior spirituality, Reb Shlomo also showed people a new way of living, grounded in the sacred rites of Jewish observance that express inner devotion. He did not rebel against the practices of Orthodox Judaism, but rather against its intellectual small-mindedness, its rote or perfunctory approach to religious service, and its failure to recognize the paramount importance of the inner world, all of which he saw as being tragically widespread within contemporary Orthodoxy.[13] The years Shlomo had spent in Lakewood were very much apparent to the more Jewishly educated among his listeners. He had a unique talent for bringing forth a vibrant spiritual message from a page of Talmud or a paragraph in the Shulchan Arukh, texts that others understood simply as dry codes of law.

Reb Shlomo's recasting of Hasidism was also very much informed by the tragedy of the Holocaust. Through Hasidic teachings and stories, he emphasized that there is meaning beyond absurdity, that life may be full of joy and exaltation even after the aporia and immeasurable loss of the Holocaust. Every moment, and each action, be it ritual or seemingly mundane, should be vested with meaning and transformed into a sacred encounter with God and a true and intense connection with another human being. He also stressed the practice of absolute and unconditional love of others, the infinite capacity of human kindness, the devotional interconnectivity across members of a community (and between individuals of different circles), and joyful compassion toward all. All of these would become key elements of his spiritual legacy.

The issue of universalism, or legitimacy of other religions, was a point of deep ambivalence. On some level, Reb Shlomo was very open to the idea of sharing and learning from other faith traditions—a perspective constituting at least as big a break with his past as his rethinking of women's roles. And the many stories about Reb Shlomo's infinite kindness to his "holy beggar" street people extended beyond Jews, raising the question as to whether some greater inclusive theory of his lay behind his well-known practices. He had in effect translated Hasidic notions of *ahavat Yisra'el*, the love of all Jews that characterizes Hasidism, into an all-encompassing posture of love and acceptance. All humanity, he felt, embodied sparks of the Divine.[14]

Still, while extending his love and openheartedness toward non-Jews, he did not truly accept the legitimacy of other religions. To those close to him, he would confide that he was appearing publicly with Eastern spiritual teachers in order to wean their Jewish followers away from them and bring them back to Judaism. Unlike his more Aquarian-minded colleague Reb Zalman, something in Reb Shlomo stopped him from incorporating elements of other religions into his spiritual teachings. In this way his legacy remains very much an intensely—and intensively—Jewish project.

Above all, Shlomo Carlebach is most widely remembered for his stirring and inspiring music,[15] which blended folk traditions with an innovative Hasidic style. Understanding both the pedagogical value and the aesthetic power of song, he once explained: "I began to sing my songs, and in between one song and another I realized I could talk to people about Judaism, because when they sing their hearts are open."[16] This Neo-Hasidic devotional aim of opening an audience's hearts to a spiritual message is clearly visible in the accompanying notes from his 1965 album *Mikdash Melekh*:

> Now a vibrant new Jewish personality has emerged to express the Hassidic heritage in the context of our times. Rabbi Shlomo Carlebach, directly descended through a noteworthy rabbinic line of scholars, seeks to make manifest the original message of Hassidism. Shlomo is an Orthodox rabbi, a man of God—but he is also a folk singer in the truest sense of the word. A bard who utters, from the fibers of his own being, music and

words that speak with the world around him, Shlomo is a link in our time to the heroic figure of the Baal Shem Tov. In his presence one may experience that glow of warmth and courage, the Hassidic spark of divine fire that melts estrangement and soul weariness.[17]

The many hundreds of tunes Reb Shlomo composed have seeped into Jewish communities across the globe. Some have essentially supplanted the traditional melodies of prayer, and many have become so universal that they are no longer associated with him. Many of them are deceptively simple and appealing, although some, particularly his early works, are quite musically complex. Throughout his career he was very careful to ensure the correct preservation of the melodies, demanding absolute precision from his students and followers.[18]

Reb Shlomo was also famous for his original renditions of Hasidic tales. His appearances always included a selection of Hasidic stories, chosen for their thematic links to his musical numbers as well as for the occasion. Unlike Martin Buber, who reworked the stories in written translation to make them accessible to a broad readership, Reb Shlomo was an oral storyteller who mastered the art of live performance. Reb Shlomo was additionally less explicit about the creative element of his tales than Buber.[19] But he too had inherited the notion that Hasidic stories are meant to inspire, and therefore one must always fuse the ethos of Hasidism with the needs of the contemporary listener.

Some of Reb Shlomo's tales were included on musical discs, though many were printed in written form only after his death or continued to circulate among friends and disciples. The message uniting all his stories, often heartrending and always inspiring, is quite clear: life in the face of death, meaning in the face of absurdity, intimate connection in the face of intractable loneliness, and sublime altruism and unquenchable goodness in the face of unspeakable cruelty and destruction.

The following story (told in his own idiosyncratic English) is Reb Shlomo's rendition of a tale about Rabbi Kalonymous Kalman Shapira of Piaseczno. This Hasidic teacher, murdered in the Holocaust, was esteemed for his legendary dedication to cultivating children's ethical lives and inner worlds.

Open your hearts, my friends. One day, one day a few years ago, I walked out on the Yarkon, the street by the beach in Tel Aviv and here I saw a hunchback, so broken, so broken. His face was beautiful and most handsome, but his whole body was completely misfigured. Sweeping the floor, sweeping the streets. I had a feeling this person was special and I said, *"Shalom lekha"* [Peace unto you]. He answered back in very heavy Polish Yiddish, Hebrew, he says, *"Aleykhem shulem"* [And peace unto you]. I said, "Are you from Poland?" He said, "Yes, I am from Piaseczno." I couldn't believe it, "Piaseczno!" I said to him, "Have you ever seen the Holy Rav Kalonymous Kalman?" He says, "What do you mean have I saw him? I learned in his *yeshivah*, in his school from the age of five until I was eleven. When I was eleven I came to Auschwitz. I was so strong they thought I was seventeen. I was whipped and kicked and hit, and I never healed. That's the way I look now." He says, "I have nobody in the world; I am all alone." He kept on sweeping the floor.

I said to him, "My sweetest friend, do you know my whole life I have been waiting to see you, a person who saw Rav Kalonymous Kalman, a person who was one of his children. Please give me over one of his teachings." He looked at me and he says, "Do you think I can be in Auschwitz for five years and still remember teachings?" I said, "Yes, I am sure, the *heylikker* [holy one] Rav Kalonymous Kalman's teachings, how could you forget them?" He was a real *hassidishe yid*, so he says, "Okay, wait." He went to wash his hands, fixed his tie, put on his jacket, and he says to me one more time, "Do you really want to hear it?" So I said to him, "I swear to you, I will give over your teaching all over the world." I have never seen such big tears in my life.

He said: "I want you to know, until the Messiah comes, until *Moshiah* is coming, there will never be such a *Shabbos* again. Can you imagine the *heylikker* Rebbe, the holy master, dancing *boi be-shalom* [Come in peace, from "Lekha Dodi"], dancing with hundreds, maybe thousands of children? Can you imagine the *heylikker* Rebbe singing Friday night '*Shalom aleykhem, malakhey ha-shalom*' [Greetings to you, holy angels!]. I want you to know the Rebbe said *Toyrah* between the fish and the soup, the soup and the chicken, and then the chicken and the dessert. The *Toyrah*, the teaching, on the Torah portion of the week, I don't remember." But here he says, "Open your heart." He pierced my soul, like he gave me over the deepest depths of his heart. He says, "I want you to know, after every teaching this is what the Rebbe said, '*Kinderlakh, tayyere kinderlakh* — children, most precious children — *gedenkt zhe* — remember — *di greste zakh in di velt iz, ti'en emetsen a toyvah*' — children remember, the greatest thing in the world is to do somebody else a favor." [Reb Shlomo to the audience:] Join me — "Children, remember, the greatest thing in the world is to do somebody else a favor."

"I came to Auschwitz, I knew my parents were dead, my whole family doesn't exist anymore. I wanted to commit suicide. At the last moment I could hear my Rebbe's voice saying, '*Kinderlakh, Kinderlakh*, the greatest thing in the world is to do somebody else a favor.'" He says, "Do you know how many favors you can do in Auschwitz at night, when people are lying on the floor crying and nobody even has strength to listen to their stories anymore. I would walk from one person to the other and say, 'why are you crying?' And they would tell me about their children, about their wife, things they will never see in this life again, until *moshiah* is coming. I would hold their hands and cry with them. Walk to another person. This gave me strength for a few weeks. When I was at the end, I would hear my Rebbe's voice. I want you to know I am here in Tel Aviv and I have nobody in the world. But you know, there are moments when I take off my shoes and I go down to the beach, and I am already up to my nose in the ocean, but I can't help it, but I would hear my Rebbe's voice again saying, 'The greatest thing in the world is— remember precious children—the greatest thing in the world is to do somebody else a favor.'"

He looked at me for a long time and says, "Do you know how many favors you can do on the streets of the world?" He kept on sweeping the streets.

This was before Rosh Hashanah. I had to go back to New York. The first night of Hanukkah, I came back the next morning, early, I am back on the Yarkon looking for my holy hunchback. I couldn't find him. I asked some people, "Have you ever seen the holy hunchback, the street cleaner?" They said, "Don't you know, don't you know, on the second day of *Sukkos*, he left the world." Listen to me children, the *moshiah* is coming—let it be today, let it be tonight, let it be soon—when God will redeem the world and all the holy people will come out of their graves, and the holy hunchback and the holy street cleaner, he will come back again, and he will clean the streets of the world. And you know how he will clean the streets? By teaching the world that the greatest thing in the world is to do somebody else a favor.[20]

In every Reb Shlomo story, there is a crux—a moment in which he invites his audience to open their hearts. And even the most hardened and apathetic of listeners cannot hear a sentence such as "Do you know how many favors you can do in Auschwitz at night?" without being touched.

In the process of teaching and touching listeners, Reb Shlomo also creatively deployed Hasidic teachings. Frequently he invoked the sermons of Rabbi Mordecai Yosef of Izhbitz, Rabbi Nahman of Bratslav, and Rabbi Kalonymous Kalman Shapira of Piaseczno, helping to popularize their more modern works among a contemporary readership. He also often quoted from a variety of early Hasidic masters and the leaders of Polish Hasidism, but he never quoted those teachings verbatim or simply paraphrased their contents. Always he summarized and repackaged these messages in ways that spoke to his audience. On a number of occasions, in fact, he handed out copies of Hasidic books to his followers, directing each selection to his intended recipient and thus suggesting that this particular work held a key to that person's spiritual growth.

The following is one of the innumerable teachings by Hasidic masters that Reb Shlomo offered over the decades of his career. It begins with Rabbi Mordecai Yosef Leiner's teaching on the biblical prohibition against a priest coming in contact with a dead body. Reb Leiner notes that the confrontation with death makes one sad, whereas the priests are charged with serving God with joy:

> "Speak to the priests, sons of Aaron, saying to them: Do not defile yourself for a person among your people" (Lev. 21:1). The priest is called one who serves God. He sees that all the things that happen in the world are not random, but are divine providence. He knows that God's will is only to do good things for His creations. Such a person can come to anger with God when he sees some happening that is an expression of the blessed Holy One's stern judgment. One who has concluded that the world is but happenstance cannot be so angry when he sees something against his will. He can say that it was random. But one who knows that everything is in the hands of Heaven can become angry.[21]

A second teaching from Rabbi Mordecai Yosef continues as follows:

> Seeing death is the opposite of joy. Thus "Speak to the priests" —
> they should see to it that they do not cause the opposite, since they
> are chosen to draw forth the flow of joy, and to bring pleasure to
> the blessed Holy One through their service.[22]

Rabbi Mordecai Yosef of Izhbitz suggests that a *Kohen* must not be
allowed to encounter death because it induces anger about the seeming
injustice of God's providence. This attitude of enraged protest would
make it impossible for the priest to perform his religious function. In
the second teaching, the Hasidic master adds that priests have been
tasked with serving God in a state of pure and constant joy.

Reb Shlomo, however, combines these two distinct homilies into a
single teaching and then extends their relevance into the present day.
We serve God through prayer and study, he says, and our worship must
be founded in joy. Yet this pure joy is impossible after the Holocaust,
to which our response can only be anger. But all is not lost:

> And you know, my sweetest friends, today we don't have a *Beit
> HaMikdash*, a Holy Temple, and although we still have *kohanim*,
> priests, we don't have animal or incense offerings to serve God in
> the Holy Temple. Today we serve God through offering words of
> Torah study and words of prayer. Today our rabbis are like our
> priests, serving God through teaching Torah. But if you are angry
> with God, you can't teach Torah. You can say the words, but the
> love and light within them do not flow through them.
>
> So please open your hearts. The saddest thing is that today our
> teachers and rabbis haven't just touched [just] one dead person.
> They've been touched by Six Million dead people. And they are
> so angry with God, so angry with god. *Gevald*, are they angry with

god! And because they are so angry with God, all their words of Torah are just that: words. There's no light, no taste, no meaning, no melody in them.[23]

But young people today are so hungry for that light, for that meaning, for that melody—for the deepest inner dimensions of truth. And if they can't get it from Judaism, they'll go anywhere that love and light are to be found.

Thank God for our hungry, searching, younger generation who found some traditions that weren't so angry with God. . . . And today in Judaism, *Baruch HaShem*, thank God, we have a whole new generation of teachers who haven't been touched directly by the Six Million (or maybe they have taken Six Million *mikvahs* from tears of sadness and then another Six Million *mikvahs* from tears of joy). And their words are filled with light and joy and love.[24]

Optimism and happiness, Reb Shlomo asserts, must be maintained despite the brokenness of the Holocaust, despite the world having been turned upside down. In the wake of Auschwitz, things cannot continue as they have always have; it is not enough to recreate the worlds of Eastern European piety from the shattered pieces. In its stead, the vital spirituality of contemporary seekers, running from new rivers and holy places untainted by anger at the Nazis, needs to be embraced.

Reb Shlomo knew that Jews would go to other sources of inspiration if they could not find an authentic Jewish language for their quest. Remarkably, he did not condemn them for that. Rather, he acknowledged that the shattered Jewish people was in need of the new generation's type of pure joy and illumination.[25]

Reb Shlomo embodied the itinerant Hasidic master in the modern world, constantly moving from place to place and illuminating the people around him.[26] Through personal interactions and Neo-Hasidic performances infused with stories, teachings, and music, he transformed the lives of hundreds of people and affected many thousands more.[27] He also trained a number of individuals, ordaining some as rabbis and others as different kinds of spiritual leaders.[28] Notably, he gave rabbinic ordination to women as well, taking such a bold step far before the issue arose in the mainstream Orthodox community. These disciples have continued to carry forward Reb Shlomo's message of hope, kindness, and spiritual uplift throughout the world.

Another side of Reb Shlomo's life must also be addressed. Allegations of behavioral impropriety and sexual misconduct began to surface shortly after his death. Some date back to the 1960s, and new allegations have continued to emerge into the present day. There is no disputing that Shlomo sometimes acted toward young women in his orb in unacceptable and deplorable ways, taking advantage of his personal charisma and of the very great trust his followers had in him. This is the case even by the standards of the time in which the events occurred, but is magnified when judged by the ethos of our own day. This should be stated without equivocation or defense.

A decade after Reb Shlomo's death, Reb Zalman Schachter-Shalomi delivered a multifaceted eulogy. Having known Reb Shlomo across some fifty years, Reb Zalman spoke glowingly of the impact of his personal charm and the enduring intellectual and spiritual message he had bequeathed the Jewish people. As a fellow traveler and friend who had come to the States shortly before the wholesale destruction of European Jewry, Reb Zalman also deeply understood and reflected upon the resilience—and creativity—of Reb Shlomo's soul. At the same time, he touched upon some of the complicated elements of Reb Shlomo's personal legacy.[29]

"Can you imagine what it was," said Reb Zalman, "for his soul to be judged by God after his life. There one is so totally transparent, there is no place to hide, and the good and the evil of a person's life is weighed at that time." Without papering over the negative elements of Shlomo's legacy, Reb Zalman proceeded to highlight his unique Neo-Hasidic contribution to contemporary Jewish life.

The impact of Reb Shlomo's teachings and music has not abated in the years since his death.[30] His project cannot easily be described in full, and a host of very different disciples claim to be carrying forward his mantle.[31] His devoted followers, all of whom may rightly be called Neo-Hasidim, run the gamut from Orthodox to liberal and avowedly heterodox.[32] Reb Shlomo's own perspective, however, tended toward a traditional—if unconventional and expansive—religious ethos.[33] He maintained close connections with many parts of the Orthodox and Hasidic world. And although Reb Shlomo disregarded particular laws or customs, especially those that erected boundaries between people (metaphorically as well as physically), his commitment to Jewish practice was quite traditional.

Reb Shlomo experimented throughout his life, but in the end he never made a full break with his past in the Orthodox world. In this sense he may be said to have interpreted an idea central to the theology of the Izhbitz Hasidic dynasty to which he so frequently turned. We may still live within the framework of *halakhah*, he taught, but our dreams reach far beyond it. In rare times and under circumstances, the will of God and the *halakhah* as codified are not identical, and in those moments we must have the audacity to break free and answer the call of the hour. He saw himself as living in such a moment.[34]

Reb Shlomo's public career as an energetic performer and teacher spanned nearly five decades, but the fact that he wrote very little has made it difficult for those coming after him to appreciate his contributions. His thoughts must be pieced together from oral testimonies or from fragments of teachings recorded and transcribed by private individuals.

One such teaching, entitled "Torah of the Nine Months," is outstanding in every way, and thus serves as our chapter's single example of Reb Shlomo's erudition, wisdom, and heart. The following comments preceding the selection, by scholar Nehemia Polen, offer readers the needed background to understand the arc of Reb Shlomo's teaching.

Introduction to "The Torah of the Nine Months"

While Shlomo Carlebach's music is now universally known and his stories are widely told, his work as an innovative teacher of Torah in the Hasidic tradition is just beginning to be appreciated. To be sure, a number of books have been published that present his thoughts, primarily on Torah and the festivals, but these are generally excerptions, rearranged and edited. The bursts of illumination are moving and impressive, but the dazzling flashes are not always fully contextualized or presented in their original sequence. It is true that during concerts—when words must not overwhelm or displace the music—Carlebach's remarks did have an aphoristic character. But there is another, less well-known genre of Carlebach teaching—the expansive discourse, delivered at a measured pace, often unfolding over a period of hours. The setting would be a postconcert gathering in a private home, or a stand-alone "learning"—that is, an event whose primary focus was the transmission of an extended teaching on a specific theme rather than a musical performance. At these events Carlebach could be seen intently studying a *sefer* [book], then lifting his eyes off the printed word, gazing at a point far removed in space and time from the book or his immediate surroundings, in a reverie of soaring spirit. Eventually he would speak, beginning with a signature phrase, such as "Everybody knows. . . ." He would introduce a theme—perhaps a single biblical term or rabbinic passage—that announced the "home key," then develop the theme, juxtaposing related texts, sharing stories and anecdotes that held implications for the religious life and the human situation. After perhaps twenty minutes he would fall silent, closing his eyes in deep reflection. This might be followed by a *nigun*, accompanied by gentle guitar strumming if the teaching took place on a weekday. It could be discerned, if one took care to notice, that the *nigun* was related, by words or mood, to the theme of the discourse. After allowing the *nigun* ample opportunity to stretch open, spread its wings, and nestle in the hearts of all present, he finally set it free so that it rose above the sonic horizon into silence. Then the process would begin again, for another long segment of teaching, exposition, reflection, *nigun*, and silence. Depending on the setting, the segments could be repeated for the better part of a day or evening.

These sessions were unscripted, undetermined, largely unplanned. Like the most riveting and accomplished jazz musicians, Carlebach seemed to have little conscious control over what was going to emerge at the next moment, nor memory of the content after the teaching ended. Such an event was an extended channeling, a transmission from a plane beyond, an open conduit from the kabbalistic Ayin, the realm of sacred Nothing.

Those present at such moments were aware that they were witnessing unparalleled virtuosity, the fresh conjuration of a tradition of electrifying discourse whose lineage comprised the great masters of Hasidism, the sages of early Midrash, arguably traceable as far back as the biblical prophets themselves.

Yet awareness is not the same as understanding, much less is it analytic comprehension. It was not easy to grasp the sweep of such expansive teachings as they unfolded, and to this day their full significance has eluded both Carlebach devotees and the scholarly community. The first step is to realize that for all their scope and variety, each discourse is generated by a core idea that launches the exposition, hovers continuously in the background, and returns at the end for a coda of resolution. The genre is theme-and-variation, as some aspect of the basic motif is brought repeatedly into surprising and supple juxtaposition with other motifs and classic texts, all in service of addressing spiritual challenges, illuminating the vagaries of religious journeys, and navigating the joys and pitfalls of interpersonal relationships.

The teaching offered here was delivered one summer in the early 1970s at Tannersville, New York, a small community in the Catskill Mountains, where Jews fleeing big-city heat owned vacation homes or rented bungalows; the summer community was largely Orthodox. Carlebach's discourse unfolded at an unhurried pace over several hours. The participants formed a small and intimate group: Carlebach himself, Zalman Schachter (later Zalman Schachter-Shalomi), and their wives. The protected intimacy of the location, the trusted closeness of Carlebach's interlocutors, and the open-ended spaciousness of the occasion encouraged Carlebach to develop his theme unhurriedly, allowing for the full flowering of his expository brilliance. The teaching, called "Torah of the Nine Months," showcases Carlebach's interpretive powers, inexhaustible creativity, and unique gift for transposing ancient themes into a contemporary key.

The foundational passage that launches the teaching is a talmudic *aggadah* (b. Niddah 30b) describing the life of the embryo in its mother's womb. The passage reads in part:

A lamp is kindled for the embryo above its head, and it foresees and gazes from one end of the world to the other, as Scripture says, "When His lamp shone over my head, and by its light I walked through darkness (Job 29:3)." ... And a person experiences no happier days than those days [in the womb], as Scripture says, "O that I were as in months of old, in the days when God watched over me" (Job 29:2). ...

They teach [the embryo] the entire Torah, complete, as Scripture says, "He instructed me and said to me, 'Let your heart hold fast My words, Keep my commandments and you will live'" (Prov. 4:4). And it further says, "When the secret of God graced my tent" (Job 29:4). ...

As soon as the newborn reaches the airspace of the world, an angel comes, slaps it on the mouth and makes it forget the entire Torah, complete. ...

The prooftexts that propel this *aggadah* come from the Bible's wisdom literature, especially the book of Job. This book is an outlier in the biblical canon, a counterpoint to the typical assurance that piety assures felicity. Job invites us to test received wisdom against experience and to ask difficult questions about human existence and the trajectory of our lives. A central theme is one's place in the world—at first Job enjoys a place of esteem, then loses it in a painful and humiliating manner, and finally regains place and stature. The theme of chap. 29, upon which the talmudic passage draws, is Job's reminiscence of his role in the community, his depiction of the respect and deference he commanded. The first bold interpretive move is thus already made by the *aggadah* itself—recasting Job's aching nostalgia for his earlier prominence into a reflective commentary on the embryo's life in the womb.

Like many earlier Hasidic masters, Carlebach lifts up and extends the thematic lines already laid down in the *aggadah* and midrash. For the great theme of the "Torah of the Nine Months" is human individuation and the struggle of each individual to find his or her place in the world. This is the *torah*—the instruction—cultivated in the womb. While not exactly in opposition to the Torah of Sinai—the commandments and rituals of normative Jewish practice—the Torah of the Nine Months may be in fruitful, sometimes tense, dialogue with it. Only by struggle, only through trial and error, can each person uncover his or her *torah*, his or her unique perspective, voice, role, and place in the world. The full realization will arrive only at the moment of death. That is why the embryo gazes "from one end of the world to the other"—scoping out a congenial spot to inhabit, to make its own, from which to grow, learn, teach, and shine. Because that site has never been settled before, the process inevitably involves both acute pain and intense exhilaration.

Carlebach makes explicit what was implicit in the talmudic *aggadah*—that the period of gestation in the womb is not a time for conceptual book learning; the developing embryo is not studying Gemara! Only an exclusively scholastic culture could have misread the passage as referring to mastery of textual material. Already in the Bible, the "lamp" is a figure for the spirit or soul (Prov. 20:27), but in Carlebach's telling, the lamp that accompanies gestation becomes a metonym that appears at all of life's nexus points, including one's wedding day and the day of death but also in sacred home-based rites such as kindling Shabbat candles and searching for leaven the night before Passover. And this suggests that the real function of the lamp or candle is to allow the person to see his or her place in the world.

As his exposition unfolds, Carlebach invokes major biblical figures, often in dyads: Rachel and Leah, Moses and Aaron. The piece in its entirety sheds light on every aspect of the Judaic tradition, infusing it with new meaning and significance. Everything is now bathed in a sacred aura: the neonate, the bride and groom, the home, spoken words of promise and commitment. The "Torah of the Nine Months" suggests a personalism that is not indulgent. There is a call to actualization, but not in a self-centered manner. Personal *torah* prompts noble aspiration, finding oneself for the benefit of others and the fulfillment of the world.

Perhaps the longest and most sustained of Reb Shlomo's extant spiritual teachings, "Torah of the Nine Months" resonates with his creativity, his tremendous erudition, and his ability to grasp the difficult yet ever-present quest of the human spirit in a post-Holocaust world full of complexity and failure.[35]

The Torah of the Nine Months (Undated, 1970s)

Now I want to talk to you about the Torah of the individual. Where do you find this Torah? This is the Torah of the Nine Months. Because I was always thinking: "What is the baby learning during the nine months?"[36] Basically, we were on Mt. Sinai, and then we come back to this world and we had to learn the words to the great light which we had on Mt. Sinai.[37] But what is it that we have to learn in the nine months?

The *Gemora* [Talmud] says *"ner doluk"* —there's a little candle burning, and the baby [inside the womb] sees from one corner of the world to the other. First of all, where does it say when you learn Torah, you must have a candle? *Torah she be-'al peh* [the Oral Torah], that's where you learn by heart, and you don't need a candle. The RaMBaM [Maimonides] says that the most important learning is *Torah she be-'al peh*,[38] which you can learn when it's dark.[39] And where does it say that you have to see from one corner of the world to the other? Where do you have a Torah that you have to look from one corner of the world to the other?[40]

Basically, if I learn Torah, I have to know exactly what to do, what not to do, what to learn; I know what the *Ribbono shel 'Olam* [Master of the World] wants me to do.[41] Where does it say I have to look from one corner of the world to the other?

So obviously we are talking about a completely different Torah, which this child is learning. There's a Torah which you can learn in darkness also. And there's a Torah, *mamash* [truly], that you must have a little light when you're learning it.[42]

This Torah [of the Nine Months] is the Torah of what I have to do in this world. What is the shape of my soul? The shape of my soul is what I have to do in this world. So in the nine months when the *Ribbono shel 'Olam* is forming the body, the *Ribbono shel 'Olam* is also shaping my soul. Shaping my soul is what I have to do in this world: my shape, my spiritual shape.

And I want to say something, a *gevalt* [an amazing idea]: Maybe before we were driven out from paradise, maybe there was no such thing as being an individual. *Le-'ovdah u-le-shomrah* ["to work it, and to keep it," Gen. 2:15] —everybody is doing the same thing.[43] We all had the same soul.[44] Obviously, the *Ribbono shel 'Olam* didn't want us to stay there. Like the Izhbitzer says,[45] "If God wanted us to stay there, he could have made us stay there." I'm sure you remember, the Izhbitzer says that the *Ribbono shel 'Olam* wanted us to make the *'egel ha-zahav* [the Golden Calf]. Otherwise, He would have made us stop.[46]

And why didn't Moshe Rabbenu come in time? Here *kelal Yisro'el* [the community of Israel] are the holiest *yidden* [Jews], the *dor de'ah* [the generation of knowledge], why can't Moshe Rabbenu come down? Why can't they make this clear? So the Izhbitzer says one thing: Eventually we would have made an *'egel ha-zahav*, but we would have never been able to go back. So the *'egel ha-zahav* had to be made by the *yidden* of *Har Sinai* because they knew [i.e., so that they would learn] how to go back.[47]

It says *le-khol ha-mora ha-gadol asher 'asah Moshe le-'eyney kol yisro'el. Be-Reshis bara Elokim* ["all the great awe, which Moses wrought in before the eyes of all Israel," Deut. 34:12; and "In the beginning God created . . ." Gen. 1:1].[48] So the Midrash says *le-khol ha-mora ha-gadol*—what's the most awesome thing Moshe Rabbenu did? It's *sheviras ha-luhos*—he broke the tablets.[49] What does that mean? That means that Moshe Rabbenu taught us two things. On Mt. Sinai, he taught us how to begin. But when he broke the tablets, he taught us *le-'eyney kol Yisro'el, be-reshis bara Elokim* ["before the eyes of all Israel" . . . "In the beginning God created"]. He taught us how to start all over again, which only Moshe Rabbenu can teach.[50] And this Torah is the most awesome Torah in the world. And you know, the thing is like this, you can teach the world how to start. [But] to start all over again, this is specific to every individual.

What's the individual's problem, what's our problem? The problem is not when we are high, but what do we do when we are low. Before, when we were in *Gan 'Eden* [the Garden of Eden], we didn't die. But that means also, spiritually, whenever

I was high I would never get low again. You see, after *Shabbos*, I would stay *Shabbosdik* [on the level of *Shabbos*] until next *Shabbos*, and then I would get higher.[51] After the *het 'ets ha-da'as* [the sin of the Tree of Knowledge], dying means, *mamash*, for five minutes I can be the highest, as holy as Reb Shimon bar Yohai, and then five minutes later, I can be *mamash, has ve-shalom* [God forbid], you know....[52]

The Torah of the individual is two things. First of all, I have to know exactly what did my *neshamah* [soul] come here for? Exactly what am I here for? What's my *tikkun* [repair], and what I am supposed to do.[53] And, second, I will not know how to do this unless I learn my elevator Torah: I'm going up and down, and not to give up. My *tehiyas ha-meysim* Torah [my Torah of resurrection]. How to, *mamash*, stand up again all the time. And one more very important thing, which is also actually the Ishbitzer Torah: there is a Torah which I can learn, just by learning it. But then there's also a Torah of *eyn adam 'omed 'al divrei Torah ela 'im ken nikhshal bah* ["one cannot fully understand the words of Torah without failing at them"].[54] There's a Torah which I only learn by making mistakes.

Which is the Torah which I only learn by mistakes? The Torah which I need the most, that's the one I learn only by mistakes.

Because the Torah which I don't need for fixing my soul, it's enough if I learn it—I learn it and I know it. Obviously that Torah which has to get into me the deepest, that's the one I always fail in. The Izhbitzer says in *Sod Yesharim*,[55] it's also the way the Torah lets you know. He says we always think that the things you always do, let's say putting on *tefillin* every day, means I'm strong in *tefillin*. But the things [where] I fail all the time, that's the things I'm *shvakh* [weak] in. He says *punkt farkert* [just the opposite]. Putting on *tefillin* every day, that means this is nothing.[56] This is not where your *neshamah* is.

But all the things which you always fail in, and you still didn't give up, that's the thing [where] you are the holiest.[57]

So he says, he says a *gevalt* Torah on Sukkos, which is *hag ha-assif* [the Festival of Gathering]. With what am I going into the *Kodesh ha-Kodashim* [Holy of Holies]?[58] He says I'm not going in with my *mitsvos*, I'm going in with *vidui* [confession]. With all the things I'm failing in—this is my *Kodesh ha-Kodashim*.[59]

That part of me, this is when I'm sitting in the *sukkah*, the *or makif* [the surrounding light].[60] I'm sitting in it. It didn't get in yet; it didn't get into me yet. But the surrounding light is so strong that it is my *sukkah*. I'm sitting in it, completely surrounded with it. And obviously I'm not home yet, because if I were at home, I wouldn't need a *sukkah*.[61] But I'm outside. And I'm not in the sun, I'm in the shade.[62] It's always dark. But there I'm getting to the level of realizing that this is my *Kodesh ha-Kodashim*—that part of [me] which always fails. And the *skhakh* [the roof of the sukkah] is made from *pesoles goren ve-yekev* [the leftovers of the threshing floor and winepress].[63] Everything which I can't do anything with. It doesn't grow, you can't eat it, everybody throws it out. So this is the Torah of the Nine Months.

Ya'akov Avinu, before he went *huts la-arets* [i.e., before he left the Land of Israel], went back to [the yeshiva] of Shem and Ever for fourteen years.[64] I want to say this: first he learned the Torah of *Har Sinai*, and the second time he went back, he learned the Torah of the Nine Months.[65]

But what was driving Ya'akov to do this before meeting Rokhel? What's the whole idea of a *bat zug* [your fated beloved]? The *bat zug* is the one who also knows your Torah of the Nine Months. But what's your connection to your *bat zug*? She has the *same* Torah of the Nine Months. Because if I just need the

Torah [of Sinai], I can marry any girl in Boro Park. The Torah
of the Nine Months is something else.[66]

And I want you to know Reb Leybeleh Eiger's Torah [his
teaching], which is a *gevalt*.[67] He says, why is the *taba'at kiddu-
shin* [the wedding ring] round like a letter *samekh*?[68] Because,
he says, the *samekh* refers to *somekh Hashem le-khol ha-noflim*
["Y-H-W-H *supports* all those who have fallen," Ps. 145:14]. He
says the first time there is a *samekh* in the Torah is *va-yisgor
basar tahtenah* ["God closed up the place with flesh thereof,"
Gen. 2:21], and He created Havah [Eve]. He says that a woman
was created to be *somekh Hashem le-khol ha-noflim*, a supporter
to all those who fall. Then he says, this is the Fifteenth of Av.[69]
In the future, the blessed Holy One will make a *circle* of the
tsaddikim–it will be on the Fifteenth of Av.[70] That's the whole
giluiy [revelation] of *somekh Hashem le-khol ha-noflim*. This is
from the last Lubliner, Reb Shloymeleh Eiger.

Everybody knows that Leah was Ya'akov Avinu's soul mate
after he was named *Yisro'el*. *Yisro'el* is *ki sarisa 'im Elokim ve-
'im anashim va-tukhal* ["for you have wrestled with God and
man, and have prevailed," Gen. 32:29]. But she was not his
soul mate on the level of the Nine Months. She was his mate
on [the] level of *moshiah*, when everything is OK [i.e., in a perfect world]. But, Ya'akov Avinu, outside the land of Israel, he
needs a soul mate like Rokhel. In *huts la-arets* [outside of the
land] he needed *somekh Hashem le-khol ha-noflim*.[71]

We see at *keri'as yam suf* [the splitting of the Sea of Reeds], the
sea split because of Yosef.[72] And yet it was Yehudah who jumped
in first.[73] So the first time *Moshiah ben Yosef* and *Moshiah ben
David* got together is the splitting [of] the sea.[74] Yosef Avinu was
splitting the sea, he is doing something, and Yehudah comes
right after that, *mamash mesires nefesh* [with total and absolute
devotion],[75] because obviously *moshiah*'s Torah is even deeper

than the Nine Months. With the Nine Months, God shows me a little bit of what to do. But *moshiah* is so completely given to God, *mesires nefesh*. It's Leah, the *'alma de-iskasiya* [the world of hiddenness]. It's *mamash* "I don't know anything." It's like *Yud Kay Vuv Kay*.[76]

So why do we fail? Because I believe *loshon ha-ra* [evil speech] about myself. I believe *loshon hu-ra* about the Torah, I believe *loshon ha-ra* about God. "And Yosef brought evil report of them unto their father" [Gen. 37:2].[77] And so obviously Yosef ha-Tsaddik, *Moshiah ben Yosef*, has to fix this *loshon ha-ra* thing. This is the Torah of the Nine Months, to give me strength. *Va-yar Elokim es ha-or, ki tov* ["and God saw that the light was good," Gen. 1:4] — to show me that it's not true. It's not true, I'm not bad.[78]

A father can teach his children everything holy, but it's the mother who's strongest in not believing *loshon ha-ra* about her children. This is unsurpassed. The whole world can say *loshon ha-ra* about a baby, and the mother, *mamash*, doesn't believe it, the mother doesn't believe it. And this is the holiness of Rokhel — *Rokhel mevakah 'al baneihah* ["Rachel weeps for her children . . ." Jer. 31:14].[79] She's crying *ki eynenu* [. . . "because they are not"]. I wouldn't say *ki eynenu* means that she doesn't believe in them. The whole world says *ki eynenu*, and she doesn't believe it. She *mamash* doesn't believe it. Yosef ha-Tsaddik [who is the son of Rokhel] brings us back, because we don't believe *loshon ha-ra* about ourselves.[80]

This is *kedushas ha-avos* [the inherited sanctity of our forebears]. How do I bring back *kedushas ha-avos*? First I have to believe that the *yid* is *Kodesh ha-Kodashim*, that the Jew is not dead. Can't be dead.

When we *daven*, we say *Elokei Avraham, Elokei Yitshak, ve-Elokei Ya'akov* [the God of Abraham, the God of Isaac, and the

God of Jacob].[81] Reb Nahman [of Bratslav] says *tefillah le-El hayai—davenen* [prayer] gives life.[82] I want to say something very strong. What is the sign of a living Jew or a dead Jew, *has ve-shalom*? Not that he keeps the Torah. The sign of a dead Jew or a living Jew comes from whether or not he *davens*. The question is, *how* are you in *davening? Tefillos avos tiknum* [prayer was established by the patriarchs].[83] The Torah was given by Moshe. A father gives you life, and a *rebbe* gives you Torah. Okay, so the Torah is *hayyim* [life] also, you know what to do. But the *tamtsis ha-hayyim*, the depths of life, is *tefillos avos tiknum*.[84]

Everybody knows that Pesah is *emunah* [faith]—it's *davenen*. On Pesah the *Ribbono shel 'Olam* gives us *davenen*, and on Shavu'os the *Ribbono shel 'Olam* gives us the Torah. Why is the whole thing on Pesah Sheni, why isn't it on Shavu'os Sheni?[85] Pesah Sheni is when the *yidden* realize, *mamash, anashim asher hayu teme'im le-nefesh ha-adam* ["people who were rendered impure by contact with a dead body," Num. 9:6]—I am lost, I can't *daven* anymore.[86] They were impure from carrying *arono shel Yosef* [the ark of Joseph's bones].[87] This is what *arono shel Yosef* did to them. Yosef ha-Tsaddik brought down to the world this Torah—that the *Ribbono shel 'Olam* opens the gates even after, *has ve-shalom, tumah le-nefesh ha-adam*, when you can't *daven* anymore.[88] You cry to the *Ribbono shel 'Olam*. You know, there's a *davenen* that you can *daven*, and then there's a crying that I don't *daven* anymore, I lost it.[89]

Rosh Hashanah is *ha-yom haras 'olam* ["on this day the world was born"][90]—the day that we are born. On *Rosh Hashanah*, the *Ribbono shel 'Olam* gives us the Torah of the Nine Months.[91] But on *Yom Kippur*, the *Ribbono shel 'Olam* gives us back the Torah of Mt. Sinai.[92]

What happened, why did we make the *'egel* [the Golden Calf]? Because the *Ribbono shel Olam* gave us first the Torah of Sinai, and then maybe, eventually, we would get to the Torah of the Nine Months.[93] But this time the *Ribbono shel 'Olam* realized first I've got to give them the Torah of the Nine Months, and then the Torah [of Mt. Sinai]. So *Rosh Hashanah* is the Torah of the Nine Months—*ha-yom haras 'olam*.

And when a baby is crying, what's the first cry? The first cry is, *mamash*, the crying of the Torah of the Nine Months. I want to say the deepest depths. How come Torah has to be taught when you grow up, and *davenen* doesn't have to be taught? Because the baby is *davening* all the time! *Davenen* is the Torah of the Nine Months; what the baby is taught for nine months is how to *daven*. This the *malakh* [angel] can't take away from me! The *davenen*, nobody can take it away from me. Nobody can take it away from me. It doesn't have to be taught. *Tumas mes* [the state of coming in contact with the dead] means, like the Izhbitzer says, I stop *davenen*. I give up, I don't *daven* anymore.[94]

So Yosef ha-Tsaddik brings you back—*tefillah avos tiknum*.[95] Yosef ha-Tsaddik brings you back, brings you back to *davening*. That is *Moshiah ben Yosef*. And then comes *Moshiah ben David*, and he connects me to *moshiah*'s Torah. *Moshiah*'s Torah is that Torah which has no words. Nobody learns it from somebody else, obviously there is no *rebbe*. But it's *ka-mayyim le-yam mekhasim* ["like water covers the sea," Isa. 11:9].[96] There's no words.[97]

Everybody knows that the meeting of *Moshiah ben Yosef* and *Moshiah ben David* is on *Tisha be-Av* [the ninth of Av], because *moshiah* is *tes* [nine]; it's the Nine Months. *Va-yar Elokim es ha-or, ki tov* ["And God saw the light, that it was good," Gen. 1:4]—*ki tov le-ganzo* [it was good to hide it].[98] *Ki tov le-ganzo* means the *Ribbono shel Olam* says it's better to teach such a holy light when everything is hidden. The best time to teach the Torah is when the baby is still hidden.[99] So *Tisha be-Av* is on *tes* [the ninth day of Av], and it's the birth of *moshiah*.[100] We're not learning Torah on that day.[101] Because on that day is the getting together of the Torah of the Nine Months and the Torah of *moshiah*.[102]

The difference between the *avos* and the *imahos* [the patriarchs and the matriarchs] is like this. The *avos* give us life, but *tehiyas ha-meysim* [resurrection] is given to us by the mothers.

[But] what was the difference between Avraham and Yitshak? Avraham Avinu, his whole thing was that the world should know that there is one God, right?[103] This was his whole thing. For Yitshak, there is no world.[104] What happened to Yitshak at the *akeidah*? Suddenly, Yitshak realized, I must have a son— Ya'akov. The highest meeting—between "there is no world" and "there is a world"—is children. Because children are so holy. Unless you taste the holiness of children, it's either there is a world, and you want to bring God to the world; or there is no world. . . .[105] And what's *moshiah*? *Moshiah* is that there is only one God, *and* there is a world. This is the revelation of *moshiah*.[106]

There are two kinds of *kedushos* [holiness], you know. There is one kind of *kedushah* that, *mamash*, I make you holy. There is another *kedushah*, [which is] how much I'm ready to sacrifice my *kedushah* for you. That's also *kedushah*. A different kind of *kedushah*. So basically this is the difference between Moshe and Aharon.[107]

The *parshah* of Moshe Rabbenu begins *kedoshim tihiyyu ki kadosh ani Hashem Elokeikhem* ["You shall be holy, for I Y-H-W-H your God am holy," Lev. 19:2]. The *parshah* of Aharon begins *emor el ha-kohanim benei Aharon . . . le-nefesh lo yitama . . . ki im le-she'ero ha-karov elav* ["Speak to the priests, sons of Aharon . . . none should defile himself for the dead . . . except for his kin, that is near to him," Lev. 21:1–2]—*mes mitsvah*.[108] The holiness of Aharon is that he can give up his *kedushah* for the impurity of death, for a *mes mitsvah*. This is his *kedushah*. The first one who gave up his *kedushah* for a *yid* was Aharon ha-Kohen. He made the *'egal ha-zahav* [the Golden Calf].[109]

Why are the people who bury someone called the *hevreh kaddisha* [the holy fellowship]? Why them? Why aren't people with *tefillin* called *tefillin kedoshim* [holy tefillin-wearers]? Because this is a special kind of *kedushah*—the *hevreh kaddisha* make themselves impure for a *mes*, for a dead person. This is the highest *kedushah*.

Yosef ha-Tsaddik, his holiness is *pakod yifkod* ["God will surely redeem you," Gen. 50:24–25]. What's *pakod yifkod*? *Pakod yifkod* is two things. Yosef ha-Tsaddik, the *Gemora* says, could have told them also, "Bring me out of Egypt to *Erets Yisro'el*" [the Land of Israel]. But he said, "As long as *yidden* are in *galus* [exile], I have to be in *galus* also." That means Yosef was the first *yiddelleh* who gave up his holiness for *yidden*. Therefore Moshe Rabbenu says [to Yosef, as it were], "You're the one to get the *yidden* out." He is the one who walks with them through *keri'as yam suf* [the splitting of the Sea of Reeds]. And he's the one who brings them Pesah Sheni.[110]

If you give up your holiness for a *yid*, for somebody else, then you taste the Pesah Sheni.[111] In fact, you tasted, *mamash*, the coming of *moshiah*. Moshe Rabbenu says to [the people who were made impure by carrying Yosef's bones], *'imdu ve-eshme'ah mah yetsaveh Hashem la-khem* ["Stand by, and let me hear what command Y-H-W-H has for you," Num. 9:8]. This is already *moshiah*'s Torah.[112] Why didn't Moshe Rabbenu answer them right away? This is already on *moshiah*'s level, when Moshe Rabbenu speaks straight to everyone. Just *'imdu ve-eshme'ah mah yetsaveh Hashem la-khem*. This doesn't go through the channels of *Har Sinai*. This is a different kind of channel. A Pesah Sheni channel.[113]

This is the whole thing of the *benot tslofhad* [the daughters of Zelophehad].[114] *'Imdu ve-eshm'ah mah yetsaveh Hashem lakhem* is *moshiah's* Torah. Moshe Rabbenu realized that the *Ribbono shel 'Olam* is talking to every *yid* privately.[115]

And what was Havah's [Eve's] thing? Havah was *broygez* [angry]: Why did God speak to me via Adam ha-Rishon [Adam, the first being]? Okay, Adam ha-Rishon was like a *rebbe*. But she was ready, she was tasting *moshiah's* Torah—I wonder why He wouldn't talk to me straight? So therefore the *nahash* [snake] came to Havah, because she knew there's something wrong here. What do you mean He tells me through Adam ha-Rishon?[116] So, the *nahash* told her, "If you eat the apple, the *Ribbono shel Olam* talks to you straight." This was where the whole thing went wrong, you know. *Benos Tslofhad* was the *tikkun* of Havah. *'Imdu ve-eshme'ah mah yetsaveh Hashem la-khem. . . .*

This is *moshiah's* Torah, when it's given to you, it's not given to everyone. . . . When a *nevu'ah* [prophecy] is given to one, it's given to everyone. This is the sweet Mt. Sinai Torah, you know, *va-yeddaber Hashem el moshe lemor* ["Y-H-W-H spoke unto Moses, saying"].[117] But this *nevu'ah*—*'imdu ve-eshme'ah mah yetsaveh Hashem lakhem*—is only for me. This is the Torah of the Nine Months. Just for me.[118]

I want to say something very strong. Basically there are two *rebbes*. There's Yehoshua and then there's Pinhas. Yehoshua is the Torah of *mamash*, everyone, right? Pinhas is the Torah for that one *yiddelle*. Because it says *va-yar Pinhas* ["And Pinhas saw," Num. 25:7]. So what did he see?[119] Basically, everybody knows that according to the Izhbitzer, Zimri ben Salu was the holiest of the holy, and Kozbi bas Tsur was really his *bat zug*. So what did he see? Pinhas saw in the Torah of the Nine Months that at this time, it's true she is his *bat zug*, but they are not meant for each other yet.

The difference between the Torah of the Nine Months and the Torah of *Har Sinai* is like this: In the Torah of *Har Sinai*, I can only tell you what you should do. If you don't do it, it's an *aveyrah* [sin]. With the Torah of the Nine Months, ultimately, you don't know what all your *aveyras* were leading to. Something else, a different kind of Torah. In the Torah of the Nine Months, it doesn't say, "This is forbidden." This is already like touching *moshiah*'s Torah. It's the closest to *moshiah*'s Torah that you can get . . . for the individual.

Yosef ha-Tsaddik, obviously he merited to walk with the *yidden* forty years through the desert. You know, what does it mean? He was teaching them the Torah of the way. *Moshiah* is in *Erets Yisro'el*. *Moshiah* is when you get there. But Yosef ha-Tsaddik is teaching the Torah of the way.[120]

Now this is another *Torah-leh* that I have to add. The whole thing between Efraim and Menasheh. Menasheh is *ki nashani Elohim es kol amali* ["for God has made me forget all my toil," Gen. 41:51]. Everything you do wrong, how do you do *teshuvah*? You forget what you did wrong. But Efraim is *ki hifrani be-erets onyi* ["for God has made me fruitful in the land of my affliction," Gen. 41:52] is that, on the contrary, you don't forget anything.[121]

How do we do *teshuvah* on the Mt. Sinai Torah? *Teshuvah* is to forget.[122] The Torah of the Nine Months level is, *mamash*, I see where all the *aveyras* were ultimately leading me. So I cannot forget, *eyn adam 'omed 'al divrei Torah ela im ken nikhshal bah*. To remember the Torah of *ela im ken nikhshal bah* [the Torah of stumbling and failure].

Now listen to this. I want to say the highest Torah. Why is Yosef ha-Tsaddik the one who is the Torah of the Nine Months? Because there is nobody in the world who was *takke mamash* never *nikhshal* [really, truly never made a mistake]. Yosef ha-

Tsaddik was *takke mamash* never *nikhshal;* he never did an *'avey-rah.* What is the biggest *sekhar* [reward] that the *Ribbono shel 'Olam* can give a *tsaddik* who never did an *'aveyrah?* That he should become the *rebbe* of this Torah of the *ba'al ha-'aveyrah* [transgressor]—of the Torah of *ela im ken nikhshal bah.* Yosef ha-Tsaddik wants to do everything for *yidden,* right? What's the highest thing he can teach them? That he can teach them this Torah which even he didn't have. If I did it, it's not the *giluiy mi-le-ma'aleh* [revelation from on High]—I went through it. Yosef ha-Tsaddik merited a *giluiy mi-le-ma'aleh.* Ya'akov gave him the Torah of *ela im ken nikhshal bah.*

[Let's go back to the] *Ner doluk* [the lighted candle in the womb]. *Mi-sof ha-'olam ve-'ad sofo* [with which the baby can see from one end of the earth to the other]. It's very simple, because, *mamash,* I have to know the whole world. What's the whole idea of *ela im ken nikhshal bah* [the Torah about where you have stumbled]? How am I *nikhshal?* Because my *'asarah ma'am-aros* and my *'aseres ha-dibros* didn't get together.[123] Because the way I saw the world, I said listen, it doesn't make sense. But if I see from one corner of the world to the other, from my world to the other, *mamash,* then the whole thing makes sense to me.

Now *hodesh av* is called the *hodesh* of *aleph beis.*[124] The *aleph* is *anokhi Hashem Elokecha,* and the *beis* is the Torah of *Bereishis.*[125] Basically, the Torah of *Bereishis* is, *mamash,* the Torah of the Nine Months. What am I doing in this world?[126]

It says *ner Hashem nishmas adam* ["the candle of Y-H-W-H is the soul of man," Prov. 20:27]. Then it says *ner mitsvah ve-torah or* ["a commandment is a candle, and the Torah light," Prov. 6:23]. How come the *neshamah* isn't the light? Why isn't the *neshamah* like the Torah? *Yidden* are *hekher* [higher] than the Torah, right? If the Torah is the great light, not the candle, so why shouldn't my soul be a bright light? The answer is very simple. When my soul is connected to the Torah of Mt. Sinai, then definitely my Torah is not a candle—my Torah is a light! But my Torah, my *neshamah*, on the level of the Nine Months is *ner Hashem nishmas adam*.

What's the whole thing of *bedikas homets* [the search for leaven before Pesah]?[127] Walking around, *mamash*, with my Torah of the Nine Months, you know. Looking for my *homets*, for everything I did wrong.[128] And this is a candle. So for that Torah it says, *mamash, ner doluk*. And I want to say something of the deepest depths: Why is it, when you go to a wedding, the parents carry a candle? To let *mamash*, tell the child, you know, *mamash*, you know what I'm giving you, with you on the way, *mamash*, your Torah of the Nine Months. And also, *has ve-shalom*, a person who's dying, why do we walk out with candles all the time? Because this is the Torah of the Nine Months. And this is the whole thing of *hevreh kaddisha*.[129]

Moshe Rabbenu is *ke-penei hamah* ["like the light of the sun," b. Bava Batra 75a]. Moshe Rabbanu is a great light. But Aharon is *'omed u-metiv es ha-neros* ["stands and lights the candles," m. Tamid 3:9].[130] Aharon is candles—Aharon is the Torah of the candles. *Ad she-tehei shalheves olah me-eleihah* [so that the flame rises up on its own].[131] Aharon ha-Kohen, is *mamash, va-yar elokim es ha-or, ki tov* ["and God saw that the light is good"]. God saw that the candle is the greatest thing. Not the sun, not the moon, not the great lights.[132]

And this is *ner Shabbos*. You know *ner Shabbos mi-shum shalom bayis* [the Sabbath candles were instituted to keep peace in the home].[133] Why was there not *shalom bayis*, do you remember? I told you that the Torah of the Nine Months is [something that] I have to hear directly from God. And Havah knew that she has to hear it from God, because the Torah of the Nine Months, *mamash*, you have got to hear it from God Himself.[134] *Yatsta bas kol me-ahor*[ey ha-pargod], *shuvu banim shovevim* ["A heavenly voice went out from behind the curtain, saying 'return, wayward children'"].[135] This is the Torah of the Nine Months.

Why was there no peace in the house? Because if the people are not connected to the Torah of the Nine Months, to each other, then they hate each other. But if they know the Torah of the Nine Months, then, *mamash*, they love each other.[136]

Listen, when I see someone, *nebekh*, falling, I'm getting angry at them, *has veshalom?* I'm trying to help them, right? Will I get angry with, *has veshalom*, say if my Neshama-leh [Shlomo's daughter] falls? Would I yell at her? *Gevalt*, I lift her up because she's crying. So, basically, if the *yidden* would be connected to the Torah of the Nine Months, in their house, they would be connected, it would be the biggest *shalom bayis*, right? So therefore, *ner Shabbos mi-shum shalom bayis.*[137] Remember that Havah was the one, she was yearning for the Torah of the Nine Months. But, so, therefore the *Ribbono shel 'Olam* told her, kindle the light of *Shabbos*, kindle candles. Don't make a great light. I'm giving you candles. Candles are the Torah of the Nine Months.

Why do women put their hands on the light? How did Moshe Rabbenu break the tablets? Because he let them go from his hands, right? And how come that the Torah of the Nine Months is not connected anymore to the Torah of Mt. Sinai? Because of Havah, right?[138] She has to fix the Torah of the Nine Months, and she has to fix the breaking of the tablets with her hands. *Va-yeshaber es ha-luhos le-'eyneyhem* [Moses broke the tablets before their eyes].[139] When a woman holds her hands against the candles, she fixes the breaking of the tablets, and *mamash*, *mi-shum shalom bayis.*[140]

Now I'm coming really to the crux of the whole thing. I'm coming back to the Torah of the *nedarim* [vows]. This is the

Torah of the Vow. Remember we were learning that the Izhbitzer says, When do I make a vow? I make a vow when I *mamash* see I don't make it. I *mamash* see I can't make it anymore, the way it is.[141] I realize that the Torah, the Torah of Mt. Sinai, doesn't help me. So what's the *nedarim* about? Basically the *nedarim* is the Torah of the Nine Months. *Mamash*, I'm taking, my whole life, you know. *Va-yehi ha-adam le-nefesh hayah–le-ruah memalela* ["and Adam became a living being—a speaking being," Gen. 2:7 and Onkelos's translation].[142] *Mamash*, my words, I'm taking my whole life in my hands, and I connect my whole life to that one thing which I have to do.

Remember the Torah that *for nedarim*, the Izhbitzer says, this is *mamash* my own individual holiness. This is like, my own *Torah-leh*. This is, *mamash*, the highest Torah there is. And, I want to say something very beautiful, for my holy daughter Nedareleh, that you can have children on the level of Mt. Sinai. It says in the Torah that you must have children, so you have children. But you can have children on the level of a vow, *mamash*.

Hannah was the first one, *va-tidor neder va-tomar* ["and she made a vow, saying," 1 Sam. 1:11]. That she *mamash*, said *Ribbono shel 'Olam*, I must have children, you know. On the *neder* level, on her Nine Months level. So, therefore she had a son, Shmuel, who found David ha-Melekh. *Heikhan matsasi? Bi-Sedom.* [Where did I find him? In Sodom, i.e., the seat of iniquity and imperfection.][143] That's the whole thing.

Everybody knows that Korah made a *ta'us* [mistake] because he saw Shmuel was his grandson.[144] What did Korah see? Korah saw that Moshe and Aharon are very good on the Torah of Mt. Sinai, but [he said to himself], "I am on the level of the Nine Months because I'm the grandfather of Shmuel." But he didn't know that the whole thing of Shmuel is *ela im ken nikhshal bah* because he was the *nikhshal*. Korah was *takke* the *nikhshal* that made Shmuel so holy.[145]

Reb Zalman: That's such a fantastic paradox. This is so beautiful. It's Shmuel who is serving as priest, and he comes out because his mother made the vow. Now, his mother felt that I need this child and I want to give him to the *Ribbono shel 'Olam*, and without that my life is no life, you know? So they begot out of that, Shmuel. Shmuel is the one whose power it is to connect us with *moshiah* because he anointed David. So you get a sense of the great link that Shmuel is? His grandfather is Korah.

Reb Shlomo: Korah saw that Shmuel is his grandson, and he is greater than Moshe and Aharon, because Moshe and Aharon— *Moshe ve-Aharon be-kohanav, u-Shmuel be-kor'ei shemo* ["Moshe and Aharon among His priests, and Shmuel among they that call upon His name," Ps. 99:6].[146] Yeah, keep on going brother.

Reb Zalman: So, that was the connection that he had to the Nine Months Torah, right? The Torah of the Nine Months [that you learn in the womb] is the kind of Torah that you get prepared for, learning about the struggle and failings that your life is going to be all about. That's the shape of the soul to come.

So Korah figured, therefore he should be able to have the right to lord it over Moshe and Aharon, because ultimately his Torah wins. But one of the nature-things [i.e., the essence of] of this Torah is that failure teaches, right?

So there *has* to be someone who fails. What Korah overlooked was that he was going to be that failure that would teach his grandchild. That is so fantastic, like a *koan*. It's a total Möbius strip of what you have to know.

Reb Shlomo: [Returning to the theme of the Sabbath candles], why do women have to put their hands against the fire? Because what does it mean, *ela im ken nikhshal bah*? Why am I falling? Why am I failing? Because my action, my hands and my head were not together, right? So, *ner shel Shabbos mi-shum shalom bayis* is that my hands and the fire, *mamash*, go together.[147]

Now I want to say something else very deep. There is a Torah and there is my place in the world, which is also Torah. Which is the highest *giluiy* of Torah, my place in the world. *Borukh ha-makom, borukh hu. Borukh she-nasan Torah le-ʿamo Yisroʾel* [Blessed is the Omnipresent, blessed is He. Blessed is the One who gave the Torah to His people Israel].[148]

Ke-Neged arbaʿah banim dibrah Torah [The Torah speaks about four children].[149] *Ehad hakham, ehad rasha* [One wise, one wicked]. Which Torah are we talking about? Which Torah are we talking about? We're talking about the Torah of the Nine Months, right? Because the Torah of the Nine Months is *borukh ha-makom*. My place, my place in the world, this is the Torah of the Nine Months.

Yetsiyas mitsrayim [leaving Egypt] first was the *geʾulah* [redemption] in the house, parents and children. This is *mamash* the Torah of the Nine Months. The next morning is the *geʾulas mitsrayim* [the redemption from Egypt], for the world. That's something else, this is a political thing, even a holy political thing, getting out of Egypt, but the first thing is, *mamash*, connecting parents and children. *Ve-heshiv lev avos al ha-banim, ve-lav banim al avosam* ["And he [Elijah] shall turn the heart of the fathers to the children, and the heart of the children to their fathers," Mal. 3:24]. This is Eliyahu ha-Navi the *seder* night, and the next day is *moshiah, Moshiah ben David* coming out. But this is first—a connection.[150]

There's *tsaddik yesod 'olam* ["the righteous is an everlasting foundation," Prov. 10:25],[151] the one who did the most right. And then there's Aharon ha-Kohen, the most *tsebrokhenne yid* [broken Jew]—*la-kakh nivharta* ["for this you were chosen"]. This is the *Beis ha-Mikdash*; David ha-Melekh is the most *tsebrokhenne yid*. *Hekim 'olah shel teshuvah* [He established the offering of repentance].[152]

Obviously it's very strange, David ha-Melekh and Aharon ha-Kohen have something very, very strong together, you know. Because David ha-Melekh built the house for Aharon ha-Kohen, and the house gets broken all the time.[153]

And our having *Erets Yisro'el* has to do with *Beis ha-Mikdash*. So what's the highest, my place in the world, *Erets Yisro'el*, is my place in the world, this is the Torah of the Nine Months. The Torah of *Erets Yisro'el* is the Torah of the Nine Months.[154]

[I want to talk] about our generation a little bit . . . I want to say a *gevaltige* Torah. On the level of the Torah of *Har Sinai*, I have nothing to do with my last *gilgul* [a previous lifetime]. Right now what I do, I put on *tefillin*, keep *Shabbos*, I have nothing to do with my last *gilgul*. The Torah of the Nine Months is everything which I went through, *mamash*, every time I went back. So I want to say that according to the Torah of *Har Sinai*, without the Torah of *ela im ken nikhshal bah*, you can't understand the Six Million. . . .[155]

Our problem today is we don't have the Yosef ha-Tsaddik, who is the *rebbe* for *ela im ken nikhshal bah*. We do have the *tsaddik yesod 'olam*, people who are holy [and perfect and have never sinned]. But we don't have people who are that holy that they can be the teacher of *im ken nikhshal bah*. And we don't have a little *moshiah-leh* who is himself *im ken nikhshal bah*. So anyway, I just want to bless you and me that our children should have it right, with two big *rebbes*.[156]

So this is *Mishneh Torah* [the Book of Deuteronomy]. Because the first four *seforim* [books of the Torah] are, *mamash*, the Torah the way you have to do it. But *Eleh ha-devarim asher dibber Moshe el kol Beney Yisro'el* ["These are the words that Moses spoke to all the children of Israel," Deut. 1:1] — *eleh posel es ha-rishonos* [the word "these" renders obsolete everything before it][157] — *ela im ken nikhshal bah*. Here Moshe Rabbenu begins to teach, to teach the Torah of the Nine Months to *klal Yisro'el*.[158] And I want to say something very strong, there is the Torah of the Nine Months of every *yiddeleh*, and the Torah of the Nine Months of *klal Yisro'el*. Aaron ha-Kohen is an expert on the Nine Months of every *yiddeleh*, but the expert of the Nine Months of *klal Yisro'el* is only Moshe Rabbenu. And this is the *Mishneh Torah*.[159]

And why when we get married [do] we say *ke-das Moshe ve-Yisro'el* [according to the law of Moses and Israel]?[160] Why couldn't we say "according to the Torah?" *Ke-das Moshe ve-Yisro'el* means that we should be married according to the Nine Months of *klal Yisro'el*, and that of every single *yiddeleh*.

Why didn't Moshe Rabbenu go into *Erets Yisro'el*? Because he wanted to be there when we are *nikhshel*, even if he can't help, he couldn't help yet. He says, "I want to be there when they fall, I want to be with them."[161]

But why is it that on Shavu'os we don't dance, and on Simhas Torah, when we don't even read the Torah, we dance so much?[162] Sukkos is basically the Torah of the Nine Months.[163] On Simhas Torah we dance in a circle, because *somekh Hashem le-khol ha-noflim*. In the future the blessed Holy One will make a circle of the *tsaddikim*.[164] And therefore on Simhas Torah we read that Moshe Rabbenu was there. He wants to be there when they're falling.

Suggestions for Further Reading

Carlebach, Shlomo. *The Torah Commentary of Rabbi Shlomo Carlebach*. Edited by Shlomo Katz. Jerusalem: Urim, 2012.

Coopersmith, Aryeh. *Holy Beggars: A Journey from Haight Street to Jerusalem.* El Granada CA: One World Lights, 2011.

Mandelbaum, Yitta Halberstam. *Holy Brother: Inspiring Stories and Enchanted Tales about Rabbi Shlomo Carlebach*. Northvale NJ: Jason Aronson, 1997.

Ophir (Offenbacher), Natan. *Rabbi Shlomo Carlebach: Life, Mission, and Legacy.* Jerusalem : Urim, 2014.

5

Zalman Schachter-Shalomi

Introduction

Rabbi Zalman Schachter-Shalomi (1924–2014), founder of the Jewish Renewal movement, was an exceptionally creative and dynamic spiritual teacher.[1] He was gifted with a quick mind and a voracious appetite for absorbing new ideas, approaches, and technologies, gifts that remained undiminished into his ninetieth year.

Born in Poland but raised in Vienna, he came of age in a diverse Jewish environment. His family had connections to the Hasidic world, but living in a major metropolitan center, the young Zalman was exposed to a wide variety of Jewish religious and cultural expressions. After passing through Belgium and France to escape the Nazis, Zalman's family moved to America in 1941. There he became close to the Lubavitch leadership, which recognized his brilliant intellect and charismatic talents.

Reb Zalman, as he was affectionately known, enjoyed a short career as a rabbi and educator within the American Chabad system. By the 1950s and 1960s, however, exposure to the wisdom of other faith traditions, through writings and living teachers, as well as the American counterculture movement, fundamentally changed Reb Zalman's paradigm of Jewish spirituality. His openness to new forms of learning led him far beyond the Chabad community, eventually beyond the bounds of Orthodoxy altogether. Still, throughout the spiritual quest that was his life, Reb Zalman maintained a deep sense of rootedness in Jewish and Hasidic tradition, looking to Hasidic teachings for inspiration and seeking to recast them in a modern key. He devoted himself to inspiring a spiritual renewal among North American Jews based on the Hasidic model.

The young Zalman had grown up in a world where religious observance and learning were unquestioned values; the family's roots were in the Belz Hasidic community. Yet even in Vienna he was sent to a modern school and began reading the works of the European intellectual world. To him, the Hasidism he saw in his youth appeared to be compromised; its creative vitality had been sapped by the dynastic inheritance of leadership and the attempt to combat modernity in all of its forms.

His perspective changed during his family's sojourn in Antwerp while fleeing from Hitler. Encountering for the first time a community of Chabad Hasidim, Zalman was impressed and inspired by their spiritual depth, their commitment to contemplative prayer and religious experience, their relative openness to modernity, and their holistic approach to intensive spiritual education. And in Marseille in 1941 he also met the young Rabbi Menachem Mendel Schneerson, the son-in-law of Rabbi Yosef Yitzhak Schneersohn and the future Rebbe of Chabad, whose personality and homiletic/gifts made a significant impression upon him.

These meetings—both with the religious community and the future leader of Chabad—were critical moments in a very tumultuous period in his life. Like thousands of other Jewish families who had made it to Western Europe, the Schachters were on the run, and their fate was by no means clear. The young Zalman was overwrought with disappointment at the collapsing dreams of progress in what he saw as "noble" Western culture in the wake of Nazi bloodlust. This Chabad group allowed space for his anger and bitter questioning without disdain, and in this community Reb Zalman saw a new model of Hasidic devotion that left room for personal inquiry and inner work. He later recalled:

I was drawn to the Lubavitch tradition, a form of Habad, because of its promise that one could become adept enough to attain certain mystical experiences in this lifetime. . . . I also liked the nature of the relationship between the Rebbe and the individual Hasid. In this kind of Hasidism, the Rebbe shows you the way, but you have to do the work yourself—rather than hang onto his coattails.[2]

Reb Zalman was particularly attracted to the Chabad notion that the inner life of the Hasid (and not just that of the *rebbe*) is of paramount importance. This emphasis on the spiritual journey of each individual, thought Zalman, provided an alternative to the exclusive reliance on the *rebbe* he saw in other Hasidic communities. Having met and been deeply impressed by Rabbi Menachem Mendel Schneerson, remembering the thoughtfulness and spiritual inspiration in the Chabad community of Antwerp, Zalman enrolled in the Habad yeshiva in Brooklyn in the 1940s.

Along with Reb Shlomo Carlebach, he spent several of his formative years as a Chabad emissary, sent out to American colleges to expose students to the teachings of traditional Judaism. By the 1950s he was working as an Orthodox pulpit rabbi in New Bedford and Fall River, Massachusetts, while also enrolled in graduate school at Boston University. There he studied with the great theologian and preacher Howard Thurman, who exposed him to other religious traditions, particularly the powerful piety of his own mystical, African American Christian faith. Thurman also taught him a great deal about spiritual leadership in community, in particular how religion could be taught in an experiential manner.[3] In spirituality "labs," group meetings in which the class learned practical religious exercises, Reb Zalman became acquainted with different modes of devotional reading, singing, and dance, amplifying the spiritual skills he had found and honed in Chabad. These proficiencies accompanied Reb Zalman throughout his career in communal leadership and university positions all over North America.[4]

In the late 1950s Reb Zalman began to look for a form of educational work that was both more open and challenging than that of the small

Orthodox communities he had been serving. He turned to working with college youth, following up on the mission his *rebbe* had defined for him. Becoming Hillel director at the University of Manitoba, Zalman was immediately exposed to Hillel colleagues, including a number of serious intellectual seekers who were non-Orthodox rabbis. While he saw himself still part of the broadly defined Chabad community, he had begun to push against the boundaries of Orthodoxy. He felt confined by its intellectual limitations and rigid approach to many issues, particularly those concerning religious pluralism; followers were prohibited from learning from other religions as well as from non-Orthodox forms of Judaism. Zalman was also increasingly troubled by the Orthodox views of gender and sexuality.[5]

At the same time, Zalman continued looking to the teachings of Hasidism—and Chabad in particular—as storehouses of religious wisdom. He devoted much time and energy to translating Hasidic and other mystical sources for teaching purposes, producing copies of them on his Hillel office mimeograph machine. In a significant essay from the period, written for an audience unfamiliar with this world, he outlined the major tenets of Hasidic spirituality, including the Hasidic approach to study, song, introspection, and contemplative prayer. One can become a Hasid only through apprenticing to a veteran member of the community, and ultimately to a particular *rebbe*, he explained, since the inner life of devotion is a skill that cannot be absorbed through books alone.

The following remarks from this essay regarding the nature of Hasidism and its relationship to Jewish practice and Orthodoxy may constitute the clearest statement of his early thinking on the subject:

Hasidism really relates perpendicularly to any form of Judaism, including Orthodoxy. It defines its teaching as the interior Torah, the Torah's innermost part. It views its mode of prayer not in terms of liturgical dissent from the Ashkenazi ritual,[6] but in terms of the service of the heart. Its field of action it views with an inner aliveness, with *kavvanah* (intention). It views God, Israel, and Torah as one, but with two aspects—the outer manifest one and the inner hidden one. It strives to impose interior recollection, joy, and discipline on outer traditional forms. The spontaneous is preferred over the dryly habitual. Yet it demands a higher awareness, and paradoxically, a pre-meditation within the spontaneous.

While basically Hasidism has no quarrel with Orthodox Judaism, it feels that the latter is neither vital nor profound enough. Orthodoxy, while it teaches what ought to be done, does not, however, show its adherents *how* they may do this. Hasidism corrects this. . . .

While Hasidism affords its adherents great individual freedom, it gives this only within the traditional framework. Latitude is given as to whether one prays earlier or later, depending on one's interior recollectedness, or whether one wishes to pray with song or chant, rhythm or motion, or meditatively: but it does demand the praying of the liturgy in *tallith* and *t'fillin*. . . . It would be a mistake to assume that Hasidism frees anyone from divinely given obligations: what it does is to provide him with the joyous, fervent wherewithal to fulfill them.[7]

This is a beautiful summary of how the inner path of Hasidism seeks to infuse existing rituals—indeed, the entirety of Jewish practice—with new religious meaning. Performance of sacred deeds does not ever replace the inward glance, but neither does contemplation or mediation supersede the obligation to act. This nascent understanding of Neo-Hasidism, not wedded to any particular mode of practice or denomination, views Hasidic teaching as a reservoir of spiritual wisdom that may be drawn upon in all religious actions and settings.

By the early 1960s it was clear to Reb Zalman that his ever-expansive spiritual vision would not allow him to remain with Chabad forever. The well-known and much-discussed reason why Reb Zalman left—

his experimentation with and high regard for the power of psychedelic drugs, a path rejected by the Lubavitcher Rebbe—is only part of the story.[8] His frustration with the intellectual myopia of Orthodoxy—especially in terms of other religious traditions—only grew as he continued to explore multiple religious vistas, having increased contact both through reading and living encounters with spiritual figures from many traditions.[9] He began to see the human outreach toward God in universal terms, to understand Judaism as a particular "*derekh* in '*avodah*," one specific way of serving the Divine among many generated by religious geniuses in cultures throughout the world. The Jewish path was his own, of course, and Reb Zalman had mastered its spiritual vocabulary and practices, but he came to recognize Jewish devotion and piety as one voice among many authentic pathways.

He had come to realize that classical Hasidism, even in its somewhat more forward-looking Chabad version, would not suffice to fuel a Jewish religious renewal in contemporary America. Some of this had to do with aspects of Hasidic doctrine, especially its religious exclusivism (teachings on the uniqueness of the Jewish soul, etc.). But he also had a sense of the patience required to follow the Hasidic path, and its distance from the quick rewards offered by the many other spiritual and self-help options that were increasingly becoming available.

Although his perspective on this subject changed over time, it was also clear to him that *halakhah* as understood within Orthodoxy was no longer compelling and useful for the majority of American Jews. As he came to work with ever-larger numbers of non-Orthodox followers and students, he did try to convey to them a respect for halakhic process, often with mixed success. This was especially difficult around issues of women's status, questions he tried to confront head-on, offering various creative solutions to complex and long-festering legal questions.[10]

The encounter with Chabad was Reb Zalman's earliest exposure to living Hasidism, but he also read the works of Martin Buber, Hillel Zeitlin, and Abraham Joshua Heschel.[11] When he first read them (while still a Chabadnik), his admiration for Heschel and Buber was tempered by a critique of their versions of Neo-Hasidism. He argued that Buber was alienated from Jewish practice and remained an outsider to the lived experience of Hasidism. Heschel, Reb Zalman maintained, spoke with the Jewish vocabulary of an insider, but in order to emphasize the idea of a transcendent God to whose call mankind must respond with sacred deeds, he had forsaken Hasidism's mystical aspects. In what may be Reb Zalman's most trenchant critique, he castigated Buber and Heschel for expressing their Neo-Hasidic projects in books rather than in charismatic leadership. Reb Zalman felt strongly that a Neo-Hasidic Judaism must foster a living spiritual master in order to offer guidance and spiritual counseling, as well as to model the life of piety it was proposing. The writings of Buber and Heschel could inspire their readers, he recognized, but without a living leader to demonstrate embodied practice, a Hasid in search of religious growth could only progress so far.[12]

Reb Zalman focused on the relationship between a spiritual leader and his (or her) disciples over the course of his life. His doctoral dissertation and several subsequent books were devoted to the subject, and Reb Zalman spent much of his career cultivating and inhabiting his role as a living Neo-Hasidic teacher. His explorations of a charismatic leader's role were personal as well as academic. Drawn in his youth to the charisma of the last two Lubavitcher *rebbes*, he was well aware that he too had the potential to draw others into his orb in parallel ways. He did this with rather little hesitation, offering blessings and prayers to his disciples in the manner one might expect of a Neo-Hasidic *rebbe*.

Concerned, however, with how this model could flourish in an American culture that valued democracy and egalitarianism, he sought to develop ways of communicating the spiritual tools of the Hasidic leader to others in his circle, and, more broadly, to the contemporary American rabbinate. The modern rabbi, he claimed, has more in common with a Hasidic *rebbe* than an official Eastern European rabbi, whose primary tasks concern deciding points of law and adjudicating disputes:

> Today's suburban congregational rabbi is more like the rebbe than he is like a rav. He is more concerned with presiding at liturgical celebrations and with counseling congregants than with ruling on points of law. Like the rebbe, his counsel centers around a specifically Jewish set of values. Like the rebbe, his task is both to help his congregants integrate his assumptive structure, and to help them function within the appropriate mythic structure. . . .
>
> If he [the spiritual leader] were consistent, it would be at his congregants' expense. The working hypothesis that all people have a theology of their own that arises from the root of the soul and the position it holds in God's service is not bad theology. On the contrary, it is good pastoral psychology; if he can trust himself and dilate his own thought system enough, the rabbi can help his congregant map his or her myths. In doing so, he must take care not to reduce the myth to a laissez-faire relativism or nihilism, or to stress a fascistic one-creed-for-all; by avoiding this he can design with his congregant a structure that allows for further growth and movement, retaining some tensions while, at the same time, relating the congregant to *klal Yisrael* and tradition. . . .
>
> The myth must be viable enough to allow for ethics, mitzvoth, synagogue involvement, and prayer.[13]

The ideal leader, Reb Zalman taught, can articulate a dynamic theology—rooted in tradition but flexible, adaptable, and growth-oriented. Modern seekers will not be satisfied with rigid answers of dogmatic creed, on the one hand, or with the assertion that no belief is necessary to live an authentic Jewish spiritual life, on the other. And since the contemporary rabbi is called upon to offer spiritual guidance, he or she must be schooled in the practical arts of pastoral psychology and learn how to interpret the dynamic spiritual world of Jewish theology in a modern (and postmodern) context.[14] At the same time, Reb Zalman portrayed the *rebbe* in functional, not essential identity terms: the same person might be the teacher one moment and a disciple in the next.[15]

Reb Zalman was also interested in establishing a devotional community.[16] Influenced by Trappist and other Catholic spiritual works, in 1964 he published a call to found a Jewish monastic (but noncelibate) order. The goal of what Reb Zalman called the B'nai Or community, similar in many respects to Zeitlin's dream of Yavneh, was to serve God wholeheartedly and with undivided attention. Reb Zalman defined the aim of such worship as "so that He, be He blessed, may derive *nahat* (pleasure) from us. Or, to put it differently, to realize God in this lifetime; to achieve a higher level of spiritual consciousness; to liberate such hidden forces within us as would energize us to achieve our highest humanity within Judaism."[17] In these sentences we find, presented in traditional Jewish language and then translated into counterculture spiritual terms, the ultimate goal of Hasidic devotion in the modern world.

Reb Zalman noted that members of his imagined community were to be drawn to this new life out of dissatisfaction with the materialism and self-centeredness of contemporary secular and religious cultures. The cure, he suggested, was a community offering unmitigated devotion to God. The day was to be divided equally into eight hours of rest and respite, eight hours of labor, and eight hours of divine service and spiritual work. Both men and women would devote all aspects of their lives to God.

This vision of B'nai Or was never realized, but it had a lasting impact on the lives of several young people who came to share in its dream.[18] This vision also continued to evolve as Reb Zalman grew and changed over the years. When he finally did establish such a community, and then a network of communities, beginning in his Philadelphia years (after 1977), the model was significantly looser and less disciplined than the original vision. These later B'nai Or communities eventually morphed into the Jewish Renewal movement, which continues to thrive and embody Reb Zalman's spiritual teachings.

Many aspects of the original call to establish B'nai Or accompanied Reb Zalman over the course of his career. He became increasingly devoted to expanding the role of women as equals in all religious settings. He remained concerned with the practical methods for cultivating the art of prayer, another central aspect of his Neo-Hasidism.[19] To achieve his goal of making prayer meaningful for the contemporary Jewish community, he worked to develop tools, practices, and techniques that could inspire greater levels of devotional attunement.

Finally, although his approach to Neo-Hasidism is primarily Jewish in thrust and practice, and the heart of his spiritual vocabulary was grounded in particular in the Chabad Hasidism of his youth, Reb Zalman readily borrowed from other traditions when necessary. His vision of a common core of human spirituality led him to draw upon experiential elements of other faith communities,[20] such as Sufi and Buddhist techniques of meditation and chant, yoga methods imported from Hinduism, and prayer forms adapted from American Christian practice. All found their way into Jewish Renewal in varying degrees.

Reb Zalman's version of Neo-Hasidism also included a radical element that became more pronounced in later years. Simultaneous to his own uncoupling from the boundaries of Orthodox thought and praxis, Reb Zalman came to believe that humanity was undergoing a transformation of consciousness. Describing this as a "paradigm shift" or later, in Buddhist language, a "turning," Reb Zalman pointed to a process of fundamental reorientation in which religious individuals were now called to look beyond the specifics of each faith tradition and into the deepest structures of human spirituality.[21]

In a work published shortly before his death, Reb Zalman interpreted the passionate devotion of Hasidism as a specific manifestation of a universal human drive toward the life of the spirit.[22] He felt that humanity was on the verge of another such shift, in which the essence of Hasidism (itself a deeper human phenomenon) would become manifest in surprising and courageous new ways. He saw himself as a teacher and leader in this new era, one that 1960s gurus had already dubbed the Age of Aquarius. In later years Zalman adopted the language of emerging Gaian or earth-centered spirituality for the new universal awareness that he saw emerging before his eyes. He was happy to be the chief presenter of this universal teaching in its Jewish garb, or to make the distinctive Jewish contribution to the collective articulation of this old-new wisdom teaching.

It is hard not to notice, in this aspect of Reb Zalman's vision, an echo of his years in Chabad, just as its messianic message was beginning to emerge. His teaching is essentially a New-Age and universalized adaptation of that vision, a messianism that leaves behind any sense of Jewish exclusivism or triumphalism but carries forth its dream of the fast-approaching day when "earth will be filled with knowledge of Y-H-V-H, as the waters cover the sea."

Hasidism and Neo-Hasidism (1960)

The three selections that follow span more than fifty years. The first essay represents some of Reb Zalman's earliest thinking on the importance and relevance of Hasidic spirituality for contemporary religious people and seekers. Taking issue with the more literary projects of Martin Buber and Abraham Joshua Heschel, yet deeply engaging with their writings, Reb Zalman suggests that a new Hasidism must also make room for Neo-Hasidic *rebbes* or spiritual leaders.

This year marks not alone the 200th *Yahrzeit* of the Baal Shem Tov but the 150th *Yahrzeit* of Rabbi Nahman of Bratzlav, his great-grandson. In three years, we shall observe the 150th *Yahrzeit* of many of the Hasidic masters of the Napoleonic era. (According to Buber, in *For the Sake of Heaven*, all of the principals died in the same year.) This is, then, a good time to evaluate the Hasidic movement and its survival to our day, despite the many premature obituaries which have been published during the past fifty years, announcing its decadence and demise.

Hasidism, once defined as a pietist reform or a revolt of the unlettered, today is usually dubbed as ultra-orthodox. Like many of the resurgent orthodoxies of our time, it has acquired a hyphenated, *neo*-prefixed school. Heschel and Buber have often been defined as Neo-Hasidic thinkers. Buber has been responsible in a large measure for present knowledge about Hasidism. His translations, his retelling of Hasidic tales, and his studies in comparative mysticism have added to Western man's familiarity with Hasidism.

Buber's development led him from his earlier "Ecstatic" and "Unitive" period to his later "I-Thou" period. At about the same time, Rabbi Shalom Dov Baer Schneerson wrote *Kunteres ha-Tefillah*, a treatise on prayer dealing with unitive contemplation. It was an era when many a Hasid and Yeshivah student in Lubavitch experienced the beholding of the *living* God. However, Buber did not know this, as he had never permitted himself to be immersed in the type of *agape* community which he later celebrated.

For reasons that seemed imperative to him, illustrated in his introductory essay to *Pointing the Way*, Buber changed his views to a dialogical approach. The unitive experience is not given to many men. We live in a world in which the monistic way is unreal and in which the dualistic way is the real dimension of living. But the dualistic way, too, does not lend itself to a fulfilled life. Thus, the step from the dualistic to the dialogical way was necessary for Buber. When Nietzsche said that "God is dead," he was of course referring to the "It" to which he had reduced Him, since for Nietzsche the *living* God had ceased to live among men. The Infinite It of God is meaningless for all those who cannot attain to *Unio Mystica*. Buber's insight into the God who can be met and "Thou-ed" (addressed in the second person) is very helpful, especially when we realize how seldom one finds oneself in the relationship which is occasioned by the *primary word* (I-Thou). Suddenly God is no longer dead: He is in hiding; He is eclipsed. He "comes where He is let in." To Buber, this saying of the Kotzker Rabbi means that He comes where man is ready to engage, or to be engaged, in dialogue.

But for Buber, there is no *conversation* in this dialogue. There is only a confrontation. God does not say "do this" or "do that, "become this" or "become that." The dialogue is wordless. Perhaps Buber is afraid that the "word" would become "flesh," leaving only a non-dialogical Halakhah. This seems to be the point in his correspondence with Rosenzweig. "God is not a law-giver, and therefore the law has no universal validity for me." However, the problems encountered in the Unitive decidedly remain in the dialogical realm though man very seldom lives in the dialogical universe. The objective, "*itty*" universe awaits him. Buber gives not bread, but stones to the man who lives in the "*itty*" world. True, the model of meeting other men is always in Buber's mind. He can confront the other man by yielding to that one's "it" the inherence of an unconditioned "thou." But man can do only one thing at a time. When facing the "it" of another, he can yield him a "thou." When facing the "It" of God, he cannot yield Him a "Thou." Man becomes so absorbed in the process of conceptualizing God's "It" that he cannot meet "It" as "Thou." Yet, is not God notorious for not providing man with an "It"? "Take heed, for ye saw no image."

The scholastics had it better. Man is actual and potential. The actual in man is yielded to him; the potential in man is confronted as an "it." But God, being pure actuality, is granted aseity of being. Thus, He is not eclipsed but can be met. Man, in this case, does not have to project *and* meet at the same time. And so, "*das Zwischenmenschliche*," despite its attraction, cannot really serve as the only good model for the relationship between man and God. Buber's reduction of one Hasidic idea into a miniature system is not Hasidism. The latter is organic, having been created by the striving of more than *one*. It is rich with many coordinates. There is, for example, the saying of the Kotzker Rabbi: "If I am I because I am I, and you are you because you are you, then I am I, and you are you. But if I am I because you are you, and you are you because I am I, then I am not I, and you are not you." And this is only one of the infinite coordinates of God. Buber felt that he had to reject the "gnostic" coordinates, as he argues against Jung, but in Hasidism there is room for the Immanent (*memalle' kol 'almin*) as well as the Transcendent (*sovev kol ʿalmin*) in the shadow of the Infinite (*Eyn Sof*).

Heschel corrected this in some measure. He added the coordinates of timespace. God becomes Time in the twenty-six hours of the Sabbath. (The Sabbath begins earlier and ends later than the ordinary day.) God is incarnated in the twenty-six hours of the Sabbath of Sabbaths, Yom Kippur. Then is He available. Whoever enters the "palace of Time" from the world of space is *in* God. The time of prayer each day is a miniature Sabbath, where the father and the child can meet in the intimacy of the private domain.

Admittedly, Heschel goes beyond Buber. Heschel employs many Hebrew terms and allows conceptually Jewish associations to be formed. Furthermore, Heschel adds an everyday coordinate, in terms of a "*He-me*" relationship. *He* is the center of the universe, yet to every man it is his own *I*. However—and this is the great contribution of Heschel—in the moment of "radical amazement," *I* discover that *I* am only a *me*. Thus do *I* become aware that *He*, the Ground of all and the Center of all, deigns to see *me*. This is so because I have availed myself of the opportunity of "making myself visible to *Him*." By intending to be seen, by praying, I make myself visible to God. This begets the emotional response of respect (*yir'ah*). It is a looking-back and an awareness that I am being seen: retrospect. From this moment on, I find myself in a *situation*. This mode of thinking is altogether different. Man is obligated when he is in the situational predicament of being seen. This is not true for the mere conceptual assent to the *idea* of being seen.

In Heschel's thinking there is room for coordinates like "faith," "prayer" (liturgical and spontaneous), "revelation" and "Halakhah," I am "responsible for" and "answerable to." He *sees* me and I am amazed. He, the only *real* Center and pronominal

Subject, reveals and decrees, and I (rather me, the mere object) cannot help but reply *na'aseh ve-nishma'*, (I shall do and I shall obey) and begin to act. "My problem is not whether my soul has attained salvation. My problem is what is the next *mitsvah* that He wants me to do." Having been seen, my *me* is hooked, committed. Yet, where can my *me* commune with Him? I can meet him whenever He becomes a *Thou* in time, and my *me* becomes an *I*. Then He can tell me what He demands of *me*. This is revelation. I can make my splintered self visible to Him and He can mend and fulfill it. This is prayer. Prayer and revelation go hand in hand, depending on whether at this moment I am praying *out* (praying myself out to Him) in petition, or praying Him *in* to me, in the revelation of liturgy or the revelation of Torah. Heschel is not afraid that the word will become flesh. He wants it to become incarnate, not in *space*, but in *time*.

Of course, compared to the tradition which begat him, Heschel, too, is self-limiting. He has incorporated only such traditional coordinates as he needs. There are still difficulties in store for those who want to proceed from his system and become what the God to Whom *they* have made themselves visible wants them to be. Heschel may have recovered for us "the question to which the Torah is the answer." Nevertheless, now that we know that "the Torah is God's anthropology, not our theology," now that we know *what He would have us become*, we still need competent direction and guidance. In short, we need a *rebbe*.

We cannot become Hasidim from Buber and Heschel. As wife implies husband and as child implies father, so the term "Hasid" implies a living and continuous relationship with a *rebbe*. In Hasidic parlance, one is *a rebben's a hasid* [a disciple belonging to a *rebbe*], as one might be in Yiddish a *tatten's a kind* [a child belonging to the parent]. And one cannot claim exemption from this relationship by pointing to the example of the Bratzlaver Hasidim, despite the fact that their *rebbe*, Rabbi Nahman, entered the Super-Substantial 150 years ago. He is *still* their *rebbe*, and to *him* it matters little whether *he* is on this plane or not. Bratzlaver Hasidim are certain that *he* presides over their prayer, seated in *his* chair, the very same one in which *he* sat while in the flesh. Yet there are those who claim to be Hasidim, though they have no *rebbe*. To paraphrase Theodor Gaster, if a Hellenist is not a Greek and a Judaist is not a Jew, then *a Hasidist is not a Hasid*, and a Neo-Hasid is only a Hasidist.

The real world of the Hasid has many other coordinates, all of which define his *Hasiding* and his *rebbe's rebbeing*. The cosmology and psychology of the Hasid's world are larger than those of either Buber or Heschel. Its morals and ethics embrace the unconscious (as Dr. Hurwitz of Zurich has shown).[23]

God is both Person and Non-Person for the Hasid. God becomes Person by emanating the world of *atsilut*, in which He assumes intellect and emotions in order to become known to man. God is Absolute and unrelating Infinite (*Eyn Sof*) before the contraction (*tsimtsum*) of His Light. *Before* is not a temporal but a *present-eternal state*. God's Light is and is not identical with the *Eyn Sof*, just as the sunlight is and is not identical with the sun. In the lower worlds, in "creation," God's Presence is the *shekhinah*. Here on earth, the *shekhinah*, the Divine Spouse, Who is our Divine Mother, is in Exile, just as in the world of *atsilut* our Divine Father is in Exile. The *Shekinah* is held prisoner in innumerable little sparks, awaiting redemption at our hand. Whenever a *minyan* is convened where she is, "She radiates so powerfully that an angel, even from the highest of angelic hierarchies, would be annihilated."

This is the world where the deistic truth is learned: "There is none comparable to Thee, O Lord our God, in this world." In the spiritual universes of Creation, Formation and Function, the theistic truth is made manifest: "There is none beside Thee, O our King, in the life of the world to come." The truth of pantheism waits for the days of the Messiah to be demonstrated: "Nothing but Thee exists, O our Redeemer, in the days of the Messiah." Then the level of *atsilut*, in which God, as Person, is each man's attainment, will be made manifest, fulfilling Him as the water covers the sea. The final parousia of the Impersonal Infinite is to be demonstrated at the resurrection of the dead: "There is none like Thee, O our Savior, at the resurrection of the dead."[24]

All of these are equally true for the Hasid, depending on the level of attainment. The Hasid sees himself reincarnated again and again. If he is to progress, he needs the help and the guidance of a *rebbe*. The *rebbe* knows the purpose of the Hasid's present incarnation, as well as the levels and rungs, the advances and setbacks experienced in previous ones.

For the Hasid, there is no point in arguing whether the way of Torah is greater than the way of service (*'avodah*) or the way of deeds of lovingkindness (*gemillut hasadim*). This depends entirely upon the root of the Hasid's soul. We say "Our God and God of our fathers" because we, in our lives, must make living contact with the God Whom our fathers served, that He be both the God of tradition and the God of personal experience to us. Then we say "God of Abraham," because He is the God of those who are rooted to the right, those who serve Him with deeds of loving kindness. We say "God of Isaac" because he is also the God of those who serve Him through prayer and sacrifice, rooted to the left, in service (*'avodah*). We say "God of Jacob" because He is also the God of those who serve Him with Torah, being rooted in the middle. Abraham, Isaac and Jacob were the only pure archetypes. Therefore, one cannot divorce himself from any of these ways of serving. Only a *rebbe* can establish the exact balance of Torah, service and deeds of loving kindness for his Hasid.

Thus does Hasidism meet the problem of the usual incompatibility of religious intensity and tolerance. Without this approach, the intense adherence to one way would be heresy to the others. Hasidism teaches that there is integration (*hit-kalelut*) in the present order of the world (*tikkun*). The former order of chaos (*tohu*) carried the seeds of its own destruction, causing the "shattering of the vessels" when various objects collided with one another in their onesidedness.

Out of the junk pile of chaos God fashioned man's animal soul. It can be of the "sheep," "ass," or "goat" variety. The Hasid cannot choose his own way unless he knows the root of that other part of his being. Only a *rebbe* can prescribe his way for him. No book can be written about such things. Rabbi Levi Yitzhak said long ago that the *rebbe* of the generation is the "Tractate of the Love and Awe of God."

Neither Buber nor Heschel can replace the *rebbe*. They can lead a prospective Hasid to one or another *rebbe*, preaching one or another way. But without a *rebbe*, the *becoming* of the Hasid is frustrated. The "world" has no knowhow; it cannot show the Hasid the way. When Hasidism first appeared, it found a Jew fettered by discipline, unable to become one with his inner destiny. The Baal Shem and his disciples began to free the devout, in accord with the realities of their divine soul, animal soul and conscious soul. Under their direction, an over-disciplined Hasid bloomed into spontaneity. But it is nonsense to say that Hasidism cast *all* control aside. One need only glance at the middle chapters of Rabbi Shneur Zalman's *Tanya* or Rabbi Elimelech's *Tsettel Katan* to see that Hasidism taught the undisciplined how to gain control of themselves. The Maggid of Mezritch first taught his disciples "to discipline the horses so that they will know that they *are* horses" and then "to discipline the horses so that they will no longer *be* horses."

Techniques of prayer must be learned. Hasidism realized that it was not enough to say *what* one ought to do; it had to show *how* to do it. Prayer, during the weekday, is a laboratory for the refinement of the animal and the rational soul. On the Sabbath, it is the laboratory for a soul's absorption in God. The ultimate, for the Hasid, is not "Heaven" or the "world to come." The ultimate is to be absorbed in the Being of God. Under the *rebbe*'s guidance, the Hasid practices that he might become a virtuoso in his own field. In prayer, he not only prays to God, but he makes *Him* whole, for the sake of bringing about the union of the Holy One, blessed be He, and the *Shekhinah*. Thus, as Rabbi Pinhas of Koretz said, "God *is* prayer."

Hasidism is not an ultra-orthodoxy, but it cannot give up the need for Halakhah, since Halakhah serves the most vital function of disciplining man's will. In the mystical literature of the East, the solution to the problem of ridding oneself of the limiting self-will which keeps God out is sought in the realization that "He alone *exists* and naught else has *real* existence." When man identifies with the great Self of the Infinite, he too is That. Hasidism holds that *some* can achieve it this way. However, this way is barred to most of us. The West believes that it comes through the Cross, through mortification and consequent *apatheia*, for when there is no feeling of self, there is no will. Or, another way, counselled by St. Augustine: "Love God and do what you like." Hasidism says that this, too, is not given to many. Not everyone has mortified his desires by fasting and not everyone is able to love God like a perfect *tsaddik*. Most of us are somewhere between righteousness and wickedness. Therefore, Moses implored God to give Himself to man in His Will, construed in the leather of the *tefillin* and the wool of the *tsitsit*. God acceded and clothed Himself in *mitsvot*, which have now become the "limbs of the King." He who shifts to a *mitsvah* centered life has no will of his own. Thus is the problem solved for him, who is neither righteous nor wicked. Yet he must constantly attune himself, to be capable of fulfilling the Will and of understanding the Mind. The Hasid sees God's Will and Wisdom in Torah.

First he surrenders his will to the *rebbe*. He gives the *rebbe* the "power of attorney" over his self, vowing obedience to him. The *rebbe* soon transfers this obedience to God.

Perhaps Buber and Heschel can bring the Jew to the verge of accepting the yoke of God's kingdom. But they cannot make him capable of accepting the yoke of *mitsvot* and of continuing to function and develop. For spiritual direction, the Hasid must seek out his *rebbe*. And each of the *rebbes* has received a "double portion" from his predecessor, as Elisha did from Elijah. In the 200 years since the assumption of the Baal Shem, they are said to have acquired considerable experience in this area. Despite Buber, there is anything but decadence to be observed in active Hasidic communities today.

Toward an "Order of B'nai Or": A Program
for a Jewish Liturgical Brotherhood (1964)

This document is Reb Zalman's call for a Jewish monastic order. His imagined devotional fellowship never came to be in exactly the form he articulated, but it served as the inspiration for the B'nai Or and P'nai Or communities of Winnipeg and then Philadelphia in the 1970s, which eventually transformed into the Aleph Alliance for Jewish Renewal.

The article also influenced the founding in 1968 of Havurat Shalom in Somerville, Massachusetts by the newly married Art and Kathy Green. A novel type of Jewish intentional community and institute for learning and prayer that drew on the spiritual legacy of Hasidism, Havurat Shalom welcomed Reb Zalman as a guest member during its crucial first year. This visit—together with his writings—assured that Reb Zalman's vision had a lasting impact upon the national *havurah* movement that would emerge from this initial group.

There are ample precedents in Jewish history for liturgical brotherhoods—*havurot*. Josephus and Philo have apprised us of the work and lives of the Essenes; and the Dead Sea Scrolls, of course, have yielded a *Manual of Discipline*, increasing our knowledge of the constitutional and functional aspects of liturgical group-life. Even within normative Judaism there are many examples of such societies. The following pages are the result of the discussions of concerned individuals who see it as their vocation to establish such a community—an "Order of *B'nai Or*" (Sons of Light)—and to live its life, in our own time.

We take it for granted that the present "business-as-usual" status quo does not express the highest and most desirable dimension of Judaism and that this condition does not necessarily meet with divine approbation. On the contrary, it must act as a stimulus challenging us to overcome it. To be moti-

vated by a wish to "save Judaism," "to make for a more meaningful Jewish survival"—or whatever the current formulation
of the *shelo lishmah* is—may have salutary effects; but we want
it clearly understood that we are interested in *shelemut ha-
'avodah*, the perfection of our service to God, so that He, be
He blessed, may derive *nahat* (pleasure) from us. Or, to put it
differently: we are concerned to realize God in this lifetime;
to achieve a higher level of spiritual consciousness; to liberate
such hidden forces within us as would energize us to achieve
our highest humanity within Judaism. Regardless of the particular formulation of the meaning of *shelemut ha-'avodah*, we
regard ourselves as not only working out our own concern,
but in our concern we also see God's blessed Providence in
action, calling us to the life of the *hevrah* as well as His abiding
involvement in it. Responding, we see ourselves as yea-saying
partners with Him.

The most serious reason urging against the establishment of
such a brotherhood is that this constitutes a forsaking of the
larger community. But this is not our intent. In a later section,
describing community services, we will deal with this in detail.
For the moment, suffice it to say that the means of earning a
livelihood for the total community and its individual members
would be found largely from serving in areas of urban Jewish
tsorkhey tsibbur—community needs.

There may be others who will be called to service in a rural
setting. From a contemplative point of view, this is certainly
more satisfying. On a farm one is far away from the contami-
nation of the city; one lives closer to the cycles of nature and
is involved in more wholesome physical activity. However, this
is a luxury which we at present cannot afford.

It is not for us to train to become the Jewish religious shock-
troops and to step into the many breaches left by the fact

that the average Jew does not consider himself a *klallmensh*. Untrained shock-troops may give vent to what may appear to others as fanaticism, haste and impatience, as well as lack of gentle spirituality. Yet, despite their imperfections, there are, thank God, some groups of this type already at work in America, Europe and Israel. It is our hope that some will be moved to *train* for this type of work, but this is not our task.

"All of Israel are responsible (hostages, guarantors) for one another." At this time, when *teshuvah* is so urgently needed, it is conceivable that some may wish to be engaged in the work of making reparations to God by accepting for themselves an "exile" of vagrancy and poverty, suffering and pain. According to Vital (*Sha'ar Ha-Gilgulim*), there are now many branches of one and the same core-soul active in different persons. Reparative *teshuvah-tikun* makes sense, but we are not called to do this.

Nature of the Brotherhood

Groups like ours are usually bound by the three vows of *poverty, chastity* and *obedience*. To us *poverty* means no private individual ownership of resources. These will be pooled in a common treasury (and shall be guaranteed in the event of leaving). That which is owned by the group is considered to be *hekdesh*, dedicated to God. A waste of these resources amounts to desecration.

Chastity, to us, means no mitigation of the full implication of this word. The eyes, the mind, language and the senses have to be guarded, so that they remain in the condition of chastity. Such sexual activity to which the Torah obligates us must be engaged in with chastity. Thus we interpret chastity not to mean total sexual abstinence, but that the fulfillment of such *mitsvot* as are tied to sex are to be engaged in a manner befitting God's continual, even more intense Presence as it obtains between husband and wife in the joyous fulfillment of the *mitsvah*.

Obedience, to us, takes on a Halachic character. Any Jewish society receives sanction for its *takanot*, constitution and statutes by virtue of the principle *shavia 'al nafshey hatikha de-issura*, in that whatever the statutes forbid takes on the forbidden aspect of *trefah*. Positive levels of obedience take on a character of positive commands. As God's delegate—*mora rabbakh ke-mora shamayim*—the ultimate arbiter of the *takkanot* will be the overseer chosen by secret ballot by full members of the community. Any immediate superior delegated by him will also be accorded the same obedience. The overseer's rule will, God helping, not be a capricious use of power. In this sense the overseer is accountable to God and the community.

As various income functions become more clearly defined and take on dynamics of their own, it may very well be that other *B'nai Or* groups will have to split off from the original group. As it is, we have quite a bit of work to do, which may turn out to be more than we can well handle. We expect that functions will be split off according to the planning of the group and the promptings that come through the individual member's heart from Him Who ultimately is the holder of our destinies.

There may be some who in their own life at home, in the world, will live as partners with us in liturgical and contemplative enterprises. Chances are that if they are not moved to join us completely in the community, they are the greater souls for their independence. To legislate for them in this outline may be, therefore, both presumptuous and premature. They will have to plan with their directors the combination of work and the times in which they are suited by nature, predilection and circumstances. When they see fit to spend some time in the community proper, they will take their places among probationary members.

Time and time again we must consciously and deliberately center down to our main calling which is the service of God in prayer. There are Torah *Kollelim* who organically represent the head—the "apostolic" shock-troops representing the mouth and language—but we must be the heart. It is for this reason that our excursions into such income-bringing functions as will be mentioned later are at best economic means. True, we will want to choose such means as will be closest to our central vocation, but *it* must remain central and be pursued in sober seriousness.

We are basically dissatisfied with "the world." Our dissatisfaction stems mainly from the fact that as well-adjusted members of it we would have to live as ardent consumers of goods which we do not really need but which in fact inhibit our best possible functioning in terms of *shelemut ha-ʻavodah*. We have to isolate ourselves from a contaminated environment. Only then can we make sure that the laboratory conditions will be met which will permit us to proceed in our chosen direction.

We believe that the experience of the cosmic and the divine is potentially given to all men and that, depending on one's style of life, one can become a receptacle for the Grace of God. We believe that there is enough psychic and pneumatic know-how available to us within the Jewish framework. To serve God better, we will not even hesitate to borrow extensively from the know-how of others. We feel that the seriousness of the vocation to serve God has largely become lost in the exoteric assertion of the reception of the unique gift of grace which is the revelation possessed by a group. To put it differently, if I am sure that I possess the clear statement of what God demands of me, this possession ought only humble me and challenge me to fulfill the demands of that revelation. Yet some "guardians of the revelation" see themselves as exempt from the humbling challenge to live up to it, as if their chosenness implied that they need not struggle with their own recalcitrant will, slothful habits, etc. For us, the need to establish a liturgical community actually means that we have become aware of what William Law calls "the serious call to a holy and devout life"—issuing daily in the *bat kol* from Sinai.

Not only are we dissatisfied with the secular world, we are also dissatisfied with the "religious" world at large. That world lives under the same consumer compulsion as the secular world. Under this consumer compulsion (and kosher goods and their producers are as relentless in driving us to consume them as are others) one is far too busy to obtain the means for consuming and then far too busy to consume all the means. One consumes without having any time left for 'avodat Hashem. One may become a kosher sensate reprobate. Economically, four hours of work per day, five days a week yield enough of the necessities of life for people whose only "Joneses" are those who live as frugally as they. With twenty hours of work per week one should have enough for one's self and one's family to give one all such necessities as will prompt one to be in the best shape for 'avodat Hashem. We will work forty hours. It is our hope that in the absence of all sumptuousness there will be no need for ascetic self-denial in the vulgar sense.

Another reason why we are dissatisfied with the religious world is that it lives the religious life of hardly more than verbal assertion, at best a feeble vote *for* the good, *for* God and *against* sin. We are not interested in formulating a new religion; what we seek is to live the esoteric implications that inhere in our religion as it is. The esoteric side of any religion not only tells about the core-experiences behind the exoteric façade but also how one is to achieve such experience. It may not be "democratic" to hold that the esoteric experience is not given to the masses, but masses are not given to the highest functional striving in the religion to which they give assent. Their assent is static. The static view does not recognize that as a person progresses and grows new emphases are necessary. Mass people are frightened by the seeming inconsistency in balancing emphases that strike them as contradictions. No static philosophy can express all the levels of the dynamic range of the process of inner growth. This is another reason why we cannot anchor ourselves in any specific philosophy and why our psychological ceiling must remain open.

The exoterically minded will accuse us of antinomianism. We are as antinomian as Yom Kippur and Pesach. If they were to fall on one and the same day, it would be quite impossible to fast and eat *matsot* at the same time. But there is half a year in-between.

To gauge the level of the postulant will be the responsibility of his spiritual director; he will give him a temporary theological-conceptual framework. There are some souls who may ultimately not fit the contemplative life but who nevertheless will need to be set into growth by being associated with us for some time. We pledge ourselves not to be possessive about them but to allow them free egress whenever they feel that the time has come. Thus, besides being theologically and psychologically open, we must be socially open. It is also conceivable that non-Jews will wish to spend some time with us. They may run into some functional difficulty on their part, but we have no intention to demand from them that they give up their present faith (or lack of faith) before they join us.

We are not pledged to any particular philosophy. However, in order to communicate with one another and with the Jewish past we need a comprehensive, subtle and precise language. We are aware that the terminology of Habad Hasidism embraces both rationalistic and mystical ends of the continuum of Jewish thought. It is best suited for our purpose. To become proficient in the use of this terminology will be important to those who join us. We hope that a postulant will outlive a dozen philosophies in his progress from level to level.

All this may give the impression that only persons of high I.Q. are suitable for the work of the *hevrah*. This is not so. Spiritual generosity is a far greater prerequisite for the communal contemplative life. Simpler souls often have as God's gift to them a better intuitive grasp of unseen realities than intellectually complex ones.

A Repository for Spiritual Know-how

If our community were to be "busy" and wanted to heal all the ills of the world, it would not have time for the very time-consuming exercises with which our purpose burdens us. We must not be "busy." We hope to divide our day into eight hours of livelihood-work (which we will describe later), eight hours for bodily needs, sleep and food, and eight hours of intensive and serious spiritual work. We are not worried about recreation in the vulgar sense. We feel that living the cycle of the liturgy, we will experience joys such as are not given to the pleasure-chaser, and that the Sabbath and holy days will suffice to recreate us in a far more natural and soul-satisfying way.

We are sure that no one will survive for long in the community if he were not to be engaged in a noticeable process of sober growth. There must be no emergencies occasioned by the other day-segments (except, of course, when a problem of the actual preservation of life arises) which would cut into the eight hours of 'avodat Hashem. This is the sole purpose of our community, and nothing must interfere with it. This aim, then, would be pursued as relentlessly as we have been pursued by the "Hound of Heaven."

There has been far too much romanticism in religion in connection with spiritual advancement. We intend to proceed with this work to achieve a level of craftsmanship that will equal other precise professional skills. Yet we are aware that despite their apparent vagueness such inner promptings as are authentically experienced by certain souls are often far more valuable than any book knowledge. These promptings will have to be clarified by spiritual direction, but the work proceeding from these promptings will have to be pursued soberly and consistently.

We are also convinced that life makes for adaptability and the readiness of organisms to accept education. To have been given the privilege of the use of the bodily senses means to us that these, too, must be educated to enhance the spiritual life. We will, with God's help, want to find the sensory triggers which are capable of opening us to a wider consciousness. We hope with His blessed help to learn in the spiritual laboratory what physiological fulcra to utilize that will be of help in our work. Any kosher means that our community will decide as proper and helpful we will want to study in their application and usefulness and learn to control. Depth psychology has given us many insights and placed good tools at our disposal, and we hope to use them.

We dare not give Him worse service than that which is expected on other levels of life and vocation. We hope to winnow out of our own Jewish and general religious literature such *etsot* (counsels, hints, bits of empirical advice) as are to be found in them, to classify them and to apply them where conditions indicate their use. We hope, God willing, to use every phase of life for the bettering of our service for Him—food, sex activity and rest, breathing and body posture, dance and song, sight-light and dark-color schemes, olfactory stimuli, etc.

As a result of spiritual direction we hope to chart our own mind-body-spirit phases and to apply such positive or negative feedback as seems indicated. We hope in this manner to be able to rediscover some of the pneumatic clues which are to be found in the observance of *mitsvoth ma'asiot*—which transform them into *hovot ha-levavot* and thus to relearn the art of achieving *Yihud*, the God-one-ing function, which will enable us to be more intensively, more frequently, and over a greater range, in *devekut*—absorptive union with our God. All this, then, is based on the assumption that it is still feasible in our day and age to fulfill the commandment of *kedoshim tihiyu*—"Holy shall you be."

Reading Room and Retreat House

We need to maintain contact with the Jewish world at large and to offer a service that many do not find in their synagogue. Furthermore, there [are] a great number of unaffiliated people who may be able to overcome their reluctance to seek information and guidance if they were offered such outside the regular synagogue setting. In short, a reading room in a downtown area may supply this need.

People are reluctant to sit down in the sanctuary of a synagogue simply to relax for a while from their pressing cares and burdens. A chapel in conjunction with a reading room would make this possible for them (and ultimately serve as a model for synagogues). The chapel would also serve as a laboratory for classes to be conducted in the reading room.

An experienced counsellor may lend a sympathetic ear to allow a heavy-laden soul to unburden itself. It is conceivable that some psychotherapist will at some juncture wish to refer people with value-problems to a counsellor affiliated with the reading room. This counsellor will, besides possessing clinical training and native ability, need to be an integrated person with a rich inner life. He will be on good terms with people who are situated in the world and will have to avoid being a soul-trapper for the *hevrah*. He will, we hope, as a result of his contemplative training, be able to look at his counselee as he stands in God's primeval thought and lead him to realize that potential in himself.

Such souls as will be moved to enter the community will be tested through a probationary period to see if they are motivated by a divine stirring in them or by a need to escape some unwholesome immediacies. In case the two coincide, it would be our principle to have the person resolve first the problems that immediately face him and only then enter the community.

For many Jews it is an unknown fact that Jewish answers in depth are available to them. Non-Jewish esoteric and pneumatic societies that promulgate one or two esoteric insights are full of Jews. We acknowledge that we are pained by this, for we think that the majority of Jews who frequent these societies do so not because they are pneumatically fulfilled by them but due to lack of available Jewish facilities. It is hoped that at least some of them will find their way to the reading room and chapel.

We need, too, *'atsarot*—weekend retreats—for our men and women. The object of these *'atsarot* would be to become reacquainted with one's inner self, and with one's early struggles to live a God-directed life. Here they could become acquainted with an enlarged repertoire of Jewish experience and striving. Here they could relearn how to *daven* with *kavvanah*, and how to learn Torah. Here they could sharpen their spiritual sensitivities. Until such time as we have ample facilities for retreat guests, we may have to conduct our *'atsarot* at some kosher hotel during the off-season.

An *'atseret* program might begin with a briefing, a spiritual housecleaning, to be followed by an earnest *Minhah*. A half-hour of representative study could be followed by a joyous *Kabbalat Shabbat*. After *Ma'ariv* all the participants would then gather at a *tish*; with the exception of conversation pertaining to Torah or prayer, silence would be desirable. Now *zemirot* could be introduced. The *tish* would take up the entire evening. Instruction as well as questions and answers could take place right there. After the *bentshen* the group would retire right on the premises. In the morning there would be a *shi'ur*, a time for meditation before the *davvening*; the service would be with all the group, followed by *Kiddush* with another *tish*. After the second meal a silent rest period with books would be desirable; another *shi'ur*, and the third meal with *Ma'ariv*, and *Havdalah*. A *Melaveh Malkah* would provide an outlet for discussion and evaluation. Perhaps the retreat ought to extend through Sunday in order to present an extension into the week of the renewal of the spirit. A group might perhaps wish to experiment with other modes of inner expression, thus bringing to light some of the gems contained in our spiritual storehouse.

Perhaps, and this is not such a remote possibility, we could again infuse the observance of *Yom Kippur Katan* with contemporary relevance. A *Yom Kippur Katan* retreat would serve as a periodic stocktaking experience. Most of our self-employed professionals and businessmen can and do, when they so desire, take a day off for whatever purpose they choose. They could convene at the retreat house in the evening, eat in silence, in fact impose silence for the entire stay, while someone reads to them a passage of, let us say, the *Mesillat Yesharim*. After a period of Torah study, they could, as a *minyan*, and taking their time, retire with *Kri'at Shema' Shel Hamittah* awake at about 5:00 a.m. and, perhaps for the first time in their life, recite the *Tikkun Hatsot* (for most of us the *Tikkun Hatsot* has the emotional connotations of a romantic legend). Then, after reciting *Tehillim*, they could study some more, *daven* without hurry, and return to study. They could fast during that day, spend some time on *heshbon ha-nefesh* meditation, and proceed with the *Yom Kippur Katan* liturgy at *Minhah* time. *Ma'ariv* and supper could be followed by a discussion, after which they would return home.

The idea behind the *'atsarot* is not only to give a one-time experience but to demonstrate the practicality of transferring and incorporating in one's own home and synagogue observance some of the dimensions experienced during a retreat.

Repository of Nussah

We are disturbed to note the gradual decline of the comprehensive liturgical repertoire once alive in the synagogue. We feel that we must prevent its complete loss. Who knows whether a generation which is yet to come would not have to resurrect for use, or at least find roots in, a non-European synagogue tradition? Idelson and others had the holy restlessness that moved them to collect and record for posterity such things as *Die Synagogengesaenge der orientalischen Juden*. We think it imperative to acquire and perpetuate the skills of praising God in the *nussah* [liturgical tradition, both verbal and musical] of Italy, Cochin, Baghdad, Yemen and Rhenish Ashkenaz style, etc.

We are also painfully aware of the lack of *piyyutic* material created in the last 250 years. People engaged in praising God with a vital and joyous desire are always on the lookout for new modes of expression of love and longing. How incongruous is it that in the last thirty years mostly people who lived in a secular world have found it necessary to find poetic expression for spiritual and liturgical feelings that welled up in their hearts. We hope to make these two problems our own.

We think the solution lies in alternating the different *nusha'ot* liturgically, musically, and rhythmically six out of seven years.

The seventh, the Sabbatical year, would be devoted only to a skeletal framework of Talmudic liturgical institutions, which would then be enhanced and clothed with the sinew, flesh and skin of contemporaneous liturgical expressions from the realms of poetry, prose, music, chant and rhythm—on days when instrumental music is Halachically permissible to the accompaniment of "harp and the timbrel" (even to the inclusion of such experiments as *musique concrete*). We hope that the people who will be exposed to retreats from time to time will take their impressions with them and bring about the adoption of such liturgical modes as fill the contemporaneous needs of Jewry at large.

The Arts as a Creative Expression of Spiritual Discipline

Currently the ideal artist is the one who expresses himself. Herman Hesse clearly points out the danger of an age of the "feuilleton," which is basically one of undisciplined self-expression. Expression that comes too soon, that does not build up a creative dam of incubatory tension, at best expresses itself prematurely, even if it has substance to offer. Avant-garde cliches are none the less cliches. It is quite obvious that only the individuated person has a unique self to express. For us an individuated self that is not also sanctified has no warrant to clamor for expression. Besides the contribution that sanctified art can make to religious art in general and to Jewish religious art in particular in stimulating other art aspects, there are particular liturgical values that can be realized through rededicated sacramental artistic expression that springs from real spiritual sophistication.

Hasidic masters have already shown the way of what can be done in the field of musical creation. Taking ethnic tunes they found appealing, they transformed them into profound religious paeans of praise. But these creations have largely been of an ecstatic nature. They may not lend themselves to a more "Appolonian" mode of worship. On the other hand, their uncomplicated rhythms are also not quite contemporaneous; even on the ecstatic musical side, the lively syncopation of jazz has for the most part introduced vulgarities to the Jewish scene. The field still awaits its artist. The same holds true even on another level: the De Rossis patterned themselves after Palestrina; Sulzer, after his friend Schubert; and Lewandowsky, after Brahms. These men were not involved in living Jewish contemplative lives. The imagination contains the only barrier to the kind of musical creativity that awaits us as a result of the activity of *B'nai Or*.

In poetry dilettantism shows up in the predilection for blank verse. One who has teethed on sonnets could perhaps be in the position to use blank verse with skill. To produce second-rate poetry would not be worthwhile. Already some of the most sublime outpourings of the spirit appear in *piyyutim* as doggerel.

From a Halachic point of view, abstract painting is to be favored. After some of our people will have become adepts, we hope that they will see fit to arrest and project that which happens in their interior contemplative eidetic field through their skills in painting. The *Zohar* and the entire Kabbalah with their visual (as differing from the Talmudic aural) emphasis offer countless themes for the artist who prefers abstract forms.

Nowadays, there are far more and more pliable media available than ever before. It will be our task to utilize them. Much philosophy and science has been redeemed and made serviceable to God in our faith. The "muses" are still awaiting redemption.

The Synagogue and Sacral Appurtenances

Many synagogue appointments, such as arks, *parokhot* and Torah *mentelach*, are now mass-produced. Though from time to time Jewish artists are employed to design new patterns for them, these do not always correspond to the spiritual business of the *shul*. To design and produce them is a work of love and ardor that stems from the awareness that these things will be utilized in a palpable way for the greater glory of God. This is motivation enough for some of us to pursue this work as a means of livelihood. It is quite conceivable that one of the people who will join us will be an architect (interior designer) or will have leanings towards that field plus innate talent. He would be sponsored by the community to study this field and pursue it. Perhaps much of the bizarre would be obviated and objects more simple and spiritual take their place. It stands to reason that people who work at prayer would be able to distinguish between that which enhances worship and that which distracts the mind. At the same time a person who is engaged in sinking his roots in the classical experience of the past will be able to make use of such traditional forms as are available in our heritage without necessarily copying them.

For whatever work we do inside our own home we would design such khaki or denim work-clothes as would permit us to attach *tsitsit* to them. For occasions of spiritual work a *tallit*-like coat will be worn. For studying and spiritual work during weekdays we want to reintroduce the practice of wearing the *tefillin* all day (even after prayer). Wherever possible, we would like to fulfill the dictum of our Sages: "'This is my God, and I will beautify Him.' Beautify *Him*? Beautify Him in *mitsvot!*"[25]—a beautiful *tallit* and a well-wrought pair of *tefillin*, the *tallit*-stripes in many colors.

Teaching

Some people at present involved in the teaching of Hebrew do this for extrinsic reasons. It is as good as any other job and better than some. The hours may be convenient and the surroundings congenial—all in all, a good way to get through college or seminary.

Every sermon on education points out that we stand in need of dedicated educators capable of empathy with their students, transferring to them information and, what is more, the proper attitude to utilize this information. Teaching is a holy act, a *mitsvah* in itself. Members of our community will be particularly well-suited for the profession of teaching, if this coincides with their talents and inclinations. Knowing that they are engaged in a *mitsvah* they will know how to resist the temptation to kill time. And besides making sure that the information transfer involves authentic Judaism, i.e. Torah, the skill drills will be in their direction of *tefillah be-tsibbur* and *limmud ha-torah*. They will foster the stance of piety of body, mind and soul.

Many virtues not usually considered to be "religious" need to be implanted in the child. Besides, it is one thing to teach the skill to recite prayers and quite another thing to teach to pray. For this one must oneself pray.

One or two of us in a Hebrew school or a day school may be capable of involving the entire staff of that institution in a wholesome change. We pray and are hopeful that some day there will also be teaching orders. To us, however, the income derived from teaching will afford an opportunity to engage in a contemplative life: and the contemplative life will influence our teaching.[26]

What we have presented above is a tentative program for our projected "Order of B'nai Or." It is not yet a rule of our Order. That will have to be fashioned as a result of actual communal living; at the present we have not yet begun as a group in any permanent sense. You who read this are asked to help us by letting us know your reactions. And if you are sympathetic toward our hope but feel yourselves not called to join us, we will request your prayers for our sake and reciprocate with ours for you.

Foundations of the Fourth Turning of Hasidism: A Manifesto (2014)

This third selection was published shortly before Reb Zalman's death. Though aimed at a popular readership of both Jewish and non-Jewish seekers, it is Reb Zalman's most mature description of Hasidic spirituality as a particular flourishing of the mystical yearning inherent to the human heart. Key to the contemporary message of Reb Zalman's inclusive and expansive vision is his embrace of individuals who are lesbian, gay, bisexual, or transgendered. The book as a whole draws upon the spiritual well of Hasidism in order to break down boundaries, answer the moral call of the hour, and stand in the presence of the One.

Hasidism

Hasidism is a movement of the spirit that arises in us as a yearning for God and the sacred, and which expresses itself through acts of lovingkindness and service to the same. Hasidism is the willingness to make ourselves transparent to God's grace and will, to live in the authentic Presence of God—*nokhah peney ha-Shem*—as if facing God in every moment, allowing this awareness to change our behavior, to make sacred acts out of potentially profane and purely secular moments.

This movement of the spirit, at the core of the Hasidic tradition, is also a universal impulse, as is the attitude of active-receptivity to the divine which it fosters. Thus, what has been called "Hasidism" over the centuries is only the story of the evolution and manifestation of that universal impulse and attitude among the Jewish people—for whom it has become a communal *ethos*, wedded to the primary revelation of Judaism, to the Jewish myth and *magisterium*—with unique characteristics and experiential outcomes.

From this perspective, Hasidism is both the origin and fulfillment of Judaism's spiritual potential, arising and developing in different periods to meet the unique needs of a specific time and place. Through the millennia, Judaism has witnessed the emergence of numerous Hasidic movements, both large and small, some bearing the name, and others not. Among the former are four significant Hasidic movements which represent the Hasidic ideal as it existed in three different paradigms and historical periods: The classical period of Greco-Roman Palestine; the medieval period of Muslim Egypt and Christian Germany; and the pre-industrial period of Eastern Europe and Russia.

We call these movements "turnings," literally, revolutions that demonstrate the adaptation of the Hasidic tradition to a particular time and place.[27] Judaism, as we have already suggested, has seen three such turnings of Hasidism (in four separate movements), each an appropriate expression of the highest and most integrated levels of spirituality available in that period, which is to say, informed by the spirit of the time and influenced by the chthonic element of the place.[28]

The First Turning of Hasidism

In the Mishnah, we are told about the Hasidim ha-Rishonim, the "First Hasidim." Although this expression is likely a general reference to the "pious of times past," the examples given of their actions are consistent with what we know of Hasidism in other periods.[29] Moreover, in the classical period of Greco-

Roman Palestine, we find references to a Jewish sect known as the *asidaioi* or *essaioi* in Greek, which may be the first actual community to be called Hasidim, as these words are generally believed to be Hellenized versions of Hebrew and Aramaic originals (most likely, *hasidey* or *hasya*, both meaning "pious").[30] In the Book of Maccabees, they are called "stalwarts of Israel, devoted in the cause of the Law."[31] And in the writings of Philo of Alexandria, it is said that they are "above all, devoted to the service of God" and seek "a freedom which can never be enslaved."[32] It is generally accepted that these Hasidim (usually called Essenes, based on their Latin name, *esseni*)[33] are the authors of the Dead Sea Scrolls and the sect whose practices and beliefs are described therein.

The Second Turning of Hasidism

The Second Turning of Hasidism is best seen in two moments of the medieval period, emerging independently in separate geographic areas and cultural climates which clearly influenced the particular expressions of Hasidism in those places. These were the *Hasidey Ashkenaz* in Christian Germany and the *Hasidey Sefarad* in Muslim Egypt.[34] The *Hasidey Ashkenaz* were led by the famous Kalonymous family of kabbalists (most notably, Rabbi Yehudah he-Hasid, the author of the *Sefer Hasidim*) who practiced an almost monastic form of Hasidism. The *Hasidey Ashkenaz* planted seeds in Europe that would spring up in many smaller Hasidic movements in the centuries that followed. Similarly, the *Hasidey Sefarad* were led by the philosopher-mystics of the Maimuni family (most notably, Rabbi Avraham Maimuni of Fustat, the son of Maimonides, and the author of the *Kifayat al-Abidin*), who forged a community of Hasidic contemplatives whose teachings and practices paralleled those of Muslim Sufis, whom they openly admired.

The Third Turning of Hasidism

The Third Turning of Hasidism flowered in the pre-industrial period of Eastern Europe and Russia under the leadership of Rabbi Yisra'el ben Eliezer, called the Ba'al Shem Tov, and his successor, Rabbi Dov Baer, the Maggid of Mezritsh, whose lives and teachings set the pattern of Hasidism for centuries to come, even into our own day. Integrating and building on the spiritual work of previous Hasidic movements like the *Hasidey Ashkenaz*, as well as generations of kabbalistic endeavor, Hasidism exploded with creativity in the eighteenth century. Its approach was characterized by a new embrace of the material world as a divine manifestation, by an acceptance and celebration of the potential of the common Jew, by a joyous engagement with life, by prayer and contemplation of extraordinary depth, as well as stories and teachings that turned conventional thinking upside down. Owing to its positive approach and popular appeal, the movement spread like wildfire over Eastern Europe and Russia, making it the most influential of the three Hasidic movements.

The Fourth Turning of Hasidism

With the emergence of a global consciousness in the twentieth century, perhaps best articulated in the work of the philosopher Pierre Teilhard de Chardin, and symbolized by the first images of our planet as seen from outer space, the paradigm of every known religion began to shift irrevocably. Before the dawning of this global consciousness, every religious tradition followed a more or less independent trajectory, or could at least maintain the illusion of doing so. But once the "shape and sharing of the planet" was known, all trajectories began to align, causing upheaval in every religious tradition and spiritual lineage. Thus, a global consciousness is both the primary catalyst for and the defining characteristic of the Fourth Turning of Hasidism.

The following are common elements shared by all the previous turnings of Hasidism in the view of the Fourth Turning.

Repentance: The beginning and the end of a Hasid's spiritual path is *teshuvah*, continually "turning" one's awareness back to the divine source, remembering from whence we come and our common identity in the divine being. *Teshuvah* is also repentance, a reorientation to a radical humility that serves as the foundation for true righteousness in our world. No matter how righteous one appears or feels oneself to be, there is always room for repentance; for the paradox of true righteousness is the requirement of self-abasement, realizing one's utter inability to serve God perfectly and humbling oneself in response.[35]

Prophecy: Nevertheless, the primary goal of Hasidism is a direct connection to God, often characterized as *nevu'ah*, "prophecy," or *ruah ha-kodesh*, "the spirit of holiness." Hasidism believes that the prophetic consciousness is still available (though the Sages declared the prophetic period closed at the time of the closing of the canon).[36] If Hasidism, as we have said, is a genuine "openness to the divine will," then prophecy is the product of such openness (as seen in the root of the word, *navi*, "open" or "hollow").[37] This suggests both the method and the means that allow for prophecy, or as we might characterize it today, deep intuition.

Prayer: The primary means of cultivating one's "openness to the divine will" is prayer, which is central to Hasidic life. In the Hasidism of the Ba'al Shem Tov, prayer is generally spoken of as 'avodat Hashem or davvenen, "divine service" or "prayer in which one is deeply connected to God."[38] In the Fourth Turning, we are also inclined to emphasize what we call "davvenology," the investigation of the inner process of prayer, including all aspects of worship and the Jewish liturgical life. Today, it is not enough to be able to connect in prayer; we must also understand the sacred technology which allows us to make the connection.

Practices: Nevertheless, Hasidism has always embraced a variety of supererogatory methods or *hanhagot*, "spiritual practices" that are not required in Judaism, but which are taken on by the Hasid to continue the process of making oneself transparent to God's grace and will, and to facilitate an awareness of living in the authentic Presence of God. Such *hanhagot* were often given in the form of traditional and intuitive *eytsot* or "prescriptions," to remedy particular spiritual maladies and to promote particular spiritual effects.[39]

Guidance: Spiritual prescriptions and guidance in the ways of Hasidism are given by one's rebbe, a *neshamah kelalit* or "general soul" who is able to locate and connect with the souls of individual Hasidim because they are part of the same "soul-cluster," allowing for relationships of deep spiritual intimacy. The *rebbe* gives his or her guidance to the Hasid in the private encounter, *yehidut*, and in public gatherings, *farbrengen*. In the past, the person serving others as *rebbe* was often indistinguishable from the "*rebbe*-function" they performed. By the Fourth Turning, it is recognized that the *rebbe*, though "called to service" and to function as a *neshamah kelalit* through the cultivation of their own spiritual attunement, is nevertheless not identical with that service and function. For the projection of such a static identity limits the *rebbe*'s personal freedom, creates unrealistic and unhelpful expectations, and allows the Hasid to yield personal responsibility in a way that is not conducive to spiritual growth.

Because the ability to function as a *rebbe* is rare, requiring particular spiritual gifts and a significant cultivation of them, Hasidism also recognizes the need for the *mashpiyya'*, the mentor or guide, as well as the *haver*, the spiritual friend. The former is an individual who has achieved maturity on the spiritual path and is thus able to help others in negotiating many of its paths and pitfalls. Likewise, friends who share the same spiritual values, and with whom one can share the journey, are also critically important.[40]

Community: The communal context for spiritual growth in Hasidism is the *farbrengen*, literally "time spent together." The Hasidic gathering may take place on Shabbat, other *yamim tovim*, or at any other time of the year. Likewise, it may be led by the *rebbe* or a *mashpiyya'*, or simply be a gathering of *haverim*. It is a time for spiritual guidance, cultivating both joy and introspection during which meditation and Hasidic *niggunim* are used for tuning consciousness to the right frequency for receiving Torah, and where Hasidic *ma'asiyot* and *meshalim*, stories and parables, open the heart and imagination to the possibilities of living a more virtuous reality.

Law: The norms of Hasidic life and behavior are oriented around a radical engagement with Jewish law, or *halakhah*. Contrary to some modern misconceptions, Hasidism is not anti-legal and has never been casual about *halakhah*. On the contrary, Hasidism stresses the most integral, elevated, and meaningful applications of every aspect of Jewish law and tradition to Jewish life. This is also the view of the Fourth Turning, which seeks to engage and examine every law and tradition, taking the needs of the time, the place, and the people into consideration, looking at the original function of the law in its original context to see how it may be best applied today to achieve similar ends.

Providence: Finally, the view of Hasidism is providential. In each turning, Hasidism has embraced an idea of providence in keeping with its own experience of divinity, as well as an awareness of the "miraculous order" in creation. The holy Ba'al Shem Tov spoke of *hashgahah peratit*, a "specific personal providence," in which all events are seen as happening with a specific or particular purpose, beyond appearances of "good" or "evil."[41] This is in keeping with his pantheistic worldview, wherein there is nothing in existence but divinity; therefore, nothing happens that is not divine or divinely ordained (however we may judge it according to our limited vision). Our own understanding of "organismic pantheism" is but an extension of this view, merely acknowledging the dynamic and sophisticated organizing principle of ecological systems within the whole of possibility, always serving the Greater Purpose.

In one form or another, these elements have been present in every turning of Hasidism. And yet, each turning always contributes something new—new interpretations, new teachings, new practices and new ideas. The following are some of the new ideas on which the Fourth Turning bases itself:

Renewal: More than ever before, Hasidism needs to maintain an awareness of its own evolution (of which the various turnings are evidence) in the context of the greater evolution of spiritual traditions on the planet. As consciousness evolves over time and the world changes, traditions must reclaim their primary teleological impulse in order to adapt to the needs of the evolving consciousness. This process of unfolding within and adapting without, we call "renewal."[42] Renewal itself is characterized by the struggle to marry the magisterium of a religious tradition, i.e., its inherited body of knowledge and wisdom, to a new reality map or paradigmatic understanding of the universe. On a small scale, renewal is happening continuously; but it is also a process that we witness on a larger scale in certain epochs or axial moments in history, like ours, when religions and religious forms are breaking down and slowly re-organizing and reforming over time.

An awareness of this process can help to keep our current religious and spiritual traditions healthy. For as we engage and become aware of the process of renewal, we must re-evaluate our traditional spiritual teachings and practices, considering their "deep structures," analyzing their function in different historical periods to better understand how they might apply, or be adapted for use in our own time.[43] This new understanding and adaptation allows us to utilize the maximum of our historical traditions, without at the same time turning a blind eye to the true needs of the present.

Deep Ecumenism: However, as we explore the deep structures of our own traditions, revealing the basic functionality beneath the specific wrappings, we cannot ignore their similarity to those of every other religious and spiritual tradition on the planet. Providence, as well as our own evolutionary perspective, demands that we acknowledge a similar sacred purpose at work in these deep structures, that we learn how others use them for the fulfillment of the greater Purpose, and how others can aid us in understanding our own use of them.

While dialogue with other religious traditions undoubtedly took place in our past, it had no legitimizing basis or support in the tradition, and could rarely take place openly. Today, it is nevertheless embraced by many Jewish leaders, being seen as a salutary attempt to achieve a measure of understanding between religions, discerning similarities and differences through dialogue and close observation. However, the Hasid must go beyond such surface knowledge, seeking the spirit beneath the external forms and teachings, undertaking the more intrepid explorations of "deep ecumenism," in which one learns about *oneself* through participatory engagement with another religion or tradition.[44]

Judaism can no longer afford to see itself as the only valid religious tradition, or even as the most important. For such a view is ultimately self-defeating and destructive to the ecological system of the planet which prefers diversity and depends on it for its own health. From this ecological perceptive, every religion is like a vital organ of the planet; and for the planet's sake, each must remain healthy, functioning well in concert with the others for the health of the greater body. Thus, Jews must be the best and healthiest Jews they can be, doing their part in the planetary eco-system; but they must also do it in a way that recognizes the contributions of other religions and supports their healthy functioning.

Egalitarianism: As we embrace this larger "organismic view," seeing Judaism as a contributor to the health of the planetary system, we must not, as we have already said, forget to support the health and diversity of the internal Jewish ecological system. Judaism has, for too long, excluded women from the full participation in the religious life of the community, denied the basic rights of individuals who are lesbian, gay, bisexual or transgendered, and erected high walls to protect Judaism from so-called "outsiders." Although there may have been times in our history when the exclusion of these groups served to preserve a fragile social order or seemed less important amid greater concerns for health and safety, today, their exclusion is untenable and acts like a cancer in the body of Judaism. If Judaism would be healed and give its most healthy functioning back to the planet, it must embrace all of these groups. And in doing so, it will find that much of its new vitality and creativity will come directly from them.

Conclusion: But all of this is just a beginning. It is not definitive, not the final word, nor the only view of the matter. Our words are not "the word" of the Fourth Turning of Hasidism. They are merely the product of a longing to serve God as deeply as our Hasidic ancestors once did, recognizing the needs of our time and attempting to call the future into the present with a name. It is only Hasidism itself—i.e., making ourselves transparent to God's grace and will, and living in the authentic Presence of God—that can do the rest.

Selections from an Interview with Reb Zalman Schachter-Shalomi (ca. 2000)

The final piece is a previously unpublished interview that Arthur Green, one of the editors of this volume, conducted with Reb Zalman circa 2000. Green was then planning to write a book to be called *After the Kabbalah*, on the directions taken by Jewish seekers in an age when Kabbalah no longer provided an overall framework for such a quest. While that book never came to be (his EHYEH: *A Kabbalah for Tomorrow* took its place), this book and its companion, *A New Hasidism: Branches*, may be seen as a reformulation of that intent. Fortunately, especially in light of R. Zalman's passing, the tape of this interview is a great blessing. In it Reb Zalman describes some of his earliest encounters with Chabad; reflects upon his close, intense relationship with Reb Shlomo Carlebach; and speaks frankly about his own spiritual quest after his break with the traditional Hasidic community, as well as his growing awareness of the new, expansive forms Hasidic devotion might take in the modern world. The following transcription has been edited; a full version is available at artgreen26.com.

I. Zalman and Shlomo

ARTHUR GREEN: In some ways, you and Shlomo Carlebach reinvented Neo-Hasidism for America, and all of us who turn to Hasidism, who have rediscovered Hasidism in a non-ultraorthodox way, are your disciples. You were certainly the first ones in America to be doing it. The myth is that the Lubavitcher Rebbe sent you and Shlomo out to convert the American college campus. You were the two people he trusted enough to do that, and you each eventually broke away from Lubavitch's point of view, became intellectually open to other things, and went your own ways. Rather than making Lubavitchers out of the world, you made this new kind of Hasidism, this American version of Neo-Hasidism. But I want to unpack this . . .

ZALMAN SCHACHTER-SHALOMI: [I first met Shlomo] when I was twelve years old. I went with a chicken from Bad Voeslau[45] on a "Toonerville Trolley" to Baden bei Wien to ask [Rabbi Naftali Carlebach, Shlomo's father] a *sheilah* [a rabbinic question] about whether the chicken was kosher. That is when I met Shlomo and Elye-Chaim,[46] and we were playing for a while, until his mother didn't like me and sent me away. She continued not to like me several years later . . . When they came to America, they lived in Brooklyn, but the shul was in Manhattan . . . Mama Carlebach had a bookbinding business. In fact, I have a few books that she bound or that her business bound. So the Bobover *rebbe*[47] spiritually embraced these two boys, and they went in and out freely at Bobov, before Bobov was bigtime . . . Then they both went to Reb Aharon Kotler.[48] Elye Chaim left [R. Aharon] sooner, and I was a lot closer to Elye Chaim first. When you looked at Shlomo, [you asked]: "Why are you sitting there with such great [yet seemingly old-fashioned and irrelevant] learning?" Shlomo was saying at that time: "You don't understand. The business of that kind of brilliance is being lost. It is burning in Europe and it is not going to be there. I have an opportunity to take this on from R. Aharon to the next generation. I don't want to lose that."

AG: When you say Elye Chaim left first, does this mean that he came to Lubavitch?

ZSS: Yes, and Shlomo didn't. So for a while, we had sort of a complaint against Shlomo, until he too left and went to Rav Hutner,[49] who had given him *semikha* [ordination]. Now Hutner had an arrangement with Rav Menachem Mendel [Schneerson of Lubavitch], learning Hasidus together. Do you know about that? Hutner spoke about this. He came to Rav Yosef Yitzhak [the prior Lubavitcher Rebbe], and asked "I want to learn Habad." He said "You learn with my son-in-law." So they had a *shiur* [lesson] every *shabbos* morning for an hour and a half.

AG: What year was this?

ZSS: Must have been forty-four to forty-five. So Hutner had a connection with Habad at that time. By the time Shlomo got the *semikha* from Hutner, I was already at Fall River,[50] after Rochester. Shlomo got a job in New Jersey at a *shul*. That *shul* had a piano. I had an accordion at that time, and I was playing an organ. I had one of the early tape recorders, and I recorded Hasidic *niggunim* [melodies] on a Hammond organ, and so on. So I had all that. I had translated some letters from the Rebbe Rav Yosef Yitzhak at that time. Shlomo at that time had a fellowship group that was called "Taste and See that God is Good." It used to meet at the Carlebach Shul. Once I was in New York, and he got me [to celebrate] with his *hevra*. It was the earliest such group around.

AG: 1950?

ZSS: Slightly before, because the Rebbe was still alive.[51]

AG: Late forties. So you and Shlomo are twenty-two years old?

ZSS: I am two years older than Shlomo. Yes, 1948, I was twenty-four and Shlomo was twenty-two. Then he started to play piano, and make some of his *niggunim*. The early *niggunim* that he made were really great compositions. Later on, in Winnipeg, I got his first record . . . So it is *yud tes Kislev* [a Habad holiday], we are in Lubavitch,[52] and there is a *far-brengen* [celebration] in a small room . . . That year we had the *farbrengen* in that little room because the *rebbe* wasn't well enough to have lots of people . . . So Shlomo and I get called in. We made a *le-hayyim*, so he said *le-hayyim*. [Then the rebbe asked us to go out to the] "colleges and see what you can do to make publicity for Judaism."[53] So I gathered up from the *shuls* thirteen pairs of *tefillin* which I refurbished a bit. Then, on Chanuukah, Shlomo came in to Providence, and I picked him up. So the two of us went on our first trip to Brandeis.

AG: Brandeis was brand new. Only a ycar old thcn.[54]

ZSS: Everything was on the hill . . . We had to carry everything up. The accordion, the tape recorder, the printing,[55] up to the castle where there was a cafeteria. The lights were low in the cafeteria. Someone was playing with the spotlight on the couples that were dancing there. So here Shlomo and I come in with some snow on us, and lugging all the packages. The jukebox that was playing stopped for the moment. Everyone stopped and looked at us. Before long we found a table and set up, on the table, the brochures, the tape recorder, and this and that, and people hung around. They listened first to the music and they started to ask questions, and Shlomo started to tell stories. While Shlomo was telling stories, someone said "That sounds like Indian Mysticism." So I pull this guy aside, and I asked him "Do you read the Upanishads? Did you read the Gita?" and so on, and then I would say, "Yeah, ours is better."

Shlomo was telling stories and it was wonderful. People gathered around him. So we said to the people, "Come at three o'clock at night to the commons room of a certain dorm, and anybody who wants to have a pair of *tefillin*, we will give out as many as we have." But in order to earn a pair of *tefillin*, you have to put them on three times and put them together, and if you know how to do it you get them. Thirteen pairs of *tefillin* went at that time. About five in the morning we wound up in a hotel room in Boston, tired, and went to sleep . . .

AG: Had you read those things [like the Upanishads] then?

ZSS: Yes, because this was toilet reading at that time.[56] But I was interested.

AG: Could you talk with Shlomo about the questions that outside reading raised for you?

ZSS: Shlomo and I never had that level of conversation. It was hard to have any kind of conversation with him because he would go into his *mayses* [stories] and to his *hiddushim* [new interpretations], which was always true.

AG: That was my experience of Shlomo. I didn't know that it was yours.

ZSS: It was always that way. We had a *shabbos* once in Houston, Texas. We weren't "on" until Saturday evening, and we stayed in the same hotel, next door to each other. But we still couldn't. . . . Here I thought, "I've got him. We will be able to talk." Because I really wanted to talk to him all about different things. But he was pouring out. He wasn't asking the question: "How does the listener take it? What can the person who hears him do with all that he is leaving him?" We had a dispute later on. I would say: "You come in and yes, you inspire people, but you don't give them what to do after the inspiration. I may inspire less, but I teach them the 'how-tos.'"

AG: Right. If there was a "what to do" from Shlomo, it was to become *frum* and go to Yeshiva.

ZSS: It didn't come that way either. It was the people whom he touched. That was their trip. I called Shlomo a genius in virtuous reality, because when he would paint the picture of someone who was doing acts of great self-sacrifice, who gave away the last penny, who is doing the great thing, there would be such longings in us. "If only we could merit to this kind of thing!" That left you hungry and thirsty for it, and people were looking for a hit. Then they found that hit in the *shul*.[57] That is when it got into *tsitsis* [wearing ritual fringes] and all the rest. But I never heard Shlomo do much of that [telling people to become observant]. Even in the House of Love and Prayer, they emulated him, but he didn't tell them.

II. Outgrowing Habad

AG: Let's go back. When did you start reading those [non-Jewish] things?

ZSS: New Haven. 1945, forty-six, forty-seven. In forty-eight I went to Rochester . . .[58] Then I read about Ramakrishna. [I thought:] "The *goyim* have a Rebbe!" From that time on, I started to look across the fence. But don't forget, I was raised in Vienna, and when I was a kid, I felt that all the women are Catholic, and all the Jews are male.

AG: Was there a Lubavitch Yeshivah there already in New Haven? Or were you part of the group that founded it?

ZSS: No. I was part of the group that founded it. That is right. We got the kids from released time, then we got them into afternoon schools, then we started to build a day school. In the day school, I felt that I needed to know more about child development and teaching. So I went to the library on the green in New Haven to get books by Norman Gesell.[59] Gesell was at the time the child development man at Yale. I did it so I could learn more about how to be a good teacher. I find in "Recent Acquisitions" in the library two new books. One was by Father Eugene Boylin, *Difficulties in Mental Prayer*.[60] The other one was *The World Bible* by Ballou.[61] So, "Difficulties in Mental Prayer!" "Who knows about mental prayer?" I asked myself. Even Belzer[62] Hasidim don't know [about mental prayer]! This is very much Habad. So I picked up the book and I read it. I see he talks there about distracting thoughts during prayer, and meditations, and so on, and the prayer that does not get said with words, that comes from the heart,[63] and of course [I said:] "*Goyim* know from that?" That was amazing, and that was the beginning of my "downfall."

AG: Who could you talk to about this discovery?

ZSS: Nobody . . . At that time, I still saw myself very much as a recruiter for Lubavitch. But I was not [so much] interested to make people Lubavitcher Hasidim as to get them to repent, to return [to God and to Judaism]. So when I was singing these songs, the *niggunim* with the people, I would see them singing them, but without knowing why there were such longings in the *niggun*. So I put words to them [singing], "For the sake of my soul, I searched for a goal, and I find another in thee Oh Lord." In the meantime, I was also exploring spiritualism and ecumenical connections . . .

So [one Friday in 1950] I get the call from Moshe Pinchas Katz [saying] that we should learn that *maimar bosi le-gani* [the teaching on "I have come into my garden," Song of Songs 5:1], before praying that *shabbos* morning . . .

AG: This was when the Rebbe was still alive?

ZSS: That was the time of his departure. He died that *shabbos* morning, but I didn't know anything about that. Moshe Pinchas called after *shabbos*, saying that the Rebbe had passed away from the world, and that I should come to New York. My first thought was "How can this be? Messiah hasn't come yet!" So I call the [Chabad] guy in Providence . . . and we drove to New York and we came in time for saying *tehillim* [psalms] while the washing of the body was going on. . . . Then was the *levaya* [funeral]. When they came to the cemetery, there was a guy who was taking tables from the *Beis Midrash* and breaking them down to make the coffin. . . . This guy was a carpenter; a *hasidisher yid mit a bort* [a Hasidic Jew with a beard], he was taking it on. The word was that he was undertaking the job of building the coffin because he was going to die that year. When they came to the cemetery, they took the coffin apart, and laid the *rebbe's* body on the ground itself and used the sides of the coffin to put the dirt up.

Do you remember that story of the RaMasH[64] meeting me outside [the gravesite]? It was Purim, and I [had] come back again to New York. After reading the *megilla* in the morning, I got in the car to drive to New York . . . Yuppie[65] was born three days after the *rebbe's* passing. . . . Feigel[66] was under gas [anesthesia] at that time, and she sees the [recently departed] *Rebbe*. The *Rebbe* says to her "*Mazel Tov*, you have a son. You should live now in New York." She says to him in the trance, "Who [is to be *rebbe*]?" She sees the letters *Resh Mem Shin* [= Reb Mendel Schneerson] in fire. You can imagine all that . . . So I come to New York on Purim, go to the *Ohel* [the late *rebbe's* gravesite] first, and I am washing my hands at the outside to go in. So he [Reb Menachem Mendel] stands near the door, and he says "Nu Reb Zalman, Have you been to the grave?" I say yes. He said: "May God help you, what did you pray for?" . . . I said, "I asked for three things. I asked that one, we should have a *rebbe*, two, that you should be the *rebbe*, and three, that you should be blessed with children."[67] He held my hand at that time, and I was crying and he was crying. He said "We have a *rebbe*. What difference does it make where he is?"[68]

So I fixed him with my eyes, and I said "Why did God take Moses our Teacher and hide his burial place? So that Joshua would not be able to send people on to Moses!" It was a Kotzker answer.[69] So he says "It will be good, it will be good, Reb Zalman." So, I just felt very, very much . . . I liked him, and I had a lot of hopes, because I had met him yet in France . . .

I am saying all this because it didn't come as a [sudden] break. So being out in . . . Fall River, I get a call from the Conservative rabbi.[70] "Would you pinch hit for me? I have to go for a Bar Mitzvah." I said, "I can't give you an answer yet. I will call you back." I call my president who clears it with his people and says "It's an honor for us that you should speak at the Temple."[71] I call Hayyim Lieberman, the *rebbe*'s secretary, because I want to talk to the Rebbe. This was still with Rav Yosef Yitzhak. I ask whether I should accept this thing or not? Because [I was] one of the *rebbe*'s guys, so how could I go into a Temple like this? So he calls me back [saying] that I should go, that I should make some kind of a *shinui* ["difference"; a public sign indicating that this is an exceptional event], but what the *shinui* is, is my choice, and that I should not prepare a talk . . .

So I figure "What do you mean?" A Conservative Temple! [They must all be] Professors, and I have to have stuff ready. I had no concept at that time; I was just new in this thing. So [I decided I would speak on the question of] divine foreknowledge and free choice.[72] The *shinui* was no organ; the choir was okay. I didn't prepare, but I had a whole lecture in the back of my mind. I come there and I see these are just ordinary folk; these are all the people I'd seen at UJA meetings, at funerals, and everywhere—so it certainly wasn't the place [for such a philosophical talk]. So now I don't know what to say. The president is already introducing me, and I still don't know what to say. While I get up there it hits me that if someone would have stood at Mount Sinai with a stopwatch, how long would it have taken "until they fainted, their souls passed out of them."[73] So I made a whole nice sermon, about moments of eternity, how every *shabbos* we can take in a moment of eternity.[74]

AG: You hadn't read Heschel. Heschel's book *The Sabbath* wasn't out yet!

ZSS: It was wonderful, but it just came, so I remained a faithful servant for the Rebbe ...

So here you hear it: there in New Haven all these things started, and I am now in Fall River, and I am already meeting with an Episcopalian priest. Then there is the Rebbe's passing.

AG: The Rebbe did not know about the Episcopal priest. These things you didn't say to him. And what you were reading you also didn't talk about to the Lubavitcher.

ZSS: No.

AG: So already from the late forties, there was a part of your spiritual life that you sort of know would not be kosher with Lubavitch, and you were not telling.

ZSS: That is right, and I stopped reading English in the toilet.

AG: You started to read it out of the toilet ...

ZSS: Later on, in New Bedford, I joined the ministerial association, took chaplaincy training, did some psychotherapy along with the chaplaincy training, which was very good. There was some group therapy, in which I participated. I went into a mental hospital and worked with people. Pastoral psychology was important. That was when I went to Boston University, to do that, and met Howard Thurman ...[75]

III. Moving beyond Orthodoxy

AG: What I am learning from all this, in terms of the order of how things happened in your life, is that at this point *Hasidus* is *Hasidus*, it's Habad in particular that knows what Judaism should be.[76] But there are also other religions and other people and to be able to communicate the message of *Hasidus* to other people and to share it with other religions, the way that others are sharing, would be your goal.

ZSS: Right, and to learn the language of the other people.

AG: This happened before you began thinking about Neo-Hasidism or different kinds of Judaism or anything like that.

ZSS: I hadn't yet gotten to the place of being critical of *Torah mi-Sinai*. The split between *Torah mi-Sinai* and *Torah min ha-Shamayim*[77] occurred much later. I hadn't yet gotten into the historical so much.

AG: So Jewishness was defined pretty much by Habad and that was okay?

ZSS: Not quite, not quite, because I used to be on those panels of Orthodox, Conservative, Reform to talk. I said after a while that I don't want to be on a panel where I start and the Reform guy comes next and breaks down what I got to say, and then comes the Conservative and picks up all the pieces. I want it to be like this. The Reform guy should start, [talk about] what he is for, the Conservative should come after him, and I should come at the last. That was my condition, so it would be a building up and not a breaking down. One of my claims in those dialogues was that religion is in the business of producing saints, and you can hear already the Catholic and the Protestant influence coming in. "Show me the saints that you have produced," I would say to the others. Bruce Irman, who was a Reform Rabbi, said to me, "What about Leo Baeck?"[78] At that point I said "You are right." That already was a strong break.

It caught my tongue. What could I say at that point? So I stopped playing that game . . . Some Conservative rabbis — I hadn't gotten to know any good ones yet. That came later on when I came to Manitoba, there was Oconomowoc[79] and all the other stuff. At that time, it was very clear to me that I still was in the service of the rebbe RaMaSH. I would bring Hillel directors or the people from Okonomowoc to the Rebbe. I was sometimes an interpreter, because he spoke Yiddish; he didn't want to speak to them in English. And he would correct me sometimes, finding a better word.

I sent letters to him. When I would write to someone a spiritual letter, I would send him a carbon copy. He would send me back those carbons, sometimes with a note on them. One of them was to a guy in India from the Bnei Yisrael,[80] who had said that he feels strongly attracted to Hinduism. He wants to be a Hindu. What can I say to him? I said "I can't be your guru, I can only be your sub-guru," and I told him about my *rebbe*, the real guru. Then I said to him: "You chose in this incarnation to be a Jew. Be a Jew. Next incarnation, you be a Hindu. Speaking in that language." So I sent this to the Rebbe, and the Rebbe writes back: "A Jew is never reincarnated as a gentile."[81]

At that point, I already felt that I had had prior incarnations which were not Jewish and I had become sensitive to that. What was happening to me when I would walk into a church where I felt something there, you know? So maybe the "incarnation" was when I was a child and my parents' maid Greta in Vienna took me to the church—but it felt strong.[82] In Vienna, I read a book about a guy who was doing a Yogic thing by smoking hemp, with a cobra, a whole story. All this lies in the background.

Another time a woman wrote to me that some *Habadniks* had come to Cornell, where she was in Medical School, and they were denying evolution. I had written back to her again. "What do you mean? We are all for evolution, [described by the Kabbalists as] emanation," and this and that. The rebbe wrote back "No! You have to stick to a literal reading of the Torah's Creation story." By that time, I was not ready to agree to that. I felt that we were out of synch.

AG: By then you were already in Manitoba? Was that 1953?

ZSS: 1956 to fifty-seven. Then I was in Israel in 1959.

AG: So when I met you, you had been in Manitoba for a year. You came to Brandeis in fifty-seven to fifty-eight, my freshman year. After just one year in Manitoba.

ZSS: Max Ticktin[83] and I already had a strong connection by that time. I would go to his school, he would come to mine. I would do retreats, the little booklet, *The First Step* was already out by then.

AG: In the years when you were in Fall River and New Bedford, were you still sometimes going to college campuses for the Rebbe?

ZSS: Yes. That continued.

AG: With Shlomo?

ZSS: Sometimes with, sometimes without. Because that was my entry to Hillel. That was how I first met some of the Hillel directors.

AG: You had already spoken on their campuses.

ZSS: They were good people, and I really enjoyed them. I met Moishe Pekarsky[84] later on, and oy, was I impressed with him. Moishe Pekarsky said, "Beneath your beard there dwells a beardless heretic."[85] And I said, "Beneath your clean-shaven face there dwells a bearded Jew." So we had a wonderful connection.

It was the ecumenism—the intra-Jewish—that opened me up a lot. At this point I was feeling a breakpoint. I had written to the *rebbe* that I didn't want to stay in Manitoba anymore and I asked if he would sponsor me for two or three years in the financial district [of New York], for a room, a space like the Christian Science Reading Room It could be a halfway house on the way to Habad at 770—and it should be in Manhattan. There should be a place with tea for people to drop in, a little place to pray, to meditate, and I would be able to counsel people, to be a spiritual director for those who have been for *yechidus* [private meeting with the *rebbe*], on how to work out this stuff. He said no.

At that time, the Bnei Yisrael in Bombay were looking for a Rabbi, and I wanted to be that Rabbi.

AG: Dick Israel[86] went for a year.

ZSS: Right. And I wanted to be that Rabbi. Because I was a member of the RCA [the rabbinic wing of Orthodoxy] at that time, and I got that announcement . . .

At the same time, [a new type of religious community] was in the back of my mind. Don't forget that the Dead Sea Scrolls were out at that point, and I had written that first manifesto, in 1961, about Qumran USA.

AG: "Toward an Order of B'nai Or." Is this the same one?

ZSS: Yes, it was the same. Qumran USA is the subtitle.

AG: I remember reading it in *Judaism* magazine.

ZSS: Yes, It was in *Judaism* . . . By that time it was forming in my mind, that *hasidus* as it was, wasn't going to make it. But I had [not] yet written *The Yechidus*.[87] Then when I started to write *The Yechidus* and got involved with Linsey,[88] it was for me like the psychoanalysis of my relationship with the Rebbe.[89] Portions of *The Yechidus* I wrote in the scriptorium of the Trappist in St Norbert in Winnipeg. . . .

AG: You saw that *Hasidus* wasn't going to work. Talk a little more about what you mean by that, what you meant by it then.

ZSS: First of all, history had come in,[90] and I understood the feudal element.[91] I saw for instance the Dukhobors.[92] They had a rebbe: Piotyr Verigin.[93] He was their spiritual nobility.

AG: So you saw that the model of dynastic *rebbes* was based on a kind of European nobility, and it wouldn't work in America . . .

ZSS: But what did I see that didn't work? The business of separating women from men. At Hillel house, I was always able to do men and women together, and that was what I saw later on. Other Orthodox rabbis came into Hillel later on, using it as their decent exit [from the rule of Orthodoxy]. If you took a shul without a *mehitzah* (gender separation barrier), that was a no-no.

AG: But at Hillel that was okay.

ZSS: Already in New Bedford, at the Friday night services, which I did not call a service, but an Oneg Shabbat, but the Oneg Shabbat was a service.[94] *Kabbalas shabbos*, and men and women could sit together, but I did not let them do that in the shul itself. I only allowed it in the vestry. Labs, I started to use that a long time ago, at New Bedford.[95] Quaker [silent meeting style] and all that stuff. At this point, in 1962, I had acid [LSD] for the first time. That was for me something stupendous ... Because I wanted acid in Fall River, and in New Bedford.

AG: You had heard of LSD already then?

ZSS: I had read Huxley's *Doors of Perception* there. It was quite something then. I had a doctor in New Bedford who was going to get it—mescaline sulphate—and he already had checked out my health, the liver. You know, in those days they were really worried about these things. So yes, I wanted it. When I came to Manitoba, I wanted it, and I could have gotten it in Saskatchewan, where Abe Hoffer and Humphry Osmond were working. But they said they could take me in their mental hospital if I wanted. And I didn't want to do it there. Because it felt like it would be like opening up for major surgery in a dunghill ...

AG: [That would have been a setup for a] bad trip.

ZSS: So I had met Gerald Heard ... He wrote the marvelous *Gospel according to Gamaliel*. Then he wrote *The Five Ages of*

Man. That was for me the beginning of the eldering work. It was wonderful. He said "I have some friends at Harvard, and my suggestion is you do it with them, and you don't do this thing with Kappel," and he mentioned a name.

So I took the kids on a trip from Ramah, in 1962,[96] and we did this wonderful trip through all the shuls we would come to. My secretary at that time was Sheila Cantor and she had been to the ashram [in Cohasset MA] . . . That is how I had met Mataji [the abbess there]. So we came to the ashram, with the kids. We *davvened* outdoors, then we do a puja with them. There is this guy with blue jeans walking around and with him was another guy. Later on I found out this is Professor [Timothy] Leary. Alpert wasn't there. The guy with him was a Reform *hazan* [cantor] that he had taken on a trip. Leary teased me about monotheism; he didn't like monotheism much. So I said "Come let's go for a walk." Remember all the pastoral stuff I was reading? Pastoral psychology stuff. He had done some fine things with recidivism[97] and he talked about inmates and penal institutions. [I said:] "But Gerald Heard had mentioned you and your work." He said, "I just had come off a trip with this other man. I will meet you here next week." That was when I did that. In between there was this *farbrengen* when the *rebbe* said "Have a good retreat, have a good meditation . . ."[98]

Suggestions for Further Reading

Magid, Shaul. *American Post-Judaism: Identity and Renewal in a Postethnic Society.* Bloomington: Indiana University Press, 2013.
———. "Between Paradigm Shift Judaism and Neo-Hasidism: The New Metaphysics of Jewish Renewal." *Tikkun* 30, no. 1 (2015): 11–15.

Schachter-Shalomi, Zalman. *Credo of a Modern Kabbalist*, with Daniel Siegel. Victoria BC: Trafford, 2005.

———. *Davening: A Guide to Meaningful Jewish Prayer*, with Joel Segel. Woodstock VT: Jewish Lights, 2012.

———. *My Life in Jewish Renewal: A Memoir*, with Edward Hoffman. Lanham MD: Rowman & Littlefield, 2012.

———. *Paradigm Shift: From the Jewish Renewal Teachings of Reb Zalman Schachter-Shalomi*. Edited by Ellen Singer. Northvale NJ: Jason Aronson, 1993.

———. *Wrapped in a Holy Flame: Teachings and Tales of the Hasidic Masters*. Edited by Netanel M. Miles-Yépez. San Francisco: Jossey-Bass, 2003.

Schachter-Shalomi, Zalman, and Netanel Miles-Yépez. *A Heart Afire: Stories and Teachings of the Early Hasidic Masters*. Philadelphia: Jewish Publication Society, 2009.

6

Arthur Green

Introduction

Rabbi Arthur Green (b. 1941), one of the editors of the present volume, describes himself as an unorthodox Jewish theologian of the Neo-Hasidic persuasion.[1] Founding dean and current rector of the non-denominational Hebrew College Rabbinical School in Boston, he has taught Jewish mysticism and theology in both university and seminary settings for nearly half a century, there educating several generations of American rabbis and scholars. As a living thinker, he straddles these two volumes of *Roots* and *Branches*.

The son of a staunchly atheist father, he was deeply drawn to Judaism already in childhood. His Jewish education came first through the Conservative movement and continued at Brandeis University, where he studied under such Central European luminaries as Nahum Glatzer and Alexander Altmann. He then enrolled in rabbinical school at the Jewish Theological Seminary, where he studied privately with Abraham Joshua Heschel and was ordained in 1967.

Green has charted his own course as a spiritual seeker. To date he has devoted much of his five-decade career to the study of Hasidism and its contemporary relevance. He has been deeply influenced by Buber and Zeitlin, whose works he read in his youth.[2] Yet Green is more directly a disciple of Heschel, and also learned a great deal from his mentor and fellow-traveler Reb Zalman. Green and his wife Kathy were part of the small cadre of young people with whom Zalman had hoped to establish the devotional community described in "Toward an Order of B'nai Or" (chap. 5).

Instead Green and Kathy became the principal founders of Havurat Shalom, a new type of Jewish intentional community and institute for learning and prayer in Somerville, Massachusetts. They were not alone in feeling alienated by the hyper-institutionalization and formality of American synagogue life that reached its peak in the 1950s. The seekers who joined Havurat Shalom in its early years, many of whom later became well-known Jewish scholars and communal leaders (among them Michael Fishbane, Barry Holtz, Edward Feld, Joseph Reimer, Michael Brooks, James Kugel, Lawrence Fine, Daniel Matt, and David Roskies), sought to create a new, participatory Jewish religious experience, meaningful for the individual in the context of intense fellowship.

The trajectories of Schachter and Green's lives had them at different places. Zalman was in the heady days of escaping the confines of Chabad's disciplined and restrictive framework. In the *havurah* years Green was in the mode of reexamining and gradually reembracing tradition, coming at it from the outside for the second time. While both had been influenced by countercultural spirituality, and especially by encounters with psychedelic drugs, Green felt that Zalman's burgeoning Jewish Renewal was too casually syncretistic, incorporating language and practices from other faith traditions, and too little demanding of Jewish depth and knowledge.

Over the many years that followed, Green devoted himself both as a theologian and scholar to carrying forward the legacy of the "founders" of Neo-Hasidism—specifically to reshaping Jewish learning, particularly that based in Hasidic sources, for contemporary Jews. Ever attracted to the authenticity and great power of Hasidic teachings to both challenge and inspire, he still believes they must be selected, reinterpreted, reframed, and experienced in our day if they are to remain a compelling voice for new generations.

Green draws particular inspiration from the textual sources of early Hasidism. He values the teachings of Kabbalah and Hasidism more for their deep insights into the human psyche and spiritual life than as literal statements of metaphysical or cosmological truth. He rejects elements of the mystical tradition, such as the degradation of non-Jews or the disenfranchisement of women, which he feels conflict with fundamental Jewish morality. Green understands them to reflect the historical contexts in which the texts were written, and insists that the modern seeker need not accept them whole cloth. The insights of Hasidism, he writes, are too valuable to be left to the Hasidim alone.

This selective reading allows for the possibility of rediscovering the beauty and potential contemporary relevance of the sources. As Green contends, the teachings of Jewish mysticism give us access to some of the deepest wellsprings of human creativity and spirituality. In a specifically Jewish symbolic language, these sources point toward a mysterious, elusive reality within them that we humans call by the name Y-H-W-H, or "God." He thus refuses to draw a strict line between divine revelation and human creativity as the source of spiritual insight, drawing instead on Hasidic readings of "the *Shekhinah* speaks from within his throat" or "eternal life has He implanted within us."

The earliest stirrings of Green's Neo-Hasidic project are found in a pair of short, provocative essays written in 1968 and 1971.[3] Clearly influenced by the ethos of 1960s youth culture, they already contain many of the core themes of his theological project. They evince Green's thought as it had crystallized during his time at Havurat Shalom. Still, today Green considers these "juvenilia," and it took some convincing for him to permit their republication here.

In the pieces, Green combines the language and theology of Jewish mysticism with the empowerment and freedom articulated by modern writers like Friedrich Nietzsche and Nikos Kazantzakis, both of whom were important in his early education.[4] Calling for a nondualistic Judaism that embraces both spirit and body, he argues that while patterns of Jewish ritual life may indeed still be meaningful, a vibrant Jewish life will depend on a radical and bold reimagining of both Jewish theology and praxis.

Green's theology continued to mature and deepen throughout his early career: during his graduate work in Jewish mysticism at Brandeis, then as a faculty member of the University of Pennsylvania, and from there serving on the faculty of the Reconstructionist Rabbinical College (RRC).[5] In 1984, as RRC dean, he published a brief but important article on the nature of Neo-Hasidism and its place in the contemporary Jewish world,[6] asserting that neither obeisance to tradition nor a fleet-footed run toward all aspects of the modern world will work for the contemporary Jewish seeker. Such a careful balance of criticism and commitment, he avowed, reflects the very struggle of the Hasidic masters in their own day: true religious renewal emerges from "a sense of reverence for the past, combined with openness to growth toward a potentially very different future."[7]

In the same piece Green also reflects on why, in his quest to articulate a contemporary Jewish theology, he turned to the symbolic language of Jewish mysticism, and to the teachings of Hasidism in particular. Here he affirms the language of Hasidic panentheism—that there is no place devoid of the One, that God is totality of being and yet infinitely more as well. The Divine infuses the world and is expressed through the cosmos, but nothing—not even the name Y-H-W-H—can adequately convey the infinity of the One. The theology of Hasidism, he writes, enables modern seekers

to view religious awareness as an added or deepened perception of the world, one that complements rather than contradicts our ordinary and "profane" perception. It seems to be nurtured by an openness to a more profound rung of human consciousness rather than needing the "leap of faith" requisite for theism. The theology that would emerge from such a re-appropriated Hasidism could be characterized as belonging to religious "naturalism," in that it entails no literal belief in a deity that is willful or active in human affairs. On the other hand, it is a naturalism deeply tempered by a sense of the transcendent, an openness to the profundities of inner experience, and a humility about the limits of human knowledge.[8]

Green is ultimately a monist, interpreting the Jewish faith in one God as pointing beyond itself toward the ultimate oneness of all being. This understanding of the infinite and expansive Divine, grounded in Hasidic theology, offers an alternative to classical notions of a personal God. Such a mystical understanding of the Divine could, of course, restrict the theologian or worshipper to silence, for it would seem that no words can adequately convey the infinite sweep of God's majesty. Yet Green argues that we are called upon to describe the infinite Divine through a variety of forms and metaphors. These are drawn, as water from two wells, from the springs of ancient symbolism and personal religious experience. Each enriches and lends meaning to the other, without which it could not be sustained or would be of little value. We are the ones who give the faceless One expression as "God" (a view with which Maimonides and some Kabbalists might agree) through our theological and religious language; we humans conceive and construct the infinite number of "faces," or names, of the Divine.

Of course, these conceptual structures constitute acts of projection, in which we attempt to describe the mysterious and infinite Divine through limited, human-created frameworks and words, and then reflect upon it. Green celebrates such a theology. "God creates us in the divine image," as he likes to say, "and we are obliged to return the favor." He thus returns to the use of personalist images of God, as well as to the language of traditional Jewish liturgy, but with the understanding that the personal God is a symbolic construction, a "bridge," as he calls it, between the seeker and the abstract and inconceivable divine Self.

Green's greatest contribution to contemporary Jewish theology is his three-part book series, written over the course of several decades. The first volume, *Seek My Face, Speak My Name: A Contemporary Jewish Theology* (1992),[9] is poetic and especially personal, welcoming readers into the depths of his heart and religious life in evocative, almost experiential ways. Embracing what he terms "projection theology," Green builds on the Jewish mystical mythology to understand the creation narrative. God, he writes, withdrew some measure of the infinite divine light so that the world might have a place. In this moment the nameless One both gave birth to and was born into the diversity of the physical world.

Here he adapts the notion of *tsimtsum* as understood in Hasidism: the infinite divine consciousness is also making room for the human other, although this process may be viewed from either direction. This transition from the infinite (but inexpressible) divine unity into dynamic multiplicity[10] is mirrored by the process of Revelation. Torah, the ever-flowing font of divine wisdom, was first expressed in language—which by its very nature both limits and reveals—through Moses's prophecy on Mount Sinai (understood metaphorically, as we shall see). Thus he views Creation and Revelation as twin self-limitations of the ineffable divine mystery, resulting in the finite world and sacred language (Torah) as we know them. The joining of these two through human agency, the bringing of wise and sacred teachings to bear upon the world as we know and live within it, leads to the most important step in the process: the movement toward redemption. This is a universal human process, though Green depicts it fully in the language and symbolic structures of Judaism.

Green offered *Ehyeh: A Kabbalah for Tomorrow* (2003), the second entry in the series,[11] as an answer to the needs of Jewish seekers attracted to Eastern religion in its various manifestations. In a very different way, this book is also a reply to certain contemporary groups that claim the mantle of the Kabbalistic tradition but remove its wisdom from the Jewish historical and devotional context. Green sees great opportunity in the modern revival of interest in Jewish mysticism. The question, he insists, is *how* that revival should take place. What elements of the kabbalistic heritage are useful to the contemporary seeker, and how might they be reread in a contemporary context? Moreover, he dares to ask, what elements of that tradition might best be left behind?

Ehyeh also presents a small number of devotional practices and specific exercises, something quite rare in Green's writings. Both as teacher and theologian, Green generally demurs from prescribing how others should act in the realm of religious practice.

The third volume in the series, *Radical Judaism: Re-thinking God and Tradition* (2010), is Green's most mature theological work.[12] Though the picture he draws is largely consistent with his earlier writings, and his vantage point remains personal, *Radical Judaism* is written in a more sophisticated style. As he explains in the introduction, he feels compelled to outline a Jewish theology that is still viable after the two great intellectual defeats of traditional religion in the twentieth century. First, evolutionary biology (and with it a host of other sciences, including astrophysics and geology) has triumphed over traditional views of Creation in accounting for the age and origin of our planet and the emergence of life upon it. Second, there has been wide acceptance of biblical criticism, with its inherent challenges to literal belief in the Divine and in Mosaic authorship of the Torah. The challenge to a serious Judaism in the postmodern era is how to move on following those defeats, rather than seek to diminish their importance or to relitigate them.

The first chapter of *Radical Judaism* presents Green's fullest spirited embrace of the theory of evolution, a view that itself evolved over the course of several earlier iterations.[13] His interpretation of evolution is still creative and selective. He does not attempt to engage scientifically with the varied nuances of Darwinian thought; doing so would undermine his entire project of providing an old-new mythic alternative that complements rather than competes with science. Rather, Green describes the development of species and biodiversity as integral to the sacred drama of Creation. The expansion and unfolding of greater complexities of species represent an inbuilt divine desire (or drive) for ever more diverse and intricate self-manifestation. The ongoing evolutionary process is the continual self-revelation of the divine One in infinitely varied garb.

More broadly, Green calls for twenty-first-century Judaism to move forward beyond higher criticism of Scripture, beyond attempting to disprove academic theories and rehash old debates. In both its laws and theology, he says, it is clear the Bible reflects the historical context in which it was written. As a corollary, the biblical text has evolved, by means of multiple authorship, editing, and transmission over time. Most importantly, the Torah text itself is humankind's response to a sacred encounter with the Divine. Indeed, like several other important modern theologians, Green contends that Revelation (like Creation) is not a single historical event but rather an ongoing and continuous process.[14] We recreate and relive the encounter with the Divine on Mount Sinai whenever we attune ourselves to the infinite One—whenever we seek, find, and create words to embody that silent presence.[15]

Throughout these works, though particularly in *Radical Judaism*, we find Green struggling with issues of intellectual honesty. He wrestles with his identity as a postmodern thinker and a monistic Jewish theologian, grappling with the tension between his creative Jewish reinterpretation of mystical literature on one hand and his reverence and attachment to the tradition on the other. Understanding the quest for religious truth to belong more to the realm of art than science, Green attempts to persuade the reader less by logic of argument than by grandeur of vision. Like Heschel, Green cares that ideas be beautiful and imaginatively appealing. The majesty of the religious narrative is inextricably interwoven with the "truth" of religion, as he understands it.

Writing from the heart of his own religious experience, Green uses the storehouse of traditional teachings and rubrics to endow these encounters with theological language and then share them with others. In the array of books and articles he has penned over the past thirty years, he has sought to create an honest, accessible, and authentically Jewish spiritual language for modern religious seekers. Today he continues to carry this project forward, with several new irons in the fire, including work on a long-standing goal of writing a devotional commentary on the liturgy.

Notes from the Jewish Underground: On Psychedelics and Kabbalah (1968)

The two provocative essays that follow constitute Green's first attempts to describe what would emerge as his Neo-Hasidic project. They are reproduced here as they were published, including the author's original notes.

"Notes," the first exploration, was published in *Response* and attributed to Itzik Lodzer. Green's choice to publish it under a pseudonym reflected the controversial nature of the work at the time, and his choice of pseudonym is a variation on Avraham-Itzik, the great-grandfather from Lodz for whom Green was named.

In this essay Green suggests that psychedelic drugs can offer the religious person a different perspective on the world, one that can help greatly in the development of spiritual insight. But, he reminds the reader, drugs on their own cannot truly provide inspiration; they only have the power to confirm experientially the descriptions of mystical insights widely found in the teachings of prior generations.

Here we see Green as revolutionary turned reinterpreter. He draws upon the language and theology of Jewish mysticism, combining it with the empowerment and freedom of modern writers like Nietzsche and Kazantzakis. In addition, Green is already reflecting upon the relationship of the infinite Divine and the world of the *sefirot*, the progressively self-limiting expressions of that ineffable One. The possibility that human experience can replay and embody this process lies at the heart of the mystical devotional life and seeker-friendly Judaism — themes Green would continue to articulate throughout his later theological writings.

Mysticism and words are strange bedfellows. They have always had to live together, neither ever being quite comfortable about the presence of the other. Mystics have ever been wary about the limitations of language: words seem to bind them to earth, forcing them to discourse in neatly boxed categories on that which by nature seeks to flow, to soar, transcending all possible verbal boxes. And words, as it were, have always been suspicious of that which they are told they cannot apprehend; they can admit of no reality beyond their own ken.

From the modern mystic's point of view, the most problematic words of all are the words associated with religion. "God," "Holy," "Love" — and all the rest. The words have become prisoners of synagogues and churches where their overpowering reality is unknown. So long have they been read responsively that they evoke no response. Even the more sophisticated words now used in their stead suffer from guilt by association; "Numinous" and "Sacred" are too respectable — they turn no one on.

When coming to speak of the deeply religious quality of the experience many of us have had through the use of psychedelic drugs, I balk before conventional religious language. Members of the religious establishment have been too quick to say that any experience brought on by a drug is necessarily cheap. I rather tend to fear the opposite: to speak of psychedelic/mystic experience in terms familiar to religionists might indeed cheapen that experience. (Now that the mystic in us has voiced his objections and we have duly apologized, we may proceed.)

Perhaps the first key to understanding what psychedelic insight is all about is the notion of *perspective*. Leary, Watts, and others have written at great length about the point of view one achieves during a psychedelic session. In the experience, consciousness and ego become detached. One comes to view the world no longer from the contextual position of the self, but rather as an outsider. "I" can somehow stand aside, somewhere in the back of my head, and watch "me" at play. The "I" who watches is liberated from the context of the "me" who acts. Associated with this generally cute busybody "me" (who sometimes seems to belong to the kind of toy world one sees when taking off in an airplane) is the entire active material universe: on the side of the "I," to one of a Western background, stands He who looks on from beyond. The most distinctively non-Western aspect of this God-image, incidentally, is that here He who looks from beyond cannot suppress a smile. The world is simply much too cute to be an object of cosmic wrath. Visions of the laughing Buddha who knows it's all a joke . . .

Together we look from beyond. God and I are not yet one at this point, but I have taken the first step: I am learning to see things from "His" point of view. That which I thought was all terribly real just a few moments ago now seems to be part of a great dramatic role-playing situation, a cosmic comedy which this "me" has to play out for the benefit of His audience. I am overwhelmed by my dramatic style, and the world's. I suppress my desire to applaud, waiting patiently for the end of the act. I no longer think that anything is "real" down there on stage, but I feel truly awed by the artistry of it all.

This perspective has a particularly close analogue in the history of Jewish thought. One of the great systems of *HaBaD* mysticisms is that of Reb Aaron of Starroselje, who bases much of his thought on a distinction between truths and realities "from God's point of view" and "from man's point of view." Reb Aaron hesitates, along with so many other Western mystics, to call our world of time and space mere illusion. (The Zohar, in calling the universe of ordinary consciousness the *Alma-De-Shikra* or World of Deception, is more radical here.) Rather, says Reb Aaron, we must learn to speak of two levels of reality. In order for "down" consciousness to function, this world must be seen as somehow real. From man's point of view, time, space, selfhood, and God's otherness are all to be taken quite seriously. Seen from beyond, however, world and ego are but aspects of the same illusion. From God's point of view, only God can be called real. The mystic must learn to balance himself between the two standpoints, never falling *too* far off the tightrope into either one. Of course the Kabbalist would never have been so immodest as to tell us openly that he personally had been "high" enough to see the world from God's point of view. He doesn't have to tell us. Assuming that the Jewish mystical literature embodies real inner experience and not just a body of empty theosophic doctrine (and this is my assumption throughout), the point is quite obvious: with the proper pneumatic keys, man can come to see the world as it is viewed from above. One who has read Alan Watts' description of psychedelic experience in *The Joyous Cosmology* might feel much at home with Reb Aaron.

Now the serious Jewish theologian might rise in protest: How can you dare to equate the vision of Reb Aaron, who labored humbly for years and meant his system to encompass answers to timeless theological issues, with something you describe in such terribly frivolous terms? I would admit, of course, that there is a tremendous difference *in tone* between the writings of the Kabbalist and that which we seem to experience. This is precisely one of the great advantages or drawbacks of psychedelics, depending upon where you stand. Because mystic insight came so hard to most mystics, their words came out heavy and awesomely serious. Only a rare figure, a Bratzlaver for example, could make his theology dance. But when one can flip into mystic consciousness as easily as one swallows a pill, the whole thing is so much lighter that it almost cannot be "serious." Indeed, nothing *remains* serious: on the next wave of acid one can flip out again, go another rung higher, and watch Reb Aaron's system too become part of the Joke.

Turning now from a description of psychedelic perspective to a discussion of the *content* of the religious insight that comes to the psychedelic voyager, our first encounter is with the age-old metaphysical/mystical problem of the nature of change. As we step back and view the world as outsiders, we observe that everything about us, including our own selves, is involved in a seemingly never-ending flow. All is becoming, moving. I blink my eyes and seem to reopen them to an entirely new universe, one terribly different from that which existed a moment ago. I think of Hesse's image of the river of life with its countless changing forms. Yes, but at the same time one seeks a metaphor that makes for bolder colors. Everything that is stands constantly ready to reorganize itself into new molecular patterns, to burst into hitherto undreamed-of forms of life. Kaplan's "God as Process" becomes attractive (has he been there?), but only for a moment. For behind the constantly changing patterns of reality, or—better—within them, something remains the same. If there is a "God" we have discovered through psychedelics, He is the One within the many; the changeless constant in a world of change.

On one level I perceive this duality through the perception of external (or relatively external!) phenomena: the face of the friend in front of me may change a million times, may become all faces or may become The Face. All this *happens*—I do not *experience* it as "hallucination"—yet somewhere in the bottom of my consciousness I know that before me stands my friend, unchanged. *Everything has been changing, but nothing has changed.* On a still more profound level, one experiences this paradox of change and constancy with regard to oneself. I encounter my own consciousness at any given moment in a psychedelic voyage only in terms of its contents. My mind, now more than at any other time, is filled to overflowing with fast-changing images and countless interweaving patterns. In the face of this, the continuity of consciousness from one moment to the next is, to me, the greatest of miracles. All is changing, and my mind seems constantly on the verge of bursting into the shrapnel of its own perceptions—and yet somehow "I" remain. Space, time, and consciousness, insofar as they can be distinguished from one another, are all going through this same infinitely majestic but terrifying process; they are all rushing constantly toward the brink of "Bang!" disintegration, but just as they reach the far limits of existence they turn around and smile. Relax; we haven't moved at all. *'Olam-Shanah-Nefesh;* Space, Time, and Mind, says the *Sefer Yetsirah,* are playing the same games. The miracle of how all three remain constant in their change, how their oneness persists through their never-ending multiplicity of forms, is the essence of religious wonder. Somehow the Principle of Paradox which allows for this coexistence seems to want to be capitalized . . .

Now it seems to this reader of the Jewish mystical literature that here we have encountered one of the basic motifs of Kabbalistic thought. The Kabbalah speaks of two aspects of the divine Self: *Eyn Sof* or "The Endless," and the *sefirot,* the various aspects of God's active inner life. Insofar as God is seen as *Eyn Sof*, He is in no way subject to change or multiplicity. He is eternal oneness, possessing no attributes, no personality, no specific content of any kind. And, in a certain sense, He is all there is. The seeming reality of God as *sefirot*, let alone the illusory reality of this "World of Deception," are nothing in the face of the One. It is only through the veiledness of the One that the many are granted some form of existence. The enlightened are at moments able to peer through the veils and catch a glimpse of the Reality within. Insofar as God is the *sefirot*, on the other hand, the near-antithesis is true. In the Kabbalists' descriptions of God as *sefirot* we find a brightly colored picture of infinitely varied forms of divine life. God loves, gives birth, is Himself born, unites and separates, pours forth multicolored light and withholds it when it becomes too strong, tragically causes and then combats evil, etc., etc. While *nothing* can be said of God as *Eyn Sof*, virtually *everything* can be said of God as *sefirot*. Here there is no limit to the ever-flowing and ever-changing face of the divine personality. God as *sefirot* is in a sense closer to the dancing multi-limbed gods of the Hindu myths than He is to the heavy seated God of the West, who only by cosmic Herculean effort can be moved from the Throne of Justice to the Throne of Mercy. Countless images can be used to describe the *sefirot* aspect of the Divine. God is water: the various aspects of His self are streams and rivers flowing into the cosmic sea. God is fire: the blue and the red of the candle's flame unite and rise into unlimited divine white. God is speech: from the hidden chasms of heart and throat, the Word struggles forth to emerge from the lips. Perhaps most striking: God is male and female, eternally seeking self-fulfillment through a union that has been rent asunder. In short, the Kabbalistic description of the two faces of God seems strikingly similar to that which we have met in the psychedelic experience. Reality is many-faced and ever-changing, and yet the One behind it all remains the same.

Students of the Kabbalah have generally shied away from this kind of experiential analysis of the Kabbalistic God-image. Those trained in *Religionsgeschichte* (the history of religions) have seen the duality of *Eyn Sof* and *sefirot* as a historic combining of Neoplatonic and Gnostic conceptions. Others, proceeding from a more philosophical background, have viewed this duality as an attempt to solve the *philosophic* problem of how the many proceed from the One. But since we are after all dealing with *mystics,* an explanation which takes the inner experience of the mystic into account might prove to be more fruitful. Our claim here, of course, is that on this level one can learn of the classic mystical experience from the psychedelic. When we further compare both the psychedelic reports and the Kabbalistic doctrine with the myths of oneness and change in Hindu mysticism, we can only conclude that psychedelic experiments have indeed led us to one of the major mystic insights common to East and West.

Within the context of this same distinction between *Eyn Sof* and *sefirot* in God, we might mention another parallel we find between Kabbalistic Judaism and the religious viewpoint that seems to be emerging from psychedelic experimentation. As we have seen, the Kabbalists were hardly afraid of using imagery in speaking of God. On the contrary, they were far more daring and creative in their use of religious imagery than Judaism had ever been. Yet they knew enough to maintain a free-flowing attitude toward their own metaphoric creations. Images in Kabbalistic literature are beautifully inconsistent. Intentionally mixed metaphors abound in the Zohar: in the midst of a passage describing the *sefirot* as patterns of light, the light imagery will suddenly turn sexual; at other times, human imagery will quietly dissolve into images of water. They tacitly knew well that all their images were of value — and that none of them was itself the truth. The anonymous mystic who penned the *Shir-Ha-Kavod* knew this well:

> They imaged You, but not as You are;
> They adjudged You only through Your deeds.
> They conceived of You through many visions,
> Yet You remain One, within all the images.

Images of the *sefirot* could be taken seriously without being meant literally; for *Eyn Sof* itself, no images were allowed at all. As a matter of fact, the taking of any image for God too literally, or the divorcing of a particular image from its intentionally amorphous context, was considered by the Kabbalist to be the very heart of idolatry. The Kabbalist's consciousness was sufficiently expanded (an expression often found in the later Kabbalistic literature: *gadlut ha-mohin*) that he could see through his own image games.

Similar processes seem to be a common part of the psychedelic voyage. At various stages of increasingly intensified consciousness almost anything that catches the traveler's eye can be converted into a metaphor which for the moment seems tremendously rich and significant. Looking at a picture, contemplating a certain word — suddenly we understand what it is "all" about. Like the author of the Zohar looking into the candle and suddenly discovering a new way of expressing the Great Truth, the psychedelic voyager, if he allows himself to "groove" on almost anything for a while, may come up with an image which produces great excitement. Indeed, this is one of the great "pastimes" of people under the influence of psychedelics: the construction of elaborate and often beautiful systems of imagery which momentarily seem to contain all the meaning of life or the secrets of all the universe, only to push beyond them moments later, leaving their remains as desolate as the ruins of a child's castle in the sand. No metaphor is permanent; one can always ascend another rung and look down on the silliness of what appeared to be revelation just minutes before. Most important, in this potentially constant drive upward, out-shooting all images, one can catch a glimpse of what the Kabbalists must have *experienced* as *Eyn Sof*: expanded consciousness seems to have no limit, except that of the degree of intensity that the mind can stand. Reb Nachman Bratzlaver speaks of this in startlingly contemporary language: the mind is expanded to the point where it becomes limitless (*Eyn Sof* is the term he uses!), and it has difficulty *fitting* into the brain when it seeks to return. Now again we have a difference in the degree of seriousness with which the whole mystic venture is taken. For the classic Kabbalist the images of his tradition were, if not absolute truth, nevertheless eternally valid approximations of aspects of the divine reality. For contemporary trippers, for whom all this happens so much more quickly, similar images may be nothing more than a moment's heavenly entertainment.

But this in no way contradicts the impression that the states of consciousness reached are in some manner the same. Both find that image and metaphor are the only tools that language can offer them which may be of value, yet as both confront the Ultimate they are forced to leave all images behind.

It is in part for this reason, so well comprehended by Western mystics, that most psychedelic voyagers have sought their religious guidance in the traditions of the East. In the East, the distinction between image and reality appears to have been better preserved, at least in such "intellectual" circles as those around Vedanta and Zen. Both Judaism and Christianity, as taught and practiced in the last few centuries, have neglected some of the most sophisticated elements of their own traditions, including some of those insights which would be of greatest value to us today. Judaism as presented today knows nothing of God as *Eyn Sof*; it has lost the creative mystic drive which led beyond its own images into a confrontation with the Nothing. The Judaism which contemporary Jews have inherited is one of a father figure who looms so large that one dare not *try* to look beyond Him. We have indeed become trapped by our image. The Kabbalists knew well that God-as-father made sense only in the context of God-as-mother, God-as-lover, God-as-bride, etc. They played the image game with great delicacy; their descendants have forgotten how to play. Perhaps most tragically of all, the Father Himself has lost His power. Were it not for guilt feelings and some sentimentalism on the part of His most loyal children, He might have been put to pasture long ago. Sophisticated Eastern religionists never took their god-images so seriously that they had to undergo the trauma of their decay and death.

From the perspective of this psychedelic/mystic insight, conventional Western religion seems to have fallen prey to a psychologically highly complex idolatry. In Judaism, the cult of God-as-father has been allowed to run rampant for hundreds of years. Now that the image is crumbling, Western man naively seems to think that the religious reality is itself about to die. Indeed, he has forgotten that there ever was a reality behind his image. Deeply tied to this problem of image, father image, and religious reality is the whole question of inner freedom in the religious consciousness. The psychedelic experience is generally conceived of as terribly exhilarating liberation. When one allows oneself to ascend into the rungs of consciousness associated with "God's point of view," one releases oneself from the bondage of all those daily ego problems which until now had seemed so terribly important. Conventional strivings for achievement or success seem to have been just so many meaningless webs in which the self had become entangled. Now one can see beyond them, and their emptiness lies bared. This is of course the real meaning of "dropping out" in Leary's slogan. In the face of the magnificent reality now revealed to me, I am truly amazed that just yesterday my ego was frantic about the silliest things imaginable. I try to reconstruct my life on the basis of this psychedelically induced moment of truth. I resolve to stay out of "bags," to maintain this freedom from the trivial as I re-enter my former worlds.

Mystics of all traditions have experienced this same liberation. In Judaism it is a part of the "negation of the Is" (*bittul he-yesh*), or it is sometimes more specifically referred to as the "stripping off of the physical" (*hitpashtut ha-gashmiyyut*). The voyager reaches the rungs where all his physical needs, all his this-worldly preoccupations, are left behind. They no longer matter to him; their vanity has been revealed. This, for example, is the interpretation that some of the Kabbalists give to the act of fasting on *Yom Kippur:* on the day of the great confrontation, man transcends his own physical self. He has become angelic; that is to say, he has been liberated from his ordinary earthbound context. This of course is virtually the antithesis of the way *Yom Kippur* is seen in non-mystical Jewish theology. Yet generally for the Jewish mystic this liberation is carefully held in check. In the Jew's relationship to God, the image of *serving* was of tremendous power. Man's mystic liberation was not allowed to flourish for its own sake. Rather it was to permit him, by throwing off the yoke of enslavement to this world, to take upon himself the yoke of service of the kingdom of heaven. This is not to say, of course, that there is no joy in real Jewish worship. Jews know well how to "serve the Lord with gladness." But for the modern man seeking mystic awareness of the Divine, the image of master and servant is as dead as that of father and child. The nature of our religious encounter, even if it is mystic, cannot counter the fact that we are children of the post-Nietzschean world: we want to enjoy and exult in our liberation no less than others who proclaim the "death of God." Our particular form of the awareness of God can no longer be one that leads us to His *service*.

This is not to say that none of the traditional forms of Jewish religious expression can be made to work. In the spirit of Berdyczewski, Kaplan, and Richard Rubenstein, I too believe that certain symbols can be reborn if we allow them to undergo a basic reorientation in meaning. The attempt to instill the liberating effects of psychedelic consciousness into everyday life generally meets with, at best, limited success. One has the feeling that the absence of ritual makes this effort all the more difficult. Were the great ritual moments of Judaism used as reminders (or re-creators) of states of elevated consciousness, as they once were used to some extent by the Kabbalists, those of us who have gained religious insight through the use of drugs might indeed find great excitement in the ritual life. Compulsive or legalistic attitudes toward ritual we will of course find repulsive; ritual must help us to be more free, not bind us. Those of us who do know of the gentle poetry that is still to be found in the Sabbath and the Holy Days would like to open up to that poetry, seeking in it the reflection of what we have discovered within. We are wary of being "hooked," or of being tied into a religious community with which we have terribly little in common — but we do want to try.

Of particular relevance here are those rituals which have so much to do with the sacred in time. The religious view of sacred time, so essential to Judaism and yet so alien to the modern—even observant—Jew, finds its parallel deeply engrained in the psychedelic experience. As with the Hasidic Sabbath, time in psychedelic consciousness takes on a cosmic co-ordinate. The moment exists, but eternity is mysteriously contained within it. A psychedelic voyager, watching a sunrise in the woods, told me that he *knew* how Adam felt when the sun first rose in Eden. Eden was there with him; he was back at home in Eden. Watching a waterfall in New Jersey, hearing it crash through the silence, we were reminded of a midrash that speaks of the silence that surrounded revelation, and suddenly we stood at the foot of the eternal Sinai. An almost sexual (in its shocking flow of completeness) union of moment and eternity, of the here and now with the everywhere and forever, is constantly taking place. But of course. This is again one of the things that Kabbalistic theology is all about. Creation happened; creation *was a moment.* Yet creation still happens. All future moments were contained within creation, and creation is renewed in every moment since. God "renews every day the work of creation." In the Kabbalistic view, Being flows unceasingly from the Endless, through the chasm of the Nothing, into ever-new forms of life. The world in which the Kabbalist lives is, in one of his greatest symbols, a universe of eternal birth.

This is perhaps even more true of Sinai. On a certain day in the third month after the Children of Israel had left Egypt, God who is "beyond time" and who is Himself called "Place" for He is beyond the totality of place, came down upon the mountain. Cosmic space and endless time enter into union with the here and now. And then, because of that union, Sinai becomes a moment that can live forever. Every moment and every place, according to Hasidic doctrine, contains within itself a Sinai waiting to be discovered. The Torah is ever being given; the moment of Sinai, having tasted of eternity, can never die. One feels that certain of the Hasidic masters would have smilingly understood: watching the silence and rush of a waterfall in New Jersey, we stood before Sinai.

The eternal moment. Having been given ringside seats from which to witness the struggle, dance, and ultimate union of the Forever and the Now, we have the exhilarating feeling of having seen through a great illusion. We had been taking time so *seriously* until now; suddenly, having peered through to eternity, time has become a joke.

We live in temporal and trans-temporal realities at once. All that we have said with regard to constancy and change seems to apply equally to eternity and time. Both are fulfilled through their union. Alan Watts describes the experience this way: "At some time in the middle of the twentieth century, upon an afternoon in the summer, we are sitting around a table on the terrace, eating dark homemade bread and drinking white wine. And yet we seem to have been there forever, for the people with me are no longer the humdrum and harassed little personalities with names, addresses, and social security numbers—the specifically dated mortals we are all pretending to be. They rather appear as immortal archetypes of themselves without, however, losing their humanity . . . They are at once unique and eternal, men and women but also gods and goddesses. For now that we have time to look at each other, we have become timeless."

"We have become timeless . . ." Israel, through celebrating the Sabbath and fulfilling the Torah, achieves a state which is "beyond time," as is God Himself. An old Hasidic doctrine is strangely rediscovered and relived by Watts. Were those aspects of Jewish life that were once purported to be relevant to states of higher consciousness only *translated* into a symbolic language our age could read, the Jewish scene might begin to look significantly different.

As we turn to a discussion of the deepest, simplest, and most radical insight of psychedelic/mystic consciousness, we balk before the enormous difficulty of expressing it in terms that will not be offensive to the Western man, and particularly to the religiously sensitive Jew. This insight has been so terribly frightening to the Jewish consciousness, so bizarre in terms of the Biblical background of all Jewish faith, that even the mystics who knew it well generally fled from fully spelling it out. We refer of course to the realization that all reality is one with the Divine. *Tat tvam asi*, in Hinduism: "Thou are God." The Hindu mystic says it unabashedly: Self and self flow together; Atman and Brahman are one. The game of Western consciousness, including most of Western religion, is truly threatened by such a claim. We have built all of our colossal civilization on the premise of the reality of the individual ego; our very religion and ethics assign limitless importance to the decisions and confrontations of the separate human self. Judaism from the Bible down to Buber and Rosenzweig has been the religion of God's *dialogue* and *confrontation* with man. If God and man are truly one—if separate identity is really but a veiling of our true oneness—what has all the game been for?

The question is more urgent than just one of institutional vested interest. Our very notion of sanity in the Western world is here being called into question. If the self and its everyday vision are said to be illusion (or at best half-truth), what place is left for sanity as the ability to distinguish the "fantastic" from the "real"? If inner vision (drug-induced or not) is to replace sense perception as the most appropriate vehicle for man's apprehension of "reality," is not the psychotic perhaps the most enlightened of us all? These questions have deeply bothered both classic and modern mystics—as well as their detractors. They certainly form the basis for the classic Jewish fears of mystic study affecting or "burning" the unstable and the young; they also legitimately enter into the reasoning of those who demand sensible societal controls of the use of psychedelic drugs.

And yet, despite all the fears and reservations, the feeling of the true oneness of God and man is encountered with surprising frequency in the literature of the Kabbalah. The *shekhinah*, the last of the ten *sefirot* within God, also contains all the lower worlds within itself. As God achieves His own inner unity, all the worlds, experimentally implying the mystic's own soul as well, enter into the cosmic One. The human soul, according to mystic doctrine, is in some particular way "a part of God above." In an oft-repeated parable of early Hasidic literature, the true son of the King, when entering his Father's palace, discovers that the very palace itself, insofar as its chambers separated him from his father, is mere illusion. Scholem describes the stage in Zohar's thinking at which the human "I" becomes but an echo of the divine "I": "the point where man, in attaining the deepest understanding of his own self, becomes aware of the presence of God."

In a particularly poignant passage, and a most revealing one in terms of classic Jewish hesitation before the identity of God and self, the Maggid of Mezritsh asks God, as it were, to step outside of man for a moment, so that man can play the confrontation game. To paraphrase him: "I know that I have no real existence outside You, but there are times when my needs require that I feel I am standing before You. Let me be for a few moments, so that I can ask You to judge me, without Your having to judge Yourself."

Psychedelic consciousness knows this experience. We too, like our mystic forebears, are overwhelmed, exhilarated and frightened by the knowledge. There are times when we want to shout it in the streets, to turn men on to the awareness that all of them are God. There are also times when we want to come back, to live in the world where man is man. In order to do this, we are even willing to pretend that man is man and God is God. But we know that this is a game; we cannot retract. Because we have the *hubris* to admit to ourselves that we have been there, we are doomed to live here with a boundless liberating joy that we fear to express, lest we be seen as madmen. But even then we have a role to play. Our society suffers greatly from a lack of madmen.

Nikos Kazantzakis speaks of man's search for God as an ascent up a seemingly unassailable mountain. Men have been climbing for countless generations; occasionally one of them comes to face the summit. There are ledges and cliffs. The higher one goes, the greater the danger of falling. Our forefathers were experts at climbing the mountain. Kabbalists generally climbed slowly, deliberately, step after sure-footed step. They were equipped with road maps that had been tested and found good for centuries. Nearly every inch of the mountain was charted. If there occasionally was a slip-up, it was usually by one of those who tried to chart a bit of a new path for himself. The task was formidable: many tried, some fell, but a good number came near to their particular summits.

Today we no longer know how to read the road maps. In any case, they would do us little good. They were charted for hikers. We are driving up the mountain in a fast car, equipped with brightly flashing multicolored headlights. We will get there faster and more easily—if we get there at all. Perhaps you will pray for us back in our village in the valley. Strange: up there, high on the slopes of the mountain, we seem to forget how to pray . . .

After Itzik: Toward a Theology of Jewish Spirituality (1971)

Three years later Green authored a somewhat more conservative response to his original essay, this time published under his own name.

In this second essay he describes the feeling of living in two worlds at once, locked in an eternal struggle with God but at the same time trying to hide within the relative safety of academic scholarship. The young Green is drawn to the Divine but tempted to flee from the intensity of this encounter, and certainly from the restrictions of classical Jewish observance. He speaks of a transition away from a spiritual life defined by rigid constancy toward a path where the ebb and flow of Divine Presence is embodied in creative rhythms of movement between worlds.

Here Green is also defining Israel as those who struggle with God, an important assertion found in his later works as well.

In the second section "Introduction II" Green introduces a striking reading of a Hasidic text with the words: "and sometimes it happens that a man's turning begins not on his own account. Rather he is awakened to the turning by an awesome Presence which God in His bounty brings to him." The text refers to natural peregrinations of the religious journey, in which one's consciousness shuttles between moments of expansion that are often swiftly followed by experiences of constriction. When this illumination is sent from on high, it is fleeting and transient, but one who struggles along the path and presses forward achieves a religious vision that endures even after the initial flash of inspiration has subsided. Lifting up this source, Green recasts it in modern parlance to emphasize that spiritual awakenings—including those inspired by psychedelics—may have their place, but they are no replacement for the difficult work of the religious quest.

Introduction I

Denizens of two worlds have never been happy creatures. Climbing half out of their own skins in an attempt to wholly enter one world or the other has always seemed to them artificial; the attempt at a personal wholeness based on an acceptance, on the other hand, of their dual status, or even a glorification of it, often strikes them as insufficiently real. So it is with the demons of Isaac Bashevis Singer: human in the nether world and demonic in the human world, at home in neither and nowhere at rest.

Such a creature, insofar as he seeks out the life of the spirit, is man. "Half from the upper realms, half from the lower . . . ," not quite at home, we might add, in heaven or earth. The spiritual history of man can be read as nothing but a series of attempts at resolution of the internalized conflicts between worlds and life-styles above and below. Reconciliation of heaven and earth: the point where mystical union *is* personal integration. Yet instead, we try to opt for one or the other. Alas. Man's attempts both to become angel and to deny the angelic in himself may have occasioned great bales of cosmic laughter and an infinite flow of heavenly tears, but they have left us no less fragmented than before.

Once there was a moment of conversion, of knowing, of *da'at* in that most intimate sense that "above" and "below" were silly attempts at distinction, that God flows into man and man into God so fully that to try to pull them apart could only do violence to both. No, not a "moment of conversion"—many such moments, perhaps, and none of them quite conversionary. That indeed is our problem and the question with which we begin: Is conversion any longer possible for those who have so nearly been converted so often, and in whom there thus remains so little innocence?

Introduction II

"Open for me the gates of righteousness" says the psalmist. "I come through them and praise the Lord." Standing at the gate, looking through to the other side. Peering into Wonderland. Waiting. Joseph K. before the Law. "Open them *for* me."

"Open them for yourself, damn you! Push!" "What are you hollering at Me for?" God says to Moses. You think *I* open the gates for anyone? "Tell the children of Israel to get moving!"[16]

". . . and sometimes it happens that a man's turning begins not on his own account. Rather he is awakened to the turning by an awesome Presence which God in His bounty brings to him . . .

Now this Awe comes from Above, and therefore it cannot last forever. If it were indeed to last, that man's service would be only of that which comes from God Himself. Thus he takes away that Awe which he had granted him, so that man will go build up his own love of God. Then his service will truly be of his own . . . This doesn't come to man easily; it's a matter of great strength and concentration over long periods of time. When a man seeks love in this way and doesn't find it, he may cry out to God to help him as he had before. Such a prayer is not answered. A man just has to work on it on his own . . ."

Thus far a voice from the eighteenth century.[17] That which you don't work out on your own, in a struggle that has to begin way down here in the world of ordinary weekday consciousness, somehow just isn't going to last. That doesn't mean the first moment (drug-induced or not) was any less real, but it does let you know that it can't become the replacement for down here religious struggle.

Struggle. Storm the gates. No, you don't have to: a gentle push will do. Now why don't we open them ourselves? If the gates are there before us, and we're standing so close we can even see how they open—and we've even looked through them—

Try to run ... try to hide
Break on through to the other side!

We stand dumbstruck both before the gates and before the question. We remain afraid. At Sinai we said to Moses: "You go talk to that thing, man. You tell us what it says. We're not gettin' any closer ..."[18]

When I ask myself these days who we, Israel, are, I hear myself answering: "We are those who fled from Sinai." Now that is really a bit of shorthand, a one part reduction of a two part statement: "We are those who were there at Sinai and who fled." (One who has not been there of course has no need to flee. He may be involved in some other flight and flatter himself by thinking that it is Sinai he flees, but his confusion can be seen and his error felt. Still, the myth of the faith-community retains its meaning: On some other plane *all* of us Israelites have been to Sinai and fled.) I would want to reintegrate the flight from Sinai into our spiritual history, from which it has been largely expunged. We generally choose to see ourselves as those to whom God spoke, as those who listened, those who agreed (perhaps the word is "acquiesced"). But that should not be all ... We are also those who fled. This does not make us the accursed of God in any very particularistic sense; it simply makes us human. Restating firmly that at Sinai we were mere terrified mortals might give us a more complete and realistic spiritual self-image, one of less angelic perfection but one with which we might more readily identify: "We are those who stood at Sinai, who saw and heard, were scared out of our little minds (*mohin de-katnut*), and fled!"

This, you see, is why we are eternally Israel, those who *wrestle* with the Divine. Our faith is not one that hopes to reside in bliss, but rather one committed to movement and struggle. Committed and destined; I'd want to say both. Committed to struggle, because the ascent to the Endless is itself Endless[19] and we are constantly to see ourselves as climbing up Jacob's ladder, not satisfied to stand on *any* rung.[20] And destined to struggle? Because we're always falling off and starting the ascent all over again. Falling off the ladder because we refuse to ascend (each rung is only strong enough to hold you for an instant) and because of our constant silly habit of looking down and contemplating flight.

We are Israel in that life in the Presence will always be a struggle for us. The discovery of God comes to us as a constant surprise, almost a shock. For countless generations we chant: "the whole earth is full of his glory," yet each time we turn around and see the glory of God in a new place we shudder with a mixture of delight, fear, and astonishment. Our sense of wonder is always getting lost. The shallow rationalist bias creeps back in, sits tight and waits to be blasted sky-high again before he'll budge an inch. Something in us is constantly repeating the primal conflict of the Israelite Moses: "C'mon, stop wasting your time" the over-educated Jewish boy in him must have been saying. "A plain ordinary thornbush and a little desert heat. Optical illusion." But Moses is, after all, Moses, and there has to be a story. He turned aside to look. He stopped, and there was God. He looked for a minute, saw and heard, and then, like one who still half thought he wouldn't be able to stand it (or perhaps feared that he *would* be able to stand it?), he hid his face.

"You want to know what a *tsaddik* is?" asks Reb Hayyim Haikl of Amdur. "We ordinary men need the hiding, we need to have God hide His light from us. The *tsaddik* says 'No!' to hiding and stares right into the sun!"[21] Moses, *even Moses*, hid his face and said: "How about sending someone else?"

Brinksmanship, unspeakable risk, borderline madness of intensity and blindness of immersion—those are the things it takes to be a *tsaddik*. Most of us Jews prefer to be *beynonim*, plain humans, ever living in the stream of our particular dialectical movement, confronting and hiding, moments of Presence followed in rapid succession by moments of dryness and despair. In other generations the cyclical motion was interpreted differently, but our particular version of it seems to run something like this: disbelief, seduction, wonder, living-in-the-Presence, terror, flight, disbelief, and so on and so forth. Each moment in the cycle is tyrannical and dogmatic: disbelief has no faith in the rebirth of wonder, and in our moments of living in the Presence we are revolted by the cynicism and self-conscious secularism of our unbelieving periods. The twentieth-century *beynoni* lives as though bound to the cycle of wonder and doubt.

We do not seek liberation by means of breaking out of the cycle. Opting for either world, as we have said, can only lead to prolonging of fragmentation. We see spiritual ebb and flow, moments of absence and moments of Presence, as central to the human religious situation. Our desire is neither to deny nor to escape it, but rather to learn to live as religious human beings in our moments of spiritual ebb. What else can be done with the moment of disbelief in our cycle? If we are not to deny the cycle altogether, must we allow ourselves to ever be torn apart by shallow cynicisms that we should like to have transcended long ago? Can there be spiritual growth if there has to be constant return to such a coarse moment of ebb? Most basically: in viewing the ebb and flow of the Spirit's presence within us, can we step beyond conflict and see the thing as rhythm, as a rhythmic movement that brings some *excitement* to the spiritual life and inspiration to the "downs" as well as the "ups"?

Hasidic theological texts, which comprise the literature we have that is most attuned to the problems of spiritual quest, knew this problem well. *Ratso va-shov*, they called it. "Running back and forth." Man runs back and forth, in and out of the divine Presence, and the Presence itself (*hiyyut*) seems to be running back and forth, in and out of the human soul. In Hasidic terms, it seems to be largely the movement of the Spirit itself that creates the spiritual cycle. Ultimate conversion is not to be made easy for us. At the same time, the spiritual masters of the Hasidic tradition, perhaps partly through the very term *ratso va-shov*, which allowed them a theologization of the spiritual reality, were able to live with the cyclical movement and continue to build. This, then, is what we seek to articulate: a contemporary theology of *ratso va-shov*.

There was a time when the appropriate geographical metaphor for our spiritual lives seemed to be one of isolated, widely separated peaks set in the midst of broad extended flatlands. The task we then set for ourselves was that of ascending the mountain with some measure of safety to bring down its secret, hoping thereby to give some light to the vast and empty world of the everyday. Then we were rather sure that we wanted to begin with the highs, that they were the paradigm of religious awareness after which the everyday was to be remodeled. If one will permit a rather simplistic reading of the tradition: a kind of *Shabbat* and weekday model, where one clearly knows which are the peaks and which are the valleys. The goal: "the world that is wholly *Shabbos*." But the humdrum world persists; the weekday simply doesn't want to become *Shabbos!* To make *Shabbos* the model for a respiritualized weekday is eschatological. In our schema, it would mean a breaking out of the cycle, a radical spiritualism that would deny legitimacy to moments of *katnut*, of spiritual ebb.

We do not always live in the glow of spiritual *Shabbos*. When we don't, we have to begin from below.[22] There is no upper light flowing into us; we have only the world. The discovery of the Presence in the world below, in the very earthiness of the weekday, then becomes our task. This is the time of struggle, the time of *'avodah* as active work in seeking out one's religious way *in the world*. We do not mean by this an indiscriminating embrace of the secular, which has come to characterize the religious stance of a good many contemporary Christians. They (like the kibbutzniks, as Rav Kook would say) have good reason to be in rebellion against an anti-worldly spiritualism. We mean rather a more profound fusion of the religious and the secular, one which can turn inward to a real spiritual life partly in order to nurture the outer life, and one which labors with love in the secular world without granting it *ultimate* seriousness.

Religious work in the weekday world, as we would see it today, must proceed from that element within the Hasidic tradition which sought to deny the separability of matter and spirit.[23] We are not interested in redeeming the spark from any earthly prison; we need rather to discover that all is spark. Nor do we seek to rejoice in the transparency or "illusion" of material reality.[24] We do not experience ourselves or one another as body and soul, but as bodysoul; so too with matter and spirit.

We seek our exultation in the spirit that can be known in the very flesh of the material world. "The breath of all life . . . and the spirit of all flesh."

This is the quality of *ratso va-shov* that we are after, that which is most faithful both to our own perceptions and to the ongoing specific mission of Israel in the history of Western spirituality. We are Israel in that we know and insist upon the oneness of matter and spirit.[25] Sometimes we are convinced of the utter folly of such a position with its inherent optimism, yet we will not let go. Sometimes all of Jewish history seems to us one vast plot by which the nations of the world hope to convert us to their otherworldliness, making it more than painfully obvious that salvation is not to be found in this life, that the true realm of the spirit must be elsewhere. No avail; we dig in and hold on to earth. Our *ratso va-shov* is not to be seen only as a ladder; in moments of stress the picture is turned on its side and the Jew is seen scurrying back and forth across a tightrope stretched out between matter and spirit, desperately patching things up at one end or the other. Even when the link appears to be so terribly tenuous, we dare not pronounce it broken.

The transformation of the ebb into a moment of religious legitimacy may take countless forms. The *via activa* as one side of the spiritual life, recognizing itself as not more and no less than that, may then rightly seek its fulfillment through social concern and political involvement. The kinds of political stances that would emerge as expressions of the spiritual as we see it can of course not be specifically pre-determined, but would have a good deal to do both with the maximizing of human freedom and the pursuit of peace. For others the active life could involve teaching, involvement in the personal and religious growth of others: the special concern we develop for student-comrades. Still others might find their fulfillment in the redemptive robustness of physical labor, particularly such as would involve them with the realms of animal and plant.

Through all of this, the maintaining of religious perspective will be essential, and will be an uphill struggle. If the Presence is to be rediscovered in the weekday world, demands will be made upon us that will radically re-orient the direction of our lives—demands of discipline of lifestyle, of ritual patterns and interpersonal openness which hardly thrive in the context of the mechanized, isolated, and frightened lives of the American middle class. The work of redemption, no matter what form it takes, will require new and intimate communities of support, which live outside current standards of achievement and success. We would do well to look at the vows of poverty found in monastic life, though seeking to read them somewhat more broadly than has been done in the past.

Such a religious path, if not watered down to absurdity, will speak only to very few. That is for the good. Ours is not an age in which popular spiritual movements could escape terrible perversion. Just as there are moments of ebb and flow in the individual's spiritual life, there at times appear to be historical periods of ebb and flow in mankind's general awareness of the Spirit. If we are to survive this great age of spiritual ebb, it will only be by the creation of small but terribly significant religious elites who can plant the seed for what may be some more fruitful future generation.

Even for the few, the task remains formidable. Our membership cards in the Western intellectual community are parted with only with the greatest difficulty. We cannot proclaim ourselves to be traditional believers; it is hoped that we are too honest even to try to talk ourselves into that position. The fragmentation of truth is part of our legacy as twentieth-century men. Yet maintaining our roots in the current intellectual milieu while trying to overcome cynicism and detachment is easier said than done. We are calling for nothing less than the re-mythologization of our lives. While not abandoning our outsiders' knowledge of the role of myth and the way it functions, we must be able to take the leap of re-entering the world of myth, in which the constant confrontation with sacred Presence is of the very fabric of daily existence. Our *ratso vashov* can become a rhythmic rather than a fragmenting process only as we begin to take ourselves seriously as human beings of great spiritual strength. Our weakness of soul is less real than we would sometimes like to believe. Such seriousness and renewed confrontation with our inner strength will come to us as we rediscover who we are, as we claim our place as members (albeit in our own ways) of the eternal faith-community of Israel.

We have always fled because the task is too great, the burden too much to bear. When we heard the Voice say "a kingdom of priests" even before the theophany itself, we knew it was time to run away. Again, in the symbolic person of Jonah, when we saw that it meant transforming *the world*, we turned and fled. *Who, us? The world? Madness.* And so the ghetto, or at least our half of that nefarious bargain. And who is to say that transforming the self is any less a challenge than transforming the world?

Sinai is eternal, its demand infinite, and we want to reject both madness and flight. In learning to live with the rhythm of our inner tides there may be a path that brings some peace. Not the stillness-peace of a lake or a pond: those we strugglers can never attain (and thus we reject them)! Rather the peace of the waters of Ocean, ever churning, smashing, rising, and falling—finding their peace in the regular breathing of tides, seeing themselves and their beauty both in ebb and in flow.

An end to flight?

Who is the man who can stand to live with his own holiness? Perhaps Messiah. Maybe that's what he's all about . . .

Note: The student of Hasidism will note that much of this article can be taken as a rereading of Hasidic sources through twentieth-century eyes.

"Where Are We Going?": An Address to the Neo-Hasidism Conference, New York City (2003)

Green originally delivered this essay at a 2003 gathering in New York City dedicated to contemporary expressions of Neo-Hasidism. It appears in print here for the first time.

Reflecting quite personally about his experiences as a Jewish seeker, writer, and teacher of rabbis across several decades, Green recalls his deep and long-standing friendship with Reb Zalman Schachter-Shalomi, who had a profound influence upon him. At the same time, Green points to his unwillingness to become anyone's disciple. While his path ahead has been inspired by many teachers, it is also entirely his own.

In this address Green outlines elements of his personal Neo-Hasidic theology through the threefold lens of *mahashavah*, *dibbur*, and *ma'aseh*, best translated in this context as theology, religious or symbolic language, and sacred deeds. Readers are invited to consider the continuity as well as the differences, in tone as well as in message, between this mature essay and those more youthful works from an earlier stage in Green's career.

I want to begin by acknowledging how good it is to be appearing here, even via the gifts of modern communication, with my friend and mentor Reb Zalman. We all join in wishing you

arikhut yamim ve-shanim [length of days and years]. May the
days be both many and full, filled with the blessings that so
beautifully radiate upon us through your warm and generous
words. Partly because of the years, but more because of your
way of endless giving, you have stepped into the role of *arikh
anpin, mekor ha-berakhah*, source of blessing, to this emerging movement. May our blessings reach back to you, even in
that high place of *tinra di-gevanin*,[26] where you have chosen to
dwell, and from there to all the worlds, and especially to our
world, today so much in need of blessing—*birkat ha-Shalom*.

I also want to acknowledge the presence here of both *haverim*
and *talmidim*, especially *talmidim*, whom I have been privileged
to teach and learn from over the course of several decades.
Those present include Seth Brody and Dan Kamesar, *'aleyhem
ha-shalom*, along with many others whose faces you see around
you. I have been blessed by the presence of great teachers in
the course of my lifetime, but I have no hesitation in saying *mi-
talmiday yoter mi-kulam* . . . ["From my students I have learned
most of all"].[27]

My journey into the world of Hasidic sources began, partly
thanks to Zalman, more than forty years ago. I have taken a
long path, with not a few detours and seeming obstacles along
the way. To understand that these were not truly obstacles at all,
but gifts given to me that I might seek out sparks of holiness in
ever new and different places, is a lesson that I have had to learn
over and over again, often each and every day, sometimes more
than once a day. Occasionally I think there might have been a
shorter way, had I been willing to accept discipleship, to walk
in someone else's well-trodden path. Then perhaps I could have
been protected enough to go *derekh erets plishtim*, to cross the
Philistine country and emerged unharmed in the Holy Land.
But that was not my way, and in retrospect I am grateful for it.

Mahi parashah ahat ba-torah asher kol divrey Torah teluyyin bah?[28] What is the single *parashah* upon which the whole Torah stands? For the new Hasidism (and I am happy to go for "new" rather than "neo-") of which we speak, I would say it is *parashat masa'ey. Eleh masa'ey beney Yisra'el*—"These are the journeys of the Children of Israel."[29] *Masa'eyhem le-motsa'eyhem*—"Their journeys forth from whence they emerged" (Num. 33:1–2). Where are we coming from and where are we going? Where are we headed and how did we get here? There may be mysteries yet to be uncovered in the names and order of all the stopping-places in the wilderness. Our journeys are complicated in ways that prior Jewish generations could not have anticipated. We wander through our wilderness, sometimes doubling and tripling back over the same territory, sustained only by the pure faith that our journey is one that has a goal, that we are on our way to *Erets Yisra'el*, to the land of Israel. We are encouraged to discover that such journeys go back to the very beginning, that Avraham Avinu journeyed *halokh ve-naso'a ha-negbah* (Gen. 12:9), back and forth to those inner dry places. We are still journeying, still digging new wells, as Yitshak Avinu had to, and still rolling the stones off old wells, as did Ya'akov Avinu, and finding them full of fresh, living waters.

Those of us who have had the great gift of nourishment from the teachings of the Hasidic masters have learned many lessons, including the three loves—the love of God, the love of Torah, and the love of Israel—as the Ba'al Shem Tov taught. But here I want to focus on the lesson of *emet*, of deep commitment to truth and personal honesty, that is also a vital piece of the Hasidic legacy. Rabbi Pinhas of Korets taught that lying is as serious a transgression as *'arayot*, as sexual misdeed. He said that only when lying is taken as seriously as *'arayot* will the Messiah come.[30]

He also said: "Nothing was as hard for me as [to stop] lying. It took me thirteen years and I broke every limb and bone in my body, but I finally got out of it: no more lying."[31] Or, in another version, he said it took him twenty-one years: seven to learn what truth is, seven to uproot lies, and seven more to fully implant the truth within himself. Perhaps it is because I began learning *Hasidut* at a place whose motto is "Truth even unto its innermost parts" that I take this part of the legacy so seriously. From A. J. Heschel, another of my most important teachers, I learned to revere Reb Mendel of Kotsk. To revere him means to fear his scornful glance, still active a century and a half after his death. He taught that *nokhmakhn*, imitation or copying, was the greatest enemy of the spiritual life. That meant that all the *shtik* of discipleship, doing it just like one's master, were closed to me. It also has meant, as my poor students know well, that I did not look kindly on those who I thought were trying to imitate me.

"Truth unto its innermost parts" in the language of Rabbi Nahman of Bratslav, is *emet le-amito*, the *emet* you find on the other side of the *halal ha-panui*, the great void from which God is absent. We do not deny the void, the real place in our lives where we know the absence of God. We do not *deny* it, but in an act of faith we *defy* it. We assert that there is a far shore to the void, a realm of *emet le-amito*, a deeper truth than the reality of emptiness. Only you can make your journey to the other side of that void, and the only way you can do it, Rabbi Nahman taught, is in silence.[32] When you get there, however, it is good to sing a *shir ha-yam* together with all the others who have crossed over as well:

Yam le-yabashah nehefkhu metsulim
Shirah hadashah shibbehu ge'ulim.[33]

That is the true *simhah* of *Hasidut,* celebrating the fact that we have come over that narrow bridge and reached the other side. Every day should contain such a moment. That is something really worth singing and dancing about, an occasion for a real *le-hayyim.*

Since Reb Zalman took us through the four worlds in his presentation, I've decided on another well-known Hasidic rubric, that of *mahashavah, dibbur, u-ma'aseh,* the three-fold division of thought, speech, and action, for an unfolding of what I mean by this call for a new Hasidism. What is its essence in the contemplative sphere? (Note that *mahashavah* in this case means something more than "thought" or "intellect.") How do we then express it in language, *dibbur,* and how does that language relate to the classic self-articulation of Hasidism in the many books that make up the Hasidic library? And in the realm of action, *ma'aseh,* what is it that we can or need to do to make that new Hasidic Judaism a reality?

Mahashavah

Our *Hasidut* returns to the great insight of the Ba'al Shem Tov: *melo khol ha-arets kevodo—mamash;* all of earth is truly filled with God's glory, nothing else. *Leyt atar panui miney;* there is no place—no moment, no person, no event—that is not filled with God's presence. God is waiting to be discovered everywhere, always. We have only to open our inner eye, to bring ourselves to *da'at* or awareness. That effort will open us to rung after rung of deeper consciousness, teaching us the single lesson that Y-H-W-H is *Elokim,* in heaven and on earth, above and below, outside and inside: there is nothing else.[34]

That realization leads us directly to the understanding that all things can be uplifted and taken back to their root, thus becoming a path through which we return to the One. This possibility includes even those things that seem most recalcitrant and unwilling to be uplifted: wicked thoughts, evil words, defiled deeds. All of them can be transformed and uplifted, although the damage they cause still requires recompense in this-worldly terms.

The Ba'al Shem Tov taught that "God needs to be served in all ways." This means that all the complexities of our lives, all the pain, all the loss, along with all the loves and all the blessings in our lives have been given to us as an infinite number of ways to serve, of channels through which to unify the light of God, to restore the sparks to their source in the single light. Although these acts of service are to be completely selfless, for the sake of the *shekhinah*, we know in faith that we too will receive in this act of giving, that the renewed light strengthened by our *yihudim*—our unifications—will shine upon us as well.

How did we come to these insights? Of course we could have read about them in such wonderful *sefarim* as *Tsava'at ha-RIVaSH*, *Likkutim Yekarim*, or *Me'or 'Eynayim*. Indeed everything I have said thus far is to be found stated quite clearly in those holy books. But we did not learn these truths from books alone. They came to us through deep reflection, on both the positive and negative sides. We discovered the life within, the world of inner reality that mystics and contemplatives in all traditions have known. For some of us this may have happened in the course of deep learning, either in university or *yeshivah*. It may have been in the course of deep *davvenen* in a *shtibl* or a *havurah*. For many of us it happened first in Zendo or Ashram, and only later did we bring it home into a Jewish setting. The Aquarian movement of the sixties and seventies had something to do with it, including for some of us a period of psychedelic adventure. Our spiritual journeys may have begun with reading Hermann Hesse or Alan Watts, leading us to Heschel and Buber, our first inkling of the riches of Hasidic tradition. We were looking for a religious language in which to express the truths we had found in such moments of profound meditation.

That is the positive side of our turn, on the level of *mahashavah*, to a new Hasidism. But there is a negative side as well. Unable to hold onto the naive faith of childhood, we were left cold by liberal Judaism as it had been presented to us, the religion of big institutions and a self-satisfied, highly achieving, but spiritually shallow American Jewry. The crisis of faith—whether personal or collective, in facing the Holocaust—called for something deeper, both emotionally and spiritually, than progressivist rationalism could muster. The denial of faith in our era proclaimed by Nietzsche, Sartre, and Camus, and so confirmed by the ungodly society in which we live, bespoke a profound existential reality, not merely the technical failure of some proof of God's existence. The response needed to be on a similar, or even more profound, human plane. Religious existentialism sustained us in meeting this need, but also led us to a doorway that lay beyond itself, to a place where the dialogue of I and Thou is silenced as we stand before the mystery of the All, the One to which there is no other.

Dibbur

One of the many gifts I received from Zalman was permission to speak traditional Jewish language and to make it my own, to talk about—and occasionally to—Avraham Avinu and Rahel Imenu, the *Ribbono shel 'Olam* (rather than "God"), to speak of *Yiddishkeyt* rather than "Judaism." I have come to understand it all as a vast spiritual language, the basic vocabulary of which I have tried to teach in a recent volume.[35]

To be a Jew in spiritual terms is to enter deeply into this language. *Bo el ha-teyvah*, as the Baʿal Shem Tov taught. "Enter into the word" with your whole household, with your entire self.[36] That language is the language of both Torah and *tefillah*, which is to say that we need to use it both as *mekabbelim*, receivers, as God ever gives us the gift of Torah, and as *mashpiʿim*, returning the gift to God through our service. As receivers, we open ourselves to the language of tradition. Another way to say this is that we take on, or enter fully into, the myth of Judaism. Here I agree with Zalman that this entering has to be and feel real. "Living with the time" means for Shabbos to be a real Shabbos, to come out of Egypt—on so many levels—on Pesah, to receive the Torah on Shavuʿot, to be reborn on Rosh Hashanah. We have to let the language speak to us in profoundly personal ways, a talent that grows over decades of living through it with an open heart.

Our search in fact is for a more richly mythic Judaism than is known to most Jews. In taking on the language of *sefirot* and Kabbalistic "worlds," of *tsimtsum* and sparks, of breakage and *tikkun*, we are reading the tradition from the point of view of its most elaborate mythical constructs, finding in these profound insights that enlighten and nourish our spiritual lives. We thrive on myth, and the more we learn, the more deeply we enter into it.

But we also know what we are doing in living within myth. We differ from traditional Hasidim partly in that we have no interest in trying to defend the literal or historical truth of Torah. Ours is a *post*-critical rather than a pre-critical consciousness. We take for granted the bio-history of our world, the obscure origins of ancient Israel, and the evolution of our sacred texts. We are not interested in trying to "prove" either the existence of *sefirot* or the historic claim that the tribes of

Israel wandered through the wilderness. We understand our entering into the myth as an act of up-leveling, of reading reality from the perspective of a higher or more unitive consciousness, one more profound than, but not needing to contradict, that of critical or historical scholarship. We develop a way of going in and out, of living richly with the myth while knowing we are doing so. *Ashrey man de-'ayil u-nafik*, as the Zohar says. "Blessed is the one who can go in and out."

Why, exactly, do we want to live within that myth? Forgive me if I quote something I have already written:

It is in the course of our search that we turn to the wisdom and language of religious tradition. Initially, we may be less convinced by the "truth claims" of tradition than we are powerfully attracted to the richness of its language, both in word and in symbolic gesture. Through the profound echo chamber of the countless generations of its faithful, tradition offers us a way to express both the longings and the fullness that we know within. The language of sacred tradition, shrouded in mystery and awe, comes to seem like the appropriate vehicle through which we express those same feelings with regard to life itself. True, the words are antiquated, grandiose, and clearly far from anything we would choose to say if we were making up a language of our own. But precisely because the language of tradition so reaches into antiquity and is enriched by the lives of all those generations that have lived within it, it has a depth that words of our own simply cannot reach.

Cautiously, hesitantly, I began to make the words of tradition once again my own. I hesitate because I know that its story is not quite my story, that it will try to take me along on its journey as I seek to appropriate it in order to express mine. Ultimately, we will strike a bargain, the tradition and the seeker.

I will enter into its language, celebrate the weekly re-creation of the world, the liberation from bondage in Egypt, the standing before the mountain to hear God's word. I will do so not as a literal "believer," but rather as one who recognizes that all these "events" are themselves metaphors for a truth whose depth reaches far beyond them.

I know that religious language is not just a collection of stories, but an attempt to put into narrative form a truth so profound that it cannot be told except when dressed in the garb of narration. This particular narration, that of my people, I make my own. I surrender to its power and allow myself to become another link in the chain of generations. What I ask in return is only that the ongoing process of tradition not be seen as closed. I plead—a plea addressed to God, to history or perhaps to myself—that my generation too might add its hand to the shaping of that which will be seen as tradition by those who come after us.

Religion begins not with doctrine, not with tradition, but with the need to pray. Theology comes only later, the mind's reflection on what the heart already knows. But what is the relationship between that emotional need to pray, to express the heart's fullness and longing, and all the claims of religion that still seem so distant? Is vague spiritual longing the same as religious truth? Where is the bridge that leads us over the chasm that lies between them?

We no longer react to the sense of wonder and beauty in creation like the medieval philosopher, who could derive from nature the logical conclusion that the world must indeed have been made by a great and carefully planning Creator. We have no logical inference here, but only ongoing intuition. That intuition is guided by a critical choice we have made, the choice to speak religious language. The step from "wonder" to "God" is not an act of inference but an act of *naming*. In saying "God" in prayer, I give the object of my wonder a *name*. It is I, or we as a community, who have performed that act of naming. It is we who attach the word "God" to our search for meaning, to our desire to find a word for that which evokes our sense of awe and wonder, for that which humbles and inspires us, for that which calls us to its service.

Our quest is not a question, one that would require a specific *answer*. But the quest itself leads us to an act of *affirmation*. There is a point in our search at which we say, "Yes!" This is the only answer we need, and it comes forth from our own inner depths. The move from quest to affirmation may come gradually, may even seem to sneak up on us and catch us unawares. Our "yes" is an affirmation of the questing process, but even more, it is an affirmation of life itself. It is the permission we give ourselves to call upon the name of God, to open ourselves to life in this deeply personal way. Within our prayers we have found a living presence, a reality beyond words. Without breaking our inner silence in any way, it has said to us: "I am." We respond with the wholeness of our being: "You, Holy One, dwell amid the prayers of Israel." All this is contained within our silent "Yes!"

We recognize that our religious language is not the only one in which the reality we encounter could be captured or celebrated. We choose, in response to that very real encounter, to invoke the name of God. But we also remain aware that it is we—as contemporary seekers and as a traditional civilization— who perform that act of choosing and naming. I believe that this act, this turn from quest to affirmation, from appreciation of wonder to calling it by God's name, is the most ennobling and significant of human speech-acts. It is the turning point in the path, the new beginning of the quest. It is one of those places, in this great circular journey back to origins, where beginning and end are joined together.

With this we are ready to begin.[37]

This consciousness that it is we who are choosing also allows us the possibility, one we do not approach lightly, of selecting critically among the mythic claims of our tradition. The spirit of Hasidism is that of *revival*, seeking not to change but to reinvigorate forms inherited from the past. In this it differs from *reform*, which seeks to change and update the forms themselves. Revivalism is enthusiastic and generally uncritical: all of the inheritance is true and meaningful to us, once we turn on the inner lights. Here I would suggest that a middle path is the one we need. In receiving the rich language of Kabbalah and Hasidism, we recognize that it was created in an age very different from our own. It has certain values that are not consistent with truths we know and cherish, and in these places we have to challenge, and to change, the legacy of the past. I refer to two matters well known to all of you: the attitudes toward women and toward non-Jews found in many of our treasured sources, attitudes I will designate by the negative liturgical formulas *she-lo 'asani ishah* (Blessed are You . . . Who has not made me a woman) and *she-lo 'asani goy* (. . . Who has not made me a non-Jew).

The Hasidic and Kabbalistic texts were written exclusively by and for men in an age still governed by a notion that women's minds were "frivolous" or less developed than the male intellect. While the good Jewish wife and daughter may have been treated with both affection and respect in the best of Hasidic circles, they were not fully welcome as participants in the circles of those who studied and created Jewish thought. That has changed in our age, a change that we embrace fully and without ambivalence. We also recognize that this change will, as time passes, influence the reshaping of the myth, a process to which we strive to remain open.

We also recognize that our tradition bears within it deep traces of the historical situation of Jews who lived for centuries as a barely tolerated minority. The disdain with which non-Jews are treated in our sources, including sometimes even the denial to them of divine souls, must be understood as a mirror reflection of the bitter (and much more dangerous, as history has shown) dehumanization of the Jew by the majority cultures. In creating a Hasidism for our postmodern age, we need to distance ourselves from the narrowness and even xenophobia of prior generations. As we read and teach the Hasidic classics, we need to do so in a universalistic spirit, one faithful to the most essential teaching of Judaism—Rabbi Shim'on ben Azzai's *kelal gadol ba-torah*— that every human being is fully created in God's image.[38] In this way we will also be faithful to our own experience as post-moderns who have read, learned from, and come to respect religious teachers and teachings from many traditions, all of them leading to the same ultimate truth. This universalism should not preclude our retaining a special love for and loyalty to our fellow-Jews—there is no Hasidism without a place for *ahavat yisra'el*—but it should be a love that helps us be more open to others, rather than closing us off from them.

Ma'aseh

This is the realm hardest to talk about in our context. Let us acknowledge that we represent a highly diverse group of Jews on the question of Jewish observance and *halakhic* authority. In part this goes back to the divergence between the two original *rebbes* of the new Hasidism in America: Reb Shlomo and Reb Zalman. Reb Shlomo, while parting company with Orthodox convention on the very telling issue of gender borders—mixed groups for dancing and ecstatic song, where all boundaries were erased—otherwise remained quite committed to a fully *halakhic* model. While deeply unhappy with the personality distortions sometimes created by the *yeshivah* world, and at times openly mocking of them, he nevertheless sent his disciples back to that world to learn the "real" *Yiddishkeyt* he loved and longed for, even as he himself lived on its far edge. Reb Zalman called for much more innovation and variety in *halakhic* praxis and ventured more clearly beyond the bounds of Orthodoxy. In more recent years, however, we have seen him try to rein in the movement around him, especially in such areas as *ishut* or personal status, fearing that the very openness he encouraged would add to the deepening gaps in the collective body of *klal yisra'el*. If we go back another generation, we can see this division also in the two great European masters of Neo-Hasidic thought: Martin Buber and Hillel Zeitlin, between whom the cleavage on the question of *halakhah* was much more radical, almost total.

But let us begin with what we have in common. A new Hasidism, like the old, is a movement built first on a commitment to *kavvanah*, to the intense and inward direction of religious deeds. We understand that the *mitsvot* are instrumental, a means rather than an end in themselves. Their purpose is twofold: they provide forms that help bring us to the awareness of which we have spoken; they also serve as vessels in which the divine light that shines through us can come to earth and be shared with others. The Hasidic readings of *mitsvah mileshon tsavta*, a *mitsvah* as a place of divine/human togetherness, or *mitsvah* as God's name, half hidden and half revealed, are understandings that we feel are very much ours as well.

In speaking of sacred deeds I naturally turn to my teacher Heschel, who was so much a philosopher of religious action. Heschel, the scion of several great Hasidic dynasties, learned from his ancestors the power of the deed: the sense that a *mitsvah* had cosmic power, that by doing God's will we were affecting heaven itself. But in tying the Hasidic legacy back to that of the prophets, Heschel taught that the true power of *mitsvot* to move the upper worlds lay first in the realm of *mitsvot beyn adam le-havero*, the ethical and interpersonal demands of Judaism. It was here that Heschel, Holocaust survivor turned activist for justice, human dignity, and peace, expressed his deepest commitment to sacred deeds.[39]

Heschel of course remained quite traditional in the ritual sphere as well, and in this realm I am quite aware that I might be seen as an unworthy disciple. But since it was he who taught me about the Kotsker's strictures on imitation, I have little apology to make for having gone my own way. Still, despite my own checkered patterns of observance, I remain deeply attracted to the call of *kabbalat 'ol mitsvot*, accepting the commandments' yoke or the obligation to them. I recognize our covenant as beginning with Israel's calling out *na'aseh ve-nishma'*, when we agreed to do even before we read the fine print. The humility and ego-transcendence, *hakhna'ah* and *bittul*, of that moment, are essential to my own understanding of *Hasidut*. The question is always whether *bittul* before the *Ribbono shel 'Olam* and *bittul* before the *Shulhan 'Arukh* or before rabbinic authorities who choose to live in the cocoon of Brooklyn or Jerusalem is the same thing. I find that once we acknowledge that the *shekhinah* is really here (wherever our "here" is) as well as "there," it becomes increasingly hard to send to *hatam* (there) a question about how I am supposed to live in a here and now that only I can fully know, and for which only I am ultimately responsible. This inability to pass the mantle of authority and decision-making onto anyone else only increases the burden of *ma'aseh* and the ongoing sense, not diminished an iota by my non-orthodoxy, that *lefi ma'asav adam nidon*, a person is to be judged only by his deeds.

That position leaves the individual very much alone, far too alone to muster the strength for a life of spiritual discipline when *halakhic* authority itself is up for grabs. To know you are living a myth, one that you can enter and leave quite freely, and to expect of yourself the power to live there every day, even when uninspired—that is too much to expect, indeed a set-up for spiritual failure. It is for this reason that we need *hevruta* and community, another important part of the Hasidic legacy. The support of *haverim* who are engaged in the same daily struggle, a support manifest in listening, in learning, and doing together, and also in celebration, is essential to maintaining our religious lives. I have been involved since the days of Havurat Shalom in building such communities, and am indeed standing at the edge of a new such venture as we speak.[40]

If you walk into a Hasidic *shtibl* where there is a *rebbe*, somewhere on the wall you will probably see a framed copy of a print called *Ilan ha-Yahas shel ha-BeSHT*. It is a thick-trunked and many-branched tree, showing how each Hasidic dynasty and sub-dynasty can trace its roots back to the movement's founder. I recently saw a prewar Polish print of such a chart for sale by a bookseller, commanding quite a high price; I guess new *shtiblekh* are still being created and need to be authenticated by old trees.

The question is where we fit on such a tree. I do not quite want to say, as Reb Zalman has suggested, that we are another

Hasidut, as different from the BeSHT's Hasidism as it was from that of medieval Germany, or as *Hasidut Ashkenaz* was from Maccabean *Hasidut.* Our relationship to the BeSHT, to Reb Nahman, to the *Sefat Emet,* and many others is closer than that. But then where are we to find ourselves on the chart? Should we go out to the far tip of the Schneersohn-Lubavitch branch, tie ourselves to Zalman and Shlomo's apprenticeship to the late Lubavitcher Rebbe, and claim authenticity in that way? Such a move hardly seems right to me. Should I try to retrieve my great-grandfather's *yihus* as a Gerer Hasid, skipping over the two generations of fierce atheism that are also part of my family inheritance? That too seems inauthentic, even pretentious. Nor do I want our authenticity as new Hasidim to depend on that of either Lubavitch or Ger, groups that would be quick to deny any shred of relation to such as us.

I am tempted, however, by the much more bold, even audacious, move of saying that we take off from the very trunk of the tree, the Ba'al Shem Tov himself. We go back to the heart of the matter. It is the very earliest Hasidic teachings that stir our spirit, even if we came to them in strange and unconventional ways, even if we saw them first in books rather than hearing them through an unbroken chain of living masters. We also belong to Hasidism at its boldest early stage, as it was before it became threatened by modernity and began devoting so much of its energy to resisting change.

Our *yihus* in that sense is older than that of many Hasidic dynasties that exist today, which originated in the period of militant and defensive Hasidism of the later era. But here we come to understand the limits of a two-dimensional chart, hanging flat against the wall. We grow out of the Ba'al Shem Tov's heart in a different dimension, in one not given to hanging on a wall. Zalman would probably create a fancy multidimensional hologram to map it out, something that would give *nahas* to his fellow-Boulderite Ken Wilbur. I have never quite understood those things, so I go for a much simpler answer, one that suits my own spiritual tastes. I would rather admit that we have nothing to hang up on the wall; the only place we can record our *yihus* is on the tablets in our heart—*katvem ʻal luah libbekha* (Prov. 3:3 and 7:3). That will have to suffice for us as a claim to authenticity. We know that our master the Baʼal Shem Tov would understand.

Suggestions for Further Reading

Green, Arthur. "Neo-Hasidism and Our Theological Struggles." *Raʻayonot* 4, no. 3 (1984): 11–17.

———. *Radical Judaism: Rethinking God and Tradition.* New Haven: Yale University Press, 2010.

———. "Response to Richard Rubenstein." *Conservative Judaism* 28 (1974): 26–32.

———. "Rethinking Theology: Language, Experience, and Reality." *Reconstructionist* 54, no. 1 (1988): 8–13, 30.

———. "The Role of Mysticism in a Contemporary Jewish Theology." *Conservative Judaism* 30 (1976): 10–24.

———. *Seek My Face: A Jewish Mystical Theology.* Woodstock VT: Jewish Lights, 2003.

Mayse, Ariel Evan. "Arthur Green: An Intellectual Portrait," in *Arthur Green: Hasidism for Tomorrow*, edited by Hava Tirosh-Samuelson and Aaron W. Hughes, 1–52. Leiden: Brill, 2015.

Source Acknowledgments

Portions of chap. 1 were previously published in:

Green, Arthur, and Ariel Evan Mayse. "'The Great Call of the Hour': Hillel Zeitlin's Yiddish Writings on Yavneh." *Geveb: A Journal of Yiddish Studies*, Spring 2016. Used by permission of Arthur Green.

Zeitlin, Hillel. *Hasidic Spirituality for a New Era: The Religious Writings of Hillel Zeitlin*. Edited and Translated by Arthur Green. New York: Paulist, 2012, 37–43, 55–58, 71–117. Used by permission of Arthur Green.

Portions of chap. 2 were previously published in:

Buber, Martin. *Hasidism and Modern Man*. Princeton: Princeton University Press, 2015, 1–15. Used by permission of the Martin Buber Literary Estate.

Buber, Martin. *The Origin and Meaning of Hasidism*. Edited and translated by Maurice Friedman. New York: Horizon, 1960, 113–49. Used by permission of the Martin Buber Literary Estate.

Commentary 36 (1963): 218–25. Used by permission of the Martin Buber Literary Estate.

Schaeder, Grete. "Martin Buber: A Biographical Sketch." In *The Letters of Martin Buber: A Life of Dialogue*, edited by Nahum N. Glatzer and Paul Mendes-Flohr, 12. Syracuse: Syracuse University Press, 1991. Used by permission of the Martin Buber Literary Estate.

Portions of chap. 3 were previously published in:

Abraham Joshua Heschel. *Moral Audacity and Spiritual Grandeur: Essays*. Edited by Susannah Heschel. New York: Farrar, Straus & Giroux, 1996, 33–39, 54–67. Used by permission of Susannah Heschel.

Abraham Joshua Heschel: Essential Writings. Maryknoll NY: Orbis, 2011, 106–7. Used by permission of Susannah Heschel.

Portions of chap. 4 were previously published in:

"The Holy Hunchback," included in the 1980 album *L'kovod Shabbos*. Used by permission of Neshama Carlebach.

Portions of chap. 5 were previously published in:

Judaism 9, no. 3 (1960): 216–21. Used by permission of Eve Ilsen and Netanel Miles-Yepez.

Judaism 13, no. 2 (1964): 185–97. Used by permission of Eve Ilsen and Netanel Miles-Yepez.

Miles-Yepez, Netanel, and Zalman Schachter-Shalomi. *Foundations of the Fourth Turning of Hasidism: A Manifesto.* Boulder CO: Albion Andalus, 2014. Used by permission of Eve Ilsen and Netanel Miles-Yepez.

Portions of chap. 6 were previously published in:

Response 2 (1968). Used by permission of Arthur Green.

Worship (1971). Used by permission of Arthur Green.

Notes

INTRODUCTION

1. An acronym for the Ba'al Shem Tov, literally "master of the good name," an appellation given to Israel ben Eliezer (1700–1760), the imagined founder of Hasidism and ideal figure of the Hasidic master.
2. From an unpublished manuscript in the possession of the editors. The full text is included in this volume.
3. See *Butsina di-Nehora*, vol. 1 (Brooklyn: n.p., 2007), 185.
4. A full history of the Hasidic movement, long sorely lacking, is *Hasidism: A New History* (Princeton: Princeton University Press, 2017, edited by David Biale. Both editors of this volume have participated in this project as well.
5. On this phenomenon, see Nicham Ross, "Can Secular Spirituality be Religiously Inspired?: The Hasidic Legacy in the Eyes of the Skeptics," *AJS Review* 37, no. 1 (2013): 93–113, based on a Hebrew book by the same author.
6. On Rabbi Shneur Zalman, see Immanuel Etkes, *Rabbi Shneur Zalman of Liady: The Origins of Chabad Hasidism* (Waltham MA: Brandeis University Press, 2015). On Rabbi Nahman, see Arthur Green, *Tormented Master: A Life of Rabbi Nahman of Bratslav* (Woodstock VT: Jewish Lights, 1992).
7. The classic Neo-Hasidic collection is Martin Buber's two volumes of *Tales of the Hasidim*, first published in English in 1947–48 and frequently reprinted. Especially charming, though a bit harder to find, is Jiri Langer's *Nine Gates to the Hasidic Mysteries*. Zalman Schachter-Shalomi also edited several volumes of Hasidic stories, both old and new, and over the past decades increasingly more collections of Hasidic tales have been made available to English readers.

1. HILLEL ZEITLIN

1. For a collection of Zeitlin's most significant works translated into English, see Arthur Green's edition of *Hasidic Spirituality for a New Era: The Religious Writings of Hillel Zeitlin* (New York: Paulist, 2012). Scholarly discussion of Zeitlin is mostly in Hebrew. See Shraga Bar Sella,

Between the Storm and the Quiet: The Life and Works of Hillel Zeitlin (Tel Aviv: Ha-Kibbutz ha-Me'uhad, 1999) (Hebrew); Jonatan Meir, "The Book of Visions: On the Mystical Diary of Hillel Zeitlin and the Attempts to Print Hidden Treatises," *Alei Sefer* 21 (2010): 149–71 (Hebrew); Jonatan Meir, "Longing of Souls for the *Shekinah*: Relations between Rabbi Kook, Zeitlin and Brenner," in *The Path of the Spirit: The Eliezer Schweid Jubilee Volume*, ed. Yehoyada Amir, vol. 2, 771–818 (Jerusalem: Van Leer, 2005) (Hebrew). In English see Arthur Green, "Hillel Zeitlin and Neo-Hasidic Readings of the Zohar," *Kabbalah* 22 (2010): 59–78; Arthur Green, "Three Warsaw Mystics," in *Kolot Rabbim: Essays in Memory of Rivka Schatz-Uffenheimer*, ed. Rachel Elior, 1–58 (Jerusalem: Magnes, 1997).

2. See Elchonon Zeitlin's memoir, published posthumously as *In a Literar-isher Shtub* (Buenos Aires: Tsentral Farband fun Poylishe Yidn in Argentine, 1946) (Yiddish). Zeitlin's son Elchonon died in the Warsaw Ghetto in early 1942. His grave lies at the very entrance to Warsaw's huge Jewish cemetery, indicating that he was probably among the last to be buried there during the ghetto era.

3. For a fascinating reflection on the different reasons for his writing in Hebrew and Yiddish, see Zeitlin's *"A Bisl Klorkeyt un Pashtus in der Shprakhen-Frage," Der Moment* 292 (December 19, 1924): 4.

4. The bibliography of Zeitlin's publications by Eliezer Rephael Malachi, published in *Ha-Tekufah* 32–33 (1948): 848–75 and *Ha-Tekufah* 34–35 (1950): 843–48, is admittedly quite incomplete, especially regarding the "thousands and thousands" of his Yiddish articles published in *Der Moment* as well as various other Yiddish periodicals in Poland, New York, and elsewhere. Malachi makes note of having received another bibliography from Aaron Zeitlin, Hillel Zeitlin's son. This list included the articles in *Der Moment* and *Haynt*, compiled by Y. Zeid and based on the Hebrew University Library holdings. Unpublished bibliographies such as this may be found in YIVO's archive, but the most exhaustive contemporary resource for locating Zeitlin's many and varied newspaper articles is the Abraham Icchok Lerner Index to Yiddish Periodicals, compiled by the Hebrew University of Jerusalem, Beth Shalom Aleichem, and the Jewish National and University Library (http://yiddish-periodicals.huji.ac.il).

5. Both of these essays are translated in the collection mentioned in note 1.

6. See Shraga Bar-Sella, "On the Brink of Disaster: Hillel Zeitlin's Struggle for Jewish Survival in Poland," *Polin* 11 (1998): 77–93.

7. See Glenn Dynner and François Guesnet, eds., *Warsaw: The Jewish Metropolis: Essays in Honor of the 75th Birthday of Professor Antony Polonsky* (Leiden: Brill, 2015).

8. See Kenneth B. Moss, *Jewish Renaissance in the Russian Revolution* (Cambridge: Harvard University Press, 2009); Gershon C. Bacon, *The Politics of Tradition: Agudat Yisrael in Poland, 1919–1939* (Jerusalem: Magnes, 1996); Daniel K. Heller, "The Rise of the Zionist Right: Polish Jews and the Betar Youth Movement, 1922–1935," PhD diss., Stanford University, 2012; and the essays in Zvi Gitelman, ed., *The Emergence of Modern Jewish Politics: Bundism and Zionism in Eastern Europe* (Pittsburgh: University of Pittsburgh Press, 2003).

9. This call for a Neo-Hasidic mystical fellowship further distinguishes Zeitlin from Buber. The latter, writing for a broader audience, was interested in the universal wisdom of Hasidism and how it could be absorbed by his readers. Buber was a Zionist thinker, interested in the revival of the Jewish spirit throughout the Jewish people; he saw the ideals of Hasidism as representing the best values of that nation. But he was far from a Yavneh project, which meant creating a new Hasidic movement in the more specific sense.

10. The Yiddish newspaper *Der Moment* was published daily between May 1910 and September 1939. Its editor was Noah Pryłucki (1882–1941), following his father, Tsevi Pryłucki. The vastly popular *Der Moment*, associated with the Folkist Party, argued for Jewish cultural, political, and linguistic autonomy in the Diaspora, though it also welcomed the work of Zionist writers. See Mendel Moses, "Der Moment," *in Fun Noentn Over: Monografyes un Memuarn*, vol. 2 (New York: n.p., 1956), 239–99; and Nathan Cohen's entry in *The YIVO Encyclopedia of Jews in Eastern Europe*, available at: www.yivoencyclopedia.org/article.aspx/Moment_Der.

11. Jonatan Meir, "Hillel Zeitlin's Zohar: The History of a Translation and Commentary Project," *Kabbalah* 10 (2004): 119–57 (Hebrew).

12. Zeitlin, an active and sharp-tongued polemicist, was bitterly attacked by the leadership of Agudat Yisrael, the party that dominated Orthodox Jewish life in central Poland and was represented in the Polish parliament by leading followers of the *rebbe* of Ger (Gora Kalwarja), the chief Hasidic group in the Warsaw region. For one of Zeitlin's many responses to his Orthodox critics, see his "*Mayn Apikorses,*" *Der Moment* 149, July 27, 1924, 4.

13. The title of this pamphlet is based on wordplay commonly found in Hasidic literature. In biblical Hebrew *teyvah* is the word for "ark," but in

rabbinic Hebrew it can also mean "word." Early Hasidic texts often rein-
terpret Gen. 6:16, "Make a light source for the ark," and Gen. 7:1, "Enter
into the ark, you and all your household," to mean that one must illuminate and enter into the words of prayer with one's entire being; see,
for example, *Degel Mahaneh Efrayim* (Bnei Brak: n.p., 2013), Noaḥ, 18–19;
Or Torah (Brooklyn: Kehot Publication Society, 2011), Noaḥ, 18, 25–26.
Zeitlin views this new embrace of the word, and perhaps the entire
Yavneh project, as an ark in which to escape or transcend the flood he
saw overcoming Polish Jewry.

14. In 1931 Zeitlin published a collection of his poems in Yiddish entitled
Gezangen tsum Eyn Sof (Songs to the Boundless One), which included
both original material and translations of works that had previously
appeared in Hebrew in the journal *Ha-Tekufah* in 1924.

15. A Hebrew translation of *Di Teyvah* by Natan Hofshi was published in
Israel in 1962.

16. The manuscript, signed by Zeitlin, is of unknown provenance. It was
advertised and sold by the Asufa Auction House in 2014 and is currently
owned by Arthur Green. For a translation of Zeitlin's Yiddish writings
on Yavneh, see Arthur Green and Ariel Evan Mayse, "'The Great Call of
the Hour': Hillel Zeitlin's Yiddish Writings on *Yavneh*," *Geveb: A Journal
of Yiddish Studies*, Spring 2016, https://ingeveb.org/articles/the-great-call
-of-the-hour-hillel-zeitlins-yiddish-writings-on-yavneh.

17. We have been unable to locate any other record or extant copy of *Mayn
Vort*, no. 7. A letter to members of Yavneh, printed in issue no. 4, is
reproduced in this chapter. The number 7 is most likely an error, either
by Zeitlin or the printer.

18. Oskar Wolfsberg and Tsevi Harkavy, eds., *Sefer Zeitlin* (Jerusalem: n.p.,
1944), 129 (Hebrew).

19. Hillel Zeitlin, *Sifran shel Yehidim* (Jerusalem: Mossad haRav Kook, 1979),
5–6. These accounts present some difficulty in the dating of the editors'
newly found manuscript. If the attempt of 1923–24 had already failed,
who are the tens of Jews living in accord with the Yavneh principles? If
the manuscript is as early as 1924–25, reflecting the same period as the
letter to Aminoach, what is the "mystical-prophetic work" that is about
to appear? Might *Sifran shel Yehidim* have been ready by then, but the
publication delayed by several years?

20. Isaac Bashevis Singer attributed Zeitlin's failure to his desire to draw
young Jews back to the house of study, a world that they had rejected so

totally that his call for an illuminated and renewed approach to Jewish learning went unheeded; see Isaac Bashevis Singer and Robert Wolf, "Concerning Yiddish Literature in Poland (1943)," *Prooftexts* 15, no. 2 (1995): 114.

21. Reprinted in Zeitlin, *Sifran shel Yehidim*, 123.

22. Zeitlin, *Sifran shel Yehidim,*, 84–92.

23. For an interesting group of original texts, see Solomon Schechter, *Studies in Judaism: Second Series* (Philadelphia: Jewish Publication Society of America, 1908), 292–301 (Hebrew). For an English translation and discussion, see Lawrence Fine, *Safed Spirituality: Rules of Mystical Piety, the Beginning of Wisdom* (Mahwah NJ: Paulist, 1984), 30–77; Lawrence Fine, *Physician of the Soul, Healer of the Cosmos: Isaac Luria and His Kabbalistic Fellowship* (Stanford: Stanford University Press, 2003), 80–81, 300–58.

24. The texts originally appeared in Aryeh Leib Frumkin, *Toledot Hakhmei Yerushalayim*, vol. 3 (Jerusalem: Defus Salomon, 1939), 47–54 (Hebrew). See Pinchas Giller, *Shalom Shar'abi and the Kabbalists of Beit El* (Oxford: Oxford University Press, 2008), 8–9, 55, 85–93; Jonatan Meir, *Rehovot ha-Nahar: Kabbalah and Exotericism in Jerusalem (1896–1948)* (Jerusalem: Yad Yitzhak ben Zvi, 2011), 19–73 (Hebrew); Lawrence Fine, "A Mystical Fellowship in Jerusalem," in *Judaism in Practice: From the Middle Ages through the Early Modern Period*, ed. Lawrence Fine, 210–14 (Princeton: Princeton University Press, 2001)..

25. Jonathan Garb, *Kabbalist in the Heart of the Storm: R. Moshe Hayyim Luzzatto* (Tel Aviv: Tel Aviv University Press, 2014), esp. 52–55, 59–72, 83–99, 123–52, 201–25 (Hebrew).

26. See Lawrence Fine, "Spiritual Friendship as Contemplative Practice in Kabbalah and Hasidism," in *Meditation in Judaism, Christianity, and Islam: Cultural Histories*, ed. Halvor Eifring, 61–75 (London: Bloomsbury Academic, 2013); Joseph Weiss, "R. Abraham Kalisker's Concept of Communion with God and Men," in Joseph Weiss, *Studies in East European Jewish Mysticism and Hasidism*, ed. David Goldstein, 155–69 (London: Littman, 1997).

27. See Yehuda Liebes, "How the Zohar Was Written," in Yehuda Liebes, *Studies in the Zohar*, trans. Arnold Schwartz, Stephanie Nakache, and Penina Peli, 85–138 (Albany: State University of New York Press, 1993); Yehuda Liebes, "The Messiah of the Zohar: On R. Simeon bar Yohai as a Messianic Figure," in Liebes, *Studies in the Zohar*, 1–84; and Melila Hellner-Eshed, *A River Flows from Eden: The Language of Mystical Experience in the Zohar*, trans. Nathan Wolski, esp. 29–84, 105–10 (Stanford: Stanford University Press, 2009).

28. Zvi Leshem has demonstrated that *Beney Mahashavah Tovah* was
written during the 1920s, and certainly before 1928; see his discussion
in Zvi Leshem, "Between Messianism and Prophecy: Hasidism according to the Piaseczner Rebbe," PhD diss., Bar-Ilan University, 2007, 5n14.
On the importance of this work and its publication, see Daniel Reiser,
*Vision as a Mirror: Imagery Techniques in Twentieth-Century Jewish Mysti-
cism* (Los Angeles: Cherub, 2014), 179–80, and esp. note 380 (Hebrew);
and Daniel Reiser, "'To Rend the Entire Veil': Prophecy in the Teachings of Rabbi Kalonymous Kalman Shapira of Piazecna and Its Renewal
in the Twentieth Century," *Modern Judaism* 34 (2014): 11–12. The title
may mean something like "children of a heightened" or "intensified"
consciousness, in reference to the contemplative exercises outlined
within. See also James Maisels, "The Self and Self-Transformation in
the Thought and Practice of Rabbi Kalonymous Kalmish Shapira," PhD
diss., University of Chicago, 2014.
29. Rabbi Shapira himself recommends that the *hevraya* be a hidden society
that is not publicized, lest it engender negative feelings or its members
become haughty and prideful; see Kalonymous Kalman Shapira, *Beney
Mahashavah Tovah* (Tel Aviv: n.p., 1973), 57–58.
30. Shapira, *Beney Mahashavah Tovah*, 10.
31. Shapira, *Beney Mahashavah Tovah*, 48–54.
32. Shapira, *Beney Mahashavah Tovah*, 8.
33. This essay, first published in 1934, was reprinted in the posthumous
expanded version of Zeitlin, *Sifran shel Yehidim*, 240–44.
34. Zalman Schachter, "Toward an Order of Bnai Or," *Judaism* 13, no. 2
(1964): 185–97. Schachter discussed this influence in personal conversation with Arthur Green, one of the editors of this volume. While
the ascetic, pietistic community of the Essenes has long been known
through the writings of Josephus, this fascinating connection between
Jewish Renewal—Schachter's term for the rebirth of Jewish spirituality
in the second half of the twentieth century—and the discovery of the
Qumran ruins and Dead Sea Scrolls deserves further research.
35. Arthur Green, "Renewal and Havurah: American Movements, European
Roots," in *Jewish Renaissance and Revival in America: Essays in Memory of
Leah Levitz Fishbane*, ed. Eitan P. Fishbane and Jonathan D. Sarna, 145–64
(Waltham MA: Brandeis University Press, 2011); Arthur Green, "Havu-
rat Shalom: A Proposal," in *Contemporary Judaic Fellowship in Theory and
in Practice*, ed. Jacob Neusner, 149–54 (New York: Ktav, 1972), as well as

various short studies and reflections collected in that volume. See also Riv-Ellen Prell, *Prayer and Community: The Havurah in American Judaism* (Detroit: Wayne State University Press, 1989); Chava Weissler, "Worship in the Havura Movement," in *The Life of Judaism*, ed. Harvey E. Goldberg, 79–91 (Berkeley: University of California Press, 2001). See also Shaul Magid, *American Post-Judaism: Identity and Renewal in a Postethnic Society* (Bloomington: Indiana University Press, 2013).

36. On the remarkable contemporary revival among the Chabad and Bratslav groups, and their success in reaching those outside the Hasidic community, see Elliot R. Wolfson, *Open Secret: Postmessianic Messianism and the Mystical Revision of Menahem Mendel Schneerson* (New York: Columbia University Press, 2012), esp. 33–38; Chaim Miller, *Turning Judaism Outward: A Biography of the Rebbe Menachem Mendel Schneerson* (Brooklyn: Kol Menachem, 2014); Naftali Loewenthal, "The Baal Shem Tov's *Iggeret ha-Kodesh* and Contemporary Habad 'Outreach,'" in *Let the Old Make Way for the New: Studies in the Social and Cultural History of Eastern European Jewry Presented to Immanuel Etkes*, ed. David Assaf and Ada Rapoport-Albert, vol. 1, 69–101 (Jerusalem: Zalman Shazar Center for Jewish History, 2009); Yoram Bilu and Zvi Mark, "Between Tsaddiq and Messiah: A Comparative Analysis of Chabad and Breslav Hasidic Groups," in *After Spirituality: Studies in Mystical Traditions*, ed. Philip Wexler and Jonathan Garb (New York: Peter Lang, 2012), 47–78; Zvi Mark, "Contemporary Renaissance of Braslav Hasidism: Ritual, *Tiqqun* and Messianism," in *Kabbalah and Contemporary Spiritual Revival*, ed. Boaz Huss, 101–16 (Beer Sheva: Ben-Gurion University of the Negev, 2011).

37. Amos 1:1.

38. A poetic way of referring to all of Poland.

39. See Jer. 17:6; Ps. 102:18.

40. Symcha Bunem Urbach, *Toledot Neshamah Ahat* (Jerusalem: Shem va-Yafet, 1953), 170–71 (Hebrew).

41. Hillel Seidman, *The Warsaw Ghetto Diary* (Tel Aviv: Umah u-Moledet, 1946), 295–98 (Hebrew).

42. For more on Zeitlin's spiritual activity in the Warsaw Ghetto, see Hillel Zeitlin, "Evaluating the Ghetto: Interviews in Warsaw, 1941," in *A Holocaust Reader*, ed. Lucy S. Dawidowicz, 218–21 (New York: Behrman House, 1976); and a letter from 1942 published posthumously in *Bleter far Geshikhte* 1, no. 1 (1948): 183.

43. A similarly bold reading of this verse appears in a sermon attributed to Rabbi Menahem Mendel of Vitebsk; see *Peri ha-Arets* (Jerusalem: n.p., 1987), *aharei mot*, 77.

44. Rabbi Eleazar Rokeah of Worms (ca. 1160–1230) and Rabbi Yehudah he-Hasid of Regensburg (ca. 1150–1217) were the central figures of the medieval Rhineland mystical circles known as Hasidey Ashkenaz.

45. R. Hayyim Ibn 'Attar (1696–1743), a contemporary of the Ba'al Shem Tov, was a well-known Moroccan kabbalist and Torah commentator.

46. An eleventh-century mystical pietist in Spain and author of the classic *Duties of the Hearts* (*Hovot ha-Levavot*).

47. Ellipsis in the original.

48. Rabbi Nahman of Bratslav (1772–1810), a creative mystical thinker and great-grandson of the Ba'al Shem Tov. Rabbi Nahman's works held great allure for Zeitlin, who devoted several studies to exploring the spiritual path of Bratslav Hasidism. See Hillel Zeitlin, *Rebbe Nahman Bratslaver: Der Zeyer fun Podoliya* (New York: Farlag Matones, 1952); and Hillel Zeitlin, "Messiah and the Light of the Messiah in Rabbi Nahman's Thought," in *God's Voice from the Void*, ed. Shaul Magid, trans. Alyssa Quint, 239–62 (Albany: State University of New York Press, 2002).

49. *Sihot ha-Ran*, no. 52, commenting on the verse, "Tell of His glory among the nations" (Ps. 96:3).

50. It is noteworthy that 1924 was the year Stalin succeeded Lenin as leader of the Soviet state. Events in Russia were very keenly on the minds of the poverty-stricken Jews of Warsaw, who were aware of the brutal and exploitative aspects of socialism as well as its utopian allure.

51. b. Yoma 69b.

52. See b. Ta'anit 16a.

53. *Mishneh Torah, hilkhot issurei bi'ah* 22:21.

54. m. Avot 2:2.

55. Based on b. Yoma 39a.

56. From *Lekha Dodi*, based on b. Rosh ha-Shanah 27a.

57. See the opening passages of the Zohar.

58. *Hovot ha-Levavot*, by Rabbi Bahya ibn Pakuda.

59. *Mesillat Yesharim*, by Rabbi Moshe Hayyim Luzzatto.

60. *Orhot Tsaddikim*, an anonymous medieval pietistic treatise.

61. *Likkutey Amarim-Tanya*, by Rabbi Shneur Zalman of Liady.

62. *Likkutey 'Etsot*, based on the teachings of Rabbi Nahman of Bratslav.

63. Zeitlin added this fifteenth principle to the Hebrew version of *Sifran shel Yehidim* (1928).

64. Zeitlin himself offered limited notes to this essay. In this chapter, whenever possible, the editors have updated Zeitlin's references to Hasidic works to more current editions. Additional comments are presented in brackets to distinguish them from Zeitlin's.

65. Dov Baer of Miedzyrzec, *Likkutey Amarim*, Introduction. We will bring quotations from Hasidic literature *as they are*, except when wording needs to be changed due to improper usage. [*Likkutey* is also called *Maggid Devarav le-Ya'akov*. The critical edition is by Rivka Schatz-Uffenheimer (Jerusalem: Magnes, 1976). The passage is on p. 5.]

66. He means to say that it cannot be grasped by the outer soul but only by the soul within, its innermost part, its godliness.

67. *Likkutey Amarim*, no. 56, 83f.

68. [Based on a widespread play on words already found in the earliest kabbalistic sources, intentionally misreading *me-ayin* to mean "from Nothing" instead of "from where?"]

69. Rabbi Menahem Mendel of Vitebsk, *Peri ha-Arets* (Beitar Illit: n.p., 2014), vol. 1, *tetsaveh*, 357–58.

70. *Likkutey Amarim*, no. 60, 91.

71. *Likkutey Amarim*, no. 78, 134. That which the author of *Peri ha-Arets* calls "being," his master, writing in *Likkutey Amarim*, calls "Nothing." This will come as no surprise to one familiar with Hasidic writings. There are often contradictions in the use of terms, and not always even between different authors. For our purpose, however, the idea is essentially the same.

72. *Sha'arey ha-Yihud veha-Emunah* by Rabbi Aaron of Starroselje (disciple of Rabbi Shneur Zalman of Liadi), *Kelalut ha-Yihud*, 27b. [*Pele'* or "wonder" is *aleph* spelled backward; aleph is frequently taken to represent *keter*, the primal One behind the process of emanation.]

73. R. Abraham ben David of Posquieres, in the introduction to his commentary on *Sefer Yetsirah*. I have joined his words to those of the Hasidim even though he preceded them by many generations, since the Hasidim base themselves on him with regard to Being and Nothingness.

74. Rabbi Israel Ba'al Shem Tov, *Keter Shem Tov* [in *Keter Shem Tov ha-Shalem* (Brooklyn: Kehot Publication Society, 2004), no. 51a, 31, and elsewhere. This parable has been discussed extensively in the scholarly literature around Hasidism. See especially Moshe Idel, "The Parable of the Son of the King and the Imaginary Walls in Early Hasidism," *Judaism—Topics,*

Fragments, Faces, Identities, ed. Haviva Pedaya and Ephraim Meir, 87–116 (Beer Sheva: Ben-Gurion University Press, 2007).]

75. *Peri ha-Arets*, vol. 1, *bereshit*, 9.

76. *Likkutey Amarim*, no. 120, 197.

77. *Tanya*, chap. 42.

78. [He can also withdraw it back into himself.]

79. See *Kitvey Kodesh* 5b, and many other sources. A distinctive explanation of *tsimtsum* is found in HaBaD writings, but that will have to be elaborated elsewhere. Here we offer only general headings, fundaments accepted by all Hasidic systems.

80. *Likkutey Amarim*, no. 60, 89f, quoting Zohar 1:234b.

81. Ethics #4–5.

82. De Profundis.

83. *Or Torah* [in *Or Torah ha-Shalem*, no. 377 (Brooklyn: Kehot Publication Society, 2011), 405–6.]

84. Rabbi Elijah of Vilna (1720–97), the great opponent of Hasidism.

85. Rabbi Mordecai of Chernobyl, *Likkutey Torah, Sixth Instruction* (New York: n.p., 1954; reprint of Lvov, 1865), 4b–c.

86. Rabbi Meshullam Feibush Heller, *Likkutim Yekarim* 54, ed. A. Kahn, 10b (Jerusalem: n.p., 1974).

87. *Likkutey Amarim*, no. 200, 325.

88. *Me'or 'Eynayim, Likkutim* (Jerusalem: n.p., 1999), 340.

89. Rabbi Israel BeSHT. [Source not identified.]

90. Rabbo Shneur Zalman of Liadi, *Tanya*, part 2, "Sha'ar ha-Yihud veha-Emunah," chap. 1, based on the BeSHT.

91. Zalman of Liadi, *Tanya*, part 2, "Sha'ar ha-Yihud veha-Emunah," chap. 3.

92. [Commenting on the *Kedushah* liturgy of the Sabbath service.]

93. Rabbi Mordecai of Chernobyl, *Likkutey Torah* (New York: Israel Wolf, 1954), 77.

94. Zohar 3:288a.

95. Zohar 1:19a, et al.

96. See b. Hagigah 13a.

97. Referring to an ancient legend that the "lower waters" of the second day of Creation called out again the injustice of their being farther from God. See *Tikkuney Zohar, tikkun* 5, fol. 19b.

98. This interpretation of Ps. 121:5 appears in the name of the Ba'al Shem Tov in *Kedushat Levi, be-shalah*; and compare *Degel Maheneh Efrayim, be-har*.

99. Based on the teachings of Rabbi Nahman of Bratslav in *Likkutey Moharan* 21:4–7, discussed by Arthur Green in *Tormented Master: A Life of Rabbi Nahman of Bratslav* (Tuscaloosa AL: University of Alabama Press, 1979), 292.

2. MARTIN BUBER

1. Martin Buber, *Meetings*, ed. Maurice Friedman (La Salle IL: Open Court, 1973), 17–19.
2. See Buber's comments to Franz Rosenzweig in Nahum N. Glatzer and Paul Mendes-Flohr, eds., *The Letters of Martin Buber: A Life of Dialogue* (Syracuse: Syracuse University Press, 1991), 288, 290.
3. Buber, *Meetings*, 20.
4. Buber, *Meetings*, 19–20. For Buber's representations of the Hasidic *rebbes* of Sasov and Zolochev, see Martin Buber, *Tales of the Hasidim*, trans. Olga Marx (New York: Schocken, 1961), 1:138–57, 2:81–95.
5. See Buber's letter to Rosenzweig in Nahum H. Glatzer and Paul Mendes-Flohr, *Letters of Martin Buber: A Life of Dialogue* (New York: Schocken, 1992), 290.
6. See Buber's letters to Rosenzweig in Glatzer and Mendes-Flohr, *Letters of Martin Buber*, 288, 290.
7. See Martin Buber, "What Is Man?" in Martin Buber, *Between Man and Man* (New York: Macmillan, 1965), 136.
8. See Glatzer and Mendes-Flohr, *Letters of Martin Buber*, 290. Regarding the influence of Kant on Buber and his contemporaries' views of religious praxis, see Paul Mendes-Flohr, "Law and Sacrament: Ritual Observance in Twentieth-Century Jewish Thought," in *Jewish Spirituality: From the Sixteenth-Century Revival to the Present*, ed. Arthur Green, 317–45 (New York: Crossroad, 1987).
9. Martin Buber, "My Way to Hasidism," in Martin Buber, *Hasidism and Modern Man* (Princeton: Princeton University Press, 2015), 19.
10. Buber, "My Way to Hasidism," 21.
11. Buber, "My Way to Hasidism," 22.
12. See Theodor Lessing, *Einmal und nie Wieder: Lebenserrinerungen* (Prague: H. Mercy Sohn, 1935), 291–96. Compare Grete Schaeder, "Martin Buber: A Biographical Sketch," in Glatzer and Mendes-Flohr, *Letters of Martin Buber*, 9; compare Paul Mendes-Flohr, "Fin de Siècle Orientalism, the *Ostjuden*, and the Aesthetics of Jewish Self-Affirmation," in Paul Mendes-Flohr, *Divided Passions: Jewish Intellectuals and the Experience of Modernity* (Detroit: Wayne State University Press, 1991), 77, 93, 121.

13. See Buber and Paula's granddaughter Judith Agassi-Buber's comments in Haim Gordon, ed., *The Other Martin Buber: Recollections of His Contemporaries* (Athens: Ohio University Press, 1988), 21–22.

14. See Mendes-Flohr, "Fin de Siècle Orientalism," 93.

15. Mishnah Hagigah 2:1.

16. Glatzer and Mendes-Flohr, *Letters of Martin Buber*, 84–85.

17. Translated in Schaeder, "Martin Buber," 10–11.

18. On the *Neue Gemeinschaft*, see Paul Mendes-Flohr, *From Mysticism to Dialogue: Martin Buber's Transformation of German Social Thought* (Detroit: Wayne State University Press, 1989), 50, 54–57.

19. On Landauer as "prophet," see his friend Felix Stiemer's words shortly after Landauer was beaten to death by soldiers in May 1919: "Gustav Landauer was a prophet, the last great prophet in the style of our time. A man around whom the atmosphere glowed, who was himself 'atmosphere' and who brought this atmosphere to believers and nonbelievers." Felix Stiemer, "Gustav Landauer," *Die Bücherkiste* 1, no. 8/9/10 (December 1919): 99. See also Hanns Ludwig Katz's oil-paint portrait of Landauer entitled *Der Prophet* (1919–20), housed in the Jewish Museum Berlin.

20. Paula Winkler Buber, "Reflections of a Philo-Zionist," *Die Welt* (1901), as quoted in Schaeder, "Martin Buber," 10. For Paula's reflections on Zionism during the summer of the Third Congress (and the summer she met Buber), see her most fascinating letter to Buber in Glatzer and Mendes-Flohr, *Letters of Martin Buber*, 67–69.

21. For Buber's views on Zionism and Jewish-Arab relations, see Martin Buber, *A Land of Two Peoples: Martin Buber on Jews and Arabs*, ed. Paul Mendes-Flohr (Chicago: University of Chicago Press, 2005); compare Samuel Brody, *This Pathless Hour: The Theopolitics of Martin Buber from Weimar Germany to Mandate Palestine* (Bloomington: Indiana University Press, forthcoming).

22. Buber, "My Way to Hasidism," 22–23.

23. Buber, "My Way to Hasidism," 23.

24. Buber, "My Way to Hasidism," 24. Friedman's translation has been emended slightly according to Buber's original German.

25. Interestingly, the Hebrew word from the original source that Buber rendered here as "hallowed (*geheiligt*)" was actually *nithadesh*, renewed! See *"Tsava'at ha-Ribash,"* in *Shivhey ha-Besht* (Tel Aviv: Talpiyot, 1961), 317.

26. See Buber's essays "Renewal of Judaism" and "Jewish Religiosity," in Martin Buber, *On Judaism*, ed. Nahum N. Glatzer (New York: Schocken, 1972), 34–55, 79–94.

27. See Martin Buber, *The Legend of the Baal-Shem*, trans. Maurice Friedman (Princeton: Princeton University Press, 1995), 11–12.

28. Buber, *The Legend of the Baal-Shem*, 12–13.

29. See Schaeder, "Martin Buber," 12–13; Mendes-Flohr, "Fin de Siècle Orientalism," 92–93; Gordon, *The Other Martin Buber*, 22.

30. Because of the Second World War, Buber published this anthology originally in Hebrew translation as *Or ha-Ganuz* (two vols., 1946–47), then in English translation as *Tales of the Hasidim* (two vols., 1947–48), and only thereafter in his original German as *Die Erzählungen der Chassidim* (1949).

31. Translated in Schaeder, "Martin Buber," 12.

32. For an important critique of Paula's unrecognized contributions to her husband's career, see Barbara Hahn, *The Jewess Pallas Athena: This Too a Theory of Modernity*, trans. James McFarland (Princeton: Princeton University Press, 2005), 66.

33. Buber, "My Way to Hasidism," 22.

34. See, for example, Salomon's letter to Buber in Glatzer and Mendes-Flohr, *Letters of Martin Buber*, 113. On the "Lemberg period," see Gedalyah Nigal, *The Hasidic Tale*, trans. Edward Levin (Oxford: Littman Library of Jewish Civilization, 2008), 18–31; Glenn Dynner, "The Hasidic Tale as a Historical Source: Historiography and Methodology," *Religion Compass* 3, no. 4 (2009): 656–59.

35. Glatzer and Mendes-Flohr, *Letters of Martin Buber*, 70.

36. Martin Buber, *Die Geschichten des Rabbi Nachman* (Frankfurt a.M.: Rütten & Loening, 1906), dedication page.

37. See Buber, *Meetings*, 22–23.

38. See Buber, "My Way to Hasidism," 20.

39. See the letter of February 6, 1908, in Glatzer and Mendes-Flohr, *The Letters of Martin Buber*, 114.

40. Of course, this reevaluation of the monolithic "East" said more about Europeans' own identity-constructions than it did about the actual cultures they exoticized, and the discourse remained bound up with a history of colonialism and imperialism. See Edward W. Said, *Orientalism* (New York: Vintage, 1994). See also Mendes-Flohr, "Fin de Siècle Orientalism," 77–132.

41. On the reception of Buber's early Hasidic writings, see Mendes-Flohr, "Fin de Siècle Orientalism," 96–109.

42. See the chapter on Arthur Green. For reflections on American Protestant interest in Buber, see W. Clark Gilpin, "'Companionable Being': American Theologians Engage Martin Buber," *Journal of Jewish Thought and Philosophy* 25, no. 1 (2017).

43. Ran HaCohen, "Einleitung," in Martin Buber, *Werkausgabe*, vol. 18, ed. Ran HaCohen (Munich: Gütersloher Verlagshaus, 2015), 27–28.

44. Buber, *Tales of Rabbi Nachman*, 10; compare Martin Buber, "Christ, Hasidism, Gnosis," in *The Origin and Meaning of Hasidism*, ed. Maurice Friedman (New York: Horizon Press, 1960), 252.

45. On Hasidism as "agnostic," see Buber, *Origin and Meaning of Hasidism*, 178.

46. Buber, "Christ, Hasidism, Gnosis," 253.

47. On the theological significance of Buber's term *Bewährung*, see Michael Fishbane, "Justification through Living: Martin Buber's Third Alternative," in *Martin Buber: A Contemporary Perspective*, ed. P. Mendes-Flohr (Syracuse: Syracuse University Press and Israel Academy of Sciences and the Humanities, 2002), 12–32. Compare Martin Kavka, "Verification (*Bewährung*) in Martin Buber," *Journal of Jewish Thought and Philosophy* 20, no. 1 (2012): 71–98.

48. The definitive scholarship on this shift remains Mendes-Flohr, *From Mysticism to Dialogue*.

49. See Martina Urban, *Aesthetics of Renewal: Martin Buber's Early Representation of Hasidism as Kulturkritik* (Chicago: University of Chicago Press, 2008), 37–39, 181n37.

50. For thoughtful reflections on the intersection of Hasidic narrative and theological discourse, see Tsippi Kauffman, "The Hasidic Story: A Call for Narrative Religiosity," *Journal of Jewish Thought and Philosophy* 22, no. 2 (2014): 101–26.

51. See Martin Buber, *Die Erzählungen der Chassidim* (Zürich: Manesse Verlag, 1949), 16. The meaning is lost in the English translation.

52. Buber, *Hasidism and Modern Man*, 4.

53. See Gershom Scholem, "Martin Buber's Interpretation of Hasidism," in Gershom Scholem, *The Messianic Idea in Judaism and Other Essays on Jewish Spirituality* (New York: Schocken, 1995), 228–50. For Buber's response, see his essay "Interpreting Hasidism," *Commentary* 36, no. 3 (1963): 218–25; reprinted in the present volume.

54. Scholem, "Martin Buber's Interpretation of Hasidism," 244.

55. Scholem, "Martin Buber's Interpretation of Hasidism," 236; compare 249.
56. Buber, "The Place of Hasidism in the History of Religion," in *Origin and Meaning of Hasidism*, 224.
57. Buber, "Interpreting Hasidism."
58. See Seth Brody, "'Open to Me the Gates of Righteousness': The Pursuit of Holiness and Non-Duality in Early Hasidic Teaching," *Jewish Quarterly Review* 89, no. 1/2 (1998): 3–44. Compare Moshe Idel, "Martin Buber and Gershom Scholem on Hasidism: A Critical Appraisal," in *Hasidism Reappraised*, ed. Ada Rapoport-Albert, 392–93 (Oxford: Littman Library of Jewish Civilization, 1998).
59. The Hasidic sources listed in the annotations feature almost exclusively the editions of texts that Buber himself used. These are determined in consultation with Buber's unpublished notebook housed in the Martin Buber Archives at the National Library of Israel (Ms. Var. 350 04 1); the incomplete source index he included in his *Or ha-Ganuz* (Tel Aviv: Schocken, 1968), 469–96; and the critical edition of Buber's *Die Erzählungen der Chassidim*, prepared masterfully by Ran HaCohen, in Buber, *Werkausgabe*, vol. 18.
60. See *Eikhah Rabbah* (ed. Buber), 1:6 and *Pesikta de-Rav Kahana* (ed. Buber), *piska* 26. These midrashic collections were edited by Martin Buber's grandfather, Solomon Buber.
61. As noted in Buber's original text. Not considered here are the development and declension of the kabbalistic view. The focus is only on its basic content, which was decisive for Hasidism.
62. Buber refers here to the Lurianic concept of *tsimtsum* (contraction), according to which divine Infinity (*Ein Sof*) had to self-contract in order to make space, as it were, for the creation of finite existence. Poetically, Buber emphasizes that this primordial withdrawal created the conditions for otherness and thus for relationship. On this delicate dynamic in dialogue, see Martin Buber, "Distance and Relation," in *Martin Buber on Psychology and Psychotherapy: Essays, Letters, and Dialogue*, ed. Judith Buber Agassi (Syracuse: Syracuse University Press, 1999), 3–16. On the concept of *tsimtsum* in Jewish mysticism, see Gershom Scholem, *Major Trends in Jewish Mysticism* (New York: Schocken, 1995), 260–64; Lawrence Fine, *Physician of the Soul, Healer of the Cosmos: Isaac Luria and His Kabbalistic Fellowship* (Stanford: Stanford University Press, 2003, 126–34); Louis Jacobs, *Seeker of Unity: The Life and Works of Aaron of Starosselje* (London: Vallentine, Mitchell, 1966), 49–63.

63. See *Bereshit Rabbah* 68:9.

64. Buber refers here to the kabbalistic doctrine of the "four worlds" that comprise the outer and inner dimensions of existence: *'asiyah* (making), *yetsirah* (formation), *beri'ah* (creation), and *atsilut* (emanation), here called "separation." The source Buber cites stresses that these are increasingly deep realms of human consciousness, rather than ascending metaphysical worlds. Indeed, all four "worlds" are ultimately one reality insofar as *Ein Sof*, the "Unlimited," is the infinite headwater and flow of all finitude. Hasidic reflections on this fundamental oneness refer commonly to Isa. 6:3 ("His glory fills the whole earth") and to the Zoharic formulation "There is no place empty of Him."

65. The original translation of "contradiction" seems to be an error. The German term Buber uses is *Einschränkung*.

66. Buber is suggesting that three exiles echo and encompass one another. The first is cosmic exile, the exile of Creation itself from its divine Source, inherent in the fact of the separate identity of each creature. This is the meaning of "the breaking of the vessels" (*shevirat ha-kelim*). The second is the universal human exile from Eden, accompanying our sense of shame and alienation. The third is the particular historical exile of Israel. Behind this structure lies the well-known rabbinic dictum "In every place where Israel were exiled, *Shekhinah* was exiled with them." See, inter alia, b. Megillah 29a.

67. This seems to be an amalgam of early Hasidic phrases.

68. Barukh of Mezhbizh, *Butsina di-Nehora ha-Shalem* (Lvov: n.p., 1903), 64. Compare Martin Buber, "Against Mortification of the Flesh," in *Tales of the Hasidim*, 1:52.

69. On this concept of "liberating the fallen sparks," see Louis Jacobs, "The Uplifting of Sparks in Later Jewish Mysticism," in *Jewish Spirituality*, vol. 2, *From the Sixteenth-Century Revival to the Present*, ed. Arthur Green, 99–126 (New York: Crossroad, 1987).

70. Mattityahu Yehezkel Gutman, *Tif'eret Bet Levi* (Jassy: n.p., 1909, 21–22; Israel Berger, *'Eser Orot* (Piotrków: n.p., 1907), 61. These teachings are commentaries on Esther 5:9.

71. Avraham Hayyim ben Gedalia of Zloczów, *Orah le-Hayyim* (Berditchev: n.p.,1817), 26a; Natan Neta Diener, *Menorat Zahav* (Warsaw: 1904), 29. Compare Buber, "Above Them," in *Tales of the Hasidim*, 1:248.

72. Likely Buber has in mind the talmudic dictum in b. Sotah 17a: "Rabbi Akiba expounded: When a man (*ish*) and woman (*ishah*) are worthy, the

Shekhinah is between them; when they are not worthy, fire (*esh*) consumes them." The interpenetration of human sexuality and human-divine encounter expands radically in later Jewish mysticism. See Zohar 1:49b–50a, 1:228b. Compare Isaiah Tishby, *The Wisdom of the Zohar*, trans. David Goldstein, vol. 2 (Oxford: Oxford University Press, 1989), 1355–79.

73. *Shivhey ha-Besht* (Kopys: n.p., 1815), 21b; Abraham Hazan, *Avaneha Barzel* (Jerusalem: n.p., 1935), 45. Compare Buber, "After the Death of His Wife," in *Tales of the Hasidim*, 1:82. Regarding the image of a man without a wife as "half a body," see Zohar 3:7b. Compare Arthur Green, *A Guide to the Zohar* (Stanford: Stanford University Press, 2004), 97–98; Yehudah Liebes, *Studies in the Zohar*, trans. Arnold Schwartz, Stephanie Nakache, and Penina Peli (Albany: State University of New York Press, 1993), 67–71.

74. Isaac ben Leib Landau, *Zikaron Tov* (Piotrków: n.p., 1892), 16; Berger, *'Eser Orot*, 51. Compare Buber, "The Wicked Plot," in *Tales of the Hasidim*, 1:230.

75. See *Bereshit Rabbah* 9:7; *Kohelet Rabbah* 3:11.

76. Affirming the spiritual potency of joy was a foundational posture of Hasidic piety from the time of the BeSHT. See also the Talmudic teaching that the *Shekhinah* does not dwell in places of gloom (b. Shabbat 30, b. Pesahim 117).

77. Meir Yehudah Leibush Langerman, *Binyan Shelomo* (Przemyśl: n.p., 1891), 106a, 111b; Berger, *'Eser Orot*, 142. For the original talmudic dictum, see b. Berakhot 58b. Compare Buber, "The Streets of Nehardea," in *Tales of the Hasidim*, 2:50–51.

78. See Shmuel ben Avraham Bornstein, *Shem mi-Shemuel* (Piotrków: n.p., 1927), *parashat lekh lekha*. The image of Enoch the cobbler's mystical unifications through shoe-stitching dates back at least to the fourteenth century, but it became especially central to Hasidism as a call to sanctify the everyday through contemplative focus. See, inter alia, Ya'akov Yosef of Polnoye, *Toledot Ya'akov Yosef* (Medzibezh: n.p., 1817), 14a, 19a; Aaron ha-Kohen of Apt (attributed to the BeSHT), *Keter Shem Tov* (Zolkiev: n.p., 1794), 9b. Compare Scholem, *Major Trends*, 67–70, 365n101; Elliot R. Wolfson, *Along the Path: Studies in Kabbalistic Myth, Symbolism, and Hermeneutics* (New York: State University of New York Press, 1995), 106–8.

79. Buber alludes here to what he—and many others—perceived as an overall decline in the Hasidic spirit. Whereas the early Hasidic sages saw rituals and teachings as vehicles for spiritual renewal and reminders

of how holy every moment of life can be, Buber felt that later Hasidic leaders tended all too often to regard religious norms as ends in themselves to be conserved and clung to at all costs. Like so many other great religious movements that began with "awakening and revolt," Buber laments, Hasidism came to prioritize conservatism over renewal. See Buber, *Tales of the Hasidim*, 2:7–13. For Buber's distinction between institutional "religion" and spontaneous "religiosity," see Martin Buber, "Jewish Religiosity," in Martin Buber, *On Judaism*, ed. Nahum N. Glatzer, trans. E. Jospe (New York: Schocken, 1995), 79–94.

80. Here, to begin the section of this essay aptly entitled "Body," Buber insists that the core of Hasidic wisdom does not lie in static statements or credos but rather in wholly embodied interpersonal moments of instruction. In other words, the "How" of oral transmission—the gestures, tones, glances, and what Buber called the "spokenness" of genuine communication—is no less meaningful than the purely conceptual "What" of the teaching's content. A key term here is *Bewährung*, translated above as "authentication" but rendered elsewhere in Buber's writings as "putting to proof in action." In *I and Thou*, Buber writes that the meaning of dialogical or religious encounter can be known and expressed thereafter "only by becoming embodied in the whole material of life. It cannot be preserved (*bewahrt*) but only put to the proof in action (*bewährt*); it can only be done, poured into life." Martin Buber, *I and Thou*, trans. Walter Kaufmann (New York: Simon & Schuster, 1996), 163. On Buber's concept of *Bewährung*, see Michael Fishbane, "Justification through Living: Martin Buber's Third Alternative," in *Martin Buber: A Contemporary Perspective*, ed. Paul Mendes-Flohr, 12–32 (Syracuse: Syracuse University Press and Israel Academy of Sciences and the Humanities, 2002). On Buber's notion of embodied theological expression, see Sam Berrin Shonkoff, "Sacramental Existence and Embodied Theology in Buber's Representation of Ḥasidism," *Journal of Jewish Thought and Philosophy* 25, no. 1 (2017).

81. See Menahem Mendel Bodek, *Seder ha-Dorot mi-Talmidey ha-Besht* (Lvov: n.p., 1865), 46. Compare Buber, "To Expound Torah and to Be Torah," in *Tales of the Hasidim*, 1:169.

82. "Enfolding" would be a more precise translation of the German word *Einfaltung* than the "unfolding" given by the translator.

83. See Levi Yitshak Monzohn, *Bekha Yevarekh Yisra'el* (Przemysl: n.p., 1905), 5a; Michael Levi Frumkin (Rodkinson), *Shivhey ha-Rav* (Lvov: n.p., 1864),

introduction; Re'uven Zak, *Beit Yisrael* (Piotrków: n.p., 1912), 10. The "girdle" in this source (*gartel* in Yiddish pronunciation) was a simple belt worn by Hasidic men typically at the time of prayer and other ritual actions. When the Apter Rebbe reties the *gartel* around the body of young Israel, the Apter imagines that he is dressing the Torah itself (which often involves tying some fabric around the closed scroll before slipping it into its cover). Insofar as Hasidim tended to regard both the Torah and *tsaddikim* as embodiments of divinity, this anecdote might remind some readers of Christian images of incarnation. On such a connection, see Shaul Magid, *Hasidism Incarnate: Hasidism, Christianity, and the Construction of Modern Judaism* (Stanford: Stanford University Press, 2015).

84. The pairing of the words *tsaddik* (righteous) and *yesod* (foundation) in the biblical verse had a special resonance for Hasidim. Indeed, for the kabbalist, *Yesod* is another name for the *sefirah* connecting *tif'eret* and *malkhut*, or Y-H-W-H and *Shekhinah*. The union of these masculine and feminine dimensions of divinity, mediated by *yesod* (thus imagined erotically as the divine phallus), catalyzes the flows of blessing and being in the world. The biblical verse "The *tsaddik* is the *yesod* of the world," therefore, provided a powerful image for the spiritual role of *tsaddikim* in Hasidic communities. See b. Hagigah 12b. Compare Arthur Green, "The Zaddiq as Axis Mundi in Later Judaism," *Journal of the American Academy of Religion* 45, no. 3 (1977): 327–47.

85. As noted in Buber's original text: Interpretive translation of Genesis 10:21.

86. Compare to Yehudah Leib of Zaklikow, *Likutei Maharil* (Lvov: n.p., 1862), *parashat Noah*; Avraham Yehoshuah Heschel of Apt, *Ohev Yisrael* (Zhytomyr: n.p., 1863), 8.

87. Portrayals of the human being as "one who walks" (*mehalekh*) and the angel as "one who stands" (*'omed*) derive from classical biblical and rabbinic sources and become incorporated as well in later Jewish mysticism. See, inter alia, y. Berakhot 1:1; b. Berakhot 10b; Rashi's commentary on Zech. 3:7; Zohar 2:241b, 3:260a. On walking as a spiritual practice in early Hasidism, see Wolfson, *Along the Path*, 89–109. For a related Hasidic source that Buber anthologizes, see Shmuel of Sienova, *Ramatayim Tsofim* (Warsaw: n.p., 1908), 37; compare Buber, "Man's Advantage," in *Tales of the Hasidim*, 2:276–77.

88. Natan Neta Diener, *Menorat Zahav*, 98b. Compare Buber, "The Secret of Sleep," in *Tales of the Hasidim*, 1:252. This is based on the talmudic notion that "sleep is one-sixtieth part of death" (b. Berakhot 57b).

89. See Mendel Tsitrin, *Shivhey Tsaddikim* (Warsaw: n.p., 1883), 36–37. The phrase "stripping away of bodiliness" (*hitpashetut ha-gashmiyut*) is widespread in later Jewish devotional literature, deriving from its appearance in Jacob ben Asher's *Arba'ah Turim, Orah Hayyim*, no. 98. On this term and related concepts in early Hasidism, see Rachel Elior, *The Mystical Origins of Hasidism* (Oxford: Littman Library of Jewish Civilization, 2008), 74–84, 115–25; compare Moshe Idel, *Hasidism: Between Ecstasy and Magic* (Albany: State University of New York Press, 1995), 64, 127–28, 177–78.

90. On the Lurianic concept of *yihud*, see Lawrence Fine, "The Contemplative Practice of 'Yihudim' in Lurianic Kabbalah," in *Jewish Spirituality*, vol. 2, *From the Sixteenth-Century Revival to the Present*, ed. Arthur Green, 64–98 (New York: Crossroad, 1987). In the early kabbalistic context, unifications with God involved extremely complex and esoteric permutations of *kavvanot*, or mystical "intentions." One of the most radical innovations of early Hasidism was to streamline the pathway to God, so that one visceral outburst of genuine spiritual yearning was deemed stronger than the most scholarly mystical performance. Instead of numerous cerebral *kavvanot*, the earliest Hasidic masters celebrated the gravity of one full-bodied *kavvanah*. As one tale has it, if the sixteenth-century approach was like opening a kingdom's gates slowly and meticulously with a complex set of keys, the BeSHT seized the great ax of *lev nishbar*, a broken heart, to smash the locks. See Moshe Hayyim Kleinmann, *Or Yesharim* (Warsaw: n.p., 1924), 104–5; compare Arthur Green and Barry W. Holtz, *Your Word Is Fire: The Hasidic Masters on Contemplative Prayer* (New York: Paulist, 1977), 7.

91. The marriage of "Majesty" to the "Kingdom" here corresponds to kabbalistic visions of the unification between the divine emanations *tif'eret* and *malkhut*, the names Y-H-W-H and *Shekhinah*, the masculine and feminine dimensions of God.

92. See Moshe Eliyakum Beria ben Israel Hapstein, *Be'er Moshe* (Józe-fów: n.p., 1883), 148; Menahem Mendel Bodek, *Mif'alot ha-Tsaddikim* (Lvov: n.p., 1897), 30–31; Yehudah Aryeh Fraenkel-Teomim, *Oholei Shem* (Biłgoraj: n.p., 1911), 15; Israel Berger, *'Eser Orot* (Piotrków: n.p., 1932), 49. Compare Buber, "Worldly Talk," in *Tales of the Hasidim*, 1:216–17.

93. See Moshe ben Yitzhak Eisik Eichenstein, *Tefilah le-Moshe* (Lvov: n.p., 1856), 57; Yitzhak Yehudah Yehiel Safrin, *Heykhal ha-Berakhah*, vol. 5 (Lvov: n.p., 1864), 159b. Compare Buber, "Illuminated," in *Tales of the Hasidim*, 2:217.

94. Jacob Margolioth, *Kevutsat Ya'akov* (Przemsyl: n.p., 1897), 46b. Compare Buber, "The Prayerbook," in *Tales of the Hasidim*, 1:125.

95. See *Tsava'at RIVASH* (Cracow: n.p., 1896), 14b; *Likkutim Yekarim* (Lvov: 1863), 17d. Compare Green and Holtz, *Your Word Is Fire*, 104; Joseph Weiss, "The Kavvanoth of Prayer in Early Hasidism," *Journal of Jewish Studies* 9 (1958): 179ff.

96. See Moshe Hayyim Kleinmann, *Mazkeret Shem ha-Gedolim* (Piotrków: n.p., 1908), 192; Moshe of Kobryn, *Amarot Tehorot* (Warsaw: n.p., 1910), 30. Compare Buber, "The Original Meaning," in *Tales of the Hasidim*, 2:166.

97. See Kleinmann, *Mazkeret Shem ha-Gedolim*, 103; Kleinmann, *Or Yesharim* (Warsaw: n.p., 1924), 8. Compare Buber, "The Nature of Prayer," in *Tales of the Hasidim*, 2:153.

98. See Aaron ha-Kohen of Apt (attributed to the BeSHT), *Keter Shem Tov*, vol. 1 (Lvov: n.p., 1857), 27a.

99. In the "tabernacle" (sukkah) during the Feast of Booths (*Sukkot*), the benediction that Rabbi Yehudah Loeb is about to recite is the blessing over the *lulav* and *etrog* prior to shaking them together according to the festival ritual.

100. See Yehudah Leib of Zaklików, *Likkutey Maharil* (Lvov: n.p., 1862), 23a. The teaching is a commentary on Exod. 20:18. Compare Buber, "In the Hut," in *Tales of the Hasidim*, 1:317.

101. See Yehoshuah Avraham ben Yisrael, *Ge'ulat Yisrael*, vol. 2 (Ostrog: n.p., 1821), 15a; Israel of Kosnitz, *Ner Yisrael* (Vilna: n.p., 1840, 22a); Pinhas Shapira of Koretz, *Midrash Pinhas* (Lvov: n.p., 1874), vol. 1, 8b; vol. 2, 6. The teaching is a commentary on Deut. 10:21. Compare Buber, "He Is Your Psalm," in *Tales of the Hasidim*, 1:125.

102. This translation of *der Welt der Ursonderung* suggests that the rebbe is angered when confronted by the petty needs of his followers after attuning himself to the most lofty of all worlds during prayer.

103. Exod. 19:14

104. See Avraham Simhah Bunam Michelson, *Mekor Hayyim* (Bilgoraj: n.p., 1912), 45–46. Compare Buber, "To the People," in *Tales of the Hasidim*, 2:209–10.

105. A better translation might be "chariot," as in the *merkavah* of Jewish mystical literature.

106. Lev. 19:18

107. See Pinhas Shapira of Koretz, *Midrash Pinhas*, 29a; Israel Friedman of Ruzhyn, *Pe'er li-Yesharim* (Jerusalem: n.p., 1921), 6a. Compare Buber, "More Love," in *Tales of the Hasidim*, 1:129–30.

108. That is, the ancient Israelites.

109. See Nahman of Bratslav, *Likkutey MoHaRaN* (Jerusalem: n.p., 1969), 61:7. Regarding this image of the *tsaddik* as a new Jerusalem Temple, see Green, "Ẓaddiq as Axis Mundi."

110. These "slips of paper" are little notes (*kvitelakh* in Yiddish) on which Hasidim wrote down their most pressing needs and desires, such as healing, livelihood, or love. They would hand these *kvitelakh* to *tsaddikim* in hopes of receiving such blessings.

111. Jews were by law members of the *kahal* and were obliged to pay their taxes through it.

112. See Pinhas Shapira of Koretz, *Midrash Pinhas*, 4a. Compare Buber, "The Ear That Is No Ear," in *Tales of the Hasidim*, 1:126.

113. Uri Feivel ben Aharon, *Or ha-Hokhmah*, vol. 2 (Laszczów: n.p., 1815), 44b. Compare Buber, "The Bird Nest," in *Tales of the Hasidim*, 1:54–55.

114. Yeshaya Wolf Zickernik, *Sippurim u-Ma'amarim Yekarim* (Warsaw: n.p., 1903), 17–18; Kleinmann, *Or Yesharim*, 198–99. Compare Buber, "The Tsaddik and His Hasidim," in *Tales of the Hasidim*, 1:172–3.

115. See Bodek, *Mif'alot ha-Tsaddikim*, 49; Kleinmann, *Mazkeret Shem ha-Gedolim*, 73; Diener, *Menorat Zahav*, 127–28. Compare Buber, "Tsaddik and Hasidim," in *Tales of the Hasidim*, 1:243.

116. See Menahem Mendel of Rymanov, *Ateret Menahem* (Bilgoraj: n.p., 1910), 72:186.

117. Exod. 20:20–21.

118. See Israel Friedman of Ruzhyn, *'Irin Kaddishin*, vol. 1 (Warsaw: n.p., 1885), 29; Hayyim Avraham Deitschman, *Shemu'ot Tovot Razin de-oraiyta* (Chernivtsi: n.p.,1885), 23a. Compare Buber, "The Right Kind of Altar," in *Tales of the Hasidim*, 2:59.

119. Barukh of Mesbiz, *Butzina de-Nehora ha-Shalem*, 74. Compare Buber, "Fine Words," in *Tales of the Hasidim*, 1:94.

120. Scholem, *Major Trends*, 338ff, 344.

121. Most recently in the conclusion of the foreword to the new edition of *For the Sake of Heaven*, trans. Ludwig Lewisohn (Philadelphia: Meridian Books, 1953), and in the title essay of *Hasidism and Modern Man*, ed. and trans. Maurice Friedman (New York: Horizon Press, 1958).

3. ABRAHAM JOSHUA HESCHEL

1. A longer and fully annotated version of this introduction appears as "Abraham Joshua Heschel: Re-Casting Hasidism for Moderns," *Modern Judaism* 29, no. 1 (2009): 62–79. For Heschel's biography, see Edward K.

Kaplan and Samuel H. Dresner, *Abraham Joshua Heschel: Prophetic Witness* (New Haven: Yale University Press, 1998); and Edward K. Kaplan, *Spiritual Radical: Abraham Joshua Heschel in America, 1940–1972* (New Haven: Yale University Press, 2007).

2. Only recently, thanks mostly to the tireless efforts of translator and publicist Dror Bondi, is Heschel's work having an impact among readers in Israel, where he previously had been largely ignored.

3. Arranged marriages between offspring of Hasidic *rebbes* had been the custom since the eighteenth century. Heschel bore the name of the *tsaddik* of Apt (Opatow in Poland, though later in Miedzyibosh) but was also closely related to the various descendants of Ruzhin and other Hasidic dynasties.

4. In this group one might include such diverse figures as Hasidic researcher Shmuel Abba Horodezky (1871–1957), psychologist and novelist Fishl Schneersohn (1888–1958), novelist Yohanan Twersky (1900–1967), memoirist Malka Binah Shapiro (1894–1971), and perhaps Harvard scholar Isadore Twersky (1930–97), though as Nicham Ross insightfully points out, he actually served as *rebbe* in his later years.

5. See the studies collected and translated posthumously as Abraham Joshua Heschel, *The Circle of the Baal Shem Tov: Studies in Hasidism*, ed. Samuel H. Dresner (Chicago: University of Chicago Press, 1985).

6. Abraham Joshua Heschel, *The Earth Is the Lord's: The Inner World of the Jew in Eastern Europe* (Woodstock VT: Jewish Lights, 1995), 107, 109.

7. Heschel contributed an introductory essay to the Vishniac volume.

8. On the latter question, see Arthur Green, "God's Need for Man: A Unitive Approach to the Writings of Abraham Joshua Heschel," *Modern Judaism* 35, no. 3 (2015): 247–61.

9. A collection of these poems was republished in a bilingual edition as Abraham J. Heschel, *The Ineffable Name of God: Man*, trans. Morton M. Liefman (New York: Continuum, 2004), and a Hebrew translation has recently appeared as well. Heschel later distanced himself from this youthful poetry, insisting that he be treated seriously as a philosopher and not dismissed as a "mere" poet as some tried to portray him. But posthumous research on Heschel has rediscovered the poems as early settings for images and ideas that were to be developed in his later theological writings. See especially Alexander Even-Chen, *A Voice from the Darkness: Abraham Joshua Heschel, Phenomenology and Mysticism* (Tel Aviv: Am Oved and the Schechter Institutes, 1999) (Hebrew); and Alexander

Even-Chen and Ephraim Meir, *Between Heschel and Buber: A Comparative Study* (Boston: Academic Studies, 2012).

10. Heschel, *Ineffable Name of God*, 131.

11. On Heschel's use of Hasidic and kabbalistic teachings, see the recent Michael Marmur, *Abraham Joshua Heschel and the Sources of Wonder* (Toronto: University of Toronto Press, 2016).

12. See Samuel Dresner's introduction to *The Circle of the Baal Shem Tov*, xx, where the author claims that Heschel should "not be labeled a neo-Hasid, though he forsook the Hasidic enclave for the broader Western society." Already in 1956, however, he was so designated by a prominent Orthodox rabbi and professor of sociology; see Joseph H. Lookstein, "The Neo-Hasidism of Abraham J. Heschel," *Judaism* 5, no. 3 (1956): 248–55. Rabbi Lookstein defines Neo-Hasidism, including Heschel's formulation thereof, as follows: "An orientation to life which enables man to feel the unfailing presence of God is Neo-Hasidism. It is, incidentally, the only genuinely Jewish variety of Existentialism."

13. Menahem Nahum of Chernobyl, *Upright Practices and the Light of the Eyes*, ed. and trans. Arthur Green (Ramsey NJ: Paulist, 1982), 35, and 29–44 for a translation of the context. A new and complete translation of the *Me'or 'Eynayim* is forthcoming, Stanford University Press.

14. The Yiddish turn of phrase is *zayen zeyen*, a beautiful play on words.

15. *Mey ha-Shilo'ah*, vol. 1 (Jerusalem: n.p., 1995), *tazri'a* 1, 109.

16. The richest portrayal of Heschel in the context of twentieth-century philosophy and theology is Shai Held, *Abraham Joshua Heschel: The Call of Transcendence* (Bloomington: Indiana University Press, 2013).

17. See, for example, the formulation in *Sefat Emet* (Warsaw: n.p., 1905–8), *hanukkah*, 5636; *pesah*, 5634; and *pekkudey*, 5652. For further information on Ger, see Arthur Green, *The Language of Truth: Teachings from the "Sefat Emet"* (Philadelphia: Jewish Publication Society, 1998).

18. For the sources of this teaching, see *Sefat Emet, shabbat ha-gadol*, 5652, quoting from an earlier text, the sixteenth-century *Seder ha-Yom* of Moshe ben Makhir (Warsaw: n.p., 1876), 25–26.

19. Nahmanides uses this notion in fierce anti-Maimonidean polemics, opposing the philosophical coolness of the philosopher's God who remains unaffected by human actions on the lowly material plane.

20. Shai Held's work referred to in note 16, sees self-transcendence as the key theme in Heschel's oeuvre.

21. b. Bava Batra 9a. All notes to Heschel's essays are by the editors.

22. Here and below, the editors have taken minor liberties with the translation for the sake of gender inclusiveness.

23. Compare with the line from Heschel's poem "Intimate Hymn," quoted above.

24. Heschel refers here to the custom of lighting the Shabbat candles several minutes before the sun has set and waiting to end the Sabbath for some extra time, in order to "add from the profane to the holy." We cannot force Messiah but we can act as though living in messianic times.

25. Heschel is here paraphrasing a well-known Hasidic adage, sometimes attributed to Rabbi Aaron of Karlin: "The greatest 'evil urge' is when the son of the King forgets that he is a prince."

26. m. Rosh ha-Shanah 2:7.

27. See Ex. 24:7, classically understood as Israel's declaration of commitment to sacred deeds, undertaken even before they understood the contours of the divine covenant.

28. Based on I Kings 8:12 and Lev. 16:16.

29. See, inter alia, b. 'Eruvin 19a.

30. Based on b. Bava Batra 9a.

31. Heschel wrote two books on the Kotsker Rebbe (Rabbi Menahem Mendel Morgenstern, 1787–1859) toward the end of his life. The English volume, called *A Passion for Truth* (New York: Farrar, Straus & Giroux, 1973), explores the teachings of the Kotsker in dialogue with the writings of Søren Kierkegaard. The other book, a two-volume work written in Yiddish and as yet unavailable in English, is *Kotsk: In Gerangel far Emesdikeyt* (Kotsk: Struggling for truth) (Tel Aviv: Hamenora, 1973). The first part is now available in Hebrew translation.

32. Heschel means that the humanizing and sacred quality exemplified by Sabbath rest is essential for the moral education of humanity. He does not intend to imply a causative relationship between Sabbath desecration and the Holocaust, a view he would have considered detestable.

33. See Tanna de-Vey Eliyahu Rabbah, chap. 25.

34. This essay was written in 1949, just after the Jewish state was founded. While rejoicing at the miracle of the return to Zion and the re-creation of Jewish nationhood, Heschel believed that Judaism, primarily a religion built around sacred time rather than sacred space, could be lived anywhere. The pioneering spirit associated with Zionism should apply to creativity regarding Torah as well as to the land, inspiring Jews (and others) wherever they live.

35. See, for example, *Toledot Ya'akov Yosef*, vol. 2 (Jerusalem: n.p., 2011), *aharei mot*, 623; and *Toledot Ya'akov Yosef*, vol. 1, *va-yetse*, 174–75. See also Joseph Weiss, "Torah Study in Early Hasidism," in Joseph Weiss, *Studies in East European Jewish Mysticism and Hasidism*, ed. D. Goldstein (London: Littman, 1997), 56–68.

36. The secret of Hasidism's rapid success has been a key question for all historians of the movement. For an extended account of the BeSHT in historical context, as well as a summary of prior views, see Immanuel Etkes, *The Besht: Magician, Mystic, and Leader*, trans. Saadya Sternberg (Waltham MA: Brandeis University Press, 2015). For brief discussions, see Arthur Green, *Speaking Torah: Spiritual Teachings from around the Maggid's Table*, with Ebn Leader, Ariel Evan Mayse, and Or Rose, vol. 1 (Woodstock VT: Jewish Lights, 2013), 1–73; and the first chapters of David Biale et al., eds., *Hasidism: A New History* (Princeton: Princeton University Press, 2017).

37. See the story recounted in Dan Ben-Amos and Jerome R. Mintz, eds., *In Praise of the Baal Shem Tov ("Shivhei ha-Besht"): The Earliest Collection of Legends about the Founder of Hasidism* (Northvale NJ: Jason Aronson, 1993), 89–90.

38. Rabbi Avraham Yehoshua Heschel of Apt (ca. 1748–1825), called by the name of his book, *Ohev Yisra'el* (Zhitomir: n.p., 1863) or "Lover of Israel."

39. *Bereshit Rabbah* 42:8 interprets the word *'ivri* (Hebrew), first applied to Abraham, as "dissenter," claiming that "The whole world was on one side (*'ever*) and he was on the other."

40. See previous note.

4. SHLOMO CARLEBACH

1. For an excellent biography of Carlebach, see Natan Ophir (Offenbacher), *Rabbi Shlomo Carlebach: Life, Mission, and Legacy* (Jerusalem: Urim, 2014); and the informative collection of essays in *American Jewish History* 100, no. 4 (2016).

2. See the comment at the beginning of the interview with Zalman Schachter-Shalomi, where he recalls Shlomo's contact with Hasidism already in Austria.

3. His remarkable presence in American culture is attested by the Broadway musical *Soul Doctor*, based on his life story.

4. Both the move to Lakewood and then to Chabad signaled a rejection of Carlebach's German Orthodox heritage, perhaps because its embrace of rational, secular culture as a necessary complement to modern religion was shattered by the Holocaust; see Yaakov Ariel, "Hasidism in the Age

of Aquarius: The House of Love and Prayer in San Francisco, 1967–1977,"
Religion and American Culture: A Journal of Interpretation 13, no. 2 (2003):
140; Yitta Halberstam Mandelbaum, *Holy Brother: Inspiring Stories and
Enchanted Tales about Rabbi Shlomo Carlebach* (Northvale NJ: Jason Aronson, 1997), 52. Carlebach enjoyed making jokes at the expense of pious
but religiously ignorant German Jews.

5. "Practical Wisdom from Shlomo Carlebach," *Tikkun* 12, no. 5 (Fall 1998): 53.

6. In the *Tikkun* interview Reb Shlomo expressed sadness that the Lubavitcher
Rebbe was unwilling to come with him into these uncharted and unconventional waters. But in 1959 Rabbi Moshe Feinstein penned a responsum
in which he alludes to Reb Shlomo in veiled terms, referring to a prodigal
scholar whose infractions are not heretical beliefs but rather the fact that he
plays before mixed audiences. See *Iggerot Moshe* (New York: n.p., 2011), *even
ha-ezer* 1, no. 96; Ophir, *Rabbi Shlomo Carlebach*, 89, and for a different incident, 243. More broadly, see Yaakov Ariel, "Can Adam and Eve Reconcile?:
Gender and Sexuality in a New Jewish Religious Movement," *Nova Religio:
The Journal of Alternative and Emergent Religions* 9, no. 4 (2006): 53–78.

7. Ariel, "Hasidism," 141.

8. On the House of Love and Prayer, see Aryeh Coopersmith, *Holy Beggars: A Journey from Haight Street to Jerusalem* (El Granada CA: One World
Lights, 2011). In this same year Reb Shlomo took over the leadership of
the New York synagogue where his recently deceased father had been
the rabbi for several decades.

9. Abraham Joshua Heschel and Elie Wiesel were listed as spiritual advis-
ers; see Coopersmith, *Holy Beggars*, 163.

10. Ariel, "Hasidism," 156.

11. Though sensitive to the plight of the Palestinian Arabs, Reb Shlomo was
supportive of the Jewish right to settle the Greater Land of Israel. Maintaining this position throughout the 1980s conflicts, he gave concerts in
support of the settlers, performing in the West Bank alongside figures
such as the radical Rabbi Yitzchak Ginsburgh.

12. Reb Shlomo once remarked that "religion," like homeopathic medicine, "has to work from inside to outside"; see "Practical Wisdom from
Shlomo Carlebach," 53.

13. One of Carlebach's veteran students described him as follows: "Rav
Shlomo was continually pushing all those around him to strive for the
fullest Jewish experience at every moment, never accepting rote performance of any *mitzvah*. . . . He taught that every moment is a unique

opportunity to connect to God and to each other. He was a unique blend of tradition and spontaneity, *halachah* and creativity"; see Avraham Arieh Trugman, "Probing the Carlebach Phenomenon," *Jewish Action* 63 (2002): 12.

14. This fact very clearly locates him within the Neo-Hasidic tradition of all three figures discussed earlier, even though he did not make reference to them. In general, Shlomo (who did not have any higher non-yeshiva education) never made reference to thinkers or writers outside the traditional rabbinic/Hasidic canon.

15. See Sarah Weidenfeld, "Rabbi Shlomo Carlebach's Musical Tradition in Its Cultural Context: 1950–2005," PhD diss., Bar-Ilan University, 2008 (Hebrew); Sam Weiss, "Carlebach, Neo-Hasidic Music, and Current Liturgical Practice," *Journal of Synagogue Music* 34 (2009): 55–75; Shaul Magid, "Rabbi Shlomo Carlebach and His Interpreters: A Review Essay of Two New Musical Releases," *Musica Judaica Online Reviews*, September 2010. See also Ophir, *Rabbi Shlomo Carlebach*, 55–57; Ariel, "Hasidism," 141.

16. "Practical Wisdom from Shlomo Carlebach," 53.

17. Quoted in Ophir, *Rabbi Shlomo Carlebach*, 108–9. The text, from the album *Mikdash Melekh* (In the palace of the King), is by Sophia Adler. See also Robert Shelton, "Rabbi Carlebach Sings Spirituals," *New York Times*, October 24, 1961, 24, cited in part by Ariel, "Hasidism," 142; and Mark Kligman, "Contemporary Jewish Music," *American Jewish Year Book* 101 (2001): 99–104.

18. See the discography and the list of songs in Ophir, *Rabbi Shlomo Carlebach*, 463–80.

19. Perhaps his clearest statement about his approach to storytelling is his reply to a student who asked about the differences between Reb Shlomo's various tellings of the same story as well as their probable written sources. Reb Shlomo responded: "I don't change a story, but . . . sometimes you read a story and you realize that part of it is not true; it *couldn't* be like this! . . . When I tell a story as I do . . . I trust my nose that that's the way it happened." Yitzhak Buxbaum, *Storytelling and Spirituality in Judaism* (Northvale NJ: Jason Aronson, 1994), 140. Compare with Buber's "I became a filter" (p. 121).

20. This transcription is based on "The Holy Hunchback," included in the 1980 album *L'kovod Shabbos*.

21. *Mey ha-Shiloah, emor*, fol. 39b. The author of *Mey ha-Shiloah* is known for taking an extreme position on the question of religious determinism,

teaching that there is no such thing as happenstance but that everything, including seeming human choice, is in the hands of heaven. See note 25.

22. *Mey ha-Shiloah, emor*, fol. 39b. A further comment on Lev. 21:1. The "priest," meaning the *tsaddik* or even the ideal religious person, should not let himself be defiled by contact with the dead, here taken to mean depressed by the reality of death, because he is a vehicle of the joyous service of God.

23. This is a very profound indictment of the religious world in which he was raised.

24. This is based on a paraphrase and transcription by his student David Zeller, *Soul of the Story* (Woodstock VT: Jewish Lights, 2006), 148–51. See also Roger Kamenetz, *The Jew in the Lotus* (San Francisco: Harper, 1995), 156–57; Ophir, *Rabbi Shlomo Carlebach*, 203–4.

25. In reworking this teaching, Reb Shlomo excludes something present in the original teaching: the literal understanding of divine providence, a characteristic element of the Izhbitzer's Torah made frightful if applied to the Holocaust.

26. For a popular collection tales about him, see Mandelbaum, *Holy Brother*.

27. Ophir, *Rabbi Shlomo Carlebach*, 195, describes him as having "crystallized a unique style combining three types of presentation: singing-whistling-guitar playing, musical storytelling, and ethical-theological exhortations spliced with personal anecdotes." See also Ophir, *Rabbi Shlomo Carlebach*, 53–59.

28. For the story of one such person who traveled to the East and then returned to Judaism through Neo-Hasidism, see Zeller, *Soul of the Story*.

29. See Sarah Blustain, "A Paradoxical Legacy: Rabbi Shlomo Carlebach's Shadow Side," *Lilith* 23, no. 1 (1998): 10–17; and the replies in "Sex, Power and Our Rabbis: Readers Respond to 'Rabbi Shlomo Carlebach's Shadow Side,'" *Lilith*, Summer 1998, 12–16; and Sarah Imhoff, "Carlebach and the Unheard Stories," *American Jewish History* 100, no. 4 (2016): 555–60. Compare Ophir, *Rabbi Shlomo Carlebach*, 421–25.

30. Avraham Arieh Trugman, "Probing the Carlebach Phenomenon," *Jewish Action* 63 (2002): 9–12.

31. Joanna Steinhardt, "American Neo-Hasids in the Land of Israel," *Nova Religio: The Journal of Alternative and Emergent Religions* 13, no. 4 (2010): 22–42. For example, Micha Odenheimer has described his efforts for social justice as an outgrowth of the lessons imbibed from Reb Shlomo; see Tomer Persico's recent interview with Odenheimer, available at:

https://tomerpersicoenglish.wordpress.com/2015/02/11/changing
-the-world-one-bit-at-a-time-an-interview-with-micha-odenheimer/,
retrieved February 1, 2016.

32. Shefa Siegel, "Shlomo Carlebach: Rabbi of Love or Undercover Agent of
Orthodox Judaism," *Haaretz*, September 4, 2011, available at: www.haaretz
.com/jewish/books/shlomo-carlebach-rabbi-of-love-or-undercover
-agent-of-orthodox-judaism-1.382475, retrieved March 8, 2016.

33. Yaakov Ariel, "Hasidism," 155: "As liberal and inclusive as he was, Carlebach wished to remain within the realm of Orthodox Judaism and was
reluctant to go along with Schachter. With all his criticism of the lack
of flexibility and inspiration on the part of the Jewish Orthodox establishment, his goal was to bring young men and women to a traditionally
observant, if open and innovative, environment."

34. Shaul Magid, "Carlebach's Broken Mirror," *Tablet*, November 1, 2012,
emphasizes the extent to which Carlebach fabricated a "prewar Jewish
world that never existed" in order to inspire his listeners; available at:
www.tabletmag.com/jewish-arts-and-culture/music/115376/carlebach
-broken-mirror, retrieved January 20, 2016.

35. The transcription is based on a recording made in Tannersville, New York,
circa 1970. A copy of the tape ended up in the Zalman Schachter-Shalomi
archives in Boulder, Colorado, and was the basis for this transcription.
The transcription reflects Reb Shlomo's distinctive oral style, including
his somewhat broken English. No attempt has been made to alter it.

36. See b. Niddah 30b. Though he does not refer to it by name, it seems that
throughout this teaching Reb Shlomo is drawing upon a homily of Rabbi
Ya'akov Leiner, *Haggadah shel Pesah* (Lublin: n.p., 1910), fol. 4a–b, which
begins with the following declaration: "On this holiday [i.e., Pesach] the
blessed Holy One illuminates a person's eyes, allowing him to recognize his place and his root, and revealing the source of what it is that
he lacks." Rabbi Leiner explains that the light of the candle used in the
search for *hametz* (leaven) represents a spiritual light, a special quality of
illumination granted only on Passover that we may use to find our own
unique place in the world. This metaphorical candle also uncovers each
individual's singular task in this lifetime: a quest for redemption that is
hidden even—or especially—within moments of failure and lack.

37. The revelation on Mount Sinai is described here as an illumination so
powerful and overwhelming that it took Israel some time to find the
words to describe and understand it. This is a traditionally phrased but

highly unconventional view of the Sinai revelation, reflecting the style of the Izhbitz Hasidism that so influenced Reb Shlomo.

38. Maimonides, *Sefer ha-Mitsvot, hakdamah*, underscores the importance and indeed superiority of oral recitation that leads to knowledge by heart. Maimonides's great project of summarizing the law, the *Mishneh Torah*, was intended to allow the entire Oral Law to become known to all.

39. Maimonides, *Sefer ha-Mada', hilkhot talmud torah* 3:13, emphasizes that the majority of one's wisdom is cultivated at night. On the merits of nocturnal study of Torah, see also b. Hagigah 12b. The Zohar and kabbalistic traditions of Safed further develop this theme.

40. See b. Niddah 30b and b. Hagigah 12a for the rabbinic legend of Adam seeing from one edge of the world to another by gazing into the primeval light of creation. Reb Shlomo is reading of "looking from one end of the world to the other" to suggest a call for a more universal and less narrow reading of "Torah."

41. Based on a frequent Hasidic statement that *torah* means "teaching," and that it must do so to teach each generation and individual how to live.

42. The verse "the candle of Y-H-W-H is the soul of man, searching all the inward parts" (Prov. 20:27) draws the link between candle and womb. A literalization of this image seems to underlie the *midrash*.

43. Divine service, shared equally and thus uniting all life forms, was the only goal in the Garden of Eden. While there may not have been multiple souls, the multitude of life that characterizes the emergence of multiplicity from the Infinite One had already taken place.

44. According to the Midrash, all souls to be born were present in the single soul of Adam. Izhbitz sermons emphasize that there can be no free choice or human agency if one is fully aware of standing in the presence of God. To allow for struggle, growth, and divine service, this knowledge was hidden from Adam ha-Rishon; see *Beit Ya'akov* (Brooklyn: n.p., 1976), *mishpatim*, fol. 23a.

45. Reb Shlomo's sources were often, but not always, found in the printed books he referenced. He creatively reinterpreted Hasidic sources, placing them in a rich dialogue with other sources and his original insights. As here, a hallmark of Reb Shlomo's teaching was to summarize teachings in a direct and contemporary conversational tone. These were far from direct quotation.

46. While Izhbitz sources hardly valorize the sin of the Golden Calf, they point toward its preordained inevitability, as well as the fact that this

iniquity led to the construction of the Tabernacle and thus the possibility of communal repentance. This fits with the generally extreme view
of predestination in Izhbitz thought, where even the "fear of heaven" or
lack of it is preordained, in contrast to the usual rabbinic view.

47. Idolatry was inevitable, but only so great a generation as that one could
have used it to learn the possibility of repentance. That is why they had
to make the Calf, showing all future generations the way to return.

48. He quotes the conclusion and the beginning of the Torah in sequence, as
they are read on Simchat Torah. Many teachings for Simchat Torah are
about that linkage.

49. See Rashi's commentary to Deut. 34:12. Quoting *Sifrey* 33:41, he connects Deut. 34:12 to Deut. 9:17 ("I shattered them before your eyes").
The comment is on "which Moses wrought," as distinct from that which
God brought about through Moses. Rashi also refers to the talmudic passage in which God praises Moses for shattering the tablets; see
b. Shabbat 87a, which records the shattering of the tablets as one of
the three things that Moses did of his own accord and with which the
blessed Holy One agreed.

50. Despite the people's failings, Moses shows all Israel the possibility
of a new *reshit*, of beginning again, following the breaking of the tablets.
Because he too was a mortal with human imperfections, only Moshe
(but not God) could teach us how to persevere and begin again, even in
the face of failure.

51. He is using both Eden and Shabbat as ways of speaking about a spiritual
"high" from which one never falls. But because we are mortals living
after the sin of Eden, such a reality is not possible for us. We can quickly
go from the highest places to the lowest.

52. That is, one can descend from the greatest heights to becoming utterly
fallen only moments later.

53. Izhbitz sources emphasize that each person has a unique spiritual
task, a particular *mitzvah* related to the root of one's soul that must be
performed with even greater devotion. See *Mey ha-Shiloah*, vol.1, *va-
ethanan*, 57b; and idem, *ki tetse*, 62a.

54. b. Gittin 43a. In addition to its central role in Izhbitz teachings, this
talmudic dictum is a key text for the spiritual ethos of Hasidism. One
attains a higher level of Torah and religious service not through static
and perpetual perfection, as one might expect, but rather through the
cyclical pattern of stumbling and striving once more.

55. The founder of the Izhbitz Hasidic dynasty was Mordechai Yosef Leiner (1801–54), whose teachings are recorded in the *Mey ha-Shiloah*. Here Reb Shlomo refers to the founder's grandson Gershon Henokh Leiner (1839–91), author of the multivolume *Sod Yesharim* and many other works of *halakhah*, talmudic commentary, and philosophical and kabbalistic thought.

56. It required no real spiritual effort and therefore is of little ultimate value in the work of repairing your soul.

57. Many Izhbitz homilies underscore the spiritual importance of stumbling, the core message of the present teachings. These texts argue that a seeker will not grow spiritually through performing deeds that come naturally or easily. It is only through constant challenge, and indeed failure, that positive growth may take place. The static model of constant ascent, while seemingly perfect, actually prevents the true and enduring religious growth that emerges from constant effort and occasional failure. See *Mey ha-Shiloah, yitro*, fol. 26a; *Sod Yesharim, bo*, 137b.

58. Tradition recalls Yom Kippur, when the High Priest would enter the Holy of Holies in order to confess his sins and those of Israel, as the day on which the second tablets were given. See b. Ta'anit 30b, and Rashi to Ex. 33:11.

59. One enters into the innermost sacred realm accompanied not by heaps of merits and accomplishments but through confrontation with the darkest elements of one's own shadow self.

60. See *Peri 'Ets Hayyim, sha'ar hag ha-sukkot*, chap. 1. Reb Shlomo seems to be thinking of the *sukkah* as a sort of Holy of Holies.

61. The Talmud refers to the *sukkah* as a temporary dwelling place; b. Sukkah 2a.

62. The *halakhah* demands that the shade of a *sukkah* be more than its sunlight, but Reb Shlomo is treating this darkness in a metaphoric way.

63. b. Sukkah 12a. Compare *Sod Yesharim, pesah*, fol. 65a. The life force and transformation that emerges from the seemingly useless agricultural waste is read as a symbol for the rebirth after one stumbles through a thorny patch of life. The roof, the holiest part of the *sukkah* and the individual's own Holy of Holies, is a phoenix reborn of one's spiritual refuse.

64. Rashi to Gen. 28:11, drawing upon *Bereshit Rabbah* 68:11.

65. He seems to be implying that Ya'akov could have learned the Torah of Sinai from Avraham and Yitzhak, who knew and kept it before it was given, but he had to go to Shem and Ever, the keepers of the tradition

of Adam and Eden, in order to learn the more intimate and fault-driven Torah of the Nine Months. Their wisdom, including the lessons of Adam's fall, was rooted in the memory of Eden.

66. Your true mate knows and shares not only the Torah of Judaism, that is, the Torah of Mount Sinai, but your own inner Torah, including your struggles and the places where you fail. Boro Park is an ultra-Orthodox neighborhood in Brooklyn.

67. Rabbi Leibele (Yehudah Leib Eiger, d. 1888), a grandson of the great talmudist Rabbi Akiva Eiger, became a Hasidic *rebbe*. Many of Rabbi Mordechai Yosef Leiner's disciples moved their allegiances to Lublin and became his students after their master's death in 1854.

68. The letter samekh is written as a circle.

69. The Fifteenth of Av is described in rabbinic literature as a day of courtship and love. m. Ta 'anit 4:8 records that on this day—as on Yom Kippur—young maidens would come out and dance in circles in the vineyards. These circles are the connection to the samekh and the round figure of the wedding ring.

70. b. Ta'anit 31a.

71. Leah was his soul mate after he was victorious in the wrestling match with his shadow side, a victory that leads toward *Mashiach*. But Rokhel was his mate "outside the land," when he was his lower self, because she shared his "nine months" Torah and could support him when he was low.

72. Moshe had brought Yosef's bones along with Israel when they left Egypt (Ex. 13:19). Numerous rabbinic traditions interpret the verse "the sea saw, and fled" (Ps. 114:3) as a reference to Yosef's bones or his casket; see *Bereshit Rabbah* 87:9 and *Tanhuma, va-yeshev*, no. 9. Yosef is the son of Rachel; Yehuda is the son of Leah.

73. Nahshon ben Aminadav, the brother-in-law of Aaron, was the prince of the tribe of Judah. He was the first to enter the Sea of Reeds. See b. Sotah 37a.

74. Tradition has it that there are two messiahs. The *Mashiach* from the House of Yosef has to die before the *Mashiach* from the House of David can bring about the final redemption.

75. The moment of redemption from Egypt is understood as anticipating, and perhaps even sowing the seeds, for the future messianic redemption. But all along the way, when the "Yosef" in us creates an opening, the "Yehuda" joins in and makes progress toward redemption as well.

76. Y-H-W-H, the most sacred name of God, is mysterious, transcendent, and always hidden.

77. Instances of "their father" in the Yosef story are taken already by the Zohar as referring to God; see, for example, Zohar 1:183b. Yosef believed and brought before God the evil things that were said. Yosef is being read here as having the failing of lacking faith in himself. Perhaps he is even reading *el avihem* (to their father) as "about God."

78. God "looks to the heart," sees the light within the person's soul, and understands that the person is essentially good and that the "evil reports," those we too readily believe about ourselves, are not the real truth.

79. The image of Rachel pleading for her children is a common one in rabbinic and kabbalistic literature. See Seth Brody, *Zohar Hadash: The Hidden Midrash to the Book of Lamentations* (Kalamazoo MI: Medieval Institute, Western Michigan University, 1999), esp. 153–88.

80. Yosef seems to represent both the failing of bringing the evil report and (as the son of Rachel) the *tikkun* of learning *not* to believe it. Presumably this experience was Yosef's burden, as well of his healing, thus representing his own Torah of the Nine Months.

81. From the opening blessing of the *Amidah*.

82. *Likkutey Moharan* 1:9, where Rabbi Nahman reads *tefillah le-El hayai* (Ps. 42:9) not as "a prayer to the God of my life" but rather "prayer to God *is* my very life!"

83. b. Berakhot 26b.

84. Meaning that prayer is our very lifeblood as Jews, coming to us from our earliest ancestors, preceding even our connection to Torah.

85. *Pesah sheni*, Second Passover, was an opportunity for those who had been ritually impure or forcibly absent on the day of the paschal sacrifice to have another chance to offer it. See Num. 9:9–14.

86. Pesach Sheni anticipates moments in which people become so caught up in darkness, impurity, sadness, and despair that even prayer becomes impossible. This harks back to his comment quoted in the introduction about the "priest" not becoming defiled by contact with the dead; he is so "deadened" that he can't pray. Pesach thus offers a breath of hope for personal and national renewal amid brokenness and tragedy. Pesach Sheni is a second chance to awaken the life-giving prayer of the soul, unlocking a vitality to which even the Torah of Mount Sinai cannot grant access.

87. b. Sukkah 25a–b, and Rashi's comments there.

88. That is the Torah of the Nine Months, allowing for the possibility of *teshuvah* and transformation.

89. Again, Yosef is an ambivalent symbol. The pallbearers are defiled through carrying around Yosef's bones, which will remain with them throughout the forty years. Yosef represents the ill report he gave to his father (to our Father): the lack of faith in oneself. But he also represents the crying out that will lead to healing: the brokenness that will allow one to pray again.

90. From the Rosh Hashanah liturgy.

91. Recalling the original midrash of the child studying Torah in the mother's womb.

92. The second tablets of the covenant were said to be given on Yom Kippur.

93. Without discovering our own inner Torah, our individual Torah of the Nine Months, the outer Torah of Sinai becomes but an idol.

94. Reb Shlomo means a spiritual "death," giving up on the possibility of *teshuvah* and forward motion in the face of failure and stumbling.

95. Because Yosef leads us back to prayer, or the inward Torah of the Nine Months, his bones accompanied the Jewish people throughout their forty years of wandering in the desert.

96. The full verse reads: "They shall not hurt nor destroy in all My holy mountain; for the earth shall be full of the knowledge of the Y-H-W-H, as the waters cover the sea." Reb Shlomo interprets this "knowledge" as a reference to *Mashiach*'s Torah, an exalted state of attunement to be attained when the Torah of the Nine Months as well as the Torah of Mount Sinai are brought into alignment.

97. This messianic Torah of true redemption, without words and beyond all language, is thus deeper than either the general, communal Torah of Mount Sinai or the individual Torah of the Nine Months.

98. Based on *Bereshit Rabbah* 12:5.

99. Hasidic sources often invoke the hidden light as being hidden within the Torah, accessible even now but only to those of great spiritual attunement and devotion. See *Degel Mahaneh Efrayim* (Korets: n.p., 1810), par. *bereshit*. This reading is a complete reversal of the original sense of *ki tov le-ganzo*, which suggests that the initial light is too great to behold in this world.

100. See y. Berakhot 2:4.

101. Tradition prohibits studying Torah on the Ninth of Av in addition to fasting; see b. Ta'anit 30a. This is a mourning practice. Reb Shlomo, however, explains that we do not study on Tisha b'Av because we are rising above the Torah of words.

102. Tradition has it that the Messiah is to be born on the Ninth of Av. Shlomo is interpreting this notion to mean that the messianic Torah and the Torah of birth are thus joined on it.

103. Avraham's goal was to demonstrate to the people that there is only one God—and that the physical world of the cosmos is the dwelling place for the Divine.

104. Yitzhak, by contrast, was drawn into contemplation of the divine unity and thus toward the realization that, because everything is God, there is no world as such, or that this world has no real or essential validity. Yitzhak is therefore prepared to die in this world, but comes to a different realization when bound upon the altar.

105. Children remind us that the cosmos can itself become infused with holiness. Awareness of this sanctity is expressed not through world denial or mystical transcendence but rather through an embrace of the physical with all of its complexities in tow. For a teaching about children giving clarity to their parents, see *Beit Ya'akov, va-yeshev*, fol. 11b–12a.

106. The revelation of *Mashiach* is characterized by the dissolution of the false dichotomy between spirituality (a vision of God's singular unity pervading all) and embodied corporeality (an embrace of the world). Awareness of the messianic time affirms the existence of the cosmos as an expression of the infinite Divine, even if this manifestation is ultimately only an illusion.

107. The first kind of holiness, typified by Moses, entails sanctifying someone else but entails no loss to the giver. The second type of holiness, however, requires great self-sacrifice; it can only be imparted through someone relinquishing one's own innate sanctity. This second kind of holiness is the model of the High Priest Aaron, who was actually commanded to become impure when necessary to help other people.

108. b. Nazir 43b teaches that a priest is ordinarily allowed to become defiled only to bury a close relative. Special permission, however, is given to bury someone who dies without relatives and would otherwise have no one to bury him or her. This contact with the dead temporarily disqualifies the priest from performing divine service.

109. This picks up on his radical reading of the Golden Calf. Aaron sacrifices his own holiness to help Israel commit this sin—one he knows is necessary to realize the greater good of their learning the possibility of repentance.

110. Yosef could have been brought directly out of Egypt to the Land of Israel. He gave this up, however, because he understood that the Jews in

379

exile needed his bones—they needed his anchoring presence as a constant reminder of the possibility for repentance, transformation, and redemption.

111. b. Berakhot 19b–20a notes explicitly that burying a *mes mitsvah* (a corpse that no one takes responsibility for burying) takes precedence over offering the paschal sacrifice. Furthermore, b. Zevahim 100a reads: "The wife of Joseph the priest happened to die on the eve of Passover, and he did not wish to defile himself, whereupon his brother priests took a vote and defiled him by force." That presence is a *pikkadon*, something entrusted to the people Israel, who will carry it with them when they leave Egypt.

112. Direct revelation to the individual in such a forthright way is a taste of the Messianic Torah, accessible in this partial or inchoate form as Pesach Sheni.

113. Rashi, quoting the early rabbinic midrash (*Sifrey* 1:22), compares Moses to a disciple who waits confidently for his teacher's instruction. He could speak to *Shekhinah* whenever he wanted. Rashi also notes that these passages and special laws could potentially have been revealed through Moses but they were actually given through the merit of these self-sacrificing individuals who gave up their own holiness and opportunity to sacrifice the Pesach offering in order to bury someone who died utterly alone and bereft.

114. This event is recorded in Num. 27. The daughters of Zelophehad refuse to become disenfranchised just because their father died, and they seek judgment from Moses regarding whether or not they can inherit something. Notably, this story represents the first instance of God speaking to Moses after the disastrous affair of the spies. Their audacious—but just—claim allowed a new *parashah* or section to be added to the Torah.

115. He is reading the *lakhem* (for you) in these two verses as "to you." God has a private message addressed to each individual, but Moses was able to listen in and act as a conduit for each of them.

116. Eve is depicted as a proto-feminist, angry that God spoke to her through Adam rather than directly. The snake used this anger as an opportunity to place himself between her and God. The daughters of Zelophehad come to repair the damage she has done by allowing God to speak *lakhem*, to them directly.

117. The *lemor* (to say) is an indication that it is to be passed on and shared with everyone.

118. Here Reb Shlomo seems to conflate *Mashiah*'s Torah and the Torah of the Nine Months, or at the very least to place them together on a continuum of intensity, whereas previously they were contrasted.

119. See Rashi, quoting b. Sanhedrin 82a.

120. Yosef is thus the model of the seeker, who strives and stumbles along the path. The Torah of the Nine Months is Yosef's gift to all those who are on the journey and encounter the inevitable failure, and this realization is a foretaste of the total unveiling that is to accompany *Mashiach*'s Torah. Yehudah's Torah, that of *Mashiach*, only works when one has the sureness of the dwelling in the Land of Israel—a sense that one is walking on holy ground. But in the wilderness we have only our private, personal Torah of the Nine Months, in which there are not the same clear lines between permitted and forbidden. Thus we need Yosef ha-Tsaddik to guide us.

121. Menasheh represents a kind of *teshuvah* or repentance accomplished through forgetting one's misdeeds and moving on. Efraim, however, means something more: to be made "fruitful in the land of my affliction" means that one may blossom even, and perhaps precisely, in the soil of failure.

122. In this interpretation, *teshuvah* means to overcome failure by moving forward and letting bygones remain a thing of the past. Through attaining the Torah of the Nine Months, however, one understands that the trajectory of spiritual growth necessarily includes failure and stumbling. Finding one's place in the world can only happen through this awakening, not simply through erasing the past.

123. These two categories are the ten creative utterances described in the opening chapter of Genesis, and the Decalogue given on Sinai. Perhaps in this context Reb Shlomo takes them as referring respectively to the Torah of the Nine Months and the Torah of Sinai. If these two realms are not united or aligned with one another, one must wander aimlessly through a web of absurdity. This restlessness is present even though one may observe all the laws of the Torah of Sinai, until one finds the right Torah of the Nine Months. Without this knowledge one cannot accomplish the singular task that necessitated one's unique soul being sent into the world. This may also refer to seeing the Torah more broadly, in the context of the entire world.

124. Reading the word *av* as an acronym of the first two letters of the Hebrew alphabet.

125. Reb Shlomo is reading *av* as a combination of the initial letter of the Decalogue (*aleph*, Ex. 20:2) and the first letter of the Torah itself (*bet*, written as *vet* without diacritics in a Torah scroll, Gen. 1:1). This association draws together the themes of Creation and Revelation, and the individual Torah of the Nine Months as well as the cosmic Torah of Creation.

126. *Hodesh av*, remembered as a time of great tragedy for the Jewish people, actually holds the seeds for bringing together the Torah of Mount Sinai (the *aleph*, the first letter of the Decalogue) and the Torah of the Nine Months (the *bet* of *bereshit*, or the first word of Genesis). This association of the Torah of the Nine Months with the word *bereshit* suggests that God's project in creating the world is really the unfolding story of the Torah of the Nine Months.

127. Tradition has it that the search for leaven on the eve of Passover must be performed with a candle and amid the darkness of night. It thus represents the quest for God amid the "dark night of the soul" aided only by the gentlest and most subtle of lights. He means to tie this candle, as well as the wedding and Shabbos candles to come, to the candle in the womb, and hence to the Torah of the Nine Months.

128. Hasidic sources, building on earlier kabbalistic and rabbinic symbols, associate leaven (*hametz*) with pride or arrogance that "puff up" the ego and thus interfere with divine service.

129. The muted-by-illuminating glow of candles represents the fact that our Torah of the Nine Months, the Torah of our individual quest or journey, is there to accompany us in the most dramatic moments of elation and tragedy.

130. See also Rashi to Num. 8:2.

131. Rashi in the same place, paraphrasing b. Shabbat 21a.

132. The candle in the womb is left over from the light of the first day of Creation, called the *or ha-ganuz* or the hidden light. This is represented by Aaron, who lights the candles in the sanctuary, in contrast to Moshe, whose face shines as brightly as the sun. Moshe's Torah is that of Sinai, the bright sunlight; Aaron's is that of the little candle, the personal inner Torah unique to each and every person.

133. b. Shabbat 23b. Remember that the true match between husband and wife means that they share the Nine Months Torah.

134. This suggests that Havah's feminist complaint is justified. Even though husband and wife may know one another's Torah of the Nine Months,

each person needs to receive it directly from God. See Meir ibn Gabbai, *Tola'at Ya'akov* (Jerusalem: n.p., 1996), pt. 2, no. 8; and Chava Weissler, "Woman as High Priest: A Kabbalistic Prayer in Yiddish for Lighting Sabbath Candles," in *Judaism in Practice*, ed. Lawrence Fine, 525–46 (New York: New York University Press, 1995).

135. See b. Hagigah 15a

136. Integrity and authenticity even in the face of failure lead to compassion and connection, whereas denial simply leads to strife and fracture.

137. Peace, including inner tranquility and the harmony between two people, is the candle or light that emerges from the Torah of the Nine Months.

138. As above, the separation between the Torah of Sinai and the Torah of Nine Months was a result of Havah's mistake regarding the fruit of the Tree of Knowledge of Good and Evil.

139. Based on Ex. 32:19 and Deut. 9:17. He seems to be reading *le-'eyneyhem* as *"for* their eyes." The broken tablets can only be fixed by the woman who takes the light of the Sabbath candles back into her own eyes.

140. The peaceful Sabbath candles do much more than give light to a Jewish home. Kindling their flames brings together the Torah of the Nine Months and the Torah of Mount Sinai.

141. The Izhbitz tradition underscores the importance of a vow as a way for the individual to establish a unique connection to the Divine. The vow forms a unique obligation particularly suited for that person, not commanded directly by God but reflecting the unique dimensions of that individual's spiritual journey. See *Beit Ya'akov, mattot*, fol. 48b–49a, which also notes that the entire book of Numbers (*be-midbar*) is about the power of the individual.

142. The words of a vow, which are taken in order for a person to guard against failure, are thus the epitome of language in response to the human condition. Speech, associated with the *sefirah malkhut* and *Shekhinah*, is described in Hasidic sources as a sacred gift and a spark of the Divine imbued in mankind.

143. *Bereshit Rabbah* 50:10, interpreting Ps. 89:21. The Prophet Samuel first identified the archetypical king and the forebear of the Messiah while he himself was in a place of darkness and failure.

144. That is, Korah felt that he had a special claim to leadership because he knew that his illustrious grandson would be a famed prophet tied to the Davidic monarchy, associated in this teaching with the Torah of the Nine Months that can only be found in darkness.

145. What Korah didn't understand, however, was that his grandson's eventual greatness was only possible because of his own mistake. Here the grandson is being understood to be something like a reincarnation of his grandfather, coming back to correct his error.

146. See the interpretation of this verse in b. Berakhot 31b.

147. Sin and failure are the result of a rift between one's intentions and deeds. Therefore, to mend this wound and reclaim the Torah of the Nine Months, the inner world and the exterior deed (symbolized by the hands and the fire) must be brought into alignment.

148. He is reading *barukh ha-makom* to mean: the greatest of blessings is to find your place in the world. This sense of belonging, of recognizing one's mission and quest, is the gift of the Torah of the Nine Months.

149. From the Passover *haggadah*.

150. The first, and perhaps the most important, stage in redemption is that which comes from the Torah of the Nine Months. *Yetsi'at mitsrayim* is understood in the Hasidic tradition as a type of personal redemption that entails leaving the straitened or constricted places of one's own consciousness (*metsar yam*).

151. This phrase is commonly deployed in kabbalistic texts in reference to the *tsaddik*, who is imagined as the foundation of the cosmos itself and the channel through which divine vitality flows into the world ('*olam*).

152. b. Mo'ed Katan 16b. Yosef is the perfect *tsaddik*, but Aaron and King David are both repentant sinners.

153. Of course it was really King Solomon, not David, who built the Temple, but he was David's son and the structure is associated with them both. Here Reb Shlomo is interpreting the Temple as a place of brokenness and failure, but one that inhabits our dreams of rebirth and redemption.

154. Because *erets yisro'el* is "the place," as in his reading of *barukh ha-mokom*, it is a spiritual symbol as well as a physical location that represents attaining the Torah of the Nine Months.

155. One's experience of the Torah of Mount Sinai is limited to this particular lifetime. The Torah of the Nine Months, the unique inner quest of the soul, however, extends beyond the contours of this physical body from the time that the soul is hewn from the Source. There is no rational explanation for the Holocaust, no way of explaining the untold suffering of millions of Jews at the hands of the Nazis. He seems to imply that faith in reincarnation might help us to cope with it. After the Holocaust, all that we can do is remem-

ber that the Torah of the Nine Months carries us forward when we are surrounded by darkness.

156. We may have great leaders, but none of them can lead the Jewish people toward the Torah of the Nine Months. That requires either a perfect and flawless *tsaddik* such as Yosef, granted a vision of the Torah of the Nine Months from on high, or leaders who have themselves acknowledged their own imperfections and who continue to search for their place in the world with the illumination cast by the "candle" of their mistakes.

157. This phrase is discussed in Rashi's commentary on Ex.21:1, quoting Tanhuma, *mishpatim* 3.

158. Thus in essence the final book of the Torah is the Torah of the Nine Months, understood not only as a personal quest but also as a people's national search for their place in the world. *Eleh posel* is not a negation of the prior four books but a brooding sense that they will not work without this one.

159. Until this moment in the teaching, the Torah of the Nine Months is entirely personal and individual. But now he says that the Jewish people as a whole also has a secret purpose, one different from that given by the Torah of Sinai. He does not spell this out but leaves the possible impression that it has to do with a mission to uplift all the fallen.

160. This phrase is recited as part of the Jewish marriage ceremony.

161. Even after his death Moshe sought to lead the Jewish people, staying close to them and shepherding them through the darkness of loss and absurdity.

162. On the eve of Simhat Torah there is a short Torah reading, but the primary focus of the day and the lion's share of the activities focus on rejoicing through dance rather than study or public liturgical reading.

163. The *sukkah* is like the Holy of Holies, a sacred and safe space into which we enter accompanied by all of our failings and stumbling. The shelter it gives us is even "higher" than that of the Torah of Mount Sinai, given to the Jews on Shavuot.

164. On Simhat Torah we dance in circles, proceeding around and around without end. This type of rejoicing is the celebration of rebirth and new beginnings after failure and disappointment. These circles represent both the wedding ring (sealing the covenant between two destined lovers as well as between God and Israel) and the round *samekh* at the head of the verse *somekh Hashem le-khol ha-noflim* — teaching that God supports the fallen, carrying them forward in their search for

the Torah of the Nine Months even when hope seems impossible. The circles also represent the circle of the Torah, where Moses in his death is present in each of us to allow for the possibility of *bereshit*, of new beginnings, of starting over.

5. ZALMAN SCHACHTER-SHALOMI

1. Zalman M. Schachter-Shalomi, *My Life in Jewish Renewal: A Memoir*, with Edward Hoffman (Lanham MD: Rowman & Littlefield, 2012).
2. Zalman Schachter-Shalomi, *The First Step: A Guide for the New Jewish Spirit*, with Donald Gropman (Toronto: Bantam Books, 1983), 2.
3. See Edward K. Kaplan, "A Jewish Dialogue with Howard Thurman: Mysticism, Compassion, and Community," *CrossCurrents* 60 (2010): 515–25.
4. In reflecting upon the years in which he was becoming increasingly aware of other religious traditions and their spiritual "technologies," Reb Zalman invoked the same teaching of Rabbi Nahman of Bratslav used by Hillel Zeitlin in his description of the deep wisdom to be found in non-Jewish sources; see Schachter-Shalomi, *The First Step*, 10.
5. Issues of gender separation and women's participation in Jewish life were significant to Zalman, but they did not constitute the "crisis point" with halakhic authority as they did with Shlomo Carlebach. Unlike Shlomo, Zalman became involved with Conservative Judaism in the early 1960s, spending several summers at the Ramah camps. There, as in Hillel, mixed seating and women's participation (though not yet leadership) were taken for granted.
6. *Hasidim* traditionally pray according to a version of the Sephardic rite, which was said to have greater mystical significance. This divergence from local praxis was one of the major factors that led to the denunciation and persecution of Hasidism by the late-eighteenth-century rabbinate.
7. Zalman Schachter, "How to Become a Modern Hasid," *Jewish Heritage* 2 (1960): 40.
8. He met Timothy Leary and took LSD for the first time in 1962. For some time he kept this, along with other issues, from the Lubavitcher Rebbe.
9. Among many spiritual teachers from various traditions, Zalman met and carried on a correspondence with Trappist monk and writer Thomas Merton. See Or N. Rose, "Reb Zalman, Neo-Hasidism, and Inter-Religious Engagement: Lessons from my Teacher," *Tikkun* 32, no. 4 (2017): 40–45, 71–72. An interview with Zalman about his relation-

ship with Merton is available in Edward K. Kaplan and Shaul Magid, "Thomas Merton and Renewal: Jewish and Christian," in *Merton & Judaism: Recognition, Repentance, and Renewal; Holiness in Words*, ed. Bernice Bruteau (Louisville KY: Fons Vitae, 2003), 301–23, as well as some correspondence from Zalman to Merton in the same volume, 198–207.

10. Part of Reb Zalman's great font of creativity was a desire to solve problems. He was not willing to leave such vexing halakhic questions as the inequality in the Jewish marriage ceremony, divorce, *agunah*, and *mamzerut* to endless debate within the circle of closed-minded authorities. He sought to come up with creative on-the-spot solutions, sometimes implementing them or encouraging his followers to do so. Later in life he expressed regret over some of the "wilder" elements of his past, particularly with regard to issues of personal status, and at times he presented his legacy as having undergone a process of refinement.

11. Reb Zalman also knew Heschel personally; see his reflections on their friendship in Schachter-Shalomi, *My Life in Jewish Renewal*, 169–74. Heschel too eschewed the use of drugs altogether, citing the turn toward such addiction as a sign that the youth were looking for spiritual uplift and met only stiltedness and banal, meaningless religion; see Abraham Joshua Heschel, "In Search of Exaltation," in Abraham Joshua Heschel, *Moral Grandeur and Spiritual Audacity*, ed. Susannah Heschel (New York: Farrar, Straus & Giroux, 1996), 228–29.

12. See his remarks in Zalman M. Schachter, "Hasidism and Neo-Hasidism," reprinted in this chapter. In retrospect it seems fair to note that this was a somewhat self-justifying critique. Zalman's great strength was always that of an oral teacher and personal guide, one who could transform a human encounter into a sublime moment. His literary skills were certainly not on the level of Buber's or Heschel's. Zalman's most successful books were all written with the help of a long row of assistants, culminating in the very fruitful and abundant efforts of Netanel Miles-Yepez.

13. Zalman M. Schachter-Shalomi, *Spiritual Intimacy: A Study of Counseling in Hasidism* (Northvale NJ: Jason Aronson, 1991), 316–18.

14. Schachter-Shalomi, *Spiritual Intimacy*, 316–18.

15. Schachter-Shalomi, *Spiritual Intimacy*, xvi–xvii. Several of his disciples recall Neo-Hasidic gatherings in which Reb Zalman embodied the role of a Hasidic *rebbe*, giving a spiritual sermon and sitting in an honored seat at the table, only to ask everyone to move down one chair and thus allow a new *rebbe* to ascend the throne. This was a way of retaining the

value of charisma while democratizing the community, something he saw as essential in the contemporary American Jewish context.

16. Schachter-Shalomi, *Spiritual Intimacy*, xiii–xv. He saw himself (and his spiritual lineage) as a link in a long line of mystical, devotional communities of Jewish, Christian, Islamic, and Eastern seekers.

17. Zalman M. Schachter, "Toward an 'Order of B'nai Or,'" reprinted in this chapter.

18. A personal note: one of the editors of this volume was introduced by Zalman to his wife of the following fifty years as a fellow-member of this B'nai Or community in the making.

19. Zalman Schachter-Shalomi, *Davening: A Guide to Meaningful Jewish Prayer*, with Joel Segel (Woodstock VT: Jewish Lights, 2012); and Zalman Schachter-Shalomi, *The Gates of Prayer: Twelve Talks on Davvenology* (Boulder CO: Albion-Andalus, 2011).

20. Ariel, "Hasidism," 155.

21. Zalman Schachter-Shalomi, *Paradigm Shift: From the Jewish Renewal Teachings of Reb Zalman Schachter-Shalomi*, ed. Ellen Singer (Northvale NJ: Jason Aronson, 1993). See also Magid, *American Post-Judaism*; and Shaul Magid, "Between Paradigm Shift Judaism and Neo-Hasidism: The New Metaphysics of Jewish Renewal," *Tikkun* 30, no. 1 (2015): 11–15.

22. See also Zalman Schachter-Shalomi, *Credo of a Modern Kabbalist*, with Daniel Siegel (Victoria, BC: Trafford, 2005).

23. For a translation of this German article, originally published in 1952, see Siegmund Hurwitz, "Psychological Aspects in Early Hasidic Literature," trans. Hildegard Nagel, in Helmuth Jacobsohn, Marie-Louise von Franz, and Siegmund Hurwitz, *Timeless Documents of the Soul (Studies in Jungian Thought)* (Evanston IL: Northwestern University Press, 1968), 149–240.

24. Quotations are from the Shabbat morning service.

25. See b. Shabbat 133b.

26. Omitted here is a section on the role of women in the B'nai Or community. The editors of the present volume have deleted it out of a sense that these words, published in 1964, long before feminist consciousness had deeply altered his views on the subject, would be an embarrassment to Reb Zalman.

27. "In speaking of 'turnings,' we [i.e., Reb Zalman and Netanel Miles-Yépez] are consciously borrowing language from the Buddhist tradition, which speaks of 'three turnings of the wheel of dharma,' describing three phases of how the wisdom of that tradition was presented accord-

ing to the needs of different eras." Quoted from Zalman Shachter-Shalomi and Netanel Miles-Yépez, *Foundations of the Fourth Turning of Hasidism: A Manifesto* (Boulder CO: Albion-Andalus, 2014), 37.

28. "*Chthonic* (from the Greek word, *chthon* or 'earth'), referring to how the land itself, or the landscape of a place, influences expression in that place." Quoted from Miles-Yépez, *Foundations of the Fourth Turning of Hasidism*, 37.

29. "The expression *hasidim ha-rishonim* may be read both ways. It occurs many times in the Mishnah. One example is found in Berakhot 5:1." Quoted from Miles-Yépez, *Foundations of the Fourth Turning of Hasidism*, 37.

30. "Another possibility is the Aramaic word *asyah*, 'healing.'" Quoted from Miles-Yépez, *Foundations of the Fourth Turning of Hasidism*, 37.

31. "1 Maccabees 2:42." Quoted from Miles-Yépez, *Foundations of the Fourth Turning of Hasidism*, 37.

32. Philo of Alexandria, *Quod Omnis Probus Liber Sit*, sections 12 and 13. Quoted from Miles-Yépez, *Foundations of the Fourth Turning of Hasidism*, 37.

33. "As they are called by Pliny the Elder." Quoted from Miles-Yépez, *Foundations of the Fourth Turning of Hasidism*, 37.

34. "Although this group did identify themselves as Hasidim, '*Hasidey Sefarad*' is simply a name we have applied to them for the purpose of differentiating them from their northern siblings, the *Hasidey Ashkenaz*." Quoted from Miles-Yépez, *Foundations of the Fourth Turning of Hasidism*, 37.

35. "See Zalman Schachter-Shalomi and Netanel Miles-Yépez, *A Heart Afire: Stories and Teachings of the Early Hasidic Masters* (Philadelphia: Jewish Publication Society, 2009), 44–54 and 294–95." Quoted from Miles-Yépez, *Foundations of the Fourth Turning of Hasidism*, 37.

36. "See Schachter-Shalomi and Netanel Miles-Yépez, *A Heart Afire*, 180–92." Quoted from Miles-Yépez, *Foundations of the Fourth Turning of Hasidism*, 37.

37. "From the tri-literal Hebrew root, *nun beit beit*, which may be interpreted as 'hollow'." Quoted from Miles-Yépez, *Foundations of the Fourth Turning of Hasidism*, 37.

38. "*Davvenen* may be derived from the Latin word, *divinum*, meaning, 'divine work.'" Quoted from Miles-Yépez, *Foundations of the Fourth Turning of Hasidism*, 38.

39. "See Schachter-Shalomi and Miles-Yépez, *A Heart Afire*, 306–31." Quoted from Miles-Yépez, *Foundations of the Fourth Turning of Hasidism*, 38.

40. "See Zalman Schachter-Shalomi and Netanel Miles-Yépez, *A Hidden Light: Stories and Teachings of Early HaBaD and Bratzlav Hasidism* (Santa

Fe: Gaon, 2011), 160." Quoted from Miles-Yépez, *Foundations of the Fourth Turning of Hasidism*, 38.

41. "Schachter-Shalomi and Miles-Yépez, *A Heart Afire*, 26–44." Quoted from Miles-Yépez, *Foundations of the Fourth Turning of Hasidism*, 38.

42. "Another term for what we have sometimes called 'paradigm shift,' a phrase originally introduced by the philosopher of science Thomas Kuhn." Quoted from Miles-Yépez, *Foundations of the Fourth Turning of Hasidism*, 38.

43. "We have borrowed the term 'deep structures' from Noam Chomsky's discussion of transformational grammar." Quoted from Miles-Yépez, *Foundations of the Fourth Turning of Hasidism*, 38.

44. "'Deep ecumenism' is a phrase coined by Father Matthew Fox. Ecumenism, from the Greek, *oikoumenikos*, 'from the whole world,' originally referred to cooperative efforts between different parts of the Christian church." Quoted from Miles-Yépez, *Foundations of the Fourth Turning of Hasidism*, 38.

45. Seemingly a country place near Vienna where the Schachters were vacationing.

46. Shlomo Carlebach's twin brother, who predeceased him.

47. Rabbi Shlomo Halberstam of Bobov (1907–2000), who survived the Holocaust and rebuilt his almost totally destroyed community after coming to America.

48. Rabbi Aharon Kotler (1891–1962) was a great talmudic scholar, a Lithuanian anti-Hasidic sage, famous as the founder of the Lakewood Yeshiva.

49. Rabbi Yizhak Hutner (1906–80), another Lithuanian-style talmudic scholar, but known for having been somewhat more open to Hasidism.

50. Fall River, Massachusetts, where Zalman served as rabbi of a small Orthodox congregation.

51. Rabbi Yosef Yitzhak of Lubavitch, whom Zalman always saw as his *rebbe*, died in 1950.

52. Meaning the Chabad headquarters at 770 Eastern Parkway in Brooklyn, New York.

53. This seems to be the *rebbe* speaking to Zalman and Shlomo at this *farbrengen*, issuing his original charge to them.

54. Brandeis was founded in 1948. This would make it December 1949. The *rebbe* died in 1950.

55. He must mean "the printed matter."

56. Hasidic young people who were forbidden to read outside books would do so in the bathroom where they could not be seen. Tradition com-

mands that Jews not study Torah in the bathroom, and this designation clearly reveals Zalman's ambivalent feelings about non-Jewish spiritual sources at the time.

57. The Carlebach Shul on West 79th Street in Manhattan, where Shlomo led and taught.

58. The sequence of Zalman's early career: New Haven (as a Lubavitcher emissary); Rochester (also for Lubavitch); Fall River, Massachusetts (rabbi of an Orthodox synagogue); New Bedford, Massachusetts (rabbi, also of an Orthodox community); University of Manitoba Hillel (ca. 1954).

59. He means Arnold Gesell (1880–1961), founder of what became the Yale Child Study Center. The Gesell Institute of Child Development is named for him.

60. M. Eugene Boylan (1904–64), a Trappist monk and well-known Catholic author. *Difficulties in Mental Prayer*, first published in 1943, is still reprinted.

61. *The Bible of the World*, first published in 1939 and still in print as *The Portable World Bible*, is an introduction to world religions and their scriptures. Robert O. Ballou (1892–1977) was a well-known author, editor, and publisher.

62. Zalman's family had been Belz Hasidim before coming to Vienna. So to him "Belzer" meant "non-Chabad Hasidim."

63. All key themes in the Hasidic discussions of prayer.

64. Rabbi Menachem Mendel Schneersohn, the future Lubavitcher Rebbe, son-in-law of his predecessor.

65. Zalman's third child, Yosef Yitzhak.

66. Zalman's first wife.

67. "People shouldn't interfere" is a reference to the sharp conflict between Reb Menachem Mendel and his older brother-in-law, Rabbi Shmarya Gurary, who had been the presumed heir apparent and was supported by powerful interests among the community's elders.

68. Meaning that he remains our *rebbe* even in death.

69. A very sharp and direct personal retort, in the spirit of Rabbi Menachem Mendel of Kotzk.

70. Zalman was rabbi of the small Orthodox congregation in those two cities. It was considered taboo for Orthodox rabbis to lend any support or legitimacy to non-Orthodox forms of Judaism.

71. The Orthodox synagogue where he served as rabbi still belonged to the old immigrant community and was undoubtedly much smaller and

poorer than the Conservative "temple." While Hasidim in New York might object to his speaking at a non-Orthodox synagogue, his congregants had no such concerns.

72. He decides to speak on this very complex theological subject, one much discussed in Chabad thought and considered particularly abstruse, but entirely inappropriate to this audience.

73. That is, he felt ready to faint. He is referring to a legend about Sinai (b. Shabbat 88b), recounting that Israel passed out and had to be revived for each of the ten divine utterances.

74. This is a wonderful early instance of what became one of Reb Zalman's greatest talents: speaking extemporaneously and transforming an ordinary moment into a great spiritual event.

75. A prominent African American Protestant theologian with whom Zalman studied and who influenced him greatly; Zalman referred to Thurman as his African American *rebbe*. That relationship marked Zalman's passage out of seeing himself exclusively as the disciple of Lubavitch and Rabbi Yosef Yitzhak.

76. There is not yet any sense of setting out to create a Neo-Hasidism.

77. Literal belief in the text as revealed at Sinai versus a broader sense of the divinity of Torah.

78. Leo Baeck (1873–1956), a famous German Jewish theologian and rabbi, survived Nazi persecution at Theriesenstadt and served as a key spiritual voice in the early post-Holocaust years.

79. A campsite in Wisconsin owned by the Reform movement, site of a series of annual intra-Jewish dialogues in which Zalman took part, probably in the late 1950s. Other notable participants were Emil Fackenheim, Arnold Jacob Wolf, Maurice Pekarsky, and Max Ticktin.

80. The native Indian Jewish community, based in Bombay, now mostly living in Israel.

81. According to the reincarnation doctrines of Lurianic Kabbalah, preserved within Chabad teaching. This is a subtle expression of one of Zalman's great breaking-points with Chabad doctrine: its insistence on the intrinsic difference between the souls of Jews and gentiles.

82. It might have been a childhood memory, not a prior incarnation in the literal sense.

83. Then Hillel director at the University of Wisconsin, later at the University of Chicago, and then associate national director of Hillel in Washington DC.

84. Maurice Pekarsky, Hillel director at the University of Chicago prior to Ticktin.

85. That is the intent here of the Yiddish *shaygetz*.

86. Rabbi Richard Israel (1929–2000), later of Yale and New England Regional Hillel.

87. Zalman's dissertation at Hebrew Union College on the private conversation between Hasidic *rebbe* and disciple, later published as *Spiritual Intimacy: A Study of Counseling in Hasidism* (Northvale NJ: Jason Aronson, 1991).

88. Mary Lynn, secretary of Zalman's department at the University of Manitoba, later his second wife, Malka. His marriage to her (Zalman was a *Kohen*, she a *giyyoret* [a convert to Judaism], a match forbidden by *halakhah*) deepened and in some ways finalized his break with Orthodoxy and Chabad.

89. A very important, revealing statement. He is saying that his discipleship to the *rebbe* came to an end only when he allowed himself to subject it to psychological analysis, as he did in that dissertation and book.

90. He had begun studying Hasidism in historical context.

91. The hierarchical relationship of *rebbe* and disciple was now placed in its historical Eastern European context.

92. A Russian Protestant sect that flourished in a region and period close to early Hasidism. Various scholars have discussed a possible link—or at least a typological similarity—between them. The Dukhobors later settled in Western Canada, giving Zalman, now in Winnipeg, a special interest in them.

93. Piotyr Verigin (1859–1924) was leader of the Dukhobors, first in Russia and then in Canada. He was killed in a mysterious train crash in 1924.

94. Modern Orthodox rabbis of that era found a degree of permissibility for mixed seating either in the context of something that was not formally considered a service (perhaps with no quorum) or in a place that was not formally considered a place of prayer.

95. In his autobiographical retellings, Zalman testified to learning the technique of "spiritual laboratories" from Howard Thurman in that same period.

96. Zalman was employed as a "religious environmentalist" at Camp Ramah in Connecticut for several summers.

97. Leary had experimented with using psilocybin in prison settings.

98. Zalman took this as a blessing for his upcoming LSD trip. But it also represents the moment of impending break between his emerging world and that of Lubavitch. He could not tell the *rebbe* how he understood his blessing.

6. ARTHUR GREEN

1. Introduction by Ariel Evan Mayse. For a fuller treatment of Green's life and work, see Ariel Evan Mayse, "Arthur Green: An Intellectual Portrait," in Ariel Evan Mayse, *Arthur Green: Hasidism for Tomorrow* (Leiden: Brill, 2015), 1–52. The following remarks in this chapter are based on his work there. The term "unorthodox" in Green's self-description is carefully chosen; it means considerably more than its alternative "non-Orthodox."

2. On his search for an intellectual lineage, see Arthur Green, "Three Warsaw Mystics," in *Kolot Rabbim: Essays in Memory of Rivka Schatz-Uffenheimer*, ed. Rachel Elior, 1–58 (Jerusalem: Magnes, 1996); Arthur Green, "What Is Jewish Theology?" in *Torah and Revelation*, ed. Dan Cohn-Sherbok, 1–11 (Lewiston NY: Edwin Mellen, 1992).

3. These essays were republished in *The New Jews*, ed. James Sleeper and Alan Mintz, 176–92 and 193–203 (New York: Vintage, 1971). The first of these, which explores the ways in which psychedelic drugs can offer the religious person a different perspective on the world, was first published under the pseudonym Itzik Lodzer.

4. Nietzsche, it should be recalled, was important to young Zeitlin as well—and this is hardly coincidental.

5. At RRC he encountered some opposition from staunch Reconstructionists who opposed his mystical leanings. See, for example, the remarks of Sidney Schwarz, "Reconstructionism and Neo-Hasidism: The Limits of Cooperation," *Reconstructionist Rabbinical Association (RRA), Reconstructionist Rabbinical College (RRC)* (1984), 25: "Many who feel that the two tendencies are compatible and mutually enriching are quick to point out how many of the same goals we share. . . . Yet at the core of neo-Hasidism is the search for the encounter with a personal God. . . . [This is a misperception of Green's theology.] Both will find natural constituencies, people previously turned off to the more conventional Jewish movements. But the universe of discourse of the two approaches is so different that I don't see the benefit of lumping the two together."

6. See Arthur Green, "Neo-Hasidism and Our Theological Struggles," *Ra'ayonot* 4, no. 3 (1984): 11–17.

7. See Green, "Neo-Hasidism and Our Theological Struggles," 17.

8. See Green, "Neo-Hasidism and Our Theological Struggles," 15.

9. Republished as Arthur Green, *Seek My Face: A Jewish Mystical Theology* (Woodstock VT: Jewish Lights, 2003).

10. That is, from *eyn Sof* to the *sefirot*, which exist only from the perspective of humans. Here we see the influence of Hasidic thought, particularly that of Rabbi Aaron of Starroselye.

11. Arthur Green, *Ehyeh: A Kabbalah for Tomorrow* (Woodstock VT: Jewish Lights, 2003).

12. Arthur Green, *Radical Judaism: Rethinking God and Tradition* (New Haven: Yale University Press, 2010). An expanded and rewritten Hebrew version appeared in 2016.

13. See Green, *Seek My Face*, 47–94; "God, World, Person: A Jewish Theology of Creation," *Journal of Theology* (Dayton) 96 (1992): 21–32; "A Kabbalah for the Environmental Age," *Tikkun* 14, no. 5 (1999), 33–38; *Radical Judaism*, 16–33.

14. See, for example, Abraham Joshua Heschel, *Heavenly Torah: As Refracted through the Generations*, trans. Gordon Tucker (New York: Continuum, 2005); Tamar Ross, *Expanding the Palace of Torah: Orthodoxy and Feminism* (Lebanon NH: Brandeis University Press, published by University Press of New England, 2004). Rivka Horwitz's treatment of Rosenzweig's theology of revelation in her essay for Green's *Jewish Spirituality* was helpful in his own thinking on this subject; see Rivka Horwitz, "Revelation and the Bible According to Twentieth-Century Jewish Philosophy," in *Jewish Spirituality*, vol. 2, *From the Sixteenth-Century Revival to the Present*, ed. Arthur Green, 346–70 (New York: Crossroad, 1987).

15. Green, *Radical Judaism*, 164.

16. A paraphrase of Exod. 14:15.

17. Benjamin of Zalozhitz, *Ahavat Dodim* (Lemberg: n.p., 1797), 61a. Compare Rivka Schatz-Uffenheimer, *Ha-hasidut ke-mistika* (Jerusalem: Magnes, 1980), 117.

18. Exod. 20:16.

19. *Likutim Yekarim* (New York: n.p., 1963), 6a.

20. *Degel Mahaneh Efraim* (*va-yetse*) (Jerusalem: n.p., 1963), 40.

21. *Hayyim va-hesed* (Warsaw: n.p., 1891), 7a.

22. The appropriate kabbalistic term here is *ha'ala'at mayyin nuqvin*, the raising up of the "feminine waters," the waters from below which man rises up (as the new manna, one source would have it) to sustain the heavens. On the complicated relationship between Shabbat and weekday religious consciousness, compare *Sefat Emet, ki tisa*, 1871.

23. Seemingly more to be found in such later Polish traditions as those of Izhbitz and Ger.

24. This dominates in early "classical" Hasidism, particularly in the school of Mezritch. Compare Schatz-Uffenheimer, *Ha-hasidut*, chap. 3; and Hillel Zeitlin, *Be-fardes ha-hasidut weha-qabalah* (Tel Aviv: Yavneh, 1960), chap. 1.

25. Desideratum: a Judaism that allows, even accentuates, its mystical self-understanding, while at the same time radically denying the Hellenistic/Gnostic body-soul and matter-spirit dualisms that have so deeply infected us. Handle carefully and avoid Frankism.

26. Colorado. Zalman was present at the New York conference via Skype.

27. b. Ta'anit 7a.

28. Echoing the language of b. Berakhot 63a.

29. For further reflections by Green on this passage, see his "These Are the Journeys: Tales of Our Wandering. Reflections on *Parashat Massa'ey*," in Jeffrey Salkin, ed., *A Modern Men's Torah Commentary* (Woodstock VT: Jewish Lights, 2009).

30. *Imrei Pinhas* (Bnei Brak: n.p., 2003), *sha'ar emet ve-emunah*, no. 26, 351.

31. *Imrei Pinhas*, no. 22, 351.

32. *Likkutey Moharan*, 1:64.

33. From a poem by the great medieval philosopher and poet Rabbi Judah Halevi.

34. See *Tanya, sha'ar ha-yihud veha-emunah*, chaps. 1–6.

35. Arthur Green, *These Are the Words: A Vocabulary of Jewish Spiritual Life*, 2nd ed. (Woodstock VT: Jewish Lights, 2012).

36. See, for example, *Degel Mahaneh Efrayim* (Bnei Brak: n.p., 2013), *noah*, 18–19.

37. Green, *Seek My Face*, xxii–xxiv.

38. y. Nedarim 9:6. See discussion in Green, *Radical Judaism*, 123–56 and 169n18.

39. See further discussion in the introduction to Heschel in this volume.

40. The Hebrew College Rabbinical School opened its doors in the fall of 2003.